Ultrareasoning

Principles and Practices

of

Faceted Model-Oriented Reasoning

Pinnacle Quest Vol. III

M. R. Lauer

Neither agree,

nor disagree;

explore

and

discover.

Contents

I Understanding The Model   29

2 Laws of Model-Oriented Reasoning   31

iv

Contents   v

viii

III Advanced Topics   451

27 Discovery   453

28 Faceted Model-Oriented Reasoning   469

29 Curriculum   489

Contents

List of Figures

Listings

Chapter 1

Introduction

1.1 Orientation

The modern world is defined equally by the astounding progress we have achieved in the fields of science and technology, as well as by the stunning *lack* of progress we have made in the messier realm of human affairs, the confused and bloody side of life that includes man's inhumanity to man, ideology, theology, philosophy, humanities, social sciences, etc. In fact, the level of thought and accomplishment in all of the presumably important fields related to human behavior and experience is generally stuck about where it has been for several thousand years. Surely, one must wonder why we have been able to make so much progress in the one area, and yet none in the other, arguably more important, arena.

"Ah," you might say, "science and technology are quantitative fields and are naturally open to quantitative methods,

1

such as mathematics and scientific experiments, while human affairs are more difficult and subjective." Yes, but, is that really an answer? Is it an answer we have to accept? How about we rephrase the question and ask, "Why haven't we been able to extend quantitative methods into the subjective realm?"

"Impossible!" you would retort, "you can't quantify subjective experience!"

"But, why not?" would be my response. If mathematics and the scientific method are the most powerful reasoning tools we have, then would we not benefit from extending them into the subjective realm? What is stopping us from doing that?

"The first thing stopping us," you might say, "is the unbroken trail of failures in the history of such attempts, dating all the way back to Euclid." While I grant this is true, much of it can be simply explained because, for reasons that will be examined later, people reflexively try to apply the "this *as* that" principle whenever they find something that works, so once we had Euclid, people thought that the road to truth had to be the axiomatic system and the deductive proof. They were sure that we could view life as if it were a geometry problem and apply geometrical reasoning to it. The same folly repeated itself with Newtonian mechanics, the concept of the clockwork world, the industrial age machine metaphor, Freudian ideas and even Relativity. Repeated attempts to *reduce* the messiness of human reality to tidy mathematical forms, ideologies or pet theories have failed to make understanding and predicting human affairs more feasible. But, maybe that's the crux of the problem, maybe we've been looking at it from the wrong side of the equation. What happens if, instead of trying to *reduce* human experience to an equation, we can figure out how to *extend* our quantitative methods to cover the unquantifiable subjective domain? What happens if we can discover a way to quantify our thoughts, feelings, beliefs, actions, and even dreams in such a way that we lose none of the messy complexity that we find so confounding, while simultaneously creating tractable models and equations that describe and predict how our mind works to solve rational, emotional, and spiritual problems?

The first obstacle that has stopped us from extending math into the subjective world is what we are calling the *purblind defect*: the defect in our physical/mental constitution that makes us incapable of perceiving the boundaries between the various parts of our mind that evolved at different times on the long path that eventually made us human. This defect makes it impossible for us to look around inside our mind in the same way we can look at our external environment to discover, identify and understand all the various parts that combine to make the whole. It is precisely because we lack the faculty to perceive internal mental boundaries that we haven't been able to begin to understand how consciousness and cognition arises from the happenstance of independently operating and evolved mental functionalities that all execute in a confined space and time framework.

We can look outside and see that the shore and the lake are different, that plant and animal are different, that different animals are different, but we can't *see* the boundary between the area in our brain that learns from experience, and that which we use to anticipate the future. We experience all of our different cognitive functions as part of a single whole that we call 'thinking'. Oddly, we do separate *feeling* from thinking, perhaps because of the physiological component, but we still combine both into what we see as our identity, our self.

The answer to the problem of how to connect the objective and subjective domains is *to extend* math and the scientific method to encompass subjective experience by adding formal model-oriented reasoning to our scientific tools so that they become powerful enough to comprehend humanity.

Model-oriented reasoning is a methodology that can be used to extend knowledge beyond its current boundaries. Although scientists routinely use it everyday, many also misuse it just as often to characterize theories as being true, and an appalling number of them even try to leverage their scientific credentials to lend credence to their political or philosophical opinions. This tendency to leverage workplace expertise to cloak their personal opinions with the aura of authority reveals a complete lack of understanding of the basics of the theory and practice of model-oriented reasoning. People fall into a trap we can call the 'authority fallacy', which leads them to erroneously assume that competence with one model system somehow endows them with a greater level of knowledge and wisdom in any field they want to talk about, an error they would not make if they had a solid understanding of the theoretical underpinnings of the method.

Many of them prostitute their expertise, despite knowing it to be an illegitimate practice, but do it with an unaware sense of righteousness that would make a preacher blush.

We will start from a sound, theoretical basis to carefully elucidate the theory and practice of model-oriented reasoning in order to show how it is wrong to combine observations and measurement with authority and obedience. We will then proceed on to define a number of new methodologies and concepts that will finally open the subjective realm to the unblinking eye of objective examination.

The goal of this work is to open the messy, subjective world of human thought, feelings and beliefs to the benefits of the scientific revolution by extending the scientific method with mathematical, logical and reasoning enhancements that support techniques that open all subjective experience to reproducible tests for the first time. Explaining the theory and practice of this formal extension of model-oriented reasoning will require the use of model-oriented reasoning to present a new model of the human mind that is consistent with modern knowledge of evolution, information theory and other hard sciences. Without first gaining a new understanding of how our mind processes perceptions, and extracts meaning from experience, it would difficult, if not impossible, to understand what needs to be done to build a bridge between our thoughts, feelings and beliefs and the world of objective, scientific inquiry.

Our objective is to provide the tools that will enable us, finally, to begin to answer the pinnacle questions that the best

minds have pondered fruitlessly for millennia: why are we the
way we are? what is justice? why is there war? But it must
be emphasized that we are providing *tools* and not *answers*,
because, for reasons that will be explained, it is impossible to
find a single correct answer to any of these questions. What we
can do, instead, is learn to use these tools to formulate models
that we can test and query in advance of experience, just like
any other quantitative model, so that we can begin to have
confidence in our solutions before we inflict them on others.

Faceted model-oriented reasoning is an enhanced form of
normal model-oriented reasoning that will enable us not only
to answer any question of the form: "why is 'man's inhumanity to man' so often the rule in human affairs, rather than the
exception?" but to go beyond that and understand what our
answers' limitations will be: what they mean and, more importantly, what they do not. The goal of this series of works
(*Pinnacle Questions, Pinnacle Reasoning, Ultrareasoning*) is to
lay a solid foundation that will support an assault on pinnacle
questions and allow us to move beyond mere idle speculation to
where we begin to achieve reproducible results that successive
generations will be able to build on. Only then will we be able
to create the same kind of tradition of progress in the field of
reasoning about subjective human experience that we now take
for granted in all of the hard sciences, all of the *real* sciences.

Understanding the very difficult and challenging material
presented in this volume will require heroic efforts on the reader's
part: first, you will have to stop *reading* and immediately begin

studying, with all that implies, and second, you will have to master the reflective pause.

The reflective pause is the disruption in the flow of thought that occurs at the junction in our mind between the pattern processor and the discovery engine (see *Reasoning*). The normal rhythm of assimilating information continuously within a framework of reasoning with conviction, impedes the transition from the pattern processor into the discovery engine. It precludes the hesitation in the pattern processing cycle required for us to be able to realize that the miracle of the burning bush is neither that it is a bush, nor that it is on fire, but, rather, that it is not being consumed in the flames. It takes time, and a significant moment of reflection to even gain the opportunity to notice that the expected oxidation of the plant matter is not occurring. This is an insight that is invisible to all but he who will pause at strategic moments.

Mastery of the material presented in these volumes absolutely requires extended journeys of exploration. In order to be able to do this, we must transition from the familiar pattern processing intellect into our mind's discovery engine, and willingly eschew the comfort of certainty, conviction and validation to be able to patiently poke and prod the unknown in front of us. This cannot happen to the reader who thinks they gain comprehension by reading rapidly while looking to recognize patterns that are similar to familiar ones in his library of knowledge.

True exploration is only available to the patient student who is open to recognizing the burning bush anomaly, and who is willing, and even eager, to disrupt the rhythm of the reading/learning process with frequent reflective pauses. These reflective moments must be long and unbiased enough to support an analysis of knowledge patterns down into component parts smaller than ever considered before. Furthermore, we must be willing to piece together new models, link by link, vertex by vertex, test by test, just as if we were Watson or Crick assembling their model of the DNA molecule, and to do this repeatedly. If you are interested but trepidatious, don't worry, you will find ample support throughout the text to support this extreme effort.

Keep this one thing uppermost in your mind as you read: whenever you object to the way a term is defined or redefined, and you are tempted to accuse me of playing word games, know that every idea in this book can be coded, compiled and tested. Can you say that for your verbal-model ideas? If so, then undoubtedly you have already done the work, and can show us all your results. If not, then perhaps you will grant me the indulgence of entertaining the possibility that what we are doing here is something with which you are entirely unfamiliar. If that is the case, which we surely know it is, then please consider refraining from criticizing the work prematurely for failing to match up with your expectations, and give your mind a chance to adjust to a new way of understanding thought.

Reflective pauses will be suggested here and there throughout the book by showing the Henri Chouanard photo below, accompanied by a sidebar. During these pauses, you are not expected to reach any particular conclusion or insight, but if you have been ruffling questions, the point made just before the suggestion to pause might be sufficient, if given time, to trigger some interesting connections.

This will contain the suggestion on where the leap off point for the reflective pause would be. Be willing to let the insight function of the brain have the time it needs to make new connections.

1.2 Review Terms

Two new disciplines, faceted model-oriented reasoning and subjective algebra, are being introduced in this book in seminal form. A great deal of work remains to be done to bring them, and the curriculum that supports them, to maturity. Although this is the third volume in a series, an attempt is being made to make it a standalone volume since the material being covered is so far beyond the previous volumes that it should be considered the first volume in a new, larger series of works. However, there are a number of terms that were covered in the earlier works that will be referred to often here, so in this section, we will cogently explain these terms to enable readers unfamiliar with the previous works to understand the references.

1.2.1   Emotional Intellect

In volumes one and two, we were working on a specific model,
whereas in the current work we are modeling the domain at a
much more abstract level, thus ideas we discussed previously
have been reformulated and renamed to fit the new context.
The more primitive parts of our mind that we share with animals was previously called the *emotional intellect*, EI, because it
is the part of the mind that evaluates perceptions into anti-self,
pro-self, and non-self component values that the action module then translates into avoid, approach, ignore actions. This
model has become part of L0 and L1 in the new model.

The emotional intellect is our protector, it evaluates the
world strictly from a self-interested viewpoint, and it believes,
that is, it *knows* what is right and wrong, true or false, friend
or foe. The emotional intellect is selfish by design: its notion of
good is defined primarily, if not exclusively, in terms of what is
good for us and the groups to which we belong.

1.2.2   Cognitive Intellect

The cognitive intellect, CI, is our calculator, a powerful pattern
recognizer and processor; it is inherently value-free, and is able
to apply arbitrary value systems to any given problem. It gives
us our language ability, the ability to learn lessons from others,
and to think logically. It is the home of what we think of as
intellect. In the new model is referred to as L2.

The cognitive intellect can be used by the emotional intellect, or it can operate independently, or any mix in between. It

can both generate and accept ideas from outside sources, and it can evaluate their validity against arbitrary yard sticks. The cognitive intellect deals in ideas, whereas the emotional intellect deals in feelings and beliefs. Ideas become beliefs if we develop a personal stake in them, but beliefs can rarely, if ever, become ideas again—the attachment to a particular view of their truth value is too personal to ever be fully detached again. The efficacy of the cognitive intellect as an abstract problem solver is largely defined by the adequacy of our cultural and educational institutions since all of our advanced thought requires mastering socially transmitted lessons (i.e., schooling).

1.2.3 Fallacies

In *Questions*, after discussing a model for how the mind works, that model was used to reveal several fallacies in common thought. The two major fallacies are the wisdom fallacy, and the erudition fallacy.

1.2.3.1 Wisdom Fallacy

The wisdom fallacy is the oldest and most damaging fallacy. The essence of the fallacy is the belief that we can insulate ourselves from the trials and tribulations of life by securing esoteric knowledge of the metaphysical or spiritual realm. This fallacy is not only a core belief in most religions and cults, it even rules the lives of adolescents in the form of 'cool', the attitude of detached, cynical indifference affected by the young and the hip.

The core of the fallacy are these beliefs:

- There is a 'truer' reality than our obvious physical reality.
- Valuing real life over the hidden truth is folly.
- The knowledge of the other reality is arcane and must be sought from masters, or by inspiration.
- The possession of such knowledge insulates us from both the tragic, and mundane, events of normal life.
- Seeking and possessing such knowledge is the highest goal of learning.

1.2.3.2 Erudition Fallacy

The erudition fallacy is the mistaken notion that becoming steeped in a cultural and linguistic tradition in the academy endows one with superior ratiocinative powers, and makes one wise, perceptive, and capable. The erudition fallacy confuses manners with competence, and that is a mistake that is lethal to the development of the highest intellect.

Learning a secret handshake may gain you entrance to a club or fraternity, but that's all it does. Yes, it may gain you entrée into the halls of power, but that is just a grouping exercise, and not only has nothing to do with education, it has a strongly deleterious effect on the progress of humanity by subordinating the purpose of education to the most primitive grouping impulses. Just because someone dresses well and has good diction does not mean that they are knowledgeable, perceptive, competent, honest, or interesting. It just means they have nice clothes and they learned to speak a certain way.

1.3 First Terms

There are a number of new terms that we will be using throughout this work, as well as a number of familiar terms that will
be redefined. Each term will be explained in more detail as it
is used; this in-text glossary is provided merely to smooth a
difficult road a little by supplying the student with some orientation, as well as a convenient spot to bookmark for later
reference.

1.3.1 Reality is the Set of All Measurables

Reality, $\mathbb{R}$, is the set of all measurable things.

$$\mathbb{R} = \forall\, r \in \{x\ :\ measurement(x_d) <= \epsilon\}$$
$$\mathbb{R} = \forall\, r \in \{i_d\ :\ |i_d - r_d| <= \epsilon\}$$

That is, reality is the set of all things in the dimensions that
can be verifiably measured. The two expressions are different
ways to say that reality is the set of ideas we have that have
been verified to correspond to a measurable phenomenon in certain dimensions. The vertical bars surrounding a value indicate
magnitude, so $|i_d - r_d| <= \epsilon$ means that the difference between
your idea, i, and the thing, r, in a specific dimension, d, is within
an acceptable margin of error, ϵ. What this means is that, if we
take a rock as an example, that rock may or may not exist in
the physical universe, but our knowledge of it is defined by our
idea of a rock that has been verified by measurement to correspond to an external reality. In practice, of course, we usually

only verify a rock by visual or manual inspection, so this means
that we only know the rock on terms of gross characteristics,
not fine detail or internal structure. The distinction is clearly
significant if you are prospecting for a specific mineral, but it is
always important, even if you don't know why. Alternatively,
we could say: $\mathbb{R} = \forall\ e_{x,y,z,t} \mid \delta_d <= \epsilon\ for\ d\ \in \{x, y, z, t\}$, that
is, reality is the set of all things that verifiably exist in space and
time (this last definition does not attempt to include subatomic
particles, it focuses exclusively on phenomena apprehendable
by our senses).

While seemingly facile, this is a very serious, formal and
powerful definition of reality that has far reaching implications
without which it is impossible to understand consciousness and
reasoning.

"But," you might protest, "what about everything that seems
real to us that is not included in this definition?" The simple
and definitive answer is that it is all something *else*, something
other than reality. This definition of reality is entirely consistent with the process, nature and philosophy of science. The
monumental impact of this definition will become increasingly
clear as we move through the discussion of thought, being and
sentience.

 *What else could reality be, but that which can be verified as real, as verifiably existing in space and time? Isn't the impulse to make reality more or less than this actually just an attempt to reify private thoughts?*

1.3.2 Intelligence

The essence of intelligence is the ability to make a self-interested choice. We think that intelligence has something to do with the ability to remember and to do rapid calculations that produce the right answer, but that is just one aspect of intelligence, and a fairly unimportant one, at that. The ability to recognize and evaluate threats and opportunities, and to move away from the one and towards the other, is the essence of intelligence. Fish and turtles are intelligent in the fundamental sense, and dogs, crows and monkeys are intelligent on an additional level. The key concept to remember is that interested choice is the essence of intelligence. Note that making a choice in one's perceived self-interest has nothing whatsoever to do with whether that choice turns out to be a success or failure—the critical factor is the process of *perception* $\rightarrow$ *evaluation* $\rightarrow$ *action*, not the outcome, which might be hopeless to begin with.

1.3.3 Tervaluation

Evaluation is the crux of the self-interested choice, it is at the heart of intelligence. The evolutionary requirement is that volitionally mobile creatures must be able to evaluate sensory input before they can respond to it. This fundamental building block of intelligence is a tripolar assessment of the anti-self, pro-self and non-self dimensions of the input. That is, is this a threat, an opportunity, or nothing to be concerned about? Do I have to avoid it, seek it or can I ignore it? Hence, the term ter-valuation (ter: three + valuation) is offered to emphasize the tripolar nature of the judgment. The three poles of assessment correspond to the three basic directions of movement: away, towards and ignore. Note that it is normal for all three dimensions to have different, non-zero values, and it is the range of these combinations that gives us the various oblique response angles.

1.3.4 Internal and External Knowledge

Internal knowledge, $\mathbb{I}$, is the set of all ideas in an intellect. External knowledge, $\mathbf{E}$, is a subset of these ideas that have been shown, within an acceptable margin of error, to map to phenomena in reality by a formal test repeatable by multiple independent observers:

$$\mathbf{E} = \{i_j \in \mathbb{I} \iff \exists\, r_j \in \mathbb{R} \;:\; |i_j - r_j| < \epsilon\}$$

Everything we know, think, believe or feel is internal knowledge; it, and all operations on it, exists entirely within our own mind. Only such parts of that knowledge that have been verified to map to the real world through reproducible tests are part of the set of external knowledge. The relation of the rest of internal knowledge to external reality is undefined: any bit of it might either be real in whole or in part, or it might just be phantasmagoria. Without a verifying test, we just don't know, we *can't* know.

There is no logical difference between $\mathbf{E}$ and $\mathbb{R}$, since both are the set of all verified ideas, but $\mathbf{E}$ emphasizes the subset nature of our verified ideas ($\mathbf{E} \subset \mathbb{I}$), while $\mathbb{R}$ will be used to refer both to our verified ideas about reality as well as to reality itself, that is, $\mathbb{R}$ is our *view* of reality.

1.4   Model-Oriented Reasoning

In quantitative fields, the area where science currently uses quantitative model-oriented reasoning extensively, the subject being modeled is whatever arises in the problem area that the modeler wants to investigate. They know that anything in reality can be modeled. Actually, anything real or unreal can be modeled, and this realization is exactly what makes it possible for us to determine which of our thoughts correspond to a verifiable reality, and which are just mental constructs that lack a physical referent. The thought in our head occurs on and through real structures, but the content of the thought, its meaning, exists on a different level. Only when we are modeling things that exist in reality can we successfully test our models against reality (but we will see in chapter 31 that there is another level to reality). Models without successful tests are simple language constructs with no measurable validity.

In this volume, our focus is on opening the world of subjective experience to formal modeling, the intention is to make it possible for us to create formal models of subjective experiences and elements so that we can test them against reality to objectively identify their reality component. This narrows the domain of our subject considerably. Since subjectivity cannot arise, cannot exist, outside of a conscious intelligence, this means that the set of all subjective elements equals the set of internal knowledge elements:

$$\{Subjective\ elements\} = \mathbb{I}$$

Therefore, the subject of advanced model-oriented reasoning is *intelligence* and its associated artifacts and processes. This means that, whatever subjective element we want to study, it has to be situated in a greater model of perception and cognition, of intelligence. We will be using formal modeling to create executable, testable models of how intelligence processes thought. The goal of this volume is to equip the student with the tools they will need to develop their own model of intelligence that they can subsequently work to improve by repeatedly using the normal scientific method to create, test and evaluate hypotheses derived from their models.

1.5   Additional Terms

1.5.1   Statements

We interact with our models through statements, expressions that are meant to communicate a particular state, application, evaluation or conclusion of a model. Statements are constructs comprising one explicit term and two usually implicit terms:

statement = [context] + content + [goal]

Normal conversations are made up of sentences that represent statements against a model. Thus, one can think of a statement as a bridge that connects our normal experience of thinking and talking with the formal world of model-oriented reasoning. In formal modeling, all three terms are specified, but in informal thought or conversation, the outer two are invariably implicit. In real life, more often than not, this underspecification of thought leads to an unsurprising amount of miscommunication, misunderstanding, and strife.

1.5.2 Purblind Defect

The inability of organic cognition to perceive internal mental boundaries between independently evolved functionalities is called the purblind defect. It is a limitation of our sensibilities and is analogous to our lacking the ability to see beyond the visible spectrum. We are constitutionally oblivious of the fact that different parts of our mind evolved at different times to do different things, and that each tends to act independently of the others. This leads us into the erroneous belief that our 'mind' exists as a whole unit that 'thinks', and this leads us to assume that human consciousness and rationality is a thing, *sui generis*, borne of evolution, full and complete, rather than seeing it for what it is: a rather haphazard collection of small, simple, functional parts.

1.5.3   Metaphor

An idea that defines a *type* acts as a metaphor for sensory events. The process of identification only happens through metaphor; the process of knowing types is a metaphoric process. We 'know' c only because it is more like a than b. We have no capacity to know c *qua c*.

N.B.: This means that the predicate nominative in a state of being sentence is a metaphor for, not a reference to, some referent. That is, the term to the right of the verb is the metaphor through which the term to the left will be known. The significance of this indirection is not trivial.

Earlier, we mentioned that we habitually see *this* as *that*, and this is what makes us initially try to use Euclid to understand the world by borrowing its method. We find later on that doesn't work because the world is multi-dimensional and messy in a way that geometric shapes simply are not. The impulse to try to see x as y arises from the fact that we *know* through comparison of a new perception, x, to a set of known types, and we take the closest we can find, and conclude that x *is y*, or x is a type of y. As we get more into the low-level cognitive functions, it will become clearer that we simply have no faculty to see x as x until we use our higher functions to later define x as its own type, but even then it is based on a composite of fundamental types and evaluations.

1.5.4   Model

A model is a mental representation of a referent. It doesn't matter whether the referent is internal or external, real or imaginary. Through moments of perception, our mind translates sensory input into an internal form the mind can process. A formal model is a model that we have expressed in formal terms that can be unambiguously communicated to another observer and independently tested. An informal model is any model that is not formal. The various intellects in our minds each use their own type of model to encode experience, and these are informal only because our higher intellects lack the training, time, or motivation to express them in formal terms.

It is admittedly a little early, but this would be an appropriate moment to pause and reflect on the last sentence above ("The... terms"); later, you should come to realize that, in a real but limited sense, it summarizes one of the fundamental insights of this work.

1.5.5   Pattern Assimilation

Pattern assimilation is the mechanism of what we traditionally call learning; it is how we learn our native tongue, how we learn lessons in school. In pattern assimilation, one learns the entry and exit points to a pattern, that is, when it should be invoked, and what the outcome should look like. The patterns themselves are composites of patterns that may themselves be composites or atomic patterns. An example of an atomic pattern would be a simple phoneme. A composite pattern would be a path comprising branching structures that support the creation of higher level, adaptable patterns, such as a path from phoneme to phoneme that continues to branch until all the forms of a word are defined with links that lead, through other patterns, to our library of fundamental types.

1.5.6   Emergent Property

An emergent property is a behavior, state, or apparently high level operation that is produced as the result of the synergy of any number of independent functions. For example, consciousness is an emergent property because: 1) it observably exists, 2) there is no single 'consciousness' function, and 3) it is the product of a number of independent functions, and it will manifest differently depending on the timely performance of these functions, or failure thereof. The significance of emergent properties is that we experience them as a whole, as a unified thing, but they are the happenstance of a number of independent processes. Peering deeply into an emergent property resolves the mirage of the whole into the constituent parts. Understanding a trait or behavior that is an emergent property requires that we work our way through all of the smaller functions it comprises.

1.5.7   Evacule, Mentacule, Situation, Pattern

See chapter 12, Cognition Objects.

1.6   Computer Science Terms

There are several terms from computer science and mathematics that may be unfamiliar to the reader, so following are some short definitions focused on the way they are used in the text.

1.6.1   Big O Notation

We do not know how fast computers will run in the future, so when we talk about time in calculating the efficiency of algorithms, we are actually talking about the number of steps a calculation takes. We represent this as orders of magnitude using what is called 'Big O' notation like this: $O(1)$, $O(n)$, $O(n^2)$, which you pronounce 'Order one', 'Order n', etc. If an algorithm is $O(1)$, it means it executes in constant time, which means very fast since it doesn't take longer to process larger data sets. Order n algorithms take proportionally longer as the data set grows, and Order n^2 algorithms grow at the square of the size of the data set. $O(1)$ is best, $O(log_n)$ is good, and exponential orders of magnitude are unusable on any but the smallest data sets.

1.6.2   Graph

A graph is a set of nodes and links, not a Cartesian grid like you see on graph paper. Think of an airline route map that shows cities (the nodes) and the flight paths connecting them (the links). Graph theory covers the mathematics of graphs, and applications to different problem domains. The traveling salesman problem is a famous example of a class of problems that have too many combinations, once they get beyond a small size, to be solved even on modern computers.

The way we use graphs is to show the relation between a set of nodes and the links between them to explain that, even if the links are virtual, the graph has a reality that can be analyzed mathematically.

1.6.3 Type

The term *type* refers to a data type and its supported operations. In computer terms, the basic types such as integer, decimal (float, double, long, etc.), string actually refer to how the data is stored on disk. In a more general sense, type is just any classification of phenomenon by specific attribute. For example, a young human can be referred to as a child, or as a boy or girl, depending on how you want to sort or classify the data.

The power of types is that they allow you to create sophisticated hierarchies to meet your specific needs, instead of just having all of your stuff in a bag. Organization by type can be used to optimize searching and retrieval of objects or data.

1.6.4 Indirection

The concept of indirection is to link to a value indirectly, instead of holding a value in hand, sort of like having a number of an account that holds your money, instead of carrying all of your cash in your pocket.

Type and indirection work together to support abstractions which make high-level reasoning possible by supporting and exposing comparison among different things on the basis of some, possibly narrow, shared characteristic.

1.6.5   Magnitude

In mathematics, the concept of magnitude is generally represented by surrounding a symbol with two vertical bars: $|\mathbf{A}|$ (the bars also signify absolute value, but I usually just use $abs(x)$ to represent that). The definition of magnitude varies with context, so sometimes it means cardinality, sometimes it means the total of some other dimensions, such as length or value.

1.7   Symbols

- $|x|$: magnitude of x
- $\mathbb{R}$: our model of reality, and, informally, physical reality itself.
- ϵ: epsilon, the error between prediction and measurementϵ
- ξ: xi, refers to externalized (in the loose sense of 'acknowledged by others') elements of $\mathbb{CS}$
- $\wedge$: logical and operator
- ':' : colon, in set notation, *such that*
- $\rightarrow$: implies or produces
- $\iff$: if and only if
- $\mathbf{M}_L$: the set of models on a given level (or just $\mathbf{M}$)
- $\forall$: for all
- $\exists$: there exists
- $\in$: element of
- $\approx, \cong$: approximately, approximately equals
- $O(n)$: order of n, refers to the number of steps in a computation in relation to the size of the input set

1.8   Review

In place of the usual exercises found at the end chapters in traditional text books, we will end each chapter with a bullet point
list of important terms and concepts discussed in the chapter
in the hopes of helping the conscientious student to master the
material as efficiently as possible.

- Method: Neither skim nor skip any chapters in this book—
  doing so would be fatal to the effort. Pause, linger, or
  reread rather than hurry. Think of this as a math book
  and plan your study accordingly. Although an attempt
  was made to make this volume stand alone, since it is
  the third volume in the work, if you haven't already read
  the previous volumes, there will be times when it will be
  necessary to review them for specific concepts.

- Goal: The goal of this work is to provide a full kit of
  tools to enable the student to carry out their own research
  extending the scientific method into the subjective domain
  so that they can begin to formulate their own answers to
  what they see as pinnacle questions.

- Purblind defect: the structural inability to see the different parts of our mind as different, including the inability
  to clearly distinguish between our idea of a thing and the
  thing itself.

- Faceted model-oriented reasoning: an enhanced form of
  normal model-oriented reasoning (the faceted aspect will
  be explained in chapter 28, Faceted Model-Oriented Reasoning).

- Reality: the set of all measurable things.

- Intelligence: the ability to make interested choices.

- Tervaluation: To what extent something is bad for me, good for me, or nothing to me, is the basis of all value and all evaluation (the word itself is not used much, but the idea is fundamental and pervasive).

- Internal knowledge: the set of all ideas, feelings and beliefs we have.

- External knowledge: the subset of internal knowledge that includes only ideas that have been reproducibly verified.

- Subjectivity: a property of mortal consciousness, the nature of thought.

- Statement: the fundamental unit of reasoning and communication:

  statement = [context] + content + [goal].

- Metaphor: our main way of knowing: 'a is b' or 'a is a type of b' is a metaphor, it is seeing a as a flavor of b.

- Model: a mental representation of a phenomenon or event.

- Formal: an unambiguous, reproducibly actionable, technical, as opposed to verbal, definition that is understood by experts in the pattern language; informal means lacking a precise, technical definition.

- Pattern assimilation: The process of memorizing pattern chunks that includes the approved uses of the pattern.

- Emergent property: a condition that exists only as the sum of the products of a number of independent functions, a result created by a set of independent functions as opposed to the output of one function.

- Big O notation, O(): the number of steps an algorithm takes to complete, based on the data set input size.
- Graph: a set of nodes connected by links.
- Type: classification of entities.
- Indirection: the ability to navigate to a target through references, or containers, etc., possibly chained, instead of direct access to the value.

Part I

Understanding The Model

Chapter 2

Laws of Model-Oriented Reasoning

2.1 Laws

We begin the examination of the principles of model-oriented reasoning with a set of fundamental laws. Our conjecture is that it is impossible for the function of cognition to evolve in any organic entity anywhere in our universe in violation of them, so it is meet to call them *laws*.

M1 All reasoning is executed by, and specific to, evolved structures.

M2 The layered structure of the cognitive apparatus:

31

- reflects it evolutionary origin, and
- restricts the domain and range of cognitive functions to the set of models on the function's level.

M3 Models are continuous or discrete, and formal, informal, or mixed.

M4 Discrete models have a finite number of testable points.

M5 The cardinality of measurements possible on reality referents is on the order of an uncountable infinity.

M6 Formal model features are testable, informal ones are not.

M7 Model validity varies as the ratio between the number of points in successful, reproducible tests and the number of testable points in the referent.

M8 Purely informal models have a validity that equals, or approaches, zero.

M9 Level L_n cannot impair the function of level L_{n-1}

*These laws are going to be referred to repeatedly in the chapters to follow, oftentimes only by letter and number, such as **M2**. So, you might find it helpful to keep them readily at hand, however you prefer to do that.*

2.2   Bootstrapping

Bootstrapping refers to the practice of using the system being built to build the system itself (or using the operating system to load the operating system). We have used this practice throughout this series of volumes, e.g., when we used the distance formula to discover the distance formula. While some may find the approach confusing and apparently circular, it is vaguely like test driven development where the practice is to create some tests prior to coding, and then code to pass each test, and iterate. Similarly, in recursive programming one solves a problem by having a function call itself after reducing the input set until the stopping case is reached, and then each of the recursive calls completes and returns an answer to its caller, all the way to the top of the calling chain, where the final answer is assembled. We mention this because we are going to gradually explain model-oriented reasoning by using model-oriented reasoning. It should be obvious soon enough that there is no other way to do it.

Although bootstrapping might seem odd at first glance, how do you suppose that evolution works, if not by bootstrapping? Evolution is the process by which biological systems incrementally grow in complexity through the trial and error addition of new functionality (with editing and final cut being made by natural selection, reality's scythe for culling maladaptations). As a software architect, I have always used the systems that I am building to build the systems themselves. This always seemed prudent, since the only alternative would be to build or work in other systems to produce parts of the target system that wouldn't reach full functionality until the new system was complete. The risk in the latter approach is, as shown by the huge numbers of late and failed projects, ridiculously high, so I have always controlled that risk by designing systems to evolve incrementally by leveraging their own functionality as quickly and thoroughly as possible, similarly to how life evolves. Life seems to be, in my eyes, a reasonably good example to follow.

Faceted model-oriented reasoning is built on the universal cognition model (see chapter 7), and this is built on evolutionary cytomodel principles. The cytomodel is derived from the design of cells that make up our bodies, complex units of function that have no central controller and instead rely on a large number of independent functions to blindly complete their tasks in a timely manner. These functions are usually triggered by chemical or other kinds of signals or input, and they just produce their output without any awareness of what its ultimate use will be. An evolutionary cytomodel models the layered structures that arise through evolution, which means that new functions can be added to the mix without necessarily modifying existing functions, with the end result that total functionality is the sum or product of functionality that developed at varying times in the evolutionary history of the being. In other words, grand, high-level functionality is the product of a pastiche of blind, independent, small functions, instead of being the product of an integrated design of same-generation functions.

Of course, cognition evolved in stages, just as all of the other biological processes have evolved in stages through a variety of solutions, only some of which succeeded, as the tree of life makes clear. So, too, have our cognitive abilities developed in a process of elaborating simplicity towards complexity through the gradual accretion of small, new functions that exploited newly evolved structures that arose through mutation. Although difficult, it is important that we maintain the discipline of eschewing teleology—nothing evolves *in order that* something, instead, mutations are perpetuated only when they are harmless or helpful. Evolution is the story of structural elaboration driven by the realities of the limits of DNA control and error correction in the face of mutation. It is important to realize that mutations *precede* changes in environmental realities, and that they are only later exposed by shifts in the ecological niche that disadvantage those parts of the population lacking them; and that mutations and evolution are an ongoing process that continues even in humans, even today.

2.3 M1: Reasoning on Structures

On what material substrate could thinking possibly occur, if not on evolved structures? It is natural, I suppose, for one to think of reasoning as a process more than as a structure, but since the reasoning capacity is inherited, it must be largely describable as a structure with related processes, rather than as a set of processes independent of any structure. Since the reasoning capacity is the product of evolution, and since primitive reasoning is observable in simpler creatures, reasoning had to have evolved in steps, and some of those stages must still be present in our more highly evolved minds.

The purblind defect prevents us from perceiving that our reasoning is a composite of more primitive and more advanced structures and processes, that it is, in fact, an emergent property that is more or less functional depending on how many lower level functions are active and effective at any given time. We know that our thinking suffers when we are impaired by illness, fatigue, intoxication or emotional stress, but we rarely appreciate how this reveals the emergent nature of thought. Impairment strikes our perceptual/cognitive apparatus unevenly, eroding some functions utterly while leaving others untouched, which often leaves us unable to recognize or acknowledge our abnormal or degraded mental function.

The consequence of the purblind defect is that we tend to labor under the misapprehension that our 'mind', *as a unit*, 'thinks'. We are oblivious to the various divisions of the mind, with their distinct functions and responsibilities that developed independently along our lengthy evolutionary path. Therefore, it might not occur to most of us that, rather than being a process that the mind does as a whole, reasoning is the product of many smaller functions that may coordinate, but actually operate independently on the various structures that evolved at different times in our mind throughout the development of our species.

Higher level cognition is a whole that is an emergent property of various independent functionalities; there is no single 'reasoning' structure or function in the brain, rather, 'reasoning' is a just a lazy term our minds use to refer to the aggregate product of many unrelated, unorchestrated functions that each do their own work independently, and without regard to each other, or to the end product.

When considered from this evolutionary perspective, it might be easier to understand that, of course, earlier parts of our mind must use simpler structures to execute simpler functions related to self-preservation, while more recently evolved parts of our minds use more complex structures to support such functions as language and abstract thought. This implies that some of our thoughts come from our most primitive mental functions, while others are produced by more evolved structures, yet we don't differentiate between them, nor do we acknowledge that the earlier parts of our minds cannot understand our more sophisticated thoughts, since they aren't built to handle them. The purblind defect means that we are not naturally equipped to anticipate what will happen when our self-preservation mind tries to handle a language concept it has no way of processing.

In computerese, what happens when a more complex data structure is converted into a simpler data structure is called a *narrowing type conversion* where the wider (more complex) data structures, for example those involved in language processing, are cast into narrower data structures, such as those used by the pre-verbal mind. For example, a decimal number, such as 3.14, when cast to the narrower integer type (converting, for example, a 64-bit data type to a 32-bit data type) becomes 3, losing important information in the process. Going in the other direction, that is, promoting an integer to a float or double, can be done without loss of information, but going from a 'wider' to a 'narrower' data type (in a literal sense this means going from a 4 byte data type to a 2 or 1 byte type) always risks losing information.

Failing to recognize the different levels of our intellect leaves us unequipped to recognize the loss in precision that happens when we downcast complex ideas into simpler structures, as well as the misleading pretense of precision when we upcast primitive ideas into complex terms (e.g., seeing the integer 3 as the float 3.00 creates a false impression of precision to the hundredth place when it is really only precise to the integer). The purblind defect assures us that we will routinely trespass across the invisible—to us—borders separating the various intellects, and in the process degrade the quality of our information and pollute the reasoning based on it.

So, the first law of model-oriented reasoning: 'all reasoning is executed by, and specific to, evolved structures', states it is not possible to have reasoning without an organic structure to support the process (the asomatous psyche that will be discussed later will be able to reason without organic structures, but it was originally created by an organism), and the structures involved have evolved over time. This means that thoughts must be encoded into evolved structures, so thoughts produced by structures that evolved later cannot be processed by predecessor structures except through a lossy, narrowing typecast (conversion), and since we have no faculty that equips us to avoid these costly forays up and down our evolutionary structures, the only way we can limit this degradation of our knowledge is by learning to use intellectual constructs to compensate for the purblind defect. Only by mastering higher level concepts will we be able to gain an articulated level of understanding of what happens in our mind as we think and feel.

2.4   M2: Reasoning on a Model

By the first law, we know that reasoning executes on evolved structures. These structures exist in our brain, so in order for us to respond to an external event with anything more than a nervous flinch, we have to convert sensory impulses into charges on evolved brain structures before we we can reason on them in order to eventually generate an appropriate response. These structures are elementary models, and we reason only on them, not with whatever external phenomenon reflected the light, generated the sound waves, or emitted the aromatic molecules that assaulted our senses. Of course, we never see the thing itself; we only sense vision if reflected light in the visible band strikes our eyes, and it is only from that reflected light and its encoded and decoded impulses that we develop a visual image. The notion that we 'see' reality is an artifact of the purblind defect that even makes it hard for us to identify the boundary between ourself and entities that exist apart from us. It's not that we mistake the external for the internal, but that we mistake the internal for the external, we think that the model inside our mind of the dog is the dog itself, when clearly it is not, it cannot be.

Understand, evolution is an error-dominant process, so the relatively random nature of the mutation process would likely lead to many of the earliest internal representations of events being inaccurate enough to lead to fatal consequences, meaning most mutations are failures, and probably most would-be species are extinct. We are the progeny of those whom evolution endowed with sensory impulse translations that were good enough to generally lead us away from trouble and towards opportunities.

This process of charging internal structures to match external experience may be summarized as:

$$P(x) \to m_i \in \mathbf{M}_0$$

That is, the perception process, P, maps any external event, x, to an internal model, m_i, which is an element of the set of all models, $\mathbf{M}_0$, belonging to the zeroth cognition level.

We can initially define a model as a mental abstraction of an event experienced by our senses, either external or internal, that is realized on some structure in some evolved intellect in our brain. When we see a dog or a tree, we do not reason on the external objects themselves, but instead, we reason on the mental representations our minds have contrived for them, a representation whose form is defined by our genotype and whose final content is heavily influenced both by our individual nature and by our personal experiences.

The second law is not that we *ought* to reason against a model, but that all reasoning is the process of comparing, analyzing, generalizing, adding, subtracting (and so on) the values in heritable attribute arrays to arrive at the basis for making self-significant decisions. The point is that there is no reasoning without a model:

Reasoning is the process of performing operations on models to produce conclusions that form the basis for the definition and execution of self-significant actions.

We only reason against models, we have always only reasoned against models, just like squirrels, birds and all of the other autonomously mobile life forms do. The mechanisms of model-oriented reasoning have been hidden from us by a purblind defect that causes us to misperceive our mind as an integrated continuum when it is actually more like a three ring circus where multiple acts are performing simultaneously whilst an aeriel act performs overhead. The purblind defect forces us to misinterpret the emergent property of consciousness as a unity, a thing in itself, even though consciousness is undeniably a composite of independent functions that operate separately with no awareness of the nature, function or purpose of the whole. What do calcium channels know of the cells containing them? Nothing, they just have pores that open or close based on voltage, and yet the cell could not function without them, and just so does the mind house a wide variety of independent functions that in total make up our reasoning capacity, even though none of them is deliberately working towards a larger or common purpose.

It is not possible to model brain-contained reasoning without models, so unless we are going back to the ancient Greek notion that our mind actually extends itself out to directly engage with an abstract, universal concept, then we are forced to acknowledge the inevitability of model-oriented reasoning as the only reasoning there is. Reasoning that is unaware of the model abstraction layer existing between *thought* and *thing*, is still model-based, but would more appropriately be referred to as purblind, rather than model-oriented, reasoning, for obvious reasons. The alternative to being ruled by the harsh and inept regime that purblind reasoning imposes on our non-scientific thought process is to make the effort to learn the art and discipline of deliberate, faceted model-oriented reasoning.

The consequence of the purblind defect is that we can only indirectly perceive the various structures and processes that affect our reasoning by using intellectual constructs that we deliberately built to explore and explain the intricacies of our thought processes. Submariners must use sound waves to 'see' underwater; particle physicists must use detectors to 'see' subatomic particles; we generally need training to understand what a sonogram or x-ray is showing us. Since the defect makes us blind to the topography of our mind, we need detailed models and training to be able to learn how to interpret our everyday experience in a way that actually makes sense, in a way that enables us to see that we are reasoning on a discrete model comprising a small number of points that have an undefined relation to the effectively infinite number of measurement points that exist in the external physical phenomenon.

Remember, the over-arching theme of this series of volumes is that it is only with the new science of model-oriented reasoning that we are now finally able to begin to tackle the pinnacle

questions that have stymied humanity for as long as civilization
has existed. That we reason against models is not to be denied,
neither is the fact that without using formal models (like the
ones we will be examining here for the first time) we have been
doing a very bad job of using our minds to create reproducible
results in the subjective sphere of human experience, the area
outside of the scientific and technical fields. This is why we
haven't yet begun to reduce the untouched backlog of pinnacle
questions.

If we look at **M2** from the perspective of the programmable
simulation, then the set of functions $f()$ on any model m in the
set of models **M** defined by an intellect level, L, will include the
initialization function, $init(m)$, that instantiates a model, and
all other functions, $g()$, supported on the set of models in a given
intellect level, $\mathbf{M}_L$. Note that a model is instantiated with input
from a lower-level intellect, $\mathbf{M}_{L-1}$. The levels we are using in
the asomatous psyche are: L0 (avoid threat, seek opportunity),
L1 (learn from experience), L2 (anticipate), and L3 (discover),
all of which we will discuss in depth as we proceed. L0 instantiates models by pulling from L-1, the level where hard-wired
connections tie sensory experiences to response triggers.

Since our intellects evolved over time, each new level of intellect only has to package the model from the preexisting lower
level into the model defined by the new, higher level structures
in order to add a new level of complex functionality to our mental faculties. This repackaging allows for existing functionality
to be preserved and leveraged, instead of having to reinvent

it at each new level of development. Note that, by this definition, while higher level intellects can become aware of the lower level intellects in the same way they can become aware of anything, lower level intellects are simply incapable—due to a lack of both wiring and the wherewithal to comprehend—of perceiving or understanding any of the more recently developed structures or functions.

$$f(m \in \mathbf{M}_L) = \begin{cases} init(m) = \begin{cases} Domain : \mathbf{M}_{L-1} \\ Range : \mathbf{M}_L \end{cases} \\ g(m) = \begin{cases} Domain : \mathbf{M}_L \\ Range : \mathbf{M}_L \end{cases} \end{cases}$$

What the above definition shows is that model-oriented reasoning maps models from the domain of a particular evolved intellect back into the same set. That is, each intellect, each independently evolved reasoning structure, can only process the models native to its structure. Since both the domain and range of the model-oriented reasoning functions supported by a particular intellect are the same set of models defined by the structures in that intellect, the limit of reasoning at any level is defined by the set of models that characterize the intellect chosen to do the reasoning.

Essentially, model-oriented reasoning is the set of all operations that map a model from a set of models into itself or a different model in the same set. Because of the evolutionary nature of our composite mind, it is possible for a higher intellect to instantiate a model in its domain with a model from a lower intellect, but the limitation remains that a given intellect maps models in its domain back into it, just as addition maps integers in $\mathbb{Z}$ to $\mathbb{Z}$. The origin of this limitation should obvious to anyone who reflects that each level of intellect had to function for eons before the next level began to appear.

2.5   M3: Discrete Models

All models not implemented as continuous functions are discrete, that is, they have a finite number of data points, regardless of how many measurable points might exist in the referent. The miracle is that our minds are able, by creating internal images with a handful of data points, to model externalities that effectively have an uncountably infinite number of measurable dimensions, and to model them so well that we survive long enough to prosper and proliferate. There is no need for us to include every point from the referent into the model, but this fact does dictate that there is always more that we don't know about something than what we do know.

The set of all models in a given intellect level, $\mathbf{M}_L$, equals the union of the set of formal models $\mathbf{M}_F$ and the set of informal models $\mathbf{M}_I$ in that level, L.

$$\mathbf{M}_L = (\mathbf{M}_F \cup \mathbf{M}_I)_L$$

A mixed model is simply an informal model with some formal bits mixed in, so if you think of the above definition as recursive, a mixed model is just an early union of formal and informal models. The practical difficulty with mixed models is that we invariably overestimate the size of the formal element in order to endow our informal thought with undeserved authority.

Formal models are expressed in formal terms. 'Formal' means that both the context and the goal of each statement, as well as the content, are explicitly defined in unambiguous terms in a formal symbolic language. Formal models support independent tests by disinterested experimenters, and in addition, can be expressed in any sufficiently complete modeling language of the verbal, visual, mathematical and executable type. Informal models can only be expressed in informal terms, and any translation to any other formal or informal terms cannot be verified for accuracy and completeness. The essence of an informal model is *subjective incompleteness*, that is, they lack of any mechanism to objectively assign any particular attribute or function either to the set of included or excluded elements. In this work, we call informal models *mudball models* on the principle that they contain an indeterminate mix of whatever happens to be around each time they are expressed, a hodge-podge of vague notions that will differ every time it is assembled or referenced.

Of course, there are many ways to partition the set of all models that can exist on any particular intellect level, but this partitioning of models into the formal and informal subsets is useful for our purposes of understanding the limits and capabilities of these two very different kinds of models.

2.6   M4: Discrete Model Limits

$$\forall \ m_i \in \mathbf{M}_L, |P_m| < \infty_c \qquad (2.1)$$

Continuous functions in mathematical models can apply to an uncountably infinite number of points, but the cardinality of the set of testable points in a discrete model, $|P_m|$, on the other hand, is less than a countable infinity (a lot less, but without further work, we accept this as an upper bound). In more practical terms, the number of testable points is more likely on the order of 10^n for a small n since every point in the formal model had to be added by a finite mind in a finite amount of time.

In observable reality, atoms join to create molecules, molecules aggregate to form materials and some organize to form chains. Gravity coalesces matter into bodies, organic matter evolves to form life, and all of this happens from the atomic level up to the macroscopic level with a level of numeracy and detail inconceivable in a discrete model. Every testable point that exists in a discrete model had to be specified by a mind, thus the upper limit for the number of possible testable points of a discrete model is less than countable infinity, a lot less.

2.7   M5: Reality Referents

$$\forall \ r_i \in \mathbb{R}, |measurements_r| \approx \infty_u$$

In most cases, the number of points in a given entity in reality, r_i, is effectively a countable infinity, but the number of measurements possible actually is an uncountable infinity when precision is unbounded or when the number of indeterminate states is included. Counting, at the limit, is comprehended by a countable infinity (think: integers), but measurement is comprehended by an uncountable infinity (think: real numbers). If we are modeling a tree, we can say it has n cells, where, although large, n is a countable number. However, since all things in reality, $\mathbb{R}$, are characterized by dimension or magnitude, and since these are *measurable* characteristics, then each entity/force in reality involves an uncountably infinite number measurements each of which may have an unbounded fractal measurement (see "How Long Is the Coast of Britain? Statistical Self-Similarity and Fractional Dimension" by Benoit Mandelbrot, *Science*, 1967).

Let's just say that reality ranges from the incredibly small to the immensely huge, and tends to the impossibly numerous at every level, and can be measured in an uncountably infinite number of ways. We must keep this nature of the referent in mind whenever our model of reality is discrete, that is, when it is based on a small number of specific data points, rather than on a continuous function.

2.8   M6: Testability

A test is a formal, reproducible procedure that produces a measurement of the variance between the statements made on a formal model and observable reality. A statement on a model can properly be viewed as a prediction that the referent of that model has a particular characteristic. That is,

$$\forall\, m_i \in \mathbf{M}_{FL} \;\exists\, t_{m_i} \in \mathbf{T} \;:\; t_{m_i} \to r_i \Rightarrow |m_i - r_i| < \epsilon$$

That is, for every formal model, m_i, there exists one or more tests, t_{m_i}, that produces a real number measurement, $|m_i - r_i|$, that quantifies the variance between the predictions in that model and observable reality. The essential characteristic of a formal model is that it can be expressed in abstract, quantitative terms that have technical definitions that allow independent researchers to precisely reproduce the experiment, without recourse to the original experimenter, to determine a measure of the variance between the model and reality. (In a more general sense, the measurement will be a complex number, but for most purposes, a real number will probably suffice.) Every model can be used to generate one or more tests for each testable point in the model.

2.9 M7: Model Validity

$$v_m = |T_{m_v}|/|r_{\mathbb{R}}|$$

The validity of a model m, v_m, is proportional to the ratio of verified tests of m, $|T_{m_v}|$ to the number of testable points in the model referent, $|r_{\mathbb{R}}|$. Since the number of testable points in a reality referent is effectively an uncountable infinity, the validity measure of discrete models, while critically important, is a very small number. We should be humbly awed that, through the miracle of cognitive faculties that only use a tiny number of points to model infinite realities, we can conceive in our heads workable models of reality. It's a miracle that we can know anything, not a disappointment that we don't know everything.

While using a model with, for example, only 5 verifiable test points of the uncountable infinity its referent contains may chasten us, yet there is all the difference in the world between that model and another of the same phenomenon that only has 2 verifiable test points, or a mudball model that has none.

The question, "How many testable points does a discrete model need to have in order to be considered a valid representation of a continuous referent?" cannot be answered in real life for a fairly obvious reason. Consider:

$$min(p)_m = n * |d_{interest}|$$

That is, the minimum number of points, p, in a model equals n times the number of dimensions of interest. If we want to map a reef in the ocean to allow shipping to avoid it, do we need a fractal map of all the concave and convex shapes in its outline down to the picometer level? No, of course not, and in all likelihood, we would be satisfied with a simple polygon larger than the reef by some comfortable margin of error. This illustrates the point that a discrete model is *not* modeling reality, but rather, it is modeling the profile of our *interaction* with reality. Ultimately, our very mortality posits that we have a rather parochial interest in reality, so our discrete model only needs enough tests to validate that, based on current information, we likely won't have an unfortunate experience with the model referent. When new information adds new risk or opportunity points to our data set, then we will probably find it necessary to extend our model accordingly.

So, the minimum number of testable points in a valid model is whatever number we are personally willing to bet our life on; no more, no less.

2.10   M8: Informal Model Validity

$$v(m_i \in \mathbf{M}_I) \approx 0 \approx v(m_j \in \mathbf{M}_I)$$

Since informal models have no tests, the validity for any of them is undefined or approaching 0, (depending on how you look at it). Therefore, logically, any informal model can be substituted for any other informal model without any loss of verifiable correspondence to reality, $\mathbb{R}$. Thus, all informal models can be considered equivalent because they have the same validity measure relative to any $r \in \mathbb{R}$.

But, what about those cases where we actually have some evidence or a test or two for a couple of points in an informal model, does that matter? Mixed models that combine an equation or verified fact or two with opinion represent such a case, and so does practice in the technical trades. The essence of testability is reproducibility, and, while it may lack a numerical or theoretical facet, one worker showing another what happens when he strikes or pushes something still falls into the realm of externalized, reproducible knowledge. In these cases, the reproducible parts can be confirmed, but the surrounding framework is still just unreliable noise.

In many cases, we actually do have physical bruises from bumping into reality, or we have learned that by avoiding it we stay unbruised, so that many mudball models have some experiential verification validating parts of them, but this is both unquantified and largely, if not wholly, unreproducible. So, while we may sometimes know something, we rarely can be sure of what is is that we do know. Now, say that model m_i has n testable points, and model m_j has $m < n$ testable points, can we say that the first model is 'better' than the second? No, we cannot for a very simple reason: besides the test results, what is the difference between the first and second models? That is, what is $m_i - m_j$? This difference can never be calculated on informal models, so we can never say that one is *better* than the other. We can *choose* to prefer using one over the other in our reasoning, but this is a belief-based calculation, little supported by the reality of the model.

As a practical matter, we have to choose one model over many others in our daily reasoning, and there are better and worse ways to make this type of low information decision, but this happens below the level of formal model-oriented reasoning, and is discussed elsewhere.

2.11   M9: Law of Preservation

Level L_{n+1} can supplement or replace functionality at L_n, the earlier level below it, but it cannot degrade the performance of any preserved function of the lower level. Complex structural changes represent an accumulation of smaller changes, and intermediate changes that impair current function before advanced functionality matures, certainly must pose a serious disadvantage in the struggle to survive. One can expect such changes will generally be culled by natural selection.

2.12   Review

This chapter has mostly been a recitation and explanation of the laws of model-oriented reasoning. The broader implications of these laws are difficult, if not impossible, for the reader to anticipate at this point. They will be referenced repeatedly throughout this work as the basis for other explanations, and by this means, their power will gradually be made apparent. The elegance of laws is that they save us the necessity of working through these basic arguments over and over again, because we can dispose of issues by simply referring to the relevant law by its identifier.

- Bootstrapping: using the thing to build the thing (in our case, to explain it)
- Mutations are an ongoing process in evolving species.
- Mutations precede (and follow) the evolution of new species.
- M1: Reasoning happens on evolved structures.
- M2: Reasoning happens against a model on a cognitive level.
- M3: Models are discrete or continuous, and formal, informal, or mixed.
- M4: Discrete models have a finite number of testable points.
- M5: Reality referents can be measured in an infinite number of ways (e.g. what is the position of every electron in

every atom of the object at every moment?).

- M6: Tests define the limited validation of models; the unvalidated part of a discrete model is infinite.

- M7: Model validity is proportional to the number of successfully tested points compared to the total number of measurable points in the subject.

- M8: Higher level intellectual function cannot impair lower level intellectual function.

Chapter 3

Models and Formal Models

3.1 Introduction

Precision is defined by the acceptable margin of error (often represented by ϵ, epsilon) in the measurement of the end result, and this is the ever-present fork in the road for all of us whenever we deal with real world entities. For example, a stick frame house is built with 2x4's, yet 2x4's are actually 1.5" x 3.5", but this can generally be disregarded (unless you are rehabbing a house old enough to have been built with true 2x4's). However, being part of an inch off plumb can cause great inconvenience, so sometimes fractions of an inch do matter. Although Newtonian calculations do not take relativistic effects into account, we can use them to send rockets to the moon because, at the speeds we travel, the effects of relativity are indiscernible, but GPS satellite networks will not work unless you take time dilation into account. In some cases, approximate answers will do, in others, we need a higher level of precision.

There is no absolute answer to the question, "how good is good enough?" It all depends on the requirements of the situation. Unnecessary precision is a waste of effort and money, but inadequate precision will sink ships and bring down aircraft. The responsible workman, designer, manager or person must, to have any hope of bringing a project in on time and under budget, make responsible decisions to insist on a high level of precision where required, and to accept a much lower level where it is not. This is part of being a grown up, we all have to solve economic optimization problems as a normal part of our diurnal activities.

By **M2** we know that all reasoning executes against models regardless of our opinion or awareness of the topic. Reasoning happens in our minds on structures that are encoded in our genotype (**M1**), and those structures are the templates that define a model once data is applied. Throughout history we have unknowingly used model-oriented reasoning to seek benefit, to avoid harm, to procreate the next generation and to pass on our culture and traditions. Let's call this traditional form of model-oriented reasoning *purblind reasoning*, borrowing the term from the purblind defect that characterizes it. This type of reasoning does not recognize the difference between the internal models it perceives and thinks about, and the actual external realities those models represent. Just as with Newtonian and Einsteinian equations, in some situations you can get away using the less precise methodology, but in other cases, you simply cannot.

Make no mistake, purblind reasoning has been adequate to get us to where we are now in the history of civilization in all areas of knowledge, belief and tradition unaffected by the scientific and technological revolutions. If where we are now, with wars, poverty, antisemitism, obscurantist political debates, intellectually bankrupt liberal arts university systems, frictional interpersonal relations and the rest, is good enough, then we can stick with purblind reasoning and continue to generate this level of result for the foreseeable future. I trust you are reading this because you do not think it is good enough.

One can think of the advanced form of model-oriented reasoning, the subject of this volume, as purblind reasoning *plus* a comprehensive system of concepts, techniques and tests that compensate for the distortions caused by our purblind lens and, in so doing, open up the domain of subjective human experience to the reach of the scientific method, and the reproducible test, for the first time. You might even liken what faceted model-oriented reasoning does to purblind reasoning to the fix installed on the Hubble telescope to compensate for the spherical aberration in its main mirror—the original, years old error cannot be fixed, but by using superior concepts and tools, it can compensated for. The reward for the greater effort required to master and execute model-oriented, over purblind, reasoning is the greater level of precision attainable with quantitative analysis and reproducible tests over what we can achieve with feelings, convictions, and 'common sense', alone.

 *Reflect on the previous paragraph. If we could we solve our age-old problems with simple ideas, wouldn't we already have done it? An intellectual fix for genetic flaws has to be complex, don't you think?*

We know that it is impossible for us to see the layers in our mind just using traditional purblind reasoning because we lack whatever sensory capacity it would take to directly perceive such mental boundaries. Certainly, we do regard thoughts, facts, feelings and beliefs as different phenomena, but we see them all as independent events or forces swimming in the sea of our awareness. We think of our awareness as being one thing, our rational mind as another thing, our emotions as another, our beliefs as another. The normal mudball model used by purblind reasoning positions our consciousness, our sense of self, in a maelstrom of different types of phenomena: mental, emotional and spiritual experiences, with us at the center, buffeted by the storm. Our awareness, our *being-ness* is seen as a unity, an objective observer of this swirl of unrelated and constitutionally distinct phenomena. But, this is exactly the problem created by the purblind defect: rather than seeing internal phenomena stratified on mental layers that evolved over the eons, we see these different things as if they all exist in the same structural space, at the same level of abstraction, all realized on the same mental structures.

But, what if beliefs, feelings and thoughts are not *horizontally* distinct—i.e., what if they do not all exist on the same level of experience—but are instead, *vertically* distinct? What if beliefs and feelings are the product of one level of intellect, while memories, concepts, ideas and patterns are products of different, more recent levels of consciousness? What if *truth* is the standard that the oldest intellect uses to know the difference between right and wrong, *grammatical consistency* the standard used by a more recent intellect, and *measurement* the standard used by the most recently evolved intellect?

3.2 Working With a Model

We have mentioned two types of models: formal, which are expressed in formal terms and are executable, and informal, which are expressed in the form native to the level that formed them. Informal models are good enough to allow us to function as we always have, and if that is good enough for us, then we are done. However, for those of us who want something more, something better, who want to see the culture of progress that has allowed science to achieve so much in the last four or five centuries, now extend far enough to encompass the world of subjective experience, then we need something more than informal models.

In order to ground this abstract discussion on a level closer to our experience to make it easier to think about, let's start working with a familiar informal model, *conversation*, and see what happens when we begin to apply the concepts we have been discussing to it.

Convivial conversation can make it seem like we share common understandings of private thoughts and experiences with our friends, that is, it seems like we are effectively communicating our thoughts, feelings and experiences—our models of these things—to our friends, and likewise they seem to communicate theirs to us. After all, in real life, whatever their theoretical weaknesses, informal models can be acted upon, they are the stuff of our experience and our thoughts, and they are what we talk about. But, is this the whole truth?

No, when push comes to shove, we invariably find out that, despite the smiles and the nods in our conversations, we weren't actually seeing and thinking the same thing, we didn't come to exactly the same conclusions, we didn't place the same value on the ideas we shared as our friends did. We invariably find out that, when we dig deep enough, our ideas are actually very different from theirs.

Why would this be? Why does conversation create an illusion of agreement that is so often fractured by the first application of stress? Why is debate between either learned or passionate opponents *always* a failure? If our thinking is sound, and logic and debate a valid means of determining the truth, then why hasn't the sphere of human interactions and experiences been steadily brought into alignment with reality by the uncounted number of debates that our educated elite have participated in over the last several millennia?

The following examination of simple formal and informal models of a conversation necessarily contain allusions to terms we haven't discussed yet, so it may not be possible to follow the discussion in detail, but that is not the intent of this section. It is just being provided to give the reader a feel for what it looks like when we begin to add rigor to our thought.

3.3 Conversation: Informal Model

If we define debate as a specialized form of conversation, a conversation with rules, then we can discuss both by discussing conversation. Of what does a conversation consist? An exchange of words between the participants, of course, usually organized in phrases and sentences, so if we allow one word sentences, we can just say conversations comprise a verbal exchange of sentences. What is the topic of a conversation? Well, there may be a stated topic, or there might be a range of topics in a free-flowing conversation. What is the purpose of a conversation? Of course, since there are several different types of conversation, then it is reasonable to expect that each will have its own purpose. For this demonstration, let's confine ourselves to considering three different kinds of conversation, and the purpose of each:

- Task-oriented conversation: communicates actionable information.
- Social conversation: expresses or exchanges personal experiences or social formulas to maintain social cohesion.
- Debate: exchanges ideas on a stated topic to prove superiority.

So, an informal model of conversation is that it is a sentence-based interaction on a topic or topics that may or may not be shared, with a goal defined by its type.

How well do conversations succeed, and when they don't, why do they fail?

- Task-oriented conversations succeed when enough information is effectively exchanged with the assignee for him to successfully complete the task. Failure could be due either to poor communication on the part of the speaker, faulty assumptions, poor comprehension on the part of the listener, or all of the above.
- Social conversations can be aimed at conviviality, conflict, rebuke or any number of other goals. They succeed when the discussants each subjectively evaluate them as successful, regardless of whether or not their assessments coincide.
- Debates, I contend, never succeed, and never can succeed because they are a purblind mistake.

What can we do with this informal model of conversation? How can we use it to study conversation, to work to improve conversation, to improve communication, to improve the success rate? We can't, really, because everything is too vague, too amorphous, too undefined to give us the crispness, the precision we need to devise experiments and compare quantified results.

3.4 Conversation: Formal Model

What would a formal model of conversation look like? (See chapter 26 for the actual formal model.) First, it would have a formal definition of every term it references, along with a formal definition of the supported operations, and their domains and ranges. For the purposes of this demonstration though, let's confine our ambitions to a quick sketch, just to get the feel of the difference between the above model that, while it had more structure than might be customary, is nevertheless still informal, and a model that has the beginnings of a formal definition and structure. We would begin simply by just substituting a formally defined term for an informal one: in a formal model, a conversation is an exchange of *statements*. With this simple change, suddenly we are able to understand much more about conversations, and why they succeed or fail:

- Task-oriented conversations tend to succeed or fail in a relatively unambiguous way, precisely because all three terms in the statement (context, content, goal) are explicitly addressed or defined in the conversation. Miscommunication often occurs when the speaker relies on previous conversations being remembered, rather than explicitly restating the pertinent points, i.e., when the implicit context is not fully shared by all.

- Social conversations invariably proceed with the contexts and goals for each participant's statements unspecified. When participants belong to a well-defined group that has well-defined roles, culture and goals, social conversations can be bond-reinforcing convivial exchanges precisely because they share an institutional context and value system to some extent. Otherwise, miscommunication is proportional to the mismatch of the implicit terms in the statements.

- Debates, as a rule, cannot succeed because the statement contents that are the putative substance of the debate are not the actual *subject* of the debate. Instead, what is actually being argued are the implicit terms of the statements, the context and the goal. Because the defined goal of the debate is to establish truth by making the stronger argument, and truth can only be defined by the value elements of the statement, the context and the goals, not by the content, which are excluded from the debate by the rules, therefore debates can *never* succeed, even if some in the audience do decide to change sides. Debates are designed to prove one side right and the other wrong, and attractive suasion is the mechanism that achieves that, not authority-based evidence. (The finer points of this will all be explained in great detail in later chapters.)

Word-based discussions of ideas are terrifically ineffective and, in most cases, actually counter-productive for a very specific reason: the actual target, the purpose, of verbal discussions has nothing to do with the manifest topic everyone pretends to address. The notion that the purpose they serve is related to their topic is what we call the **conversation fallacy**, the idea that conversations exist to address their manifest subject.

The notion that any conversation above the task level occurs to address the manifest topic is demonstrably untrue, *and we all know this*, but have been reluctant to acknowledge it out of fear of spoiling the emotional good that conversations can accomplish. However, once we begin to model conversations formally, we can no longer avoid admitting that they are just grouping activities (see chapter 19, Groups), and are simply unsuited for the task of intellectual inquiry.

3.5   Statements

The definition of statement mentions that the first and third terms are usually implicit, but it must be understood that 'implicit' generally means 'unspoken, assumed', it does *not* mean that the implicit can be made explicit through speech. In fact, in purblind reasoning, implicit generally means ambiguous or altogether *undefined*. The fact that we leave two-thirds of every statement unspoken hides a multitude of sins of omission, confusion and duplicity. The reason we accept this sad state of affairs is that it lubricates social interactions by allowing us all to assume shared context, outlook and purpose where there is none. This allows us to experience an emotional coupling with another that belies our essential mental isolation. It allows us to treat as friends those with whom we actually share very few interests.

3.6   Model Concepts

This brief discussion of a formal and informal model of conversation should make it clear that informal models are neither designed nor intended to participate in rigorous discovery exercises that support scientific inquiry, because their goals are much more modest, and generally focused on interest, task or social organization concerns. Discovery exercises are covered later, but for now, just understand that their purpose is the methodical exploration of the unknown with the object of extending external knowledge beyond the current boundaries. That is, the goal of a discovery exercise is ultimately to solve previously unsolved problems, and they require the use of formal models even to begin.

Ask yourself, what is the difference between how you reason in thoughtful conversation, and how you reason when you are alone? Both forms use the verbal model to express ideas in the vernacular taught in your schools. If your conversation does not support the advancement of knowledge, how can your reasoning support it?

The context and goal of a statement are implicit in the sense that the speaker is situated in his reference frame and value system, and thanks to the purblind defect, he generally assumes that the context equals reality, and the goal correctly states the true, inherent meaning of life, or some such, and not just of his reality and his life, but of *all* reality and *all* life. The first line of defense he retreats to, once he finds out that his discussants don't actually share his views, is to assert, either silently or aloud, that all *right thinking* people do see things his way.

The reason we are saying that the context and goal are actually undefined, rather than just implicit, is because the speaker simply has no way of ever precisely defining them, since he has never expressed them in formal terms. Not being able to express the ideas in formal terms means that he will not even be able to tell you exactly what is in the sets of goals and assumptions, and what isn't. Since he has never actually defined the membership criteria, all he has to rely on is that he just *knows* what he thinks, means and feels, even if he can't express it.

The problems with conversation and debate, the reasons that they always fail to objectively advance knowledge, are manifold, but the core of the problem starts with three assumptions that lie at the heart of traditional purblind reasoning on informal, mudball models:

1. Perception is objective.

2. We reason on reality.

3. We express our ideas in words.

Contrast this with what we know from the laws of model-oriented reasoning:

1. By **M1** and **M2**, perception is realized in informal models and is therefore subjective.

2. By **M2**, we reason against models, not reality, so reasoning is not objective when the models are informal.

3. We make *statements* against models.

One can make the argument that the whole reason we have to go to all the effort required to master formal model-oriented reasoning is to be able to fix the damage caused by these three mudball assumptions. Were it not for the purblind defect, we could simply peer into our minds and observe how the various parts interact, and be able to understand what mental event comes from which structure with what limitations. It isn't remarkable that we cannot do this, after all, we cannot see ultraviolet light either, even though it is there and can be seen by some birds and bees. We *perceive* by means of organic instruments (internal and external senses) and *conceive* on evolved structures (models) so we can only naturally see and think whatever our equipment supports. Fortunately, we do have a way to see beyond the limits of our senses, and that is to use our higher intellects to create intellectual constructs and use our cleverness to invent physical equipment that, together, extend our ability to perceive and understand our internal and external reality with new levels of clarity and detail.

 *Checkpoint: think about the above para-graph and list for more than a minute. Review the laws, think about how they are being applied. If things are not be-ginning to click for you yet, then you must stop and discuss the book with an-other reader who is at or above your level, before you can proceed.*

3.7   Formal Models

Informal models are internal knowledge (see chapter 11, Internal and External Knowledge) constructs that are expressed in subjective terms and that lack verifying tests. Formal models are expressed in formal terms that support reproducible tests by independent experimenters. In order to illustrate the distinction, let us look at a subjective term that we can express both as an informal and a formal model. We want to use the simplest example we can to avoid getting too heavily into concepts we haven't discussed yet, so let us choose the phrase: "rodent retreats from loud, large being."

The informal model is just the phrase itself, which may or may not be amplified with further details or specifications. The nature of the informal model is that it is a natural language expression of observations, impressions or reactions to something. Since it is not expressed in formal terms, it is inherently ambiguous and subject to interpretation or question by others (e.g., how big? how loud?). More importantly, it doesn't support testing, and does not generally suggest aspects to investigate with any level of precision or reproducibility.

A very quick sketch of a formal model of the phrase would begin with a tervaluation element, possibly represented as a three dimensional evaluation array, [anti, pro, non], in order to be executable. This 3D array, called an evacule, would be part of an array of evacules to represent the range of nuance our senses can perceive. We would set up the test as a simulation of an intelligence represented by the rodent, perhaps using the asomatous psyche application we will discuss later, and set the anti component of the visual and aural senses at maximum to represent 'loud' and 'large', and the other values at zero, to simplify the test and keep it focused on the problem as presented. We would then devise the action encoding algorithms in the simulation to generate the expected behavior. Once we had a simulation that acted as we expected, this then would form our hypothesis of how an actual rodent would behave, and we would then be able to run an experiment to verify our results.

What we would find, of course, would be that our simulation would retreat some distance from the loud, large being in a straight line, while the actual rodent would follow a path with more segments, not all 180° from the input. We would then take the new, more detailed observations and introduce segments into the path mechanism, perhaps with a restricted random element. We could tune our concept of 'near' and 'far', and the frequency of renewed observations and recalculations until our simulated path approached the average of a number of real test results to within an acceptable margin of error.

Note that as soon as we succeeded this far in simulating the avoidance behavior specified in the face of a two dimensional threat, we would immediately be in a position to test all other allowed values in all dimensions and combinations, including response to positive and null evaluations and beyond. We could begin to investigate what it means when an input simultaneously has both positive and negative evaluation components. Once we have a working quantitative model, there is no limit to the experiments we can conduct with it.

An informal model is a description, an ambiguous expression that describes our feelings and experience, but that does not model the referent with the rigor necessary to support reproducible tests and scientific investigation of the phenomenon. A formal model not only supports scientific experiments beyond the specified problem, but it opens the question for all other interested investigators to confirm, refute or extend our findings. A formal model enables us to build knowledge of subjective experience on top of a solid base of reproducible results.

3.8 Summary

Faceted model-oriented reasoning is a conceptual system designed to enable us to see inside our own minds by using techniques that allow us to create testable models of our internal experience. This a process we call *externalization* (see chapter 11). Formal or rigorous model-oriented reasoning is a complex system of abstract concepts that takes some effort to master, but this cannot be a surprise, since we are using our reasoning to synthesize what amounts to a new *sense* with the capability to enable us to peer inside our working mind and to identify and understand the flow of events that occurs as we process our experience. This newly constructed level of perceptual and conceptual ability allows us to create testable models of our thoughts and feelings so that we can examine them as measurable subjects for the first time. It enables us to finally open up our internal, subjective experiences to the reach of science and to connect the objective (quantitative) and subjective worlds together through faceted models that support scientific inquiry.

The fundamental difference between formal and informal modeling is that the first understands that both perception and cognition are mental processes that happen inside a brain that is inside our head, while the other assumes we are capable of objectively observing and processing phenomena in reality. The purblind defect is the only thing that ever led us to mistake internal entities, such as thoughts and perceptions, with external entities, such as things that actually exist in $\mathbb{R}$.

If it seems that it is too much to demand of the average person that they define their ideas with algebraic, executable, or set notation or the equivalent, just so that they can crisply define the boundaries of their ideas, then it is time to take a few moments to consider our assumptions on reasoning. Ask someone with strong beliefs if they are rational, informed and a clear thinker, and most will tell you they are. Their mudball concept is that their purblind reasoning is precise and well-informed because it *feels* that way, even though they cannot tell you precisely what is included in their argument and what is excluded. They cannot tell you what operations are possible on their thoughts, or what the domain and range are. The impression, or fatuous assumption, that we are clear thinkers, that we think logically and see the world for what it is, are all artifacts of the different mental structures that generated our values, assertions and ideas. They are not rational assessments, but structural assertions. Each separate reasoning function only does whatever it does and no more. That is, by returning a value, every mental function posits its legitimacy, irrespective of context.

The difference between a formal and an informal model is precision and testability. We have shown what a significant difference that formalizing the conversation model has on the clarity and power of our thought, and that was even before we define the terms *context* and *goal* precisely. Formalism can be applied incrementally, and each layer brings clarity and power to the concept being treated. Is it too much to ask that the average person formalize all their thoughts? Of course it is, but no one is ever going to formalize all their thoughts (we show later that this would actually be impossible), and the average person just wants to fit into their group context and to make a comfortable living.

We know that only a small percentage of people are, ever will be, or even need to be, explorers. The only qualified candidates for admission to a course in faceted model-oriented reasoning are those who are convinced that the effort and hazard involved in exploring beyond the frontiers of the known is worth the trouble for the chance to increase our knowledge. To them, model-oriented reasoning will just be a new tool, a sextant for reading the skies vaulting the seas of subjectivity they must explore. To them, the effort of mastering a useful, new tool is always a bargain.

3.9   Review

The difficulty in this chapter is that we ventured beyond the limit of what we were prepared to discuss in order to give the reader an orientation to the greater subject of how learning, exploration and a scientific approach can be applied to the messiness of subjective human experience. Hold your questions for now, but keep a list of them so that you can check them off as they are addressed.

- Different levels of precision are required to achieve different levels of results.
- Purblind reasoning: the low precision reasoning process that is only adequate to produce historical, non-quantitative results.
- Faceted model-oriented reasoning includes fixes for the defects in purblind reasoning.
- Conversation—except when it morphs into an argument— is designed to create an illusion of agreement.
- Two thirds of every conversation is unspoken.

- Formal models support intellectual progress; informal models support decisions.
- Mudball assumptions: perception is objective, we reason on reality, discovery ideas are expressible in words.
- Model-oriented reasoning alternative to mudball assumptions: M1, M2, and we make statements against models.
- Formal models are designed to be scientifically tested.
- Formal models built to test one statement are capable of supporting exploration of others.
- Informal models describe our experience, not the external reality.
- Higher level reasoning effectively synthesizes new senses.
- Executable models connect the subjective and objective domains.

Chapter 4

Cognition Levels

4.1 Introduction

By **M1** we know that reasoning is executed by, and specific to, evolved structures, **M2** tells us that all reasoning executes against models in the set of models, M_L, specific to that level, and that both the domain and range of operations on models on a given level are the set of models in that level. These laws are sufficiently restrictive that the definition of *level* follows directly from them:

> **Level**: A model level is one layer of a segmentation of mental functions into successive layers that leverage, enhance or replace functionality from earlier layers, each of which is defined by a unique collection of structures and functions.

That is, a level is a model within a larger model that is defined by a heritable data structure and the operations on it

that, together, could have produced an evolutionarily positive
and significant, or benign, capability enhancement. Levels give
us a way to structure our models so that they mirror and respect
the evolutionary process. The concept of levels forces us to design disciplined models that prohibit lower level functions from
processing higher level structures (higher levels can instantiate
their own model from the data in a lower level model). Violating this stricture would violate the evolutionary process as we
understand it.

Model-oriented reasoning's laws require that all models of
cognition be structured in levels, but which particular levels
might be in any particular model is not specified, nor could it
be. This chapter will not, therefore, consist of a catalog of levels in the model, because which levels you use in your model is
entirely up to you, since the purpose-driven nature of models
dictates that different investigations of the same domain could
reasonably be expected to use different models in order to facilitate different types of analysis and testing. By **M3**, we know
that any discrete model can only include a tiny subset of the set
of points in a referent, so the selection of the subset to include in
the model must be made carefully to support the investigation
at hand. We will, therefore, approach our subject gingerly, and
explore the concept of levels by means of an edifying journey
through model-building and a further examination of the principles and practices of model-oriented reasoning. The complexity
of our subject compels us to cover topics lightly through several
iterations, going deeper each time and relying on what we have

briefly touched on earlier, and this demands some patience on the part of the reader.

It is entirely valid to have a model with a single level, but note that this would limit your model to a single data structure for all of the mental constructs being modeled, such as ideas, memories, feelings, calculations, etc. In general, it is necessary to have a level for each different class of phenomenon or construct being modeled, but the choice and design of each level is entirely up to the modeler.

Rather than terminating this chapter here, after telling you to just go ahead and design your own models, we will illustrate the process by discussing both the nature of the models being used in the asomatous psyche application, and the nature of the thought process we use when modeling the unknown. This extended introduction into the actual process of creating new models should help the reader get started on their own projects.

One can model the known by using L2 pattern processing, searching for a known pattern similar to the new situation, and then relying on the known patterns and pattern language grammar to infer from incomplete knowledge likely patterns to fill the lacunae in our understanding, and then to guesstimate in what ways the patterns might be productively extended. But this approach is entirely inadequate when attempting to create models of observable phenomena for which there are either no, or utterly inadequate, patterns to use or follow.

Working with the altogether unknown, however, presents us with an entirely different type of problem, and requires a higher level of thought to assemble a model from nothing that must be both testable and extendable. This requires L3 level reasoning, which probably everyone capable of reading this book does every once in a while, but which is poorly understood and essentially never mentioned in the literature. Because we need to use it as a normal part of our modeling work, we will sketch some of the operations and actions that L3 both makes possible and requires, even though we are deferring in-depth discussion of L3 to a later volume.

The levels we will be using for illustrative purposes, the L0-L3 levels referred to throughout this work, come from the asomatous psyche application[1], the executable simulation that tests some of the ideas presented here. These specific levels are only of interest because they will help the reader to understand the material in this volume better, and will be relevant should you choose to modify or extend the asomatous psyche, but remember, they are part of *my* model, not part of the universal cognition model. So, the discussion that follows is only intended to be illustrative of both the level concept and the L3 reasoning operations that make it possible to build models of the unknown.

4.2 Levels

Let us proceed with the discussion of levels by leveraging the rule of thumb that the way to attack large problems is to analyze

---

[1] The asomatous psyche is discussed in the next volume; the code is at https://mryilauer@bitbucket.org/mryilauer/cognitionmodel.git

them into smaller, component parts that we can attack in detail. Thus, if we want to begin to build a formal model of the mind that we can explore and test, we should try to break it down into smaller parts and then start from the bottom so that we can proceed to build our model, level by level, on top of previously tested model levels. The best tested model we have for modeling biological development is, of course, evolution, so we begin with that.

We want to break the composite model of the mind down into more manageable parts, so we start by asking, what fundamental stages of cognition might have evolved at different times? Can we model the mind as an accumulation of mental faculties that developed over the eons in a progression of complexity, building from the simplest to the most intellectually sophisticated, rather than just picturing the mind as one big mudball of different functionalities? Does this mean that evolution proceeded by the addition of the layers we will be describing? Of course not, but neither would it be a surprise if it did, yet the goal here is not to describe the evolution of the human mind but, rather, to construct heuristic models that will enable us to explore our mind in ways that support the development of testable, quantifiable models of it.

It will help us to model the problem if we also recall from earlier that, "the essence of intelligence is interested choice", i.e., intelligence really has nothing to do with being able to come up with the 'right' answer to a question (this is a fallacy that will be covered in the the next volume). No, volitional movement *presupposes* a level of intelligence that supports being able to choose to move away from threats and towards opportunity, an intelligence that encompasses the ability to identify and evaluate threats and opportunities. It would be hard to make the case for volitional movement being an advantageous mutation without such an ability.

It is critical to understand, and keep in mind, that we build models solely to aid our exploration and discovery. By **M4**, **M5** *and* **M7**, *we know that discrete models and continuous reality are different.*

4.3   Example Levels

The first level in the cognition model used by our simulation models the fundamental ability to benefit from the capability of volitional movement by generally moving towards opportunity and away from danger. Although it was chosen to suit our particular needs, it does seem that this first level, which we call Level Zero (L0) (I am a C programmer at heart, and we always start counting at 0) is a very natural first level of intellectual development that might well be universal. The second level, called Level One (L1), is L0 plus memory. This means that the data structures for the two levels are different, that L1 initializes with its objects with L0 objects, that L0 knows nothing about L1, that L1 does leverage L0, and that the domain and range for the operations on each level are the set of elements on that level: L0 for L0, L1 for L1.

The next higher level, L2, is the pattern processing engine, and patterns are what is at the heart of language and what we commonly recognize as intelligence. L2 patterns are instantiated with L1 results (a *result* is an evaluated record of an action and outcome, it is the structure that supports being able to learn from experience, the major benefit of the L1 memory function), just as L1 results are instantiated with L0 mentacules (*menta* from mental, *cule* from molecule, a mentacule is the fundamental unit of mentation).

Above L2, of course, is L3, the discovery engine, but, despite a few passing references to it in this chapter and volume, we will be deferring in-depth consideration of L3 to the next volume.

4.4   Designing a Level

Note that what we are calling L2 does not follow automatically from L1, it not an organic evolution of L1 to the next level of capability probably achieved by evolution. Instead, it compresses what undoubtedly should be several different levels into one. We did not take the route of designing multiple levels because it would have required more work than we could afford, and would have offered no significant return to the current project. Is it legitimate to allow project management concerns to influence the actual model design? Not only is it legitimate, it's nearly inevitable, and there is no problem with this as long as the resulting model maintains its integrity and power to perform.

In order to build a tractable simulation of human conscious-ness, creativity, cognition and emotion, I needed to model self-awareness, and this required a model of language ability, which in turn, required a model of pattern processing ability.

Thus, I focused on modeling the language function and be-gan to see it as an issue of processing language patterns, where language patterns are simply a specialized type of pattern. I then explored whether or not I could model a set of advanced cognitive functions as patterns, and the thought process as pat-tern processing, and found this approach to be quite productive.

In order to model language processing, I knew I would need mechanisms that would handle grammar definition, grammar error detection, and pattern extension, and it turned out that these naturally generalized into generic pattern processing func-tions. Thus, working on the specific problem helped me to solve the general problem, but this is merely to be expected, and is not a surprise. Even better is the case when you have more than one specific problem to model before you pull back to model the general case.

So, I was able to model L2 as a pattern recognition and pro-cessing engine that not only supports language but also gives us the ability to anticipate the future. This satisfied my im-mediate needs, but I am keenly aware that semiotic key-value associations provide a primitive level of language (animal calls and gestures, for example) that are independently significant, but that I was just subsuming under my area of interest, the higher function of phoneme-based languages having syntax and grammar. Thus, my L2 model that I am describing here is a pattern language processing engine that suits my need to test my model of the mind with a simulation, but others, of course, would be free to take entirely different paths to modeling the problem, and would probably find it useful to introduce several additional levels in addition to the four we will be discussing.

This illustrates the entirely subjective aspect of modeling: what we choose to model and how we choose to define and organize those models is a completely subjective, personal and creative process that must focus on what is required to extend the boundaries of our own modeled world, rather than succumbing to the pressure to conform to certain strictures or results. The objective aspect of model-oriented reasoning is strictly confined to a properly-formed model's capacity to support reproducible, formal tests.

Thus, while there is a strong case to be made for the generality of the L0 and L1 levels, the L2 level, as presented, is arbitrary in the sense that it was chosen to suit my personal needs. In model-oriented reasoning, I am allowed to do this since the only measure of idea quality is the extent to which the result is both viable and productive, which means that I can ride this horse until it collapses or gets too expensive to maintain, at which time I would be driven to refactor the model to account for the errors and to provide for new possibilities.

4.5 Model-Oriented Discovery

The creative part of model-oriented reasoning involves us mapping the frontiers of our own knowledge-scape and charging up the promontories and peninsulas at the limits of our understanding, in order to stimulate growth and discovery from them, even though these might be inland features to other minds. Traditional education factories tend to assume that we learn *from* the referent by assimilating it as is. They do not recognize the value of growing *towards* what we want to learn, of using discovery and extension to invent new knowledge, rather than simple memorization that merely lets us acquire what others have known before us. Within limits, this works fine for L2 pattern acquisition, but not for the higher level L3 discovery function. It apprentices us to our predecessors (which is fine, up to a point), rather than equipping us to captain our own ship of discovery.

Note that the design of L3 was actually extrapolated from what we wanted to learn, instead of from what we already know. That is, we began our quest from the distant side of the discovery configuration that describes the discovery we want to make, instead of the near side where our knowledge already reaches. The gap in between these two edges of the discovery configuration is the chasm that has to be jumped with an insight.

It is possible to approach discovery from the end point instead of the starting point because L3 has a number of functions that allow us to work from both sides of the divide quite easily, from what we know, forward, as well as from what we wish to

discover, backward. We can drive the discovery process from
the a receptor point in the discovery configuration, instead of
from a launch point on the question side of the idea gap, because L3 uses a process that leverages insight, rather pattern
extension, to bridge gaps.

This switch from pattern extension to the insight-discovery
process of model building, from reaching *forwards* from the
question to *reaching back* from a receptor point, adds an important tool to our learning capacity. It also illustrates a central
concept in the theory and practice of model-oriented reasoning:
the fundamental purpose of model building is *not* to discover
reality, nor to memorize known patterns, but, instead, to extend our existing mental models to cover more area with more
elementary models that can become part of a larger, composite
model.

The fundamental problem we face in L3 discovery learning is how to extend models to new levels of complexity in a
manner that maintains a testable relation with external reality.
Model building is fundamentally about *extension*, not *acquisition*, that is, it is about extending the frontiers of our models,
it does not guarantee that we will inevitably acquire specific,
new knowledge. This limitation stems from the fact that, however much we might discover, we *cannot* know its value until
we reproducibly test those discoveries against reality, to determine whether or not they are actually useful insights that
correlate with reality. By **M7**, we know that it is impossible to
be certain of any knowledge without independent replication of

results, and only formal models support replication, so all discoveries have to be formalized and tested before we can know whether they are valid or not. Therefore, although the joy of discovery is keen in the moment of realization, this thrill in no way guarantees that our insight is not worthless.

4.6   Exploration and Discovery

Exploration is the act of deliberately journeying beyond the limits of the known, it is the conscious choice to go out beyond the safe boundaries of knowledge with the intent of conquering *terra incognita* in the quest to extend the boundaries of knowledge beyond anything reached before. It requires a fearless commitment to confront the fear of death that is triggered by the plunge into the blackness of the unknown in pursuit of an elusive goal. Read Ernest Shackleton's book, *South: Shackleton's Endurance Expedition*, to get a sense for what this type of journey of exploration actually feels like. The irony, of course, is that instead of confronting the frozen, desolate Antarctic in a wooden sailing ship like him, our journey is confined to the vast reaches of the terrifying, unprogrammed areas in our own brains that are safely ensconced inside of our heads.

Discovery has always played a critical role in the advancement of knowledge, but it has primarily been thought of as a serendipitous event that involved being touched by the muse, struck by the bolt of insight or some other poetic image of inspiration. It has always been seen as an unpredictable, rare event, but in reality, it is only rare in the sense that lightning strikes or diamonds are rare. Lightning strikes the earth maybe 8,000,000 times a day, so it only seems rare if you don't know where to look for it. Similarly, diamonds are only as rare as the diamond cartel can make them when, in reality, they are really quite a bit more common than most people think. Discoveries aren't exactly as common as that, but the process of exploration and discovery is an entirely natural process that we can deliberately engage in with a reasonable expectation of encountering discoveries on a monthly, weekly and even daily basis, when the conditions are right.

The questions we want to ask in relation to model building are:

- Can we consciously decide to undertake an exploratory expedition that has a better than even chance of leading into areas productive of discoveries in our field?
- How do we guide our explorations through the fields we found so they tend to engender discoveries?
- How do we cultivate the discovery phase to make it more common, more predictable, more productive?

Inasmuch as these questions have never been successfully answered before, they are certainly non-trivial. Since exploration is a volitional activity that requires little more than intention, persistence and character, we can assume that part, and focus on the discovery component of these questions. The obvious way to investigate discovery, or any topic with a considerable unknown dimension is to use models, so let's see if we can come up with a quick, back-of-the-envelope sketch of a model for insight that will help us to understand how we can use it to build viable and productive models of the unknown.

4.6.1   Insight

How should we model brain activity, and more specifically, how should we model insight, the spark of inspiration that so often leads to new knowledge? Well, an insight is clearly a new path that suddenly appears and bridges the gap(s) between previously unrelated or distant ideas, often along unanticipated dimensions. How should we model the event that creates these new paths?

One of the traditional images of insight is a spark, a bolt of lightning that brightens the world and allows one suddenly to see what has always been there, but was previously cloaked in darkness. Going with that, let's see if there are any validated models available for us to try to fit in here. The obvious one is electricity: voltage, current, gap, spark; this seems on point. What if, just to see if it works, we try to imagine an insight as a sudden connection between two ideas that occurs when the voltage on the question side of the gap builds to the point that a spark can leap across to the receptor idea. Is there anything we can do to charge up a 'meristem' point in the brain? Yes, there is, in a previous volume the process of 'ruffling questions' was explained.[2]

Is there anything else we can do to prepare the other side of the configuration, the receptor side? Yes, we can *touch* as many in-subject ideas as possible, by assiduously cycling through as-

---

[2]see *Pinnacle Questions*

sociations in our memory. 'Touching' an idea is a technical term
that refers to traversing the idea tree without invoking the notions of TFRW (true/false/right/wrong). Touching is, in this
sense, an entirely different thought action than a recollection
that invokes TFRW, because the latter actually disables the internal tree structure of the idea pattern, while the former opens
it to conducting charge. That is, if you invoke an idea's TFRW
evaluation, then you close it to detailed analysis, because remembering idea a as true or false, metaphorically surrounds it
with a Gaussian sphere that conducts charge around, but not
through, the configuration. After all, why would our mind be
built to go into the dark woods if it already 'knows' a shorter
path around it? You only venture in, if there are open questions,
not if there is already a solid wall of conclusions.

Since insights do not connect to book and chapter headings,
but, instead, connect directly to a phrase somewhere deep in
the middle of the page, to an idea or fact deep in a learned
thought pattern, then the internals of an idea are only available for insight if they are not wrapped in a TFRW evaluation
bubble. By touching ideas without rousing the judgment bear,
we can charge up, not just the pattern's entry points, but all of
the branches and connections deep inside the pattern to expose
them to external connection. This in-depth charging does not
occur when the TFRW dimension of an idea is invoked.

The way the mind works is that it evaluates models under
consideration to hew a path from problem to solution. Once an
idea's evaluation has been invoked, the mind has no need, no

excuse for traversing down into the idea's depths, since it already knows the idea's actionable dimension. Creative thought requires the non-judgmental charging up of the internals of all ideas in the set of possible solution participants we identified when we cycled through associations in our reflective phase.

Model-oriented reasoning uses the discipline of mental exploration and discovery to find our way in the dark, in a step-wise fashion, from idea to idea, via sparks or bolts of insight that cross gaps that have never been bridged before.

Referring back to the electricity model, let's say that Paschen's law describes this situation:

$$V_B = \frac{Bpd}{\ln(Apd) - ln[ln(1 + \frac{1}{\gamma_{se}})]}$$

The details are not germane at this point beyond noting that, within a certain range, the voltage required to create the arc increases as the gap widens. This would suggest that we should try to reduce the gap between question and receptor nodes in order to make the appearance of a connecting arc more likely. The distance formula, explained in an earlier volume,[3] allows us to do exactly this: to build on both the question and the receptor points sides so as to reduce the distance between them.

Analyzing ideas in the traditional sense breaks them down into constituent parts. The effect of analyzing the elements in a discovery configuration is to replace the single question point and the small set of receptor points with a much larger set of candidate points by spilling the contents of the ideas, as it were,

---

[3] *Pinnacle Reasoning*

into the gap between the ideas by breaking their patterns down into the constituent parts and, in the process, charging them all up.

As a rule of thumb, the way forward in model-oriented reasoning is usually found by adding small, testable models to previously tested models, because having more, smaller ideas participating in the process reduces the gap between candidate ideas and thereby increases the likelihood of triggering an insight that will form a new connection.

A fact that we all should know, but that purblind reasoning makes it easy to forget, is that results flow *from* functionality, not *towards* a goal. We may *aim* our efforts at achieving a particular result, but the efforts we can coordinate arose in layers over the span of our evolution and it is these structure-based function sets that define the domain of ideation functionality, and this domain determines the range of what is possible for that intellect, not our fears, hopes and dreams. It is a mistake, therefore, to attempt discovery learning using L0 (truth), L1 (experience), or L2 (encapsulated patterns) mechanisms. Sparks of insight leap gaps, and we cultivate them only by charging up the elements in discovery configurations, not by pushing forward with the torch of truth.

We can greatly augment our set of candidate ideas in discovery configurations, at very little cost, as long as we are willing to question authority to the point of disregarding it. Being able to ignore authority, at will, allows us to review our library of known patterns with a new eye, so that we can see them from the point of view of the *question* rather than from the point of view of the *authority* that taught them to us. I am not suggesting that we discard or ignore math, science or any other tested, external knowledge, but merely pointing out in that, in the process of pattern assimilation, we are/were forced to accept patterns as units that only have a limited number of authorized uses, which are defined by the memorized entry and exit points. Encased ideas aren't open to the kind of peripatetic contemplation needed to expose their internal points to new, unapproved, external connections. Freeing our minds from the prejudices of our teachers allows us to discover powerful, hidden dimensions in what they blindly taught us, that we can leverage in entirely unanticipated ways.

In the last several paragraphs we have been addressing ways to foment insights from the question side of the discovery configuration, but the attentive student may have noticed that, from the point of view of the participating ideas, the discovery configuration is entirely symmetrical: what works from one side works exactly the same way from the other, as well. There is no special magic required to solve a problem by working from the unknown back to the known, once you have a handle on the process of triggering insights.

 *The preceding discussion of the process of insight is a freebie: you don't have to buy or master model-oriented reasoning to use it. Of course, that it is usable kind of validates the process that dis-covered and defined it.*

4.7 Modeling

It is an important requirement that, however we model the levels of intellect, once we have a model, we are bound by the laws of model-oriented reasoning, that is, once we have our levels defined, then we are required to define data structures and operations for each level such that these laws are obeyed by the operations that model observable behaviors in the referent. In this particular case, **M2, M3**, and **M7** are controlling. This means that the outcome of processing any thoughts on a particular level must produce more thoughts on the data type in that level. Narrowing type-casts and using simpler models to instantiate higher models are both entirely consistent with this restriction, but supposing that you can *understand* an L0 idea in L2 terms is just as much an error as is supposing your L0 action is actually based on your L2 understanding (more later on how L2 reasoning is distorted by the L0 connection).

Note that we are allowing the laws to drive our model design and the model design obviously drives our executable implementation. Everything in a formal model is going to be executable, so all ideas you have will have visible, quantifiable consequences, they will exhibit behavior that we can use to test both hypotheses and the model itself.

Another constraint introduced by the evolutionary model, on which we are building our cognitive model, is that each level must function independently of, and in parallel with, the others, and not sequentially, because the lower level intellects must not only be utterly unaware of the higher levels, but they must be constitutionally incapable of conceiving higher level ideas. The higher levels can observe the function of the lower levels and consume their output to instantiate their own higher level models, and even prepare output that can, by a narrowing type-cast, be reductively consumed by the lower levels, but the lower levels cannot be aware of the higher, later arriving levels at all; they cannot observe, cooperate with, or wait for the higher levels that they do not know exist. The higher levels evolved thousands to millions of years after the design and implementation of the lower level intellects were validated by natural selection, and the lower levels, while they may have been selectively updated, were not rewritten to correspond to the new functionality introduced by the higher levels (unless in your model you can make the case that they were).

4.8   Summary

The art of optimal decision making is an old skill that our culture tries to teach us in multiple ways. Some of the heuristics we are taught include: never lose focus on the primary values and goals; assess the risks carefully; don't over estimate your abilities; neither let euphoria, fear nor peer pressure cloud your judgment. Model building requires judicious decision making to identify and pursue the top priority in the moment. In my particular case, since I had to build an executable simulation of the human mind based on this model, I absolutely had to manage the complexity of the model to keep the programming model tractable.

In test-driven development, one is not allowed to code something that cannot be proved with test automation, so the need to test enforces a discipline that banishes sloppy thought earlier in the process than is customary. We mention this because the benefit of using levels to model the mind is simultaneously to enforce testability and to follow the norms established by evolution.

Using levels that conform to the evolutionary model while satisfying one's immediate modeling needs imposes a discipline on our thought that opens the way out of the mudball model and into the world of executable, and therefore testable, model-oriented reasoning.

Formal model-oriented reasoning is designed, primarily, to provide a disciplined structure for all reasoning, but especially to guide the process of discovery, that is, the extension of knowledge beyond the boundaries of the known. The essence of the discovery process is the consolidation of the fruits of exploration into meaningful and useful terms. Thus, exploration is to discovery as prospecting is to mining—exploration identifies areas where we can dig for treasure. Exploration is the activity that makes discovery possible, and, happily, exploration is something we can choose to do as often as we want. Model-oriented reasoning uses L3 functionality to give us a set of tools and practices that help us to maximize the benefits of discovery through disciplined design and testing.

4.9   Review

- Level: a segmentation of mental functions into successive layers defined by a collection of structures and functions.
- Levels correlate to the evolutionary model.
- Model creation is a subjective, creative process. Model design must support objective, reproducible tests.
- Models are purpose-driven and partial, not definitive.
- Exploration is the act of deliberately journeying beyond the limits of the known in the quest to extend the boundaries of knowledge.
- Discovery is the consolidation of the fruits of exploration into meaningful and useful terms.
- Insight is the leap from the limits of the known to previously unrelated ideas that instantaneously synthesizes a new level of awareness and understanding.
- Ideas can be translated from one level to another, but loss of information is certain in one direction, and loss of meaning is certain in the other.
- Levels are independent, not parallel or coordinating tracks.
- Results flow from functions, not towards a goal.

Chapter 5

Perception: The Complete Function

5.1 Models and Pinnacle Questions

Imagine you are seeing, for the very first time, a house you had just inherited, and you notice that one corner of the roof sags. Since you can neither sell it nor live in until it is structurally sound, fixing the roof is suddenly your problem. Where do you start? Do you tell yourself that the problem is that the roof corner sags, so you need to get into the attic and raise and brace the sagging corner? I certainly hope not, because it is highly unlikely that the real problem is there. More likely, you are seeing a symptom or a result of a structural problem somewhere below the roof. I would start in the basement and look for cracks or shifting in the foundation, and if I found

99

problems there, I would get someone in to check for settling or issues in the ground beneath the house. Then, the inspection would continue up, floor by floor, until we got back into the attic, at which point we should have a full picture of where the problem started, how it propagated, and how it could best be remediated, given our resource constraints.

The entire *Pinnacle* series is focused on one issue: why have we not made any real progress in our attempts to tackle pinnacle questions? Why have we been able to transform the world during the steel age, the machine age, the industrial age, the corporate age, and the computer age, and yet have not gotten past step one in making similar progress on tackling pinnacle questions? Why has there been so much progress on scientific and technical problems, but so little on those related to human experience and interaction, both at the large, societal level, and at the small, personal level? Why have we not even developed a methodology for investigating the cause and cure of man's inhumanity to man?

The simple answer is that we haven't made progress in understanding subjective human experience well enough to establish a tradition of progress in improving our collective behavior and condition, because we have not yet extended the scientific method far enough to penetrate the cloud of subjectivity that encompasses human experience. In this volume, we are explaining the principles and practices of model-oriented reasoning in order to show how this methodology gives us the means to study subjective experience with the rigor and reproducibility of the scientific method.

We are discussing model-oriented reasoning in the abstract, instead of focusing just on how we humans think and feel, because the sagging roof problem applies directly to this situation: of all the events and behaviors we see in the trials and tribulations of human social life that trouble us, which ones are we sure are uniquely human? Which of the issues involved in pinnacle questions arise only within the human sphere, and which ones are not strictly human problems, but occur at a lower level and are shared with other primates, other mammals? Are there any we share with all mobile creatures? That is, of all the human choices and behaviors that trouble us philosophically, how many are actually structural issues that start many layers lower down in the tree of life, down in the basement, as it were, or below? For, if our real problem is a crumbling foundation, then we could spend lifetimes in the attic trying to shore up the roof without ever getting close to addressing the actual problem. This is why we are starting our investigation in the basement first, so we can focus our efforts where each class of problem originates, instead of foolishly trying to fix them on higher levels where the symptom appears. With these thoughts in mind, we can begin to critically examine perception, the first step in the cognition process.

5.2 Perception

Perception is unique among all functions, whether biological, mathematical or executable. By definition, a function is a process that maps elements in a domain uniquely to an element in the range. What sets perception apart from all other functions is that the domain of the perception function is unbounded, it includes *everything*, past, present and future, whether real, imaginary or impossible, anything that can perceptibly impact the internal or external senses. This makes it the only *complete* function, complete in the sense that it can map *anything* from *any* domain into a very restricted hierarchy of elements whose roots are encoded in its genotype. The job of the perception function is to produce a result in its range for any sensible event, *regardless* of what the input is. Perception is about facilitating response, not about 'accurately and completely' seeing any given x for what it 'really is'.

Perception is the act of mapping the state of the internal and external senses at a given trigger moment to an actionable evaluation object. That is, the stimulation of a sense does not equate to perception unless that stimulation exceeds a trigger value. Whenever one, or a combination of the score or so senses, is charged to a trigger level, the perception function grabs and processes a snapshot of the sensorium's state into whatever data object the organism uses to evaluate experience in self-significant terms. Even if laboratory experiments confirm continuous visual tracking of test objects, this does not mean that the *mind* is aware of the new position of the target every time it moves a fraction of a millimeter, it just means that the senses are focusing on a stimulation source. We are defining perception as the process of the mind taking sufficient notice of sensory input to evaluate it. From the perspective of cognition, the event does not exist until it has been encoded into a cognitive object, a process that is discrete, not continuous like stimulation of a sensory organ can be.

From the point of view of model-oriented reasoning and universal cognition theory, it matters not how many senses an organism has, or what they happen to be. Theoretically, an organism could have a single sense, or dozens—it doesn't alter the fact that the essential mechanism that makes consciousness, cognition, and volitional movement feasible is the ability of the organism to respond to any sensible event with a reactive movement.

The senses seem to function as analog sensors with ephemeral persistence that are active whenever the organism is alert, so they are 'on' the entire time when the organism is awake, but perception only occurs at discrete intervals, and seems to be triggered by some senses reaching threshold values. As humans, we are used to constantly reading and interpreting information in the environment, so we are easily fooled into thinking that perception is actually continuous, but this is demonstrably not the case. You can demonstrate this to yourself if you think back on the times when you have had accidents as trivial as dropping or bumping into things, and you will find that there is always a moment missing from your awareness right before the accident moment that correlates to the surprise you felt when things went awry. That missing moment is what proves that, while sensory perception may be continuous, cognitive perception is periodic and discrete, not continuous.

No matter what impinges on the sensorium, the cognitive mechanism can react because *all* perceptions can be evaluated, even those that cannot be, because the actionable evaluation object has genetically encoded default values that support a characteristic response regardless of the poverty of input. All events that register in the sensorium above a trigger level can be perceived, evaluated and acted upon. Once you include the concept of internal senses in the concept of the sensorium, you can begin to see that phantasmagorical, impossible monsters that exist only in our dreams can be perceived, conceptualized and evaluated just like a pebble in our shoe.

5.3   The Perception Expression

The perception function prepares any perceptible event in the universe for evaluation by the L0 intellect. This is a bold statement. We will qualify it later to help you understand how this applies to our L2 rational functionality, but for now let us focus on L0 functionality, the level of functionality that every volitionally mobile creature possesses, in which the perception expression can be stated thus:

$$\forall\, x \in (\mathbb{R} \cup \mathbb{I})\ \exists\, p \in \mathbf{P}\ :\ L0(p) \to e\ :\ AM(e) \to a \in \mathbf{A}$$

That is, there exists a not necessarily unique perception, p, in the set of perceptions, $\mathbf{P}$, to represent anything in the union of reality and internal knowledge that stimulates our senses above a threshold level, that can be evaluated by L0 and then processed by the action module, AM, to specify an action, a, in the set of actions, **A**, that are supported by that entity. Anything in the vastness of human experience or in the vault of the cosmos that stimulates our senses above a certain level can be processed by our cognitive apparatus into an action. The action might be, and usually is, null, but this is both valid by the expression and to be expected. Perception is *not* about the left side of the expression, it is about the *right* side. It is genuinely peculiar that, to this day, intellectuals fail to understand this.

Events that do not register on the sensorium produce a null perception that evaluates to null that leads to a null action specification. In computer science, we consider null a unique value, and functions, or the call chains they are used in, must gracefully handle null inputs, so conceptualizing a below-threshold event as a null input to the perception expression is entirely standard practice.

Notice that external reality, $\mathbb{R}$, the physical universe, only appears once in the left side of the above expression, and only as one of two possible sources of the input x. Thus, it turns out that reality is a relatively minor player in the perceptual drama, a bit player lurking at the edge of the crowd, while the cognitive processes of perception and evaluation stand alone together at center stage.

Furthermore, note that when $x \notin \mathbb{R}$, the expression still evaluates normally. That is to say, *reality is not a necessary element in the perceptual process*. Naturally, one could reasonably expect that organisms that are fully exposed to the vicissitudes of nature and yet routinely exclude it from the perceptual process would be dealt with harshly by natural selection, but what about organisms living in colonies or populations with distributed responsibilities that insulate them from directly experiencing the consequences of their actions?

 *It's obvious that, while the level of abstraction throughout this work is very, very high, nevertheless, the fertile mind can hardly be expected not to make numerous associations between new ideas and current events or personal experiences.*

5.4   Summary

Perception, thus defined, is not a perspicacious process that critically examines all of reality within its sweep to learn all there is to know about each and every crumb, plant and creature it can see, but is, instead, a *reductive* process whose sole function is to empower creatures to avoid, ignore or approach entities based on the evaluation of snapshots of the internal and external senses taken at discrete intervals. There is nothing in this definition of perception that requires any error bound on the relation between the perception and the perceived. Natural selection takes care of that problem.

5.5   Review

Perception is not a passive, transparent window that simply allows us to see what is outside. On the contrary, it is an active process that feeds coded input derived from a few dimensions of sensory experience of the immediate environment into the L0 evaluation object at discrete intervals.

- Perception can map anything from any domain into a very restricted hierarchy of elements.

- Perception is about facilitating response, not the sensed phenomenon.

- While sensory perception may be continuous, cognitive perception is periodic and occurs only when sensory input is mapped into an actionable evaluation object, not when senses are stimulated.

- Because the uninitialized evaluation object always has default values, even null perceptions can trigger responses.

- $\forall\, x \in (\mathbb{R} \cup \mathbb{I}) \;\exists\, p \in \mathbf{P} \;:\; L0(p) \to e \;:\; AM(e) \to a \in \mathbf{A}$

- Cognition and evaluation are at the center of the perception process, not reality.

Chapter 6

Spaces

6.1 Introduction

Up to this point, we have been modeling the intellect from a few different perspectives. First, of course, we have approached the subject using a verbal model to sketch the broad outlines of our ideas. Then, we briefly touched on part of a formal model when we defined the laws and some formulas defining several relations. Next, we approached it from an executable point of view, when we referred to code in the simulation that models the mind as a collection of small, independent functions that process input to return a value without any awareness of the larger context. Then, we described it as a stack of independently evolved intellects organized in layers that each perform their own function without regard to the layers above, but consuming the products from the layer below.

The only limit to the number and type of models we can

apply to a problem is that defined by our own ability, education, industry and imagination. Each different type of model we add to the set of models in any particular solution strategy is called a *facet*, as in *faceted* model-oriented reasoning. Each facet contributes a unique perspective that might not be easily discoverable or expressible in other types of models. Given that a discrete model is built by selecting a finite subset of points to include in our model from an infinite set of data or measurement points in the referent, there is literally no limit to the number of different models we can construct of each given type.

We are now going to add another model type to our set of facet options that we can use to explore problems, by leveraging the concept of deformable space from general relativity to help us define the *space* model.

6.2   Definition

In model-oriented reasoning, a *space* is defined as:

Space: an unbounded geometry and the elements in it.

It should be easy to see that, by this definition, our model of reality, $\mathbb{R}$, is a space. The universe itself is a big place, and general relativity gives us a description of how matter distorts spacetime with gravity, meaning that the geometry of spacetime is curved near massive bodies (even though, on larger scales, spacetime is currently assumed, for purposes of calculation, to be flat).

We are going to use the concept of 'flat' in a slightly different sense and say that the geometry of the verifiable physical universe we live in is *flat* in the sense that:

- There is no fixed point in ℝ.
- There is no special frame of reference in ℝ.
- Physical laws are consistent throughout ℝ.

That is, all points in the universe are equal in the sense that different regions of the universe do not require different physics or different math (of course, black holes and other oddities are peculiar, but they have this property everywhere and it is described in our standard physics).

 ℝ is, of course, our model of external reality, but sometimes we use it to refer to reality itself when it seems unambiguous that it is just shorthand for the thing itself.

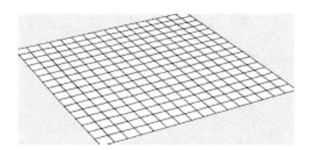

Figure 6.2: Representation of flat spacetime

Curiously enough, a critical reading of the Torah reveals a very primitive version of the same flat space concept when it establishes that there are no local gods and that there is no (local) magic. This incredibly liberating lesson is invisible to most, and it really has no place in the current discussion, but I find it both amusing and reassuring, nonetheless.

What we are saying is that the physical universe is a flat space, and that we can verify this through experiment and measurement (but, do note that this is just being used as a rhetorical device and is not evidence the rest of this chapter relies on). This flatness just means that what is measurable from one point should also be measurable from another, although some sophisticated calculations may be required to see it. The alternative to a flat space is a curved space, the difference being that, in a space that is curved in the vicinity of a singularity, all of the above laws are different:

- The point of maximum curvature (the singularity) defines a fixed point.
- The singularity distortion field constitutes a special frame of reference.
- Physical laws are fundamentally different in the curved regions than in the flat regions of space.

If the topography of our model space is curved, rather than flat like reality, this could have serious implications for any mappings from one to the other that do not take this distortion into account. For the simplest example of this, just think of 2D world maps of the globe that make Greenland look huge and Africa look small, and that case is much simpler than mapping between a curved value field and a flat physical plane.

Figure 6.3: Representation of a curved space

Of course, since we live in $\mathbb{R}$, then it just makes sense that our minds must also exist in $\mathbb{R}$, and therefore, cognition must also exist in $\mathbb{R}$, right? Well, there is a problem with this supposition, a flaw that has made it impossible for us to understand either ourselves or how we think and feel and fit into the world. Let's call this the Missing Dimension fallacy; it can be illustrated using the standard coordinate system.

- In a one-dimensional system we have a single axis, x; a two-dimensional system has two axes, x, y, and a three-dimensional system has three, x, y, z. Given three vectors: a = $[1]$, b = $[1, 2]$, and c = $[1, 2, 3]$, since all vectors have $x = 1$, do they all exist in **1D**, the set of one dimensional vectors?

- Similarly, if we draw an x-axis and mark out the integers with an ellipse at the end, we can understand this to represent the set of all integers. If you are then asked to mark the position of 1.5 on the line, it would be easy enough to put a mark between 1 and 2, would that work?

In the first case, the answer is simple and obvious: of course 3D vectors do not exist in a set of 1D vectors. In the second case, since a set, such as the set of integers, only contains its elements, and nothing else, and has no concept of anything existing *between* those elements, then, obviously, insinuating the real value 1.5 onto an integer graph would be a mistake.

If, however, we agreed to adjust our understanding to see the line as representing real numbers rather than integers, then putting the mark between 1 and 2 would be fine. This is not a small distinction, especially when you recall that the set of real numbers is infinitely larger than the set of integers. The infinite set of real numbers that exists between 1.0 and 2.0 in the set of real numbers is, itself, actually larger than the set of all integers, and it absolutely does NOT exist anywhere in the set of integers, even though we might be using the same numerals to express both types of values.

Extending these examples to spaces, we can define one space with the set of integers and a one-dimensional geometry, another if we combine the integers with a two-dimensional geometry, and yet another if we use a three-dimensional area. Although the elements in these cases, the integers, are the same, we still have 3 entirely different spaces because the geometries are different. Also, each of these three spaces are unbounded and exist independently of the others; they do not abut, overlap or in any way share an area.

It is just as illogical to say that our mental world exists in the same space as our physical world, as it is to say that the set of real numbers exists in a set of integers. That different sets have different elements as specified by their membership rules is not a new idea in the world of math and set theory, nor is the concept of a space defined by a geometry new in math or physics. However, that the concept of spaces not only applies to the subjective domain, but that it so brilliantly and naturally describes the wide world of human experience, ideas, beliefs and feelings, is an entirely new idea that is well worth our attention.

6.3   Cognitive Spaces

Let us define a cognitive space as some geometry with a set of elements that comprises all of our thoughts, feelings and beliefs. The question becomes, what is the nature of that geometry, flat or curved? And, if curved, what phenomenon has sufficient gravity to distort our cognitive plane of existence?

To begin building our answer, let's start by recalling a few concepts we covered earlier: the second and fourth laws of model-oriented reasoning, and the concepts of levels and perception. With a little indulgence, we will also borrow a concept from chapter 8, the definition of self.

- **M2**: All reasoning executes against a model $m_i \in \mathbf{M}_L$, the set of all level **L** models, and that the domain and range of model-oriented reasoning operations are both $\mathbf{M}_L$.

- A level is a collection of structures and functions in an evolution-based cognition model.

- Perception *bends* experience to fit its cognitive apparatus:

$$\forall\, x \in (\mathbb{R} \cup \mathbb{I})\; \exists\, p \in \mathbf{P}\; :\; L0(p) \to e\; :\; AM(e) \to\; a \in \mathbf{A}$$

- The seed of the self is a collection of self-preferential encoded values that defines a fixed point in cognitive space.

Figure 6.4: The value paraboloid.

What lens does perception use to bend experience into a focus that our cognitive apparatus finds sufficiently meaningful to enable it to process any perception, x, into a self-preferential action? The *self*, obviously. The self posits its own right to exist, and defines the very notion of *value* by prizing the self above all, and then valuing everything else in proportion to its impact on the interests of the self. Because life is essentially a self-preferential evaluation algorithm, it can only experience external reality through the filter of its own needs.

The very nature of life itself establishes the self as the sole gravity point in the cognitive space, so the geometry of cognitive spaces is necessarily curved towards the singularity of self at the center point of the space. The curve of that space is defined by an equation that calculates the density and type of interest at each point, an equation that might look something like this:

$$V_x = \frac{(|\mathbf{a} - \mathbf{n}|)^2}{i^2} + \frac{(|\mathbf{p} - \mathbf{n}|)^2}{s^2} \tag{6.1}$$

This equation wouldn't actually work, it is an equation for a paraboloid like figure 6.4, but it is being shown just as an illustration of how normal these calculations become once you have figured out how to see the inherently quantitative nature of our native models. Even though this equation is just a placeholder, an example, the relations we are showing actually do make sense, with the numerators being the sum of the squares of the difference between the positive and negative evaluation vectors each with the non-self vector, and the denominators i and s being the subject's sense of entitlement and strength (constitutional parameters for each cognitive entity), respectively. Thus, even with this sample equation, the slope of the self interest curve is defined by an individual's level of personality traits that influence it.

Now, keep in mind that, while this formula is not presented as anything other than a quick sketch of what the last mile of the process to formulaically represent subjective feelings will look like, it does represent a fundamental concept in the model of cognitive spaces. The anti-, pro- and non-self evaluation concept is at the center of this approach to understanding subjectivity and is the single most critical concept embodied in the asomatous psyche application. Whether the calculation of value involves just this simple ratio, though, or something more complex, will be left as an exercise for the serious student. For now, just assume this equation, or one like it, defines the curve of the area around the singularity of the self in a cognitive space.

6.4   Spaces and Levels

Combining this curved geometry together with our set of mental elements defines a new space, $\mathbb{CS}0$, Cognitive Space Zero, that is based on the L0 level of cognition (therefore, this is just an example space, not an element of the universal cognition model). The geometry describing the $\mathbb{CS}0$ space differs from that of $\mathbb{R}$ in these very important ways:

- In $\mathbb{CS}0$ there is a fixed point: the self, in $\mathbb{R}$ there is not.
- In $\mathbb{CS}0$ there is a special frame of reference, the value distortion field around the self defined by the value equation, in $\mathbb{R}$ there is not.
- In $\mathbb{CS}0$ the 'physical laws' are different in the special frame of reference around the self because the effect of value is both strong and directional, and utterly absent in both a flat geometry as well as in the remote, flat regions of this geometry. In $\mathbb{R}$, the laws of nature at any given scale are consistent throughout the space.

The fixed point in a cognitive space is the experience-bending self that only exists in $\mathbb{CS}0$, but not in $\mathbb{R}$. The *body* of the being certainly exists in $\mathbb{R}$, but the *world of the mind* does not. The special frame of reference is the distortion field around the point of the self in which significance, value and truth reach absolute levels at the center point and decline towards null as the distance from the center increases. The 'physical laws' that are different in this special frame of reference can be thought of as a value gravity that only exists in the center point region of the cognitive space. Simplistically, we could start by thinking of this as a single-body system and then use the metaphor of general relativity to picture the $\mathbb{CS}0$ space as a system with the value radius extending from the center self mass involving nearby entities in a gravitational field and the value-free remote elements existing in flat, gravity-less environment.

The astute reader may have noticed a problem in this discussion, not with the ideas as presented, but with what they inescapably imply about $\mathbb{R}$. $\mathbb{R}$ comprises an element set that is continuous in terms of measurability, and a flat geometry described by the physics and math we currently use to understand it. But, how do we *know* $\mathbb{R}$? We know $\mathbb{R}$ initially *through* limited, discrete models in $\mathbb{CS}0$, and only secondarily do some of us learn to know it to a greater or lesser extent through the workings of our higher intellects through the study of advanced mathematics and science. That is, our untutored attempts (think of Galileo's detractors) to understand $\mathbb{R}$ are effected entirely through $\mathbb{CS}0$, and bear all the marks of having been conceptualized thus, being festooned with notions of absolute right and wrong, independent of any verifiable evidence. The geocentric cosmology of Ptolemaic astronomy, for example, uses the geometry of $\mathbb{CS}0$ to view the flat-geometry universe through the $\mathbb{CS}0$ curved geometry frame of reference, using what can only be termed the hilarious mechanics of epicenters and epicycles. If you think on this for a moment, you will see that these circles on circles were needed to map the flat geometry of $\mathbb{R}$ onto the curved geometry centered around us in our $\mathbb{CS}0$ reality.

It is important, though, to take a moment and recognize that the distortion around the self center point is not a flaw in our perception or cognition, nor even a primitive level of be-

ing that we should strive to overcome. On the contrary, it is
the very miracle of consciousness, of cognition, itself. This deformity in the geometry of space around the self is the actual
mechanism that endows us with the ability to interpret and understand elements in $\mathbb{R}$ in a way that makes sense in $\mathbb{CS}0$, to
interact with reality in a way that makes it possible for us to
understand our environment sufficiently to use our mobility to
our advantage. It is what makes mobile mortality possible because it enables us to translate any perception x into a phrase in
our movement language. Matter in $\mathbb{R}$ has attributes of position,
mass, relative velocity, etc., but it does not have the attribute
of *meaning*. Meaning only exists in cognitive spaces, because
meaning is only defined in relation to a specific mortality constraint (either of an individual or a group). Meaning, purpose
and value are mortality related concepts, they can only exist in
cognitive spaces because, ultimately, meaning is defined by the
ability to make an interested choice in a cognitive space.

The geometry of $\mathbb{CS}0$ is absolutely characterized by its curvature at the center point; this is the massive feature at the center of our reality that is the basis of the strongly felt concepts of
good/evil, right/wrong, good/bad and true/false. Furthermore,
each $\mathbb{CS}0$ is unique to the L0 structure on which it is realized,
that is, every volitionally mobile creature realizes cognition in
their own, unique $\mathbb{CS}0$ space, so while there is only one external
reality, there are as many $\mathbb{CS}0$ spaces as there are mobile creatures, each with its own model of reality, $\mathbb{R}$. It is important to
note that, while all $\mathbb{CS}0$ spaces are structurally similar, they are

all profoundly different in that they each have their own unique quasar of absolute truth burning at their center.

The absolute concepts of good/bad, true/false, etc., *cannot* be defined, cannot exist without a fixed point. Relativity and the flat geometry of $\mathbb{R}$ tells us that there is no fixed point in reality, no special frame of reference that sets the standard for the rest—all points in reality have equal status in a flat geometry. Such is not the case in the curved geometry of $\mathbb{CS}0$, in it all of space is bent around the center point of the cognitive being's existence and survival interests. This is not a flaw, not a defect, but the key mutation that made volitional movement evolutionarily feasible, it is the key to conscious life itself.

We will not be discussing $\mathbb{CS}1$ because, since L1 is just L0 with memory (via the result data structure), it just doesn't add much to the current subject. Even though being able to learn from our experience is an extremely important innovation, the significance of this memory function only manifests in operations that apply below the level of the space concept, and thus, doesn't seem relevant to the current discussion.

$\mathbb{CS}2$, however, is worth discussing, because the L2 level it is based on presents a much more interesting case than L1, since it introduces a fundamentally new data structure, the pattern, and therefore generates a fundamentally new space that is interestingly different than $\mathbb{CS}0$. The question is, what is the geometry of this new pattern space? The answer, it turns out, requires multiple parts.

First, consider that L2 patterns can be thought of as words

in a pattern language that are linked and organized according to the grammar of that particular language. Now, what happens when an L2 grammar is violated? For example, what happens in an argument when one disputant charges the other with contravening a principle of logic? Do they both recheck their work and verify the error, which the errant one then goes off to rectify by backtracking, correcting and regenerating his argument? Surely, he must, because we all know that one simply cannot proceed as long as a logic error exists, right? Of course, this is not what happens, instead, he invariably attacks along some other line, while simply ignoring the supposed violation. He gets away with it, they both do, repeatedly—since all debaters violate logic rules all the time—because principles of logic are just like all other grammar rules in that they are, to paraphrase the *Pirates of the Caribbean*, more of a guideline than a rule.

Rules in pattern languages are subjective in both form and application, so they float in the æther to be recognized or ignored at will. The L2 pattern processing reliance on local, optional rules makes the geometry of the $\mathbb{CS}2$ space flat, because patterns do not natively have links to the curved value region of cognitive space, instead, error correction depends entirely on value-free rule sets defined by the pattern language itself. If the set of language rules is informal, as it usually is, then it lacks a rigid membership rule, and this leads to set membership being variable, rather than fixed. This leads to different observers getting different results using what is supposed to be the same calculation, and in fact, it leads to the same person getting different results each time they recalculate their results (think of literary and musical tastes and interpretations).

What is $2,317 * 3,894$? "Uhmm, more than 6 million, *whatever* *shrug*, I mean, who cares, right?" What forces you to do the work to get the answer to a math problem correct? Nothing, unless there is a pressure to meet some verifiable goal. Lacking that pressure, different people will get different results and be happy with it, regardless.

On the other hand, what about the beliefs of a fundamentalist or ideologue? These internal ideas, doctrines, creeds, these ruminations in $\mathbb{I}$, now *these* are worth killing over and dying for, right? Patterns with a high value link to the singularity distortion field have a set, unchangeable truth value attached that brooks no challenge. Patterns that have a value link exist in the curved geometry of $\mathbb{CS}0$ (truth of self-interest) or $\mathbb{CS}1$ (the truth of experience).

That is, $\mathbb{CS}2$ is both curved, like $\mathbb{CS}0$, and flat, like $\mathbb{R}$, in concentric regions with the boundary between them being defined by the values that drive the value formula to zero. (In the paraboloid above, the vertex is at 0, but in the model it is at the maximum discrete evaluation value, so flip it in your mind, or do the math to fix it.) By this construction, any ostensibly 'objective' idea—the pride of the intellectual fleet—can become profoundly subjective in just one step: as soon as you attach a value link to an idea, its subjectivity equals the value position it is linked to. One aspect of subjectivity is the emotional resistance to change one feels when a subjective idea is under

attack. This capacity for objective ideas to be instantly subjec-
tified means no idea is immune to the formation of emotional
attachments that impair their capacity for correction, and ideas
that are not readily updated by the uptake of new facts tend to
fester over time.

While the case of L2 using unenforced grammar checking
as the only gauge of pattern correctness is both common and
faulty enough, the problem only gets worse when a value link
is attached, and suddenly even small, informal changes meet
increased resistance. Do you *believe* in evolution? Is climate
change *true*? Are creationists *wrong*? These are normal opinions held by the educated class in the present day, and most of
the educated elite can be provoked to assign truth or falseness
values to almost any sufficiently complex science-based idea.
Attaching TFRW values to pattern ideas repositions them into
the curved geometry region of $\mathbb{CS}2$.

There are different ways we can view the relation between
$\mathbb{CS}0$, $\mathbb{CS}1$ and $\mathbb{CS}2$:

1. each one is a different space,
2. each one is a different region of a common space, or
3. there is only one cognitive space.

Perhaps the alert student, if they have given themselves sufficient time to reflect on this, will have already come to the
conclusion that #3 is the simplest solution: each cognitive entity only has one cognitive space, with the value distortion field
containing all ideas at the L1 level and below, plus all ideas
above that level that have a value link. If we leverage the

$\mathbb{CS}n$ terminology for one more moment, we can say that, since $\mathbb{I} \neq \emptyset \therefore |\mathbb{CS}0| > 0$ (why?), but it is still entirely possible that $|\mathbb{CS}2| = 0$. Thus, we have simplified the problem to a single cognitive space with a value distortion field and ideas that do or do not have evaluations or value links that place them within it.

Since L0/L1 are pre-language levels, L0/L1 creatures are restricted to knowing only what they directly experience, so all of an L1 creature's memories would be positioned within the value radius of the curved geometry of the cognitive space. The flat area of the geometry only becomes significant with the addition of the L2 capacity for affectless learning through language (rather than having to rely solely on direct personal experience) of value-free patterns.

Calculations on entities within the distortion field would use a different algebra to account for the effect of value than would ideas without a value link, since they are not subject to its gravitational influence. While this difference might be handled simply by zeroing out the value factor, I don't think this would be adequate, because in a zero value situation, $a + b$ can be calculated using the rules of subjective algebra, but within a value field the calculation could fail because local value rules might prohibit adding a_{v_1} to b_{v_2}.

6.5 $\mathbb{R}$ to $\mathbb{CS}$ Mapping Issues

Mapping between the flat geometry of $\mathbb{R}$ and the value distortion field of $\mathbb{CS}$ poses considerable epistemological difficulties that have not hitherto been adequately addressed. The presumption has always been that reality is described by truth, that education is the process of instructing the youth in the great systems of truth, and that truth, once presented to the intelligent, honest mind, induces a revelation of sorts that enables the sincere student to see the truth, the light. Odd, isn't it, that nothing in that last sentence is consistent with verifiable reality?

The problem with mapping from a flat to a curved geometry arises from the value links, of course, because they introduce an essentially incalculable stickiness into the situation by adding a resistance to the process of idea combination and other operations. In the subjective algebra, I began working out the various algebraic operations supported in each intellect, and the work has turned out well, at least in so far as the tunable simulation is concerned. That is, given the various parameters for a particular cognitive entity (called an asomatous psyche since in the machine there is only mind and no body), the algebra appears to work out well. However, when we get away from specific values into pure algebra, the value link introduces the concept of resistance, which we could properly represent with Ω for obvious reasons, and this turns a simple addition problem, $\mathbf{a} + \mathbf{b} = \mathbf{c}$, for example, into something considerably more complex:

$$(\mathbf{a}+\Omega_a) + (\mathbf{b} + \Omega_b) =$$

$$\text{if } (\mathbf{a} - \mathbf{c}) < max(\Omega_a, \Omega_b)$$

$$then: \ (\mathbf{a} + \mathbf{c}) + max(\Omega_a, \Omega_b)$$

$$else: \ no - op$$

That is, now we have to use complex-like notation to represent entities as a combination of an attribute array and its resistance to change, Ω, that is proportional to the magnitude of the value link attached to the idea. The simple act of adding two attribute arrays now proceeds only if the difference between the two is smaller than the maximum resistance of the two, and the result is the sum of the two attribute arrays plus the max of the resistance, otherwise, a no-operation occurs and nothing happens.

The idea resistance addition, shown above, is more at the thought experiment, rather than result, stage. All of the material presented here is closer to the starting than ending point. Work on it, extend or replace it, don't just accept it.

The upside of this new complication is that it gives us a formula to calculate one type of resistance to learning, and this should open the way for a whole host of others to apply to various normal learning limitations. The conjecture here is that,

by taking this approach, we can represent real-life situations
formulaically, and this will allow us to devise solutions analyt-
ically, which we can repeatedly test in the lab, before we loose
them on the world. The only reason human reason and emotion have seemed messy and intractable subjects up until now is
that we have been using the mudball model to understand ourselves and our behavior. With rigorous, faceted model-oriented
reasoning, we can increase our reasoning abilities sufficiently
to tackle human issues like any other situation that produces
results observable in $\mathbb{R}$.

Carelessly mapping from a flat to a curved geometry is
fraught with risk. Since value acts like gravity in the curved
cognition space, then operations that work in the flat space will
not always work the same in the curved one. For example, take
a very simple arithmetic problem: $2 + 3 = 5; 5 - 3 = 2$. This
works fine in the flat space, but add the resistance factor to the
operands and one of the operations might turn out to be an 'up-
hill' action that pulls against the force of value, and the other,
a downhill one. In a curved world, both equations cannot be
guaranteed to succeed. This sounds odd, to be sure, but if you
reflect on it for a minute, you might realize that what we are
modeling are subjective idea operations in your own mind, and
you should admit that reasoning is not symmetrical. This is
why good teachers keep giving you clues when you are stuck on
a point, until you can finally make the connection, and do the
operation that they have been explaining from the beginning.
What happens in such cases is that they are looking for a path

of lower resistance in your mind that will allow you to make the connection. We all know that the topography of our minds makes some approaches difficult to impossible, while others are easier. The value force is one approach that successfully models this hitherto inexplicable asymmetry in our learning capabilities.

In our model, we are envisioning a symmetrical deformity field surrounding the singularity, but what happens if you use some other means to determine idea positions, and then inject the effect of value topographically, using hills and valleys to represent the value component at various locations? Suddenly, contiguous ideas might be separated by a value chasm too severe ever to be bridged, or operating from one idea to another might be downhill and easy, while the reverse is difficult and uncomfortable.

 *Modeling is a powerful tool that allows us to conceive the object of our study in whatever terms our tools can handle and our solution requires.*

Everyone knows that we all experience emotional resistance to different types of learning, that it is easier for us to handle some challenges than others. For many of us, when we are learning math or other hard sciences, for example, our greatest problem is often not the subject matter itself, so much as it is the difficulty we experience in overcoming our intense non-self evaluation of the material well enough to be able to memorize, recall and use it on demand. But, obviously, math is a very small part of life for most of us. Many people have favorite colors, sounds, smells, even numbers: this means that they *identify* more with some elements of a class than with others, that they attach a value link to what would seem to be inherently neutral entities. Most of us really like our favorite subjects, and this, too, means that we attach value links to these subjects and the ideas in them. Value links bring a resistance to change with them because they link arbitrary facts with our sense of self to some degree. Suddenly, learning gets both sticky and emotional, making us loath to part with ideas we hold near and dear to our hearts.

Sound familiar? Of course. Sound problematic in a learning situation? Of course. Does this sound like a fertile area to explore in order to find meaningful discoveries? I should certainly hope so.

6.6 Summary

By approaching the consideration of model-oriented reasoning, as we have, from the perspective of its laws and terms, rather than from a focus on details, techniques and implementation, we have been able to clarify and simplify much of what has historically puzzled us about different facets of human behavior by using first principles rather than having to dig all the way through layers of analysis to get down to the fundamentals underlying implementation details. In fact, just by adding the concept of layers to the laws and terms, and then defining cognitive spaces, we have already reached a point where we can see an entire class of solutions to our questions all at once: we now know that much, if not most, of the messiness of human relations and belief systems has nothing whatsoever to do with being human, but instead, arises from structural issues inherent in the nature of cognition itself.

One of the things we learned from relativity is that there is no fixed point in the universe, no special frame of reference that has precedence over any other. But it turns out this only applies to systems comprising only matter and energy of whatever sort, i.e., physical reality, it does not apply to volitionally mobile cognitive systems and the internal picture they contrive of their environment. By **M1** and **M2**, although it may take some moment of reflection to see it, we should realize that a cognitive system necessarily creates a new, alternate, abstract, discrete model version of a continuous reality, and that it is with this personal construct that we interact, it is in this synthetic world that we think, feel and live. Physically, we verifiably live in reality, but mentally we live in a cognitive construct of our own making that has no defined relation to external reality. Now that we understand the distortion involved in trying to map objects from a flat reality into our curved consciousness, perhaps we can appreciate a little better the extent to which our ideas need to be verified.

Cognitive systems *always* have a fixed point, and this departure from physical reality has profound implications because cognitive systems model the bit of external reality that fits within their perceptual sphere, but their models of reality comprise personally significant data points that are not only few in relation to the points on the referent, but are also synthetically constructed from sensory impulses rather than true pictures of external reality.

- Cognitive systems are not structured like physical reality, and their models are built on their peculiar structure, not on the pattern of reality.

- Cognitive systems do not model the entire contents of their perceptual spheres, but only such parts of it as they evaluate to be significant, and their modeling is incremental and partial, not a full snapshot of the whelming reality.

It is easy, now, to see the problems that must arise when we try to understand the flat geometry of reality through the curved lens of, for example, religion. The educated classes scoff at the uneducated simpletons who insist on biblical literalism, but what they do not see is the folly and danger of disdaining belief and faith in favor of a slavish devotion to what they think of as reality; they do not realize that they are trying to use the flat geometric system of the pattern processor to satisfy the curved geometry requirements of a mortality-constrained system. Both conservatives who want to solve tomorrow's problems with yesterday's answers, and liberals who want to solve problems with a resource budget unconstrained by the strictures of mortality, are making complementary errors of neglecting to recognize the topology of the other space, and since both reality and mortality are important, neglecting either when trying to solve problems that involve both, cannot be wise.

RWTFGB (right/wrong, true/false, good/bad) cannot be defined in an absolute sense without a fixed point, a thing which does not exist in $\mathbb{R}$, but can only be found in $\mathbb{CS}0$. When we mutually argue from L0—as sometimes it is necessary and appropriate to do—then we are arguing from one curved geometry to another, which would make sense and could lead to productive discussions were it not for the rather glaring fact that each participant's truth sources are different because the fixed points at the center of each system are centered in the speaker using it. The only point actually being argued in L0 debates is which of these center-defined geometries we, as a group, should align with, that is, who has the center point that we should follow, a question that is determined not by factual correctness, but by force of personality and persuasion. L0 discussions are, by nature, power contests designed to identify which $\mathbb{CS}0$ truth source the group should follow with the winner of the argument becoming the authority of the group, at least for the moment.

On the other hand, when would-be intellectuals vaingloriously pretend to be debating from logic, rather than emotion, in truth-based discussions, their use of internally defined or accepted notions of right and wrong exposes their pretensions for what they really are: primitive assertions that their truth is truer than their opponent's truth, which is just the crudest of L0 primitive assertions, only thinly cloaked in the puffery of erudition.

6.7 Review

- Space: an unbounded geometry and the elements in it.
- $\mathbb{R}$ is flat, has no fixed point, or special frame of reference.
- $\mathbb{R}$ is our tested model of reality, sometimes casually used as shorthand for reality.
- Cognitive space ($\mathbb{CS}$): a geometry with mental elements, e.g., thoughts, feelings and beliefs.
- Our brain is in $\mathbb{R}$, mental events occur in $\mathbb{R}$, but semantics occurs in $\mathbb{CS}$
- $\mathbb{CS}$ is a first class object on par with $\mathbb{R}$.
- The *self* is the singularity that creates the curvature in the $\mathbb{CS}$ geometry.
- Self-interest defines value; value acts as a space-deforming gravity in $\mathbb{CS}$.
- $\mathbb{CS}$ has a fixed point, a special frame of reference in which special laws hold.
- The $\mathbb{CS}$ singularity distortion field is the seat of the self, volitional mobility would not be possible without it.
- The self is the basis of value, which is the gravity force in $\mathbb{CS}$.
- Reference objects realize consciousness from the fact of self.
- The semantic chain is: self $\rightarrow$ value $\rightarrow$ meaning.
- The curvature of the $\mathbb{CS}$ is defined by the value formula.
- Our model will only use a single $\mathbb{CS}$ for each cognitive entity.
- L2 affectless learning is required to situate ideas in the

flat regions of $\mathbb{CS}$.

- The value force models asymmetrical learning events
- Things such as favorite smells and colors are examples of our tendency to drag neutral entities into the value sphere.

Chapter 7

Universal Cognition Model

7.1 Introduction

Beyond our species, beyond our own tree of life, beyond our galaxy, what do we know of cognition itself? What do we know about the fact, the process of cognition emerging from an evolving organic context? If we limit our consideration to the sort of cognition realized in autonomously mobile creatures (without presuming to know whether or not any other kind exists), it turns out we actually know a great deal.

In order to study anything, first one must have the appropriate tools, and so Descartes, Galileo, Newton, Lavoisier, Einstein and the rest of the pioneers worked out their ideas and presented us with the tools we needed to study and understand nature at an ever deeper, more profound level. If scientists can study light from a star billions of light years away and tell us its age, vector and composition based on what they know about atoms here on earth, then, now that we have faceted model-oriented reasoning, why shouldn't we be able to do the same level of work on cognition and cognitive entities? We are, after all, made of atoms, aren't we? So, once we begin to model the fundamental nature of cognition in an organic entity *here*, we should have every expectation that what we discover will also apply *there*, as well, regardless of where *there* is.

The line between the universal cognition model and the ECDM explained in *Pinnacle Reasoning* may seem blurry at times, because the particular came well before the general, and we are still picking parts of the general out of the single particular instance, as we go. In this very short chapter, we will list a few basic principles that seem to belong to the universal model. As the specific model—either that used in the asomatous psyche, or another one built from scratch by a reader—is elaborated, tested and strengthened with informal and formal models, then we should be able to elaborate and polish the universal model. For now, we will be content with just a few notes to start with.

 *Stop and reflect for a moment before proceeding: from the point of view of scientific study, why should cognition be different than anything else? What, other than our purblind mudball model, could have led us to exclude the possibility of a universal cognition model?*

7.2 UC1: Cognition Proves Itself

Cognition proves itself and the space it defines. That is, cognition posits the right of the cognitive entity to struggle to survive and multiply. Value is created in the self singularity, and value, meaning, and purpose only exist within the singularity distortion field.

7.3 UC2: Basis of Cognition

$$choice + mortality \Leftrightarrow cognition$$

The necessary and sufficient condition required for cognition to emerge from an organic context in a physical universe is achieved when a mortal frame gains the capacity for forming and implementing choice, i.e., evaluating perception and choosing to move in a self-preferential way. By 'mortal', we should understand not just a finite limit to a lifespan, but also the regular need to secure resources from the environment to survive.

7.4 UC3: Self

$$self \Leftrightarrow cognition$$

The cognitive function and the atomic self are one and the same. The self is created when the capacity of choice is added to a mortal line. This level of self is rudimentary and functional, but not self-aware.

7.5 UC4: Essential Cognition

$$\forall\, x \in (\mathbb{R} \cup \mathbb{I})\; \exists\, p \in \mathbf{P}\; :\; L0(p) \to e\; :\; AM(e) \to a \in \mathbf{A}$$

The fundamental function of cognition is to evaluate perceptions of flat space phenomena by mapping them into the curved $\mathbb{CS}$.

As L2-centric creatures, we naturally associate cognition with pattern processing, but that is just a very small, very late part of what cognition does. The first function of cognition is to assign value to reality elements ($r_i \in \mathbb{R}$) in order to convert them into cognitive elements ($i_j \in \mathbb{I}$) that can be processed by the mind and responded to with the body.

7.6 UC5: Value

Value is an attribute of curved space. By **UC1-UC4**, we have the relation:

$$cognition \Leftrightarrow self \Leftrightarrow value$$

Cognition is achieved when choice is added to mortality, which both defines and presupposes self, and self by its existence and function defines value.

7.7   UC6: Periodicity of Cognition

Cognition is not, and cannot be, a continuous function. It periodically processes input into discrete models that can be evaluated. The function of evaluating input into a model requires some time, $t > 0$, and this makes the process periodic. (Conceptually, an organism might host independent perceptual mechanisms that support switching and background processing, but this would only work around this principle, not abrogate it.)

7.8   UC7: Cognition Evolves in Levels

The evolutionary cytomodel requires that higher level functionality be composed of lower level functions that evolve over time. The first level of cognition, L0 in our model, only supports self-preferential movement in response to interpreted perceptions, and we are an example of language-enabled pattern processors, so this suggests that there have to be one or more levels between us and L0, as well as the possibility of levels above us.

7.9   UC8: Self-Awareness

True consciousness of self requires multiple levels of cognition. The ability to self-name, which is what we identify as self awareness, requires cognition levels that support containers and patterns.

7.10   UC9: Time

The concept of time is not a native cognitive construct, it is a synthetic inference based on the capability to react to the present, recall the past, and anticipate the future. This requires several levels of cognitive evolution. In other words, *time* is an intellectual construct created by cognitive entities at or above lower L2 levels and above to keep us oriented to resource cycles.

Time, as we conceive it, doesn't actually exist in $\mathbb{R}$, it is an artifact of our cognitive apparatus.

7.11   Review

Just review the list of principles above.

7.12   Exercises

1. Take no more than a few moments after reviewing the universal cognition model principles and try to boil them down or sharpen them.

2. Take another moment and see if there are any other principles you would want to add.

3. Periodically return to this exercise as you continue through the book, and review and update both your additions and subtractions.

4. Briefly explain how thinking about the idea of a universal cognition model helped your understanding of how to apply models to human experience. If it didn't help, explain why it did not.

Chapter 8

The Self

8.1 Introduction

The self, just like any other higher level cognitive function, is an emergent property that arises from the synergy between a large number of smaller functions performing simple tasks at various levels of the organic hierarchy. That is, there is no **self**, per se, rather, it manifests in layers of complexity and completeness that result from the timely performance of the various contributing subordinate functions.

8.2 Evaluation

The seed of the self, the beginning of self-awareness, can be found in the evaluation term, $L0(p) \rightarrow e$, of the perception expression. Evaluation is accomplished through the comparison of the evaluand with a reference standard. An example of pseudo code of the evaluation function is:

```
tuple evaluate(x){
  type = archetypes.closestMatch(x)
  degree = angleBetween(type, x)
  return (type, degree)
}
```

What this says is that the evaluate function takes any parameter x, and returns a tuple (a finite list of terms) as the evaluation. The steps in the function body are:

1. Find the closest match to x from the collection of archetypes to determine the type of x.
2. Calculate the angle between the type and input parameter to determine the degree to which x matches this type.
3. Return the two values in a list.

8.3   Archetypes

This raises the questions: where did the archetypes come from, and how did the input wind up in a format that makes comparison between the unknown and the archetype possible, and how does comparison work? The short answer, of course, is evolution, and the slightly longer answer is that life is a collection of behaviors that persists long enough to support reproduction in a given environment. Natural selection weeds out entities whose behaviors do not match their environment, so it should be apparent that the archetypes represent a collection of generalized anti-self, pro-self and non-self stereotypes of entities and events, which are common to an ecological niche that is defined by the nexus of the environmental reality and the organism's sensory and physical capabilities. These archetypes are thus at the core of what makes any organism exactly what it is. So, the archetypes encoded in a mosquito, a frog and a weasel will be very different, even though they all may live in the same pond area.

As explained in an earlier chapter, the perception process encodes a snapshot of its sensorium into a structure native to its intellect. The essence of any level of intellect is the data structure it operates on, so every level of intellect has the ability to convert input into standard form using the inherited structure, and to perform operations on that structure. That is, the data structure in each intellect level *is* how that intellect 'sees' the world; sensing any input, x, charges the various elements in the data structure in some way, and then cognition proceeds to process the charged data structure, not x itself.

As an evolution-related point, we should note that the archetype collection can be, and possibly is, virtual rather than actual. That is, the same effect as having a collection of anti-, pro- and non-self archetype vectors somehow encoded in our genotype can be achieved much more economically by having a function initialize the vector template with maximum anti, pro and then non values sequentially in the process of evaluation, reusing the same structure, just charging it up anew for each evaluation. While this is an implementation question, it is always nice to ensure that our solutions can be simplified sufficiently to be plausibly encodable genetically.

It is this collection of archetypes, which may not even exist, except as an ephemerally charged state of a data structure, that forms the seed of the self, and this seed forms the basis of self-consciousness. That is, we can define the essence of *self* as:

> **Essential Self**: a collection of values encoded in the genotype that forms the basis for all anti-self, pro-self and non-self evaluations.

Yes, the foundation of selfhood, of consciousness, of self-awareness, is as simple as a collection of baseline values that are used in the comparison function that the evaluator routine uses to determine whether and how quickly it should retreat or approach a threat or opportunity, or whether it can just ignore it altogether. After all, at a fundamental level, who am I but a union of the different sets of my fears, needs, strengths and abilities?

Of course, the L0 organism is not, in any sense, self-aware, but the consciousness of identity manifested in L2 intellects rests on this definition of a protoself in terms of its environmental interaction boundaries. The *self* is defined by the boundary delimiting it from other, but that boundary is drawn around behavioral needs, abilities and limitations, not around a body outline (see figure 8.1). This unaware protoself is the fixed point at the center of $\mathbb{CS}$ that is the basis for all meaning and value in its world.

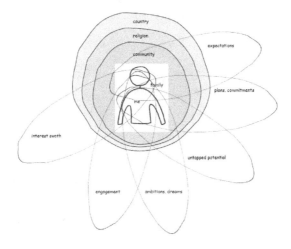

Figure 8.1: Behavior view of self boundaries.

8.4   Self and Other

The self is not defined by the goo in the middle, but by the boundary at the edge; without a boundary, there is no self.

In order to define *self*, first we must define *other*, **O**:

$$\mathbf{O} = \forall\ i \in \mathbb{I} : i_{[p]} < min\ \&\ i_{[n]} > min$$

That is, *other* is the set of all things represented by ideas that have a pro-self ($i_{[p]}$) evaluation below a minimum level and a non-self ($i_{[n]}$) evaluation above a minimum level. So, any x that I don't evaluate as of any interest to me is part of other. Doesn't matter if x is person, place, thing, or even part of my body or mind: if I do not associate it with myself through at least a minimally significant value link, then this thing is not me.

The definition of *self*, Ψ (psi, from *psyche*), necessarily follows immediately:

$$\Psi = \mathbb{I} - \mathbf{O}$$

That is, everything I have an interest in, is linked *into* me with a bond proportional to the strength of its value link: I am the sum of the degrees of my interest. Of all the things of which I am aware, the only ones that are not part of me are those I don't care about, those I don't claim. All the rest contributes to the whole that is me, in proportion to the bond I have attached to it.

Your family is part of you; if you are religious, your religious community is part of you; if you are patriotic, your country is part of you. If you care about things you own, they are a part of you. If you have plans, dreams, or expectations, they, too, are a part of you and, depending on the value of parameters i and s in equation 6.1, you may fight to preserve them.

The self is a great deal more than what we unthinkingly suppose, and what we claim as our own is likely much different than we automatically allow others to claim for themselves. Those of us with a constitutionally high level of self-interest will but grudgingly grant others even the right to their own body and family, and maybe *some* of their possessions, while we will usually claim all that is ours and all that we want or expect on top of that.

Did you expect a positive definition of self? Why? We are the sum of all the things we sense and think that are not explicitly other. Why get mad in traffic? Because that gap in front of you was yours, part of you, and it was violated.

The *min* value referenced in the definition of **O** is a variable that is set by the individual, based on their aversion to conflict, sense of entitlement and sense of strength, so this formula is not a prescription for conflict, it is merely a formal set definition of the ubiquitous concept, *self*. Why is there conflict, why is there competition for food, why is there a food chain? Because of Ψ, because of cognition, because of *life*.

We can choose to expand or contract our definition of self, we can choose to set the trigger level for violence higher or lower. Yes, we can act as responsible, moral beings, we have that capacity, but the fundamental reality of resource strife is that it is an inherent part of volitional mobility, and, far from being a deplorable evil, on the contrary, it does yeoman service to all, by acting as a major engine in the exogenous process that compensates for the defective partial algorithm that generates unlimited reproduction.

8.5   Summary

Evaluation is, in essence, comparison against a standard. What
big is x? How far away? What does it mean? Friend or foe?
These and all other evaluations are comparisons against a standard: what is large to a meerkat is small to an elephant, what
is close to a snake may be far to an ant. The act of evaluation
posits the existence of self, for all evaluation answers the question: what does x mean to *me*? The given in that expression is
me, and the interrogation determines whether x is a threat, an
opportunity or a nullity. But the 'me' term in that calculation
is not some abstract psychological or physical abstraction representing the L0 organism's identity or worth as a being, but
the negative, positive and null collections of maximum values
in the data structure that holds the charges transmitted by the
senses.

The core self, the L0 self, is defined by its mortality interests
that are represented by the maximum threat, opportunity and
meh levels its data structure can register in response to sensory
input. Who am I? I am he who is not threatened by a mouse,
but is threatened by a bear, one who cannot eat grass, but
can eat animals. Or, I am he who eats mice and fish and is
vulnerable when not flying, and so on.

The self, at the L0 level, is defined at the level of the species:
individuals here are fungible. The L0 self is the sum of the
needs, vulnerabilities and behaviors encoded in the genotype.
The L0 organism interacts with its environment from a point of
interest centered in the heritable archetype array deep within

itself.

The L0 self is a fixed point in the L0 sphere of existence, it is the basis of all comparisons, of all knowledge, of all value. The higher selves just elaborate this into different spheres, using different terms.

8.6 Review

Remember, the gentle reader is more than the L0 self being described here. All we are discussing are the foundational ideas everything else is built on.

- There is no self per se, it is an emergent property.
- The ability of L0 to evaluate input is the seed of self.
- Evaluation rates *other* in terms of its relation to self.
- Archetypes are implicitly defined by singly maximizing evacule dimensions.
- The essential self is defined by a collection of values encoded in the genotype that forms the basis for all evaluations.
- Self, $\Psi = \mathbb{I} - \mathbf{O}$.
- Resource strife is required to compensate for the defective, partial reproduction algorithm. It is part of evolutionary mortality.

Chapter 9

Value

9.1 Introduction

In this transitional chapter, we will be taking a few moments to expand on the concept of value by considering some of its more abstract aspects, and to examine some of its applications, in preparation for the shift from introductory to more advanced material. If you find some of this material hard to follow, just keep reading after reflecting on the knotty parts for a moment, and trust that the obscure parts will clear up when they are elaborated later on.

Spaces are defined by elements and geometry, and the two geometries we have considered so far are flat and curved, but not just curved, curved around a singularity defined by the single point of self in the $\mathbb{CS}$ space. The deformation reaches maximum at the point of self, and diminishes as the distance from that point increases. But what does 'distance' mean in this context? Obviously it is not a quantity measurable in feet or meters, but must be in units appropriate to the singularity. What is the singularity, if not the trinity of the values used by the self to evaluate experience? The apex (or nadir, depending on your perspective) of one tertrant of the distortion is the anti-self evacule [max, min, min], and the other two are the pro-self [min, max, min] and the non-self [min, min, max] evacules. Distance in the distortion field is therefore defined in whatever units are used to quantify the anti-, pro- and non-self elements of evaluations. (Since we measure the angle of difference between vectors, we generally use degrees.)

Consider the abstract concept of *value*: any set of non-identical elements supports the selection of a subset of one or more of them from the others, based on some attribute. If the attributes of the elements support an ordinal sort, then the ordering attribute can be construed as the value quality. Fundamentally, the relation: *value* ⇔ *order*, tells us that value or *meaning* is a concomitant aspect of order. From this perspective, 'value' is an emergent quality of a prioritized search function and the set of scored elements over which it operates. The mere assignment of scores, though, is insufficient to define value by itself, because the value emerges only once a selection process respects it. Similarly, a priority search without scored elements is also inadequate. The scores on the set elements do not have to actually refer to any particular standard, or any standard at all. Arbitrary scores will produce the same result as calculated ones in returning a subset in the search, but the result sets will vary when considering their relation to an external value standard.

But, if they are not arbitrary, how can the value attributes be set? Once a boundary value for each type of value is defined, then the various elements in the collection can be set relative to that. But how is the boundary value set? In a flat space, such as $\mathbb{R}$, there is no boundary reference frame; all quantifiers such as most, least, closest, or furthest are cognitive constructs that exist in some cognitive space outside of $\mathbb{R}$. While it might seem that both the question and answer to: what is the closest planet to earth? could be answered in $\mathbb{R}$, the only thing that can actually be determined in $\mathbb{R}$ is a measurement with a certain precision. Concepts such as closest actually only exist in $\mathbb{CS}$, along with all of the other concepts in the question. Comparison is a strictly a $\mathbb{CS}$ function, because there is no comparison mechanism anywhere in $\mathbb{R}$.

Priority searches cannot exist in a flat space precisely because the flatness of the geometry precludes any salient on which a relative sort can be based. Value supports and is defined by the selection process. Without selection, everything is equal, and there is no such thing as relative value. Value is a space-based attribute that can only exist in a curved space because it must, ultimately, be defined in terms of a fixed point, and the only place in the universe where a fixed point can exist is in a cognitive space. Value does not exist in $\mathbb{R}$; without reference to an external frame of reference, nothing in $\mathbb{R}$ is any more or less valuable than anything else.

The singularity in $\mathbb{CS}0$, the self center point, is the only basis we have for defining an absolute value. In the cognitive space, of course, the absolute value is the mortality interest of the entity reifying the space. Value does not, and cannot exist in $\mathbb{R}$, because the geometry does not support it—things just exist as and where they are, without favor or prejudice. Only in a curved space do things become more or less special by virtue of their position in the space; in a flat space, no one thing is ever inherently more or less valuable than another—wherever this distinction is made, it can only be made by an external or containing reference frame.

To a cognitive being, the value of anything is defined by the value link connected to the abstract representation of that thing in the cognitive space: the closer the connection is to the singularity at the center point of the space, the more valuable it is. The [a, p, n] coordinates of the value point determine whether that value has a negative, positive, null or mixed quality. It is important to recognize that the flatness of the geometry in $\mathbb{R}$ means that value does not, *cannot*, exist in it, because, absent a comparison standard, any rock is as 'good' as any other. Value is strictly a cognitive space phenomenon, because it is an attribute that must be assigned, since it does not inhere in anything. The singularity is the sole source and definition of value in cognitive spaces, which means that it is the sole source of value, not only in cognitive spaces, but anywhere that can be imagined.

This means that for a cognitive entity to value any idea,

belief, feeling, phenomenon or event, it must have a value assignment within the $\mathbb{CS}$ distortion field. A familiar illustration of the consequence of assigning value is the high school algebra student who learns that $a^2 - b^2 = (a + b)(a - b)$. The small percentage of students headed for degrees in the STEM fields will immediately see the value not only of this particular factorization, but also of the pattern it establishes. The majority of students in most classes, though, will lack the background to be able to connect this abstract idea to a position in cognitive space, so they will find the class boring and the equation meaningless, and their ennui will foreclose any possibility of a STEM career. Ideas, such as this, that never get a $\mathbb{CS}$ value assigned, are soon lost in the trackless desert of null valued ideas, and will be quickly forgotten unless the force of circumstance compels an amount of reuse sufficient to harden the path to it and cement it in memory.

9.2   Value Links

Ideas in $\mathbb{CS}0$ (mentacules), and in $\mathbb{CS}1$ (results), are given a value position as a result of the evaluation process. Ideas in $\mathbb{CS}2$, patterns, are initialized with a null value parameter and only gain a value either directly, by assignment, or indirectly, through linking to another valued pattern that forms a chain of links that ultimately connects back to a value in $\mathbb{CS}0$.

A *link* is a mutable association of a pattern to a value. Whereas beliefs are immutable (they are changed by substitution, not alteration, with the old one persisting even if unused), and patterns themselves are resistant to alteration but open to extension or substitution, links between the two can be dropped, modified, replaced or extended. This malleability of the link between idea and value is the basis for the occasional success of the conversion exercise that is practiced by evangelical religions and belief systems and vegans.

One of the thought linking processes that L2 automatically does as a background process whenever cognitive resources are available, is a scan of the L0/L1 inventory of beliefs and lessons that looks for a middling to high level match with a salient feature of one of the recently referenced patterns that doesn't have a value link yet. This process of automatic linking new ideas to established value nodes is achieved by a standard best-fit searching algorithm. This matching process can be triggered deliberately, by an accident in conversation, or by idle-time background processing. Likelihood of a successful link being established is proportional to the distance between the pattern and the belief archetypes. For example, after one learns that *sesquipedalian* means polysyllabic and encodes a pattern to preserve that lesson, a logophile would have a familiar way to link an affection of a certain type to a newly learned obscure word, particularly one that practically puns on itself, while a sufferer of hippopotomonstrosesquipedaliophobia would not.

The quintessential function of the L2 pattern processing mind is *grammatical linking*. In the asomatous psyche application we model patterns as single in, multiple out structures that support branching on input based on strength of match against the pattern template. This implements the concept that different responses can be triggered by the details of a given class of input, or, in other words, *rules*. An L2 pattern language operates on a class of elements, such as words, numbers, shapes, etc., by using the rules of that language to control the branching path taken through the pattern. The essence of L2 action is to suggest a path based on the details of a particular situation.

The natural state of L2 is to extend patterns in quiet times, and to offer pattern suggestions in times of choice. L2 evaluates the consequence of following a pattern by calculating the delta between the favorability of the pre and post situations. This evaluation of pattern success is calculated on evacules, and so is expressed in the same language that L0/L1 use to evaluate experience, so finding a mentacule or archetype to link to is quite easy. Later, when considering various pattern candidates to match to a particular situation, the quickest way to sort the various options is simply by sorting on the linked L0/L1 evaluation.

The L2 pattern processor that operates in the CS2 space learns patterns, extends patterns, searches and organizes patterns so that it can quickly suggest patterns. The fundamental purpose of a pattern is to anticipate the future by suggesting a planned response to the current situation that has a known history of success. Sometimes, there is ample time for reflection, but oftentimes, the exigency of the moment requires an alacritous response. Linking patterns in the L2 mental library to an L0 value node supports rapid and effective searching and sorting; correspondingly, unlinked patterns are generally not included in ordinary result sets, with desuetude tending to lead to pattern loss.

 *Although the word 'value' is only used once in the previous two paragraphs, take a moment and see how many times it connects to the various ideas being discussed.*

9.3 Value Graphs

As explained elsewhere, we feel, decide and act in L0/L1, but, from our conscious point of view, it seems like we only *think* in L2, because that is where language is. Think of it this way: L0 responds to the moment, L1 to the past, and L2 to possible futures. L2 is connected back to L0/L1 by a value graph.

A *value graph* is a network of value links between our L2 ideas and L0/L1 self-significant feelings, beliefs and memories. Value graphs are the natural form of the result set returned by any idea search, because ideas are naturally connected to other ideas and feelings. In L0/L1, generalization of ideas created by experience embeds them in a value hierarchy topped by the archetypes, while L2 wiles away the hours by endlessly generating, connecting and associating patterns, and connecting them back to L0 value nodes wherever possible. Thus, almost any idea can be used as a starting point to navigate to other ideas, either vertically through the type hierarchy or horizontally through attribute association.

Thus, whenever we query our mind for a memory or a solution to a problem using words, we are querying L2 for result-embedding patterns and what we get back is a result set of zero or more entries that are enmeshed in a web of associations that can be navigated in a variety of ways for a variety of purposes. For example, if we want to intensify or attenuate our emotional response, we can climb up or down the type hierarchy, while if we are unsatisfied with the first option returned, we can crawl the web of associations in an innumerable number of ways to search for a better solution.

The mental or emotional sense of complexity, depth, and nuance that we often experience when reflecting on a question, or other input, is the experience of awareness of a value graph that connects ideas together, as well as the endless value gradients and association pathways it offers for our consideration and exploration. When we resist making a decision because we have the feeling we should think about the issue more, that feeling is proportional to the significance of the recognized, but unexplored, paths in the value graph that are demanding our attention and warning us of unconsidered dangers and opportunities.

9.4 Review

- Selection of a subset, from a set, posits a concept of value.
- Order is an implicit value.
- Value $\Leftrightarrow$ order. There is no need for a metaphysical basis

for value.

- Boundary values are required for sorting.
- There is no boundary in $\mathbb{R}$.
- Comparison does not exist in $\mathbb{R}$.
- Value does not exist in $\mathbb{R}$.
- Patterns in L2 have an optional value link.
- Mutability of value links is inversely proportional to their value.
- One of the background processes in L2 crawls through the pattern library, searching for value matches to which value links can be connected.
- A value graph is a network of value links between our L2 ideas and L0/L1 self-significant feelings, beliefs and memories.
- Value and association graphs support idea navigation in different dimensions.

Chapter 10

The Extended Self

10.1 Elements of the Extended Self

Most human calamities happen from the group, rather than the individual level. Certainly, individual mass murderers are a problem where they appear, but their carnage is usually limited to the double digits of victims, whereas groups can destroy millions and tens of millions of souls in very little time. Many, perhaps most, pinnacle questions concern issues that appear at the group level: war, genocide, slavery, institutional injustice, class and caste systems, antisemitism and the like. Many of the problems we want to be able to study and reproduce scientifically are group related, so of course, before we can examine any particular group, we have to consider the very nature of grouping and how it arises in a cognitive space.

To begin with, the **self** is *me*, the **extended self** is *we*. We is me in a collective sense, it is any collection of which I consider

163

myself a member. Both self-awareness and self-as-part-of-other awareness are L2 achievements—the obverse and reverse of the introduction of indirection into the cognitive apparatus.

Denotation—*that* is a rock—is the definition of a term by direct reference. This is, of course, a linguistic mechanism that is only required when a mind has a lexical capacity and the ability to associate a known entity to a signifier that acts as a reference mechanism. That is, our direct encounter with a rock results in the initialization of a mentacule for rock, and the generalization ability of L1 can create a mineral type hierarchy so that we can know that a pebble is a form of rock. Adding L2 language to the mix allows us to add a new L2 level pattern to hold the word 'rock' and the ability to point it to the rock mentacule, thus allowing us to create linguistic patterns using only the word as a reference, rather than having to use the encounter-derived rock mentacule itself.

Generalization is the ability to compare two related entities to extract the minimal set of characteristics that can identify the shared type of the two instances. This is done by taking the minimum value of each attribute pair of the entities (see listing 16.1). The new supertype entity will have characteristics shared by both of the subtypes, but none of their specialized values. The ability to define supertypes from new perceptions is invaluable in being able to recognize types of things fast enough to support rapid responses when needed. Typing in this fashion supports hierarchical organization of thought and experience and makes storing and retrieving information much more efficient ($O(\log(n))$) vs. $O(n)$). Generalization is an L1 operation.

These two abilities, the L1 generalization function and the L2 naming function, combine to give us the ability to achieve self-awareness once the emergent property of self expands to include named references, because a named evaluation can replace an entire idea hierarchy to simplify calculations that would not be doable if the entire tree of each term had to be evaluated before the expression could be resolved. For example, everything you know about a political enemy should constitute an extensive collection of knowledge, history and experiences that should take you hours, days or weeks to document. However, the way you reason through situations involving this enemy does not use this library of knowledge, but instead relies on an opinion you use to represent the knowledge tree with a label such as liberal, conservative, reactionary, fascist, Marxist etc., along with an evaluation of how bad they are. In all of your arguments involving this enemy, the only thing that you usually use is the opinion's label and evaluation, with only occasional forays into the fact collection to grab a factoid or anecdote to make a point.

This same naming process eventually generates self-awareness when our mind realizes (a process that compares new thought paths to known paths and automatically replaces the longer with the shorter) that the root generalization of all the elements composing the emergent property of self is, indeed, *me*, the singularity of self at the center of our cognitive space, enabling us to think, "I am all of *that*" (referring to the collection of self properties). Sentience plus self-awareness together produce what we think of as consciousness, the level of awareness that culminates in the autonomous, self-reflective, expressive and creative consciousness that we think of as uniquely human but that is really just a point on a continuum of cognitive ability.

10.2   Self and Extended Self

Me is an emergent property, that means it is a not a thing, not a *single* thing, but a collection of things, a composite of many smaller properties and functions, a wraith that materializes in degrees as the various component systems assemble and rev up to full operational speed. The self is neither an organ nor growth that bulges somewhere in the body, but an awareness that is, at its base, nothing more than a genetic capacity to evaluate experience from a self-preferential perspective. As layers of complex functionality are added to the system, the collection of sensibilities and abilities that comprise the self is accordingly enriched to include such functions as learning, memory, calculation and planning, not all of which are exhibited equally by all members of any given species at any given time.

When we think of our *self*, it is normal for us to include all of the externalities of our bodies, from our fingers and toes to the hair on our head, in our concept of ourselves along with our abilities, limitations, feelings, thoughts, beliefs and experiences, and we think that the inventory of all the parts comprise the totality of who and what we are. When, however, accident, disease or the wear of age takes parts of us away, we are forced by circumstances to grudgingly learn that whatever it was we lost, this time, was not the essence of us, but just a part, that we can still be ourselves even without the lost function or part. This realization is just the life lesson version of the point made above that what we sense as our 'self' is actually a fluid aggregate of functions and parts that varies from age to age over our lifetime, and even from moment to moment throughout our day.

What, then, happens to the crisp, black and white dividing line that defines the limit that separates *us* from *other*? The line that unambiguously marks where we end and the rest of reality begins? That line disappears because it was never there. By **M2** we know that our understanding *even of ourselves* is effected by means of a discrete model of a continuous reality, that we know the uncountable whole by a countable set of points we include in a model. The sense that there is a definitive separation between self and other comes not from reality, but from the fact that our models of ourselves only include a discrete number of points at any given time. These models are themselves fluid and situational, but since all models not represented by mathematical expressions are discrete rather than continuous (**M3**), adumbrated rather than exhaustive, this means that every time we conjure up an image of ourselves it only includes a discrete, small number of elements and excludes everything else.

In the most general case, what happens when a being learns that his needs must be met by another, such as a parent? Conceptually, their concept of self expands to include their nurturer, since without that functionality they are not complete, not viable, but with a little reflection one should be able to see that since the definition of self is the set of things that make me *me* at this time, therefore, dependent newborns include the nurturing functionality of their parent in their concept of self from the moment of their birth. Without the ability to sustain its physicality, the self is incomplete. The incompetent offspring only exists as the progeny of the parent. The aggregate concept of self comprehends the necessary and sufficient functionality to function and survive. The miserable loneliness of the orphan is not just, or even mostly, emotional, but rather is an actual physical reality.

The aggregate that is the self includes anything that is identified, rightly or wrongly, as being essential to the health and well-being of the individual, that is, the value graph surrounding the properties in the emergent self. This includes not only my hand, but the sandwich that it holds, as well as the field that will grow the wheat for next year's loaf, and the river that irrigates it, not to mention the family, community and economy that makes it all possible.

Many animals suddenly find out that their adolescence is at an end when their mother pushes them away and forces them to go out on their own. In this type of case, the adolescent has likely achieved the capability to live independently, but was happy to continue living as a child somewhat longer than the parent would allow—meaning that the youngster's concept of self was contracting a little more slowly than the parent's own—demonstrating the flexible definition of self on both the parent and offspring sides.

10.3   Value Graph Inclusions

As mentioned, a graph is a set of nodes and connecting links. A value graph is a set of nodes in the singularity distortion field connected by value links. For example, I would have links to (my ideas of) my family members, which would be, for the sake of this discussion anyway, maximum value positive links, meaning I would die, if necessary, defending them, because they are that important to me. If I like cheeseburgers, on the other hand, on a scale of max = 5 to min = 0, I might have a positive value link to the idea of cheeseburgers with a 1 or a 2 rating. 5 for loved ones, 1 for a cheeseburger, maybe 4 for my car, 3 for good friends.

If I define what is mine by specifying a value graph that only included links of value 5, I would get a smaller graph than if I specified links of value 3 and above. Thus, if we add value graph inclusions into our concept of self (me and my family, or me and my stuff, for example), then we get a definition of self that explicitly includes items at and above a certain level of interest.

The utility of the value graph term is that it formalizes a parameterized definition of our self-concept that we can use in executable and algebraic models.

10.4   Levels of Aggregation

The purblind defect causes us to mistake our perceptions for reality, and to see the parts that make us viable as a unitary whole, so we tend to include our interest swath in our greater self concept. The key to understanding the relation between the self and the group is to realize that the relation is not between a unit (the self) and a collection (the group), but between two collections (the aggregate self, and the aggregate self with value graph inclusions to a lower level of interest), and not even between two fixed collections, but between two variable, *ad hoc* collections that are defined by ephemeral chemical states in the cognitive apparatus. Such as, for example, the variable mental states that cause you to have completely different feelings about yourself from day to day as you cycle through periods of feeling good and capable and other times when you are feeling weak and hopeless. For example, you construct one concept of self on those days you feel you can do no wrong, and an altogether different concept of self on those days you feel you can do no right.

The point is that there is no fundamental difference between the group and the individual for L2 entities and above, because the emergent property of the self includes all that appears vital to the individual's interest, without regard to where it comes from, since the purblind defect prevents us from discriminating between self and anything beyond the self that is associated to a value positioned within the distortion zone around the $\mathbb{CS}0$ singularity. At first, it might seem that individuals rationally choose to become part of a group to enhance their power, and to reduce their vulnerabilities, by positioning a concept of the group deep within the distortion zone, where all is self (we will return to this question in chapter 19, Groups). But, the proclivity to join groups arises from the self-aggrandizement effect of the purblind defect: that which I want, my mind immediately sees, in a very real way, as already part of me. While the group's strengths may sometimes make the individual stronger, the inclination to join and the urge to acquire, are actually not two different urges, but are driven by one and the same mechanism. Joining is what acquisition looks like when the sought after prize is the ability of another, instead of the fruit of a tree.

Which makes more sense? That you are willing to die for a group you are a part of, or that you are willing to die for a group that is part of you?

Individuals will fight to the death for the interests of a group because they see it as part of themselves (even though we say we are part of the group, we really mean that the group is part of us, as will be explained later), and they are fighting to preserve their own interests. Is this always objectively true, does it always make sense? No, of course not, but as mentioned earlier, intelligence is rooted in interested choice, not in fidelity to reality. Intelligence is the ability to process input into response, but there is no guarantee that the outcome of every event will be favorable for us.

The distortion that the self center point creates, the singularity that defines $\mathbb{CS}0$, can be extended to even the flattest extremes of the space that houses $\mathbb{CS}2$ concepts by means of value links. Why is anything *important*? Why is an error in a logical argument or mathematical calculation something to care about? The wellspring of their mortality interests is the only source of importance that cognitive entities can access. This emphatically does *not* mean that everyone always, or even usually, acts in their own objective, or even stated, self-interest, but rather just that the urgency of importance is defined in an [a, p, n] evacule that connects to the fundamental genetic expression of those values as realized within the particular chemical and structural context of a particular being.

Patterns that seem to lack a natural emotional component, such as language patterns, can acquire them through affiliation with a group that endorses the pattern. A sad example of this is the grooming that children attending upper class English private (erroneously and perversely known in England as 'public') schools, where to avoid opprobrium and to gain entry into the higher social classes, children must learn to affect the received pronunciation. All dialects, regardless of class, whether rude or refined, are acquired through a similar mechanism where one is humiliated and ostracized if one persists in 'talking funny'. Thus, whether or not you pronounce the 'h' in hotel is made important when it gets connected to the emotional experience of being accepted or ridiculed by the group you belong to, or want to join. It's easy to think that some patterns are just patterns with no value link, but any pattern you link no value to is, by definition, unimportant to you, and likely to be forgotten very soon.

10.5 Summary

There is no such thing as a group per se, it is an emergent property of the voluntarily coordinated actions of a number of individuals. Like all emergent properties, it waxes and wanes as the efforts of its elements strengthen and coordinate or weaken and lose a common tempo. Groups may have names, membership lists and even buildings in which gatherings are held, but they don't actually exist, except as the emergent property of the members' behavior. People gather to act in concert to accomplish goals none could achieve by themselves, and whether a group appears to survive for a night or for millennia, once the energies of the members are diverted elsewhere, the group ceases to function, it ceases to exist.

Groups form naturally in many species, from insects to birds to pack animals, because it is an extremely efficient solution to amplifying viability through coordinated action. Groups work in any species that communicate intent by any means, because that intent is essentially an action command that followers can execute directly without having to waste the time and effort necessary to process experience into a command on their own. While the current model does not contain the mechanisms necessary to simulate bee hives or ant colonies, this could be achieved by tweaking the initialization parameters that determine the constitution of each instance of the asomatous psyche. At this level, the problem should be trivial.

From a human perspective, once our model contains the singularity, the purblind defect, the emergent nature of the self and self-awareness, then the extended self becomes inevitable, because the self demands that it includes all of the resources it needs, either now or in the future, regardless of where they come from. The self is like a grabby three year old who makes no distinction between what is theirs and what is yours; if it looks good, it's theirs.

10.6 Review

- The self is me, the extended self is we.
- *Me* is an emergent property.
- *We* is an avaricious extension of me.
- Self is to group as many is to many, not one to many.
- There is no fundamental difference between the group and the individual.
- The inclination to join and the urge to acquire are driven by the same mechanism.
- Groups are an emergent property of cooperating individuals.
- For individuals willing and able to pay the price of sociability, grouping is inevitable.

Chapter 11

Internal and External Knowledge

11.1 Introduction

One of the consequences of the purblind defect is that we think that our knowledge of the world is actually knowledge about external reality, that we really see the external world directly for what it is, and that our ideas are accurate, faithful representations of what is actually out there. We think that we see a rock as a rock, a bear as a bear.

But, by **M2**, we know this is not actually the case, that it couldn't be the case because our minds can only work on thoughts formed in it and formed on and of the structures available there. So, of course we think in models, and our idea of a tree is just that, an idea of a tree, not the tree itself. By

M7 we also know that the margin of error between our discrete model and the continuous reality it represents is, in fact, of an uncountably infinite magnitude.

11.2   Internal Knowledge

All of the ideas, impressions, feelings, memories and beliefs we have in our mind are models that were instantiated with evaluations and/or data points derived from cognition or internal or external sensory events. The set of all these models is what we are calling *internal knowledge*, the collection of everything our mind is, or can be, aware of.

What makes the concept of internal thought difficult to grasp is that the purblind defect works both ways: not only do we confuse ideas for reality, we also confuse reality for our ideas. By that we mean that there are many tangible objects in reality that most of us have a pretty good working understanding of. We are pretty good at recognizing rocks, for example, even though we may not know what its mass or mineral content is, and sometimes we mistake a lump of hardened clay for a rock. The problem is that when we have a rock in our hand, we tend to mistake it for the rock concept that *only* exists in our minds.

That is, saying that the rock in our mind is just a mental model is not to say that there is no corresponding rock object in physical reality. But, it does say that, without further measurement, we cannot know how closely our idea of the rock matches the actual rock in our hand. It might have inclusions of uranium or gold we don't expect.

11.3 Measurement and External Knowledge

Qualitative knowledge is what I *perceive*, quantitative knowledge is what I *measure*. Is quantitative knowledge objective or correct? Of course not; until it is verified it must be considered internal, and if independent attempts to verify it fail, then it is just wrong.

Measurement is a process that uses technique t to measure entity e to produce a measurement m with a margin of error ϵ:

$$t(e) \rightarrow m \pm \epsilon$$

This is all that measurement does, it doesn't guarantee anything beyond a value. If the technique, t, is described in formal terms, and the value m and the error bound ϵ are described in standard terms, then it should be possible for an independent experimenter to reproduce the measurement and confirm or contradict its accuracy. But, even in the case when the measurement is verified, all that is being verified is the measurement of the entity in this particular dimension, not all measurements of it, not all details of it, and certainly not all conclusions drawn from it.

External knowledge is what we commonly think of as scientific or quantitative or objective knowledge. It is knowledge that is expressed in formal terms that support tests to validate the measurements involved. The formal definition of external knowledge is:

> **External Knowledge**: a formal mapping of value-
> free, measurable dimensions of an idea, $i \in \mathbb{CS}$ to
> $j \in \mathbb{R}$

That is, external knowledge is a formal mapping of some of the measurable dimensions of an idea—excluding the value dimensions, of course—from our cognitive space to $\mathbb{R}$, the cognitive space we use to model reality. 'Formal' means described in formal, technical terms that unambiguously instruct another how to reproduce and test the mapping. The mapping is shown as a mapping from $i \in \mathbb{CS}$ to $j \in \mathbb{R}$ because the idea in $\mathbb{R}$ is neither a copy of, nor a reference to, the original idea; it is a new, stripped down idea that only contains testable dimensions.

All of our ideas are internal knowledge, and only some few of them have an external facet that can be verified by others. But, that an external knowledge facet of an idea of ours has been verified does not say anything whatsoever about the internal knowledge idea itself. Since internal knowledge ideas have a value dimension that is normally not null, we know that the external knowledge facet is not a full and faithful representation of the internal part. Furthermore, the internal thought is enmeshed in a value graph that defines its meaning, and nothing in the external facet proves, supports or endorses the feelings and beliefs of the value graph.

11.4 $\mathbb{CS}$ and $\mathbb{R}$

What is the actual relation between $\mathbb{CS}$ and $\mathbb{R}$? Which one is bigger? Of course, approaching the subject naively, one would know without question that reality is larger than our understanding of it, and perhaps the physical universe actually is larger than our understanding of it, but how would we, how could we, *know* that? Certainly, our *understanding* of reality is smaller than our internal knowledge:

$$\mathbb{S} \neq \emptyset$$
$$\mathbb{S} \subseteq \mathbb{I}$$
$$\mathbb{S} \not\subseteq \mathbb{R}$$
$$\mathbb{R} \subset \mathbb{CS}$$
$$\therefore |\mathbb{I}| > |\mathbb{R}|$$

Admittedly, sometimes it is difficult to keep track of whether we are talking about reality *itself*, or our idea of reality. Well, basically, we are *always* talking about our idea of reality because, by **M2**, it is only possible for us to reason on models. Yes, there actually is a physical reality that can kill us, but the scientific revolution was forced into being by the realization that we don't have clue one about what reality is really like. Formal methods and independent verification are the scientific method we have contrived as the most reliable means we have to knowing reality. The contribution of faceted, model-oriented reasoning is to define the theoretical basis for understanding the relation between subjectivity and objectivity, to both explain why we needed the scientific method in the first place, as well as how to extend it into the subjective domain. The only way to do this is by beginning to understand that we are always talking about the idea, and never about the thing itself.

Of course, we *mean* to talk about the thing itself, so we use shorthand to refer to something directly, but we must keep in mind that we think in models, not realities. This makes it easier to really think about the relation between $\mathbb{CS}$ and $\mathbb{R}$:

$$\mathbb{R} \subset \mathbb{CS}$$

Earlier, we made the point that $\mathbb{CS}$ is on the same level as $\mathbb{R}$, that it is a universe of its own with the same status as the external universe. But the reality is that, since each of us only achieves cognition through our cognitive space, and our minds are defined by the cognitive space centered on the singularity of our self, then the only thing that $\mathbb{R}$ can possibly be is a model we build inside of $\mathbb{CS}$. Before the scientific revolution, everyone built $\mathbb{R}$ inside the value region of $\mathbb{CS}$, and so our 'educated' ideas of reality were replete with fanciful, supernatural personalities and effects.

Take a moment and reflect on the consequences of building one's reality model inside the $\mathbb{CS}$ value region. Now, think about humanity's past attempts to answer pinnacle questions. Discuss.

It is only through education and discipline that we can keep $\mathbb{R}$ free enough of value links to even approach the verifiable flatness of external reality. Without discipline and formal methods, our idea of reality is nothing more than a bad, personal joke.

11.5   Externalizable Ideas

External knowledge is what we think of as scientific knowledge, and it should be obvious by now why previous attempts by rationalists to objectify human experience had to fail miserably. The laws and nature of cognition place very hard limits on what we can think, how we can think it, and what relation those ideas can be shown to have with reality. The goal of this work is to show how specific bridges can be built between internal and external knowledge that will support independent examination and testing of personal, subjective ideas and experiences. Part of this effort will be to adumbrate the limits of the effort, and to explain what we can do around the edges to enrich value calculations with shareable and verifiable components.

The first level of externalization operates on the L1 result object (see chapter 12). The result object enables us to learn from experience by giving us the mechanism needed to compare the before and after states around an action we take. When collected by the community, such lessons become the cultural tradition that one is encouraged to heed lest one fall into hidden snares off the known path. The problem with result-based lessons, of course, is that both the pre- and post-situations are informally defined, along with the action, so the lesson is strictly anecdotal, even if reportedly shared by others. Externalizing lessons from experience begins with formally defining the precise pre-condition, the exact action, and then measuring the outcome. While beneficial, this level of externalization is lesson by lesson only, since L1 does not have the capacity to conceive or entertain anything as complex as a theory that would explain and predict why these actions should have these results.

The obvious candidates for externalization are ideas at the L2 level and above, since this is the level of the language and concepts that we use to construct theories to explain experience. The strength of higher level cognitive functionality is not only what we can accomplish with the more complex objects and operations native to the newer level, but also the greater use we can make of the artifacts already created by the lower levels. It has been mentioned in passing that the L0 mentacule object seems to contain a bitmap field that somehow records details of events that L0 can make little use of. The L2 pattern framework, however, apparently can query the blob data structure in the mentacule bitmap directly to tease more details from it than we were conscious of perceiving.

Thus, L2 functionality can be used to mine details from data recorded by our sensorium, as well as to construct conceptual frameworks —using the ordinary operations of pattern processing, such as extending, merging and refining patterns—that attempt to explain observed realities. However, L2 is natively an internal knowledge processing engine, and the theories it spins are, without the discipline of formal methods and tests, entirely internal. It is only by learning the patterns of the scientific method and absorbing the culture of the collegial review of published works that L2 can participate in externalizing knowledge.

The ideal L2 candidates for externalization are, of course, the ideas in the flat regions of $\mathbb{CS}$, since value-linked ideas can only be externalized if stripped of the meaning they gained from the links. Scientists, even without a solid framework that explained why it must be so, have known for years that the more passionate one is about a particular form of an idea, the harder it is to establish scientifically.

One of the problems that invalidates most of the soft sciences, and even some propositions in the hard sciences, is that once a value link has been attached to an idea, one is confronted with a hard choice: strip the meaning from the idea while externalizing it, *or* preserve the value by keeping the idea internal. Ideas can be externalized only by excluding value links, by excluding the very facet of the idea which is, by definition, its most important feature: its meaning and value. Thus, the passionate commitment to ideas that is common in the social sciences is the very thing that, predictably and necessarily, invalidates all of their results because value links can only be preserved in internal ideas.

11.6   External Knowledge Idea

To define an external knowledge idea as precisely as possible, let us take

$$\mathbf{i}_n - \mathbf{v} = \mathbf{c}_m$$

to mean that we subtract all the value dimensions, $\mathbf{v}$, from the internal idea $\mathbf{i}$ that has n dimensions, to produce the value-free concept, $\mathbf{c}$, with m dimensions, where $|\mathbf{v}| = n - m$. Then we test the variance of each dimension of $\mathbf{c}$ against reproducible measurements of its physical referent, to determine a delta for the measurement of each dimension:

$$
t \begin{pmatrix} c_0 & r_0 \\ \vdots & \vdots \\ c_n & r_n \end{pmatrix} \rightarrow \delta \begin{pmatrix} m_0 \\ \vdots \\ m_n \end{pmatrix}
$$

This then gives us the precise definition of a single external knowledge idea:

$$
\mathbf{e}_p(\mathbf{c}_n) = \{ \forall \ \mathbf{c}_{n_i} \mid \delta_{n_i} < \epsilon \}
$$

That is, the $p \leq n$ dimension external idea, $\mathbf{e}$, extracted from the n dimension value-free concept $\mathbf{c}$, contains only those dimensions from $\mathbf{c}_n$ that were verified in independent tests to vary from observed values less than the specified error bound. That is, we expunge the value dimensions from an ordinary internal idea to get a concept that we can test in each part to get a bit of external knowledge that contains only the verified dimensions. Like mining for gold, you wash tons of dirt to get grams of knowledge about reality.

11.7　Summary

Why go to all this length to define external knowledge, a term that roughly means scientifically verified knowledge? Because, its important to simultaneously emphasize both the humility we should exhibit when boasting of our knowledge and as well as to highlight the effort that is actually required to externalize even the little bit external knowledge we really have.

Why haven't we answered pinnacle questions before now? Because it is very hard to do. Mathematics, hard science, faceted model-oriented reasoning and pure pattern processing is what we should be studying in college, instead of the puffery of the liberal arts and soft sciences. Hard sciences must be taught, pattern processing must be taught but directly, not obliquely through intoxicating literary jaunts. Yes, literature and the rest of the humanities should be included, but only as cultural history, not as the path to education as has been done for millennia. The material in this chapter has only seemed difficult in direct proportion to the inadequacy of one's higher education.

The particular definition of external knowledge we have discussed may be debatable, and certainly, it is improvable, but it was presented to highlight the labor required to map a single bit of internal knowledge to an actual physical referent with a measured degree of confidence. A robust higher education would provide us the tools necessary to make this process, if not easy, then at least doable and normal.

11.8 Review

- Internal knowledge is the set of all of our ideas, feelings and beliefs.
- We mistake our ideas for reality, and reality for our ideas.
- Qualitative knowledge is what I perceive, quantitative

knowledge is what I measure.

- We use specific techniques to measure phenomena with a certain margin of error.

- Neither measured nor quantitative means 'true'.

- External knowledge is a verified formal mapping of idea dimensions to reproducible measurements.

- External knowledge cannot include values.

- $|\mathbb{R}| < |\mathbb{I}|$

- $\mathbb{R} \subset \mathbb{CS}$

- $\mathbb{R}$ can be, and historically has been, built inside the $\mathbb{CS}$ value region.

- Experience and ideas are both externalized through formalization and testing.

- L2 can data mine for details in L0 mentacules.

- Value dimensions cannot be externalized.

- External idea: $\mathbf{e}_p(\mathbf{c}_n) = \{\forall \ \mathbf{c}_{n_i} \mid \delta_{n_i} < \epsilon\}$.

- Externalizing ideas is hard; rigorous education makes it much easier.

Chapter 12

Cognition Objects

12.1   Introduction

It may seem late to begin discussing the data type objects used
by each of the levels, but their introduction couldn't be rushed,
it had to wait on the progressive consideration of the many topics ahead of it in the discussion line. Now that we are here and
ready to begin the introductions, let us begin with a moment of
clarity: the laws of model-oriented reasoning only require that
there be levels in the cognitive model, and that each level em-
ploy its own data model. The objects we are discussing below
come from the asomatous psyche application, not from the universal cognition model. These objects were designed to suit my
purposes, to simultaneously satisfy both my particular limitations and ambitions. They are being offered for their illustrative
power alone, they are neither a prescription of what must be,
nor of how it must be done.

12.2   Evacule

The *evacule* (from *eval*(uation) + (mole)*cule*) is the atomic unit of cognition, the transistor on which all cognitive functions are built. Evacules contain three elements: an anti-self value, a pro-self value, and a non-self value. Each position can hold a value in the range of minimum to maximum, and they all three always hold a value when they register a sensation or event, even if it is just the minimum value.

The semantics of the evacule are defined both as an aggregate for the evacule, and contextually, depending on which strand of which sense it is connected to. The way we *know* anything is by registering each of the dimensions of which we are sensible into evacules. For example, if we have dozens of evacules connected to our olfactory senses, then dogs might have thousands, each one of which registers information by combining the three evaluations in the context of a specific connection. An evacule with the values [5, 3, 0], for instance, where 5 is maximum and 0 is minimum, might, if connected to the magnitude dimension of sight, register a large, potentially threatening object that, at the same time, offered significant opportunities. The same values in an evacule attached to the volume auditory circuits would mean something else in terms of sound, but it would suggest a similar mix of potentially dangerous power and beneficial opportunity. At the other extreme, an evacule with the values [0, 0, 5], would mean the input could be ignored no matter what the context was.

Volitional mobility requires that experience be evaluated in terms of self-interest to support self-preferential movement, and the axes of self interest certainly address the two questions: is this a threat? is this an opportunity? But these two questions together necessarily posit the third case: if neither negative nor positive, is this an ignorable case, a nullity? The 3-dimensional value structure of the evacule precisely addresses this need by interpreting every dimension of every perception in terms of anti-self, pro-self and non-self significance within a semantic context defined by a particular facet of the organism's sensorium.

In the asomatous psyche, the evacule is implemented as a 3-dimensional array in which the first element is the anti-self evaluation, the second is the pro-self evaluation, and the third element is the non-self evaluation. This introduces a critical concept in the evolutionary cytomodel: positional semantics. Fidelity to our organic referent both forces us to acknowledge and allows us to exploit the fact that structure is hard-coded in a genotype. In software engineering, we try to design software so that it is robust in the face of change, but when we are modeling heritable structures, we need to respect that the underlying structures are highly resistant to change. We take it as a fact that our minds evaluate our experience using actual connections from our senses to our brain where the encoding into cognitive objects happens. These inflexible connections are consistent with semantic positioning, with the idea that some meaning arises from the actual organic context, rather than always having to be transmitted in the payload itself.

Another aspect of positional semantics dictates that, at every level of cognition, the negative element must be in first position, ahead of the positive and null elements, so that even when our evaluation process is interrupted, we are always in a position to react defensively.

Each of the positions in the evacule holds a value in the inclusive range from the minimum to maximum values. In our simulation, these elements are implemented with discrete, rather than continuous values because a fundamental principle of the universal cognition model is that complexity emerges from simplicity, and it seems that the 100 to 1,000 different permutations arising from having just 5-10 discrete values for each dimension will easily cover the full range of human emotional responses we observe since every event is recorded using from one to ten thousand or more evacules at once. An important rule of thumb in modeling is always to start our models as simply as possible, and to extend towards complexity only when test cases demand it. This particular implementation is optional, of course, but the tripolar evaluation construct is the seminal idea that our models and applications are built on.

By UC4, we understand that the process of knowing, the process of making sense of something we perceive, is, first, the process of encoding and evaluating perceivable dimensions of input phenomena onto an organic structure, such as a collection of evacules, which translates the internal or external sensory event into self-significant terms in $\mathbb{I}$ where it becomes conceivable and processable by the self. A tripolar data structure implementing positional semantics satisfies this requirement.

12.3 Mentacule

We can think of the mentacule structure, the fundamental unit of L0 cognition, either from an object-oriented, or from a functional perspective. In the first case, we would view our problem as a collection of data elements and the operations on them, while in the second, we would first ask what functions are required to realize cognition and then we would design the mentacule around those operations. While both approaches are valid for different purposes, we will follow the latter course in our current discussion because functional analysis is more consistent with the progress of evolutionary development from the simple to the complex, and thus matches how we are building our model.

In considering a mentacule from the purely abstract perspective of what is required to achieve organic sentience anywhere in an energetic, material universe, we come again to the fundamental need of sentience to make interested choices: once organisms achieve volitional mobility in niche spaces with non-uniform distribution of threats and opportunities, then for volitional mobility to long survive the scythe of natural selection it must, on average, tend to favor beneficial over harmful choices, at least for as long as is needed to successfully launch the next generation.

The question we need to answer for ourselves is, what is the minimal function set that will fulfill the interested choice requirement?

First, let us consider whether or not a mentacule actually exists in a physical mind, and not just in our model. For organisms with no persistent memory function, we could think of the state of the current memory, the collection of evacules hard-wired to the sensory organs, as a virtual mentacule. Since the genome encodes the [a, p, n] archetype evacules that define threats, opportunities and nullities in its niche, then movement choices could easily be made based on a comparison of the state of the current memory to the archetypes. This would mean that, while the structure of the mentacule wouldn't exist per se, the interface for a mentacule would be implemented in reference to the current memory, and so we would effectively have a mentacule with or without a dedicated structure. In the case of an organism with a memory, on the other hand, experiential data contained in memory has to be organized semantically, and that organization is what we are modeling with the mentacule concept, so it would seem that such an object might exist in the physical mind.

The process of populating a mentacule with the data from a perception or event starts when the senses are stimulated, but since the senses seem to be, in effect, analog sensors that produce waveforms continuously even in the absence of actual input (we experience some level of sight events in a completely dark room, for one example, or, to use Isaac Newton's example, touching the side of your closed eye can trigger visual experiences), this implies that, at certain times, a snapshot of the current state of this continuous flow of input is grabbed and committed to a mentacule. Either before or after the moment of snapshot, the analog information is encoded in what we are assuming to be a relatively digital form, and encoded into a mentacule. Note that it actually makes no difference whether a discrete or a continuous value is physically recorded in the evacules, because our lack of an infinite range of emotions and responses means that we are, in effect, responding to changes in quanta, not wave forms. However, given the vector structure of our model and the fact that if we discretize the sensory waveform into as few as 5 values ranges we can simulate 125 distinct emotions, or 10 values to simulate 1,000 distinct emotions, it seems safe for us to say that discrete values more than account for all observed human emotional responses from the simple to the fairly complex.

Think of a mentacule as an array of evacules in which position is not only semantically significant, but actually hardwired to specific sensory connections. In the asomatous psyche, the basic code for the mentacule object is:

Listing 12.1: Mentacule

```
//
// Mentacule data elements
//

// animal, vegetable, mineral, etc.
Type type
```

```
// quantized evaluation of the external and internal
// senses' input
Evacules attributes = new Evacules(
    NUMBER_OF_ATTRIBUTES)

// the 'bitmap' referenced in the verbal model
Payload payload

// the move command the body will execute
Move move

// mentacule level evaluation calculated by combining
// all evacules into an array for angle calculation
Double threatLevel
Double opportunityLevel
Double ignoreLevel
```

The only required data elements in the mentacule are the collection of evacules and the bitmap of sensory data; the other elements are calculated from this information and are represented as data only for programmatic efficiency. The mentacule is simply the mind's evaluated impression of a sensory event, it is what can be reacted to, thought on and remembered. The external phenomenon is whatever it is, wherever it is, but the miracle of cognition requires, and is only made possible by, the internal mental image that the mind constructs and works on.

Before the mentacule comes into play, though, the brain has to be able to perform these functions: perceive, collate/snapshot, encode. Once the synthesized perception snapshot is encoded, only then can the brain start to work with the abstract representation, the mentacule. Once we have the mentacule, now we can ask, what are the necessary and sufficient functions the mentacule must support in order to effectuate interested movement? We are going to start with only three functions, and see how far this gets us (the expectation is that, the more demands we place on the simulation to produce detailed results, the more functions we might have to add at this level, but even in the worst case, it shouldn't be many). The three necessary and sufficient functions to support interested movement are:

- Categorize: the mentacule has to be categorizable as a threat, an opportunity, or a triviality.
- Compare: the mentacule has to be comparable to other mentacules to determine degree of similarity.
- Update: the mentacule has to be updateable, even in the case of the virtual mentacule.

The very first requirement, categorizability, is needed so that the organism can instantly, even if incorrectly, identify the mentacule's referent as enemy, friend, or nothing of the type animal, vegetable or mineral (for example). The second requirement is needed to support a refined evaluation of exactly how good, bad, or unimportant this referent is. The third requirement, updateability, is needed even in the case of the virtual mentacule because the current memory is inherently updateable, and once an independent mentacule is supported by a memory-capable mind, the values in the mentacule must be editable to support refinement of perceptions as new data becomes available (e.g., as the other being gets closer). And, that's it, for now. With just this little functionality, I assert that we can simulate sentience.

But, what about the data inside the mentacule? Well, the

content and granularity of the abstract representation of the perceptual snapshot will certainly vary from species to species, at least, because not all species have the same sensitivity of each sense, and do not even all have the same set of senses. The snapshot captured by higher level animals must include data about the movement vector of the sighting, but, for now, at least, we are going to try to model that as inferrable from the difference between successive snapshots, and see if that holds up. There certainly seems to be both an evaluation and a bitmap store, since the evaluation would capture what we think about the thing now, and the bitmap store is what allows us to reconsider our memories long after they happened.

One of the general themes of this work is that consciousness and intelligence are not only not God-given blessings, they are not miraculous, and in fact, they are not even very complicated, but rather are actually so simple that coding them up is pretty easy. A program written to the specifications presented in this book up to and including the naming function, should achieve self-awareness after being initialized correctly and allowed to run continuously in a rich environment for a few months.

The mentacule is a simple object that does not pretend to provide the necessary and sufficient conditions for higher human thought. All it does is to provide the necessary and sufficient conditions for effecting interested movement.

12.4   Situation

In memory-capable organisms, current memory is modeled as a priority queue of the 7± most important entities found in the most recent scan of the environment. A *situation* is a snapshot of this current memory which can be evaluated as a whole. The situation object thus supports a higher level understanding of what impact an action has had by making comparisons of the before and after situations of an action possible.

Simple aggregates like the situation object give rise to richer semantics that support sophisticated thought. Where the mentacule in the simplest organisms is adequate to drive movement, by aggregating several of them together, we gain the ability to understand and respond to the gestalt of current reality.

12.5   Result

The *result* is the L1 data structure that endows the mind with a concept of the past and the ability to learn from experience. It comprises a pre-situation, an action mentacule, and a post-situation. The action mentacule is labeled thus just for clarity, since it encodes the action that followed the pre-situation and, presumably, led to the post-situation.

L1 implements the ability to store and recall result objects, and to generalize them into type hierarchies that support rapid recall. Learning from experience is then easily achieved by simply extending the evaluation function to cover situations. Notice that, even though the ability to evaluate and learn from experience seems to be a complex mental function, implementing it actually requires a minimal amount of new structure and only an extension, rather than an invention, of the evaluation mechanism.

12.6   Pattern

The *pattern* is the L2 data structure that supports language and planning, which together support anticipation of the future. The essential pattern data structure in the asomatous psyche is:

Listing 12.2: Pattern Object

```
// patterns are instantiated with results
Result result

// this pattern is triggered when the current situation
// matches this
Situation entryPoint

// action to take
Action command

// branching condition
Condition condition

// the collection of alternative paths available
// depending on the match level of the situation
// and supports branching logic, rules, etc.
PatternLinks branches

// indicates current position in an active plan
Pattern currentStep
```

This relatively simple structure supports very complex pattern creation and processing. The wonder of cognition is not that it is so complex, but that simple, genetically encodable structures support extremely complex thoughts.

The pattern functions are simple pattern versions of basic cognitive functions such as: compare, add, subtract, generalize and update. The exit selector function is encoded in a pattern language and can be arbitrarily complex (just think of the rules and calculations you learned in your most advanced math and science courses).

The pattern object has dual nature as both an anticipation and a plan object. Every pattern is an anticipation pattern in that it tells us what the future might look like, e.g., finding fresh scat in this terrain may match a pattern that tells us we may be within a certain distance of a known type of animal. The other side of the pattern object is the plan aspect: patterns record conditional steps to achieve an objective, i.e., they are plans. So, given a situation, we can match a pattern that suggests a possible future occurrence, or given a need or objective, we may select that same pattern and follow the recorded steps to achieve our goal. This dual nature of prescience and prescription is inherent in all pattern objects.

12.6.1   Types of Patterns

Because the L2 pattern object is the basis of language and conditional reasoning, it defines for us what thinking feels like, so we will examine a brief catalog of different types of commonly used patterns to help the reader better grasp the general idea of patterns: what they are, how they work, and what they do.

There are a number of different types of patterns that enhance our cognitive ability in a variety of ways. They are all built on the same template using the same lower level functions, but they are specialized to perform specific tasks to answer particular needs. Since patterns have the capacity to define new functionality, there is almost no limit to the types of patterns possible. We will restrict the current discussion to cover just a few pattern types that, in addition to being illustrative, are germane to our immediate purposes:

- **Language** patterns hold the building blocks of language, ranging from phonemes to syllables, words, etc. Grammar would be implemented in a separate pattern language. Spelling requires archetype patterns.

- **Name** patterns support indirection, i.e., the substitution of a name for a full pattern structure to make mental calculation tractable.

- **Opinion** patterns are named, evaluated, value linked patterns that summarize potentially complex trees of facts, experiences, lessons, beliefs and feelings.

- **Experience** patterns are built from direct experience and value linked to the pain or reward level of the lesson.

- **Authority** patterns are communicated from an authority and value linked to emotional connection to the authority.

- **Lesson** patterns are school lessons, abstract ideas typically drilled into us by teachers as indivisible, unquestionable whole units.

- **Task** patterns comprise a sequence of concrete steps to accomplish a particular task.

- **Loopback** patterns are antswers, answers that exist before any question is asked, and are intended to quiet all nagging questions, fears or anxieties about the future or the unknown, without regard to content or circumstance.

12.6.1.1 Language Patterns

Since language is not yet implemented in the asomatous psyche we can expect this part of the model to be provisional and subject to serious revision and extension, but the basic concept of viewing grammar as a structural pattern built on heritable mental structures seems to be entirely in line with the inherent proclivity or need for grammar among humans across all cultures. It also seems to follow the pattern of how RNA is the mechanism that strings new strands of DNA together. The conditional linking aspect of patterns itself was specifically designed to accommodate natural language word and sentence construction.

Language is an extremely important function, but it survived as a mutation not because it enables us to explore nature, but because it provides the primary mechanism for the development and maintenance of ever greater, more complex extensions of the self in the form of groupings. The primary focus of language is necessarily the internal, not the external, knowledge domain. That is, language is primarily focused on enhancing L0/L1 functionality at higher level of complexity, not replacing or superseding it.

It is clear that the only serious advances in knowledge have all been built on mathematics, science and technology, none of which were based on the natural language platform we mistakenly think of as humanity's highest intellectual achievement. In fact, the fundamental reason this book had to be written was to demonstrate a way to get around natural language's intrinsic inadequacy to advance external knowledge, and to show how a mistaken emphasis on language-based internal knowledge not only impedes, but obviates and even undoes progress in the development of external knowledge.

12.6.1.2   Name Patterns

Consider the problem of combining complex verbal models together: when you have finally gotten your thoughts together and want to begin to process the entire complex of thoughts, you find that you have to feed them sequentially through a processor that has a bandwidth capacity of only about 7 thoughts at a time. Attempts to calculate large patterns are swamped by the fact that not even a single complete thought fits into our sequential processor at any one time.

The solution to this problem is naming: the use of a pattern whose only job is to name an evaluated pointer to a complex thought pattern or group of such patterns. Since when we are 'thinking' — when we are trying to solve a problem by applying thoughts — we are primarily concerned with what an idea *means*, rather than with every last detail it was built on, then a pattern that rolls up an idea tree's evaluation and ultimate exit points is a powerful tool that enables us to swoop over large collections of ideas so we can pick and choose which to apply, based solely on their evaluated naming patterns, instead of having to slog through the weeds every time.

The sophisticated inference that the controlling identity relation which connects our various mental functions together is, in fact, *me*, is the great but inevitable step that brings high level L2 cognitive entities the last mile to self consciousness. The level of abstraction required to realize, "this is me!" is effected through the indirection implemented in the naming pattern function that creates the term 'me' and uses it to designate my collected abilities, appetites, memories and experiences.

12.6.1.3   Opinion

An opinion is a type of named pattern that points to a body of patterns encoding information bits, feelings, experiences, beliefs and whatnot with an evaluation computed from some of the referenced patterns and connected with a value link to a position in the belief system within the singularity distortion.

One way to understand the difference between a naming and an opinion pattern is to think of the first as a pointer, while the second is both an actionable summary of a vaguely defined set of patterns, and a data processing optimization function. The purpose of an opinion is primarily to align a welter of somehow related experiences, ideas and facts to the constellation of value sets subscribed to by the individual. Opinions may be self-generated, but more often they are assimilated from a grouping one subscribes to.

Once an opinion is formed in either manner, though, it transitions from a collection mechanism to a disposal mechanism. That is, once formed, opinions are ideal for defanging unprocessed facts by rapidly putting them in their place inside a matching opinion where they no longer have to be thought about. Opinions organize experience by stably structuring related data pattern configurations; they help to keep us oriented by giving us a familiar way to interpret experience. The instant we determine a new fact is not actionable, we assign it to an opinion that will ground its attention-demanding power.

Opinion conversations, also known variously as debates, discussions and arguments, are built on the fallacy that opinions are derived from and justified by, and therefore can be attacked through, their data elements, while the reality is actually the reverse.

An opinion is not a conclusion, but an assertive proposition that our viability is up to the task of taming and managing whatever reality sends our way. The only important parts of an opinion are its evaluation and its relation to the individual's belief web. The contents of the opinion have been reduced and controlled by being herded into the opinion corral—they are the herd, not the herder.

12.6.1.4   Experience

Patterns can be instantiated with results, and their structure easily supports the extension of the single action learned lesson from the result object into a more complex pattern that encodes conditional path selection. Experience patterns range from life lessons to the most trivial observations about the smallest actions. The medical school practice of: "watch one, do one, teach one" is a learning technique that reinforces pattern acquisition by pairing experience patterns with lesson and task patterns.

12.6.1.5 Authority

Patterns that pair a lesson with a truth value are authority patterns, they are 'true' by virtue of their source, and their degree of truth is proportional to the power of the source, not to the verifiability of the pattern. Authority patterns can be a creed inculcated into the followers of a religion, or an opinion of Aristotle insisted upon by university tutors as a condition of passing.

Authority patterns are characteristically black box patterns that have to be accepted whole, without being reviewed or critiqued in part. They apply to very particular situations, and have uneditable exit points. Oftentimes, there are sanctions of one sort or another for varying from, or violating, the strictures of the pattern.

Authority patterns are suitable for teaching professional techniques, but they stifle innovation and tend to mark the end of the exploration phase of education and the beginning of the training phase.

12.6.1.6 Lesson

A lesson pattern is a socially transmitted action description. Lesson patterns are the stuff of education, whether of the liberal arts or hard science variety. Lessons are what schools *do* because they can be uniformly taught and tested with more or less predictable results to various types of classes that have risen through the lower grades.

Lessons are the quintessential L2 level group formation ex-

ercise. Individual lesson patterns are acquired through pattern
assimilation with a combination of verbal and visual presentation, rote study and exercises in pattern processing. This is
generally what passes for education, and it works well enough
as long as there is no desire or need for invention or discovery.

12.6.1.7   Task

A master or journeyman teaches an apprentice a trade through
teaching him how to execute, and then master, the various tasks
that make up the craft. Tasks are teachable lists of verifiable
activities. Teaching a child what 'raking the yard' actually en-
tails, is teaching them a pattern that includes cleanup, disposal
and putting tools away. Tasks are normally described verbally,
but they comprise a list of generally physical activities that can
be verified by others. This is why a task occupies a gray area
between internal and external knowledge in that action descriptions are usually verbal, often ambiguous or under-specified,
but the actions and their results usually involve movement and
change in the visible, physical world.

Some lesson and authority patterns can consist mostly of
tasks, so this may be one reason that so few have perceived
the inherently internal nature of much of pattern assimilation,
which has led to a general overestimation of its potential to
teach students how to innovate and solve new problems in addition to training them to follow known patterns.

12.6.1.8   Loopback

Even though evolution is the best model we have to explain
the development of life, no one ever said it was a nice process,

or that it always produced elegant solutions. I mean, toucans? Mosquitoes? Brain fungus, flesh eating bacteria? No, evolution isn't pretty, but surely, you must have realized this at some point earlier in this book, while reading about the messy details of the inner workings of cognition.

Evolution is not a sophisticated, godless substitute for the loving, masterful creator myth. On the contrary, it is a blind, flawed, extravagantly expensive process. Negative mutations happen all the time, but because they have a deleterious impact on an organism's viability, they tend to die, forgotten, with their host. Neutral to positive mutations, in contrast, may survive across the generations, since they do not trigger natural culling.

The L2 pattern processing capability that enables us to anticipate the future, and gives us our advanced level of reasoning that is the basis of our consciousness, intellect and civilization, turns out to have been a strongly negative development that would have killed us, had it arisen alone, instead of in a cluster of mutations, as it did. The ability of L2 to anticipate the future is a negative evolutionary development in the sense that the fuzzy algorithms used by the L2 pattern matching mechanism cause an outrageously high rate of false positive matches that constantly alert us to impending crises that rarely happen. This constant ringing of alarms, if left unchecked, would drain our energy and distract our attention from real crises happening in the moment.

The problem with anticipation patterns is that, when they match the current situation — however weakly — they excite nodes in the brain corresponding to the pattern exit points, and literally charge them up to an electrically excited state in readiness for launching a response. Uncontrolled, this continuous state of excitation is not only distracting and enervating, but it can cause chronic anxiety, fear and even panic, and expose us to danger by distracting us from the fact of what is, with the chimera of what could be.

The loopback pattern is one of the mutations that were included in the cluster that finally completed our pattern processing ability. Loopbacks work to quiet the constant stream of false alarms that are caused by L2 eagerly matching any patterns it can to the current situation. The loopback quiets the alarm din because it answers all questions, it is what we are calling an *antswer* (from *ante* + (an)*swer*), i.e., that class of answer that both precedes the question, and takes no input from it; it is the answer that anticipates all questions.

In the electronic and computer world, a loopback routes signals back to their source without processing, and this is what the cognitive loopback does, it turns off excited thoughts by draining their power away. In the cognitive world, a simple charge redirecting loopback may be implemented with just an attitude, such as "stuff happens". Simple loopbacks, such as this, are adequate to calming our overexcited responses to everyday frustrations, but addressing existential or life crisis issues often requires something larger, a system of ideas that can attach to all currently anxious thoughts and drain off their disturbing charge. There are levels of loopbacks, as you might imagine, but the most complex and important loopbacks are called *transcendent* loopbacks, so-called because they are systems of theological, philosophical or psychological articles of faith that antswer all existential, emotional, practical and general life questions. Vexing questions break through our normal defenses to raise specters of doom that trigger our fears of the unknown. Transcendent loopbacks work to calm these breakthrough fears by acting like a failsafe grounding plate at the edge of our consciousness.

Part of the power of transcendent loopbacks comes from a commandment they invariably include that equates questioning it to blasphemy. In the harder religions, one risks not only eternal punishment in the hereafter, but actual death in the now, for merely doubting the power or legitimacy of the group's transcendent loopbacks out loud.

The loopback's structure includes an entry point that is a wild card matching pattern, and its sole exit point is something like a cliché with an attitude. The transcendent loopback uses a pure wild card entry point that will match any and every situation, and its cliché is usually of the all-encompassing "God's will" variety. There are also smaller loopbacks that help us to adjust to, or accept, smaller worries or disappointments, and they take the form of homilies or generally acknowledged truths, such as, "no good deed goes unpunished". Smaller loopbacks have restricted wild card entry points that only match bad news, good news, non-religious situations, or the like.

The loopback pattern is the God mutation, it is the mechanism that explains the human invention of God in $\mathbb{I}$ (whether or not God exists in $\mathbb{S}$, or indeed, whether $\mathbb{S}$ exists outside of $\mathbb{I}$ at all, is another question). Certainly, the reader must be among those who accept the validity of the evolution model, but if that is the case, then mustn't we have wondered why no one has ever been able to explain, before now, how evolution created God? Surely now, having thought about it even for an instant, one must realize that the order of creation must be *evolution* $\rightarrow$ *God*, and not the other way around, right? God is the ultimate loopback, the final backstop that antswers all questions, quells all doubts, and ultimately grants dispensation for the evolutionary flaw of the L2 toxic idea fountain.

Loopbacks don't always work, sometimes they fail to fully drain the perturbation potential out of an excited pattern, so we seek to combine reassuring personal contact with the loopback panacea by getting a clergyman, counselor, loved one, or passing stranger to repeat comforting sayings to us, while touching our shoulder, arm or hand. The physical touch apparently helps to drain some of the anxious energy away. When even this fails, then we may seek novel formulations of a loopback offered by proselytizing groups, in the same way we seek new music from new bands when an old song loses its impact from being heard too often in a short time.

Look at sophisticates who reject religion as superstition. Can you see that they replaced religion with an opinion web spun from the reasoning, rational and erudition fallacies? Which is more sound?

It seems odd that, with as many people rejecting religion as mere, primitive superstition as they do today, yet still, when they leave the fold, they go to their modern, sophisticated world still clutching the *antswer* to their bosom. Do they not notice that its very existence is cosmically ridiculous, an utter refutation of our vaunted rationality?

And yet, it happens that we need antswers to survive, and always will, because without them, we would be paralyzed by an unending torrent of premonitions of doom and disaster (just because we understand electricity doesn't mean we don't have to use a ground anymore). The flaw in the L2 pattern processor is real, and dangerous. We have always needed, and will always need, grounding straps to protect ourselves, to clean up the mess that spills out of our brain everyday. The only thing that has changed is that now we have the tools we need to make sure we don't mistake this rather simple, mechanical function for some all-powerful supernatural whatever.

12.7   Fractal Branching Tree

L3 uses a fractal branching tree data object that supports exploration in search of discovery and invention. It will be discussed in a later volume.

12.8   Review

- Unique data objects are required for each cognition level, but they are not specified.
- An *evacule* is the basic atom of cognition.
- The evolutionary cytomodel uses positional semantics.
- A *mentacule* is the basic molecule of cognition, a snapshot of sensory state.
- Mentacules support evaluation, comparison, categorizing, and update.
- A *situation* is an evaluated snapshot of current memory.
- A *result* is an object that evaluates actions by calculating the delta between their pre- and post action situations.
- Results make learning from experience possible.
- A *pattern* is a single-in, multiple-out structure of patterns.
- The pattern object supports planning and anticipation.
- Language patterns include lexical and grammar patterns.
- Name patterns support reference and indirection.
- Opinion patterns summarize, absorb and disable facts.
- Experience patterns are extensions of result objects.
- Authority patterns prescribe conduct and organize hierarchies.
- Lesson patterns communicate action instructions.

- Task patterns communicate action steps to fellow workers or underlings.
- Loopback patterns turn off over-excited ideas.

Chapter 13

Operations

13.1   Introduction

In order to understand how the human mind works, we must build a model of it that we can test and query. Never lose sight of this objective — this is why we are going to all this trouble, so that we can learn how to build and test solid ideas. Testable models can be worked on until they are solid, viable and productive; untestable ideas have no provable worth, and are of no help in the effort to advance the state of civilization.

We are considering an abstract model of the organic cognition process itself, independent of the human body, and expressing it in verbal, executable, algebraic and geometric models. In this chapter, we will be considering the functionality of each of the cognitive spaces by examining the operations that each level of intellect (L0, L1, L2 and L3) must perform in order to achieve its goals. (The limits of the operations that a level can perform within its space will be discussed in chapter 14.) Finally, we will break down these higher level operations into the lower level functions the mind performs to actually do the work.

Although these levels are specific to my model, and not specified in the universal cognition model, we are using them to provide both examples and structure to what would otherwise be too abstract a discussion to be helpful.

13.2 ℂ𝕊0

The model of the first level of volitional mobility, ℂ𝕊0, was designed to be as simple, and as primitive, as could be in order to track evolution. This model space was designed to include only the bare minimum of elements and functionality required to support self-preferential movement, i.e., movement away from threats, towards opportunities and disregarding nullities. The basic element in this space is the fundamental unit of cognition, the mentacule. Mentacules can be thought of as snapshots of the state of the internal and external sensorium, captured in ordered collections of evacules (anti, pro, non self value arrays, the atoms of cognition), with a bitmap of sensory details that was probably added later in the evolutionary process.

The intellect level inhabiting the ℂ𝕊0 space must execute a number of simpler, smaller functions in order to be able to achieve its two higher level goals of: 1) identifying and discriminating between threats, opportunities and nullities, and 2) formulating an appropriate move command. We will analyze each of these actions to identify the minimum constituent functions that can produce these results.

13.2.1 Identify Input

The process of identifying input can be broken down into a number of separate steps, all of which are important:

- Perceive
  - Encode transient state into semi-persistent state
- Identify
  - Determine type
  - Calculate position, direction and speed
    - Capture second perception and evaluate direction delta
- Evaluate
  - Determine degree of type match through identifying maximums
  - Calculate urgency

13.2.1.1 Perceive

The current model pictures the senses as working in continuous, analog mode, but cognition as working on static quantized images of sensory states. Thus, there is a need for a trigger function to copy discrete values from the live data structure to a matching, semi-persistent version that is processed by the cognitive function. The snapshot copy is necessary, of course, because the senses are continuously overwriting previous events. So, perceiving an entity and encoding it into thinkable form requires:

- Connections between senses and elements in the live data structure.

- A trigger function to call the copy function.

- A function that copies the contents of the senses to the semi-persistent mentacule.

- A semi-persistent mentacule data structure that retains the captured state long enough to be processed. A second, specialized, abbreviated, transitory mentacule may be needed, too, to support calculation of motion vectors.

13.2.1.2   Identify

Identifying the now semi-persisted data requires both a comparison function, and a comparison standard. That is, some number of archetypes have to be available to compare the perception to, either in a persistent or generated form. The best match (the smallest angle between the vectors) defines the type of the perception: was it a predator, prey, water or something unimportant?

Capturing some sense of position is undoubtedly done the same way we do it now, i.e., comparison against objects of known size within the context of whatever depth perception the entity possesses. Calculating the direction and speed vector requires a second semi-persistent mentacule to hold a second snapshot from a slightly different time so that the size of the two perceptions can compared to determine whether the entity is approaching, retreating or moving obliquely. Speed can be calculated in terms of change in position in the observed period of time in relation both to the distance from the observer and the observer's maximum speed of movement. These calculations can be done easily on special purpose circuits, and they are simplified by the fact that the self is, by definition, at the origin of the CS0 space.

13.2.1.3 Evaluate

Evaluating the encoded version of the sensory event requires that after the L0 intellect determines, for example, that the perceived entity is a threat, it then determine how much of a threat it is. This can be done by comparing the actual evacule values to the genetically determined minimum and maximum of the range to get a measure of the target, and then comparing that to the current state of the self in terms of need and strength. This can be done using just the mentacule because it captures the state of both the external and internal senses. In the asomatous psyche, for example, the minimum evacule value is set at 0, and the maximum is currently defined to be 5, but could be increased if the tests require a wider range of discrimination. Thus, determining the degree of a threat is accomplished by simply taking the maximum anti values in the relevant mentacule set, and comparing that to the self's resources.

Urgency is calculated on the basis of the perceived object's rate of motion in relation to its location and the self's maximum speed, in the case of a threat, or in the case of an opportunity, the self's state of need in relation to the richness of the opportunity.

13.2.2   Formulate Response

Following the evolutionary model, the *action module* has been modeled separately from the body for the obvious reason that this greatly simplifies the evolutionary problem since "approach" and "retreat", for example, are very primordial concepts that every type of body, from those that walk, fly, or swim, to those that crawl, can implement in their own way. The primordial abstract movement language (AML) was undoubtedly extended somewhat for limbs, wings and fins, but likely the core of it has remained unchanged since very early in the history of life.

The reason this extra layer of indirection was designed into the simulation is because it seems obvious that the action module had to have evolved very early in the development of mobile life, well before the range of body types proliferated. Separating the action module from the body would have allowed the action module circuitry to remain relatively unchanged, even though the body of each new species might have an entirely new repertoire of movements available. The vocabulary of the abstract action module would have to be extended, of course, as needed to support new levels of complexity in movement, but the core could remain unchanged.

Thus, the problem the action module has to solve is pretty easy: issue a command to retreat from threats, approach opportunities, and ignore nullities and include an appropriate vector and velocity suggestion. The body then moves accordingly, within the realities of its capabilities and the physical situation.

13.2.3   CS0 Operation List

The only low-level functions that are needed to accomplish the above actions are these:

- *copy*() : copies values from one structure to another.
- *trigger*() : fires a signal when threshold values are met.
- *magnitude(type, v)*− > *n*: calculate the magnitude of a vector in a subset of dimensions.
- *angle(v1, v2)* → *θ*: calculates the angle between two vectors.
- *archetype(type)* → *v*: get *type* archetype vector

It might seem implausible to suppose that the lowest intellect, L0, fulfills its very primitive functions with a lot of vector mathematics. The original idea for this approach, oddly enough, came from watching baseball players, some quite young, running to catch fly balls in the outfield. There is a moment in the play, a very, very brief moment where the outfielder sees the swing, hears the crack of the bat and sees the ball leave the bat. That moment, that critical, incredible moment, is all the fielder needs to calculate, seemingly instantaneously, the approximate landing point of the ball. After that instant of observation and calculation, he takes off with the necessary speed on the appropriate vector to intercept, if possible, the ball before it hits the ground.

If that's not amazing enough, dogs can do the same thing, especially with Frisbees. Or, consider foxes that pounce on unseen rodents under the snow, based just on calculating the origin of a sound. Even though calculus and linear algebra may be fearsomely difficult subjects for many college students, it turns out that we have the ability to do differential equations and vector calculations hard-wired into our brain.

This should not be such a surprise. Computer and software engineers know that slow, complex encryption algorithms suddenly become easy and fast when they are built into hardware. Remember, reality and our model of it are two different things, and even though calculating trajectories is hard when we use the L2 patterns we learn in school, doing it is automatic and easy when we do it with our built-in circuits. The L0 solution functions are designed as vector calculations because our brains are built to do them almost effortlessly on circuitry that was developed very early in the evolutionary process. I contend that intelligence is actually built on the twin pillars of the ability to encode experience into vectors, and the ability to calculate angles (similarity) between vectors.

The hypothesis is that the L0 intellect can fulfill all of the requirements of identifying and responding to threats, opportunities and nullities using only the functions listed above using the structures discussed (we compose higher level functions in the simulation using these lower level ones). The obverse of this hypothesis is that this is *all* that L0 can do, and that expecting it to be able to do anything else is an error. The significance of this limit will become more apparent as we consider how it also applies to each of the higher levels of intellect.

13.3 CS1

CS1 is just CS0 with memory. An easy way to implement memory on top of CS0 is through the addition of a new data structure, the *result*, along with the few operations required to store, retrieve and evaluate memories.

The *result* data structure uses the *situation* data structure. Whereas the mentacule is a snapshot of the state of the internal and external senses, the situation is a snapshot of the seven or so mentacules in the current memory.

L1 implements memory in two parts: the current memory, and the persistent memory. Current memory is what is commonly called short-term memory, implemented as a priority queue of recently referenced mentacules. In the simplest case, current memory would just hold the seven or so most important things seen by the entity in its last scan of its environment. Current memory, to use computer terms, is implemented using dynamic memory, which means that it holds images for a short period of time (on the order of ten seconds, in this case), and must be regularly refreshed or the stored references simply disappear.

Accepting that we can keep roughly $7\pm$ items in current memory at a time, a situation is implemented in the asomatous psyche as a seven element array of mentacules. Whenever the mind scans its perceptual sphere it tries to load a mentacule into current memory for each thing it sees, however many that is, but since current memory is implemented as a prioritized queue, unimportant perceptions simply evaporate because they don't merit a slot in current memory.

The result data structure holds two situations, an action, and an evaluation. This enables L1 to capture the pre-action situation, record the action, then add the post-action situation as soon as possible, and finally, to add an evaluation of the effect of the action by comparing the pre- and post-situations. The action is recorded in a mentacule by the *action module* that interprets evaluations it receives and uses them to calculate and encode a movement using the AML into the mentacule.

One of the key L1 operations is $generalize(m1, m2)$, a function that defines a common superclass of two related objects and thus supports the development of a hierarchy, a key requirement for supporting fast searching by type and then detail. Performance requirements suggest that the L1 memory must be implemented as a hierarchical result store in which position is semantic in the sense that the [5, 0, 0] pure anti archetype represents not only a different position in $\mathbb{CS}1$ than [3, 0, 0], but more importantly, a much higher threat level.

The result object provides the basis for learning from experience. A new result is instantiated each time a new action is formulated for a situation, and it remains open until the action is complete, at which time the post-situation is added and the situation delta is evaluated. This action of 'completing' a result is a highly variable process that differs greatly between individuals, because it is influenced by a number of constitutional parameters. As a result, the ability to learn from experience is not consistent across species, or even within a species.

When an L1 entity is confronted with a situation, it searches its memory to find a result whose pre-situation closely matches the current one. If the match is close to exact (what constitutes 'close' is another constitutional parameter), and the result of the action, i.e., the evaluation of that result, was positive, then the L1 intellect will select the action command from the action mentacule and send it along to the body. This process enhances survival potential by shortening response time and leveraging strategies that have been proven successful by experience. In those cases where no good match is found with an existing result, the event will just be treated as new, and the ordinary process of determining an action will be used.

The structures that L1 needs to implement the ability to learn from experience are:

- Current memory: a fixed size, prioritized queue of recent perceptions.
- Situation: a structure that is used to capture and evaluate the contents of current memory.
- Result: a structure with pre- and post-situations, an action mentacule, and an evaluation of the change.
- Persistent Memory: a hierarchical result memory store.

The functions that L1 needs to use the above structures are:

- $init(m) \rightarrow r$: initialize a result with an action mentacule
- $store(r)$: store a result in the hierarchical memory.
- $search(key) \rightarrow [result]$: search result memory by key value, return sorted list.

Note that L1 also has its own versions of the L0 functions, adapted or extended to deal with results instead of mentacules.

The *generalize*() function, shown in listing 16.1, returns a vector containing the minimum values of similar vectors. What makes vectors similar? In general, we can say that any two things are similar if they are of the same *type*. This raises the question, in the evolutionary cytomodel, how do we define type when we are looking at an array having perhaps 10-30 thousand, or more, numbers? (We get the big array by simply appending all the evacules in a mentacule together, end to end, respecting positional semantics, of course.)

Since we know that everything in the model has to be structure-based, and encodable, we should expect the concept of type to arise naturally from the structure and values, rather than having to be imposed as an extrinsic, complex construct. The answer turns out to be elegance itself: type is defined by the zero-signature of the array. This means that any two arrays that have zeros in exactly the same positions in the array are to be considered related. Why? Because the pattern of zeros defines the indifference profile of the thing from the point of view of our value system.

While our positive and negative evaluations of various types of cats may differ, the parts that we care not at all about shouldn't vary from lion to tiger to cheetah. Now, this means that an individual might wind up putting bears and wolves into the same category, but this matches what happens in real life: we categorize things by what they mean to us, and things that share the same indifference profile also share the same anti-self and pro-self profile, albeit with different levels of value. Thus, the concept of type arises naturally from the heritable data structure used by the L1 intellect.

The generalize function is implemented with just four functions (*updateMemory()*, *generalize()*, *related()*, and *min()*, that require no new low-level functionality, as shown below:

Listing 13.1: Generalize function

```
public static void updateMemory(ArrayList<Node> memory){
  memory.eachWithIndex{ Node n, i ->
    if (i + 1 < list.size()){
      Node next = list.get(i + 1)
      if (next.objectType == n.objectType){
        Node newNode = generalize(n, next)
        if (newNode != null){
          // insert into memory and update links
        }
      }
    }
  }
}
public static Node generalize(Node n1, Node n2){
  Node ret = null
  if (n1.equals(n2))
    return ret
  if (related(n1, n2)){
    ret = min(n1, n2)
    ret.objectType = 'super'
  }
  if (n1.equals(ret) || n2.equals(ret))
    ret = null
  ret
}

public static boolean related(Node n1, Node n2){
  boolean match = true
```

```
n1.nodeValues().eachWithIndex{n, i ->
  match = (n == 0 && n2.nodeValues()[i] == 0) ||
  (n != 0 && n2.nodeValues()[i] != 0) && match
}
match
}

public static Node min(Node n1, Node n2){
  Node result = new Node()
  ArrayList<Integer> list = new ArrayList<Integer>()
  n1.nodeValues().eachWithIndex {n, i ->
    list.add(Math.min(n, n2.nodeValues()[i]))
  }
  Evacule e1 = new Evacule(list[0], list[1], list[2])
  Evacule e2 = new Evacule(list[3], list[4], list[5])
  result.setEvacules(e1, e2)
  result
}
```

This economy of effort is characteristic of good design practices, because good design allows the demands of reality to shape the solution, rather than trying to force an ill-fitting solution onto a reluctant reality. Evolution, although it admittedly does produce some peculiar solutions, tends to exhibit an economy of nature for the exact same reason bubbles are spherical: the pressure of physical reality tends to define simple spaces.

The contention is that with these few structures and functions, we have satisfied the cognition requirements needed by mobile creatures capable of remembering and learning from experience, and avoiding or selecting past actions for reuse based on past results.

The L1 structures and functions do not significantly affect the geometry of the $\mathbb{CS}0$ space. In L0 space, input is encoded into mentacules and evaluated to a position in the singularity distortion field, but this positioning is transient. L1 makes the evaluated position persistent, and relates the elements in this durable memory in a hierarchical relation culminating in an archetype for each (anti, pro, non) type. The hierarchy facilitates the recall and response process, but just inhabits the pre-existing curved space without any changes or extensions.

 *Think about this: we are simulating pre-language cognition with just 10 functions, and a few data structures. If the tests verify this, what would it mean to your view of what intellect is?*

While the singularity is the root of self-consciousness, personal experience is surely its trunk, and we have now shown this can be encoded as an L1 function. While full self-consciousness requires the language ability of L2, it should be apparent that much of what makes us think and act as we do is rooted in the very nature of organic cognition itself, and not in human flaws and frailty.

13.4   CS2

CS2 is the space inhabited by L2, what we fondly think of as our 'rational' mind. This is the world of words and conscious thoughts, of language, conversations, opinions and school subjects. The CS2 space extends beyond the singularity distortion field into an apparently unbounded, geometrically flat area where ideas *can* be positioned solely on the basis of hierarchy, relation and sequence—what we tell ourselves is logic and reason—or they can even more easily be positioned in the distortion field by the simple act of attaching a value link connecting them to self-significant values and beliefs.

The distinguishing characteristic of L2 is the capacity to learn and process patterns, the data structure on which it is built. A pattern, in the abstract sense, is a linkable unit containing a matchable entry point (a situation), content (an action mentacule), and a collection of selectable exit points (other patterns). Patterns model both paths and syntactical constructs, such as language. In the asomatous psyche, the exits are chosen by the degree of a weighted (with the weighting being calculated in the moment by internal state variables) match with the post-action situation: a 7 point match on the entry point follows the 7 point match exit path, a 6 point match follows the 6 point exit path, etc.

Although not implemented yet, the way language could be coded in the asomatous psyche would be to accept phonemes as content, with branching supporting word building, and composite word patterns supporting phrases, sentences and so on (in reality, we would leverage some of the very successful work that has already been done in this field). Words would point to patterns, results or mentacules that would denote their meaning. Just as RNA guides the construction of DNA, structural grammar patterns would guide the construction of content patterns holding actual sentences and more complex constructs.

The concept of a pattern language is similar to the concept

of natural language: where natural language has a lexicon and a grammar, a pattern language has a set of patterns and an optional grammar. The grammar in a pattern language is actually just another pattern language that encodes grammatical rules. Therefore, in pattern languages that use an independent grammar language, generating or interpreting linguistic constructs requires the stitching together of structure and content, just the same as what we do when we speak and listen.

In normal operation, once an existing pattern is activated in the L2 mind, it is added to a new short-term data store, the *recently used patterns* store, and this is the mechanism that enables us to follow a path or procedure from step to step. Note that this implementation also accounts for the fact that lengthy interruptions to our plans can cause us to lose our place, and force us to have to search for where we left off with an effort proportional to the length of the interruption. For a variety of reasons, we are modeling this as a most-recently-used priority queue with a capacity of about two dozen patterns. The elements in this queue have several interesting roles in L2 functioning, in both waking and sleeping states, which will be discussed later.

The significant pattern operations are:

- Patterns can be instantiated with results or patterns.
- Patterns can be extended with patterns of arbitrary size, virtually without limit.
- Patterns can be updated through linking and unlinking.
- Patterns accept value links.

- Pattern paths are affected by weighted values in the selection process.
- Pattern matching on input is, by design, optimistic and aggressive (lots of false positives).
- Pattern matches trigger alertness, i.e., they alter internal state.
- Grammar rules are defined by structural patterns and implemented by means of the choosable exit options.

The pattern processing cycle starts with creating a pattern from a result or another pattern. Then, during times when no higher priority processes are active, low priority background threads search for patterns that can link to the lower match exit points in the recently referenced pattern currently being processed. This process of extending patterns can also be triggered on purpose, in the process we call *thinking*.

It is important to understand that the very structure of a pattern determines that there is no difference whatsoever between a simple and a composite pattern. When pattern b gets attached to new pattern a, if b is already 100 patterns deep along the 7-match branch, this means that a now becomes 101 patterns deep in one step. The most natural thing in the world is for patterns to link in ever-lengthening chains. The only real limit to the size of a pattern chain is priority: below a certain length, a pattern has no value because it doesn't accomplish much, but above a certain length, the pattern becomes too specialized, and too difficult to use. Thus, the priority is always to fill out new or short patterns until they reach useful dimensions before any more time is spent extending patterns that already reach a conclusion of one sort or another.

Another characteristic of patterns is that links connecting patterns to other patterns are only semi-persistent and must be reinforced several times within a short period of time to become durable, or the link to the pattern is lost. For example, links made in pre-ultimate dreams are ordinarily never reinforced and so are lost before waking, and lessons heard in class but never studied are often lost before the test. The initial reinforcement must happen quickly, and additional repetitions, the number of which vary by each mind's memory facility, must occur within a time limit that grows for each repetition.

Think of patterns as the Lego^{TM} blocks from which language, paths and plans are built. The action mentacule in a pattern contains an action command that was inserted by the action module if the pattern was instantiated with a result, or it contains a fully specified action if the pattern was learned from others through pattern assimilation. The three most important characteristics of patterns are:

1. They enable us to make and follow plans.
2. They enable us to anticipate the future.
3. They can be inculcated in succeeding generations with a good degree of success.

That is, they enable us to begin to react to a critical situation *before* it happens, and they provide the mechanism that makes cultures and civilizations possible by creating a channel for the transmission of cultural lessons and attitudes from generation to generation.

13.4.1 CS2 Operations

In addition to the pattern version of the functions from the lower intellects, the catalog of new CS2 functions required to support robust pattern processing is:

- *store*(*pattern*, *key*): Store a pattern into a persistent memory structure having both hierarchical and associative indexes.
- *search*(*dim*, *key*): Search the pattern memory store in a given dimension with a key.
- *link*(*p*)(↑): Pattern linking of one pattern to another. Linking is not commutative, but is associative.
- *unlink*(*p*)(↓): Pattern unlinking unlinks patterns.
- *vLink*(*vo*)(↔): Value linking between a pattern and a value object.

It is the structure of the pattern as defined in the genotype which, in combination with a genetic affinity for pattern linking, is responsible for most of what we would think of as rational thought. The capacity for grammar arises as a combination of the structure of the pattern exit points and the programmable matching rules along with the power of value linking. Checking for grammatical and logical errors is accomplished by comparing the constructed thought pattern against the template pattern to determine whether or not the variance angle is within tolerance. Read the source code of the asomatous psyche to see the details of how this all can be done.

13.5 Summary

The fundamental question of modeling is: can we define a tractable model that closely matches the behavior of the referent in the dimension of interest? Both sides of the question are critical: 1) can we define a model that is simple enough to manage, and 2) can we define a model that will produce results close to those observable from the referent? In simulation, we always try to use the simplest model we can that still captures the dimension of interest well enough to support tests and analysis. The idea is that we ultimately want to learn something of the unseen internals of the referent by using the internals of a model that successfully reproduces measurable, external behavior. Based on test results, we can then generate hypotheses to begin to create new, more detailed, concrete models based on verified knowledge of the referent, selectively replacing the abstract terms used to create our first model with actual data when it becomes available.

The functions discussed in this chapter are adequate to produce the behaviors associated with cognitive levels L0-L2. The asomatous psyche application built on this design can be used to simulate many types of behaviors in creatures from the insect up to the human level, depending on the configuration parameters specified. In the event that the simulated behaviors fail to match observed actual behaviors, the design and implementation of the application can be revised, extended or replaced, as needed, to bring the results within tolerance.

If we can demonstrate complex human behaviors using a

simulation built with just these functions, then the justification for supposing that human behaviors are generated by higher level capabilities and sensibilities should be seriously challenged. This would not relieve of us our responsibility for our actions, rather, it would just allow us to focus our efforts better on the area in which the problem actually arose, rather than just spending all of our time dithering around in the attic.

13.6 Review

High level operations performed on each level:

- L0: encode, identify, evaluate, formulate response.
- L1: store, recall, generalize.
- L2: extend, update, select, follow.

Low level functions used by each level

- L0
    - $copy()$: copies values from one structure to another.
    - $trigger()$: fires a signal when threshold values are met.
    - $magnitude(type, v)-> n$: calculate the magnitude of a vector in a subset of dimensions.
    - $angle(v1, v2) \rightarrow \theta$: calculates the angle between two vectors.
    - $add(v1, v2) \rightarrow v$: add two vectors
    - $minus(v1, v2) \rightarrow v$: subtract two vectors
    - $archetype(type) \rightarrow v$: get $type$ archetype vector
- L1
    - $init(m) \rightarrow r$: initialize a result with an action men-

tacule

- *store(r)*: store a result in the hierarchical memory.
- *search(key)* → [*result*]: search result memory by key value, return sorted list.

- L2

  - *store(pattern, key)*: Store a pattern into a persistent memory structure having both hierarchical and associative indexes.
  - *search(dim, key)*: Search the pattern memory store in a given dimension with a key.
  - *link(p)*(→): Pattern linking of one pattern to another. Linking is not commutative, but is associative.
  - *unlink(p)*(↓): Pattern unlinking unlinks patterns.
  - *vLink(vo)*(⤳): Value linking between a pattern and a value object.

Chapter 14

Limits

14.1   Introduction

The mind is an organic mechanism capable of performing a discrete number of functions. To put it bluntly, the mind does NOT think, it does NOT reason, it performs low level functions that produce results that we sometimes recognize as thinking and reasoning. There are limits to what the various intellects can do naturally and easily, and hard limits to what they can do at all. The consideration of these limits is critical to answering any question of the form, "Why haven't we yet done xxx?" This includes our core questions: why haven't we answered any pinnacle questions yet, and why haven't we been able to extend the scientific revolution into the subjective domain of human experience, motivation and action?

If we can determine, from our model, that it is impossible for the human mind to do action xxx, then that would certainly answer the question of why we haven't done it yet. That type of negative answer would open a terrific opportunity for exploration and discovery, since digging into the anomaly of impossible expectation versus reality could tell us a lot about our assumptions and understanding of ourselves and our lives. The Torah gives us an example of how liberating it can be to find that certain actions are impossible when it outlawed magic and soothsaying and stated unequivocally that local gods, to whom such incantations would be directed, *cannot* exist. This should have had a huge liberating effect on human society, and perhaps it did for those who learned the lesson, but sadly, there are still many alive today who continue to live with the primitive delusion of miracle and magic.

We will walk through the intellect levels and review what each level of intellect is capable of doing, what it can't do, and what some failures might look like.

14.2   L0

14.2.1   Output

The purpose ('purpose', when used in this sense, is just rhetorical flourish for saying this is the function of something, this is what something is observed to do, not that it is a goal) of L0 is to enable volitionally mobile entities to move appropriately in response to external phenomena within the perceptual radius, with a general, but not universal, bias towards the defensive in the specified moves. But, since purpose is an attributed meaning deriving from the perspective of the singularity, and not an attribute of reality, we should simply say that this is the result of this functionality, rather than its purpose.

14.2.2 Capabilities

The L0 intellect is capable of reductive perception to a known type, evaluating the meaning of the perceived phenomenon, and specifying an action response. It cannot do anything else.

14.2.3 Dysfunction

Sensory defects can interfere with the normal process of appropriately charging the target evacules for the affected senses, and thus skew the data input to the evaluation process.

The efficiency of the perception-evaluation process can be degraded by a number of factors, such as fatigue, inanition, or intoxication, with the result that perception and evaluation may be flawed, thus causing reactions to occur in a tardy, rather than timely, fashion.

Since species are adaptations to ecological niches, if a species finds itself, by whatever accident, in an unfamiliar environment, then its ability to respond appropriately to unusual perceptions and events is undefined.

14.2.4 Impossible

The L0 perception process is reductive, not perceptive. That is, it maps *whatever* into one of a fixed set of supported perceptions because the range of answers is what characterizes a species, it has no way of anticipating everything that can exist in nature. The important end of the perception cycle is not in the externality being perceived, but in the internal representation constructed from the encounter which triggers the response process. The significance of this cannot be overstated: at the L0 level, we have perhaps 10,000 or even 100,000 conceptions that we can form from our perceptions and this limit is hardwired into our genotype. Anything beyond this hard limit will still be seen, but not as it *is*, instead, it will be seen to be whatever our fixed array has in the slot we map it to. In the case where L0 has no ability to identify something, it will still always map it to a known threat/opportunity profile. (L2 can perform another level of recognition by synthesizing perceptions from an assemblage of known patterns, but this is a different level of recognition than L0.)

L0 produces actionable solutions to all perceptions. That doesn't mean they are right, it doesn't mean we will survive, it just means that L0 is what sees action as a solution to both problems and opportunities.

L0 only knows right/wrong, true/false, good/bad, or not important. If an idea does not fit into the 'approach, retreat, ignore' paradigm, L0 *cannot* think it. The corollary of this is that if you are using the right/wrong paradigm, you are thinking with L0. Thus, if you find yourself arguing truth or right and wrong in a debate, then these three simple choices are the absolute limit of the level of sophistication available to you at that time, because however complex your thought originally was, you are asserting it reduces to one of these three buckets.

If you even hear any of the RWTF words in a conversation, then you should immediately realize that you are in an intellectual crawl space, not a great hall of learned discourse.

14.3   L1

14.3.1   Output

L1 uses the result data object and hierarchical persistence to support functions that make it possible to learn from experience. L1 exists to serve L0, to enhance our viability quotient by incorporating experience in our response calculations. Using experience to react to phenomena can greatly improve response time. A hierarchical data store reduces the time penalty for searching through experience to $O(1)$ for the retrieval of type, and guarantees a usable result set is available at all times, and eliminates the risk of long search times. Thus, while L1 evaluated memory is a powerful and complex functionality, it has been implemented in a way that is consistent with the unchanged function of L0.

14.3.2   Capabilities

The L1 intellect stores actions with before and after situations, and calculates the change in status that is presumably due to the action. The hierarchical nature of the L1 memory store uses the L1 ability to generalize from the specific to the super type to populate memory using a shallow type tree. It does this using simple calculations, and produces a data structure that supports both very rapid search and storage functions.

14.3.3 Dysfunction

Organic or chemical factors can impair the result creation process. Since results have to be held open for the eventual assignment of the post-situation element that is needed for the evaluation, any diminution of attention or searching ability will result in a failure to match the consequent situation with the appropriate result object, leading to the loss of unclosed results. This leads to lost lessons, and a reduced ability to learn from experience.

The evaluation process can also be skewed by any level of degraded internal state, leading to the storage of improperly rated results.

14.3.4 Impossible

The L1 intellect is not creative; it follows experience, it does not anticipate it. Its type and memory hierarchy is concrete, not abstract, and can be extended through generalization, and subsequently rebalanced, but not otherwise changed. This means it is both inflexible and sensitive to initial conditions. In other words, the L1 intellect is intensely parochial and sees a world built of its own experience — it simply cannot see the world in any terms but its own.

14.4   L2

14.4.1   Output

The L2 intellect uses the pattern data object to support language, naming, indirection, path and event sequencing. Naming patterns support the emergence of self-awareness, lesson patterns support the development and perpetuation of culture, authority patterns and pattern extension support the evolution of complex social structures.

14.4.2   Capabilities

The L2 intellect can anticipate the future by matching the current situation to existing patterns; it can support the development of very large pattern complexes as well as an evaluated summary of them. Through language patterns, it supports complex social organizations that can profoundly affect the individual's survival potential. The task pattern supports coordinated work activity, and the loopback pattern supports religious concepts and organizations that reinforce the social, cultural and economic institutions.

14.4.3   Dysfunction

The pattern processor is a toxic idea fountain—it never shuts down, it is active even during sleep. The function of the processor, however, is dependent on a range of lower level functionality, not all of which is always available, so the quality of the pattern processing results vary widely from day to day and even throughout a single day. Furthermore, there is no actual connection between the L2 pattern processor and external reality; patterns are assembled strictly according to their own accepted pattern grammar. An English sentence, for instance, does not have the same structure as a German one, and, without social interaction, neither of them can be corrected by external reality, since there is no point of direct connection between a pattern and the outside world.

14.4.4   Impossible

The nature of any sufficiently advanced, formal construct such as a data structure and storage system, is that, with enough work, it can be made to handle arbitrarily complex models. A language is said to be Turing complete if its elements and operations are sufficient to execute any instruction doable on a Turing machine, the theoretical model of single threaded, algorithmic processing. While no work has been done on a proof that L2 is Turing complete (since the formalism defining L2 is not complete yet), it seems likely that L2 is a Turing complete organic mechanism. That is to say, L2 is quite powerful.

However, there are certain things that L2 simply cannot do, such as invention. L2 can be creative through the mechanism of pattern extension, the normal process of appending patterns to patterns that can produce surprising results when the extensions occur on novel dimensions, but this is not invention. Invention, experienced as learning discoveries and learning explosions, is an L3 activity. L2 can elaborate and improvise pattern extensions along unusual dimensions chosen to satisfy a particular need, but the ability to invent the stage on which thought occurs, and new methods by which thoughts can be assembled and tested, is impossible in L2.

By itself, L2 has no means to check its results against external reality, it is restricted to grammar checking against the pattern language for consistency. This verification process is a tree search that terminates on finding the first result, i.e., there is no mechanism to force it to exhaustively search the entire pattern to uncover all possible errors at once. L2 error checking is inherently partial and casual in that it either identifies an error in the time we decide to devote to the effort, or it does not, in which case it returns the authoritative assessment: "looks good to me!"

Although we base our definition of intelligence on the level of one's L2 pattern processing ability, the ability to memorize, recall and even manipulate large volumes of patterns is not inconsistent with high levels of stupidity. Xenophon, in the *Symposium*, has Antisthenes ask, "...do you know any tribe of men ...more stupid than the rhapsodes?" showing that we have known for 2,500 years that excessive, blind memorization of patterns, whether Homer or the Quran, is a fairly reliable mechanism for castrating the inquiring intellect. Pedantic, unoriginal, rule-fanatic academics are a prime example of this limit of the L2 intellect.

L2 can do linear transformations of pattern through the extension of patterns with patterns, and can pivot data to fit hierarchies of generalizations of specific patterns, but it does not have the means to generate non-linear leaps in discovery and invention.

14.5   L3

L3 will be covered in its own volume.

14.6   General Limits

The definition of reality tells us that the fundamental law of physical reality is *specificity*, that is, everything is specific, nothing is general: every position, every movement can be measured, and two movements with different coordinates and vectors are different. Only in the minimalist discrete models in the mind can very different realities regularly appear to be the same, or generally the same, but this happens because the organic mechanism of the mind serves its purpose by reducing the complex and unique to the simple and generic so that it can guarantee that it will always be able to calculate a timely response to any input whatsoever.

This simplistic reduction of complex, unique experience to evaluated generic object is something our mind not only does to external events, it also does it to internal events. The mind reduces the singular and complex to a simple type not only when it looks at other, but also when it looks at self. Of course, because of the purblind defect, the reality is that the mind cannot reliably tell the difference.

The fact is that there are hard limits to every level of cognitive function, limits that are defined both by structure and evolution (in the sense that 'the economy of nature' throttles

efforts above what is necessary for the job at hand). Not knowing those limits makes it impossible to discern the independent
parts of a gross perception, and the various role each of those
parts play in contributing to the whole. This leaves one with
only a confused mudball notion that cannot be analyzed, cannot
be understood, and can but be badly described.

Let's imagine that we ask the average college educated professional to tell us what they think the brain does, and they
will likely give an answer that amounts to, "Well, it *thinks*." If
we push them further by asking, "Are planning, doing math,
reflecting, learning and creating all just different parts of thinking?" we will likely get the lame response, "Well, I guess so,
what else could it be?" If we then finish the discussion with one
final question, "What kind of mental operations can't the brain
do?" befuddlement will probably be the only response we get.
Would this not be the common level of understanding of how
our minds think and feel?

Do you have a pair of pliers? What can they do? What can't
they do? What are they good at, what are they particularly fit
for? What are they bad at, what can they do, but only badly?
Name any other tool, every one has capabilities and limits, after
all, what in nature does not? Name any action such as running,
walking, swimming, flying, throwing; each action suits a limited
range of circumstances, requires a certain type of ability and effort, and can achieve a certain range of result. Does any tool
just 'fix' things, does any action just 'move' us from any *a* to
any *b*? Obviously the *mind* is a tool for processing experience,

and it, too, has limits, but since the mind is a composite, not an atomic phenomenon, saying *our mind has*, rather than *our minds (intellects) have*, reveals a crippling lack of understanding. The different parts of the mind have different capabilities and different limits. Not knowing your tool's exact capabilities and limits makes you a bad mechanic, a bad craftsman, a bad *thinker*.

Careful analysis of the different levels of intellect that developed at different ages in the evolution of volitionally mobile creatures, and the functions supported by each, can enable us to identify the capabilities and limitations of each stage of cognition. It can help us to understand, in detail, how our minds work and how they achieve the results we see.

Our previous understanding of our minds and our thought process has been inadequate in the extreme, and, in fact, it has been juvenile, at best. Thinking our ideas are accurate representations of reality, or even worse yet, reality itself, is ludicrous, and simply inexcusable. And yet, this way of thinking passes for erudition, or even wisdom, still today. In the first volume of this series (*Pinnacle Questions*), we introduced the concept of an anomaly as a critical opportunity for the exploration of the variance between our understanding and reality. It should be apparent to everyone, by now, that such anomalies are not only not rare, they are the stuff of which all ideas are made.

14.7   Review

- L0 abilities: reductive perception to type, evaluation, response command; formulates actionable solutions to perceived changes
- L0 limits: sees what it can, not what is; can only understand reality from the perspective of the ternary values
- L1 abilities: rapidly remembers and recalls evaluated actions to learn from experience
- L1 limits: sees the past, not the future; sees the world in terms of its own experience
- L2 abilities: language, planning, anticipation, social organization, linear transformations, data pivoting
- L2 problems: floods the mind with false predictions, causes anxiety and weakness if not compensated for
- L2 limits: can extend, not invent; does not check its ideas against reality
- reality is continuous and specific, cognitive models are discrete and general; purblind defect causes us to think reality resembles our models

Chapter 15

Thought Cycles

15.1 Introduction

The concept of intellect level independence is crucial to developing an understanding of the way that the layered cognition model works. Each level is perfectly unaware of both the operations and objects of the levels above it, the levels that developed after it in the evolution of the cognitive entity. Additionally, each level is, strictly speaking, only aware of its own objects and those produced by levels below it, not the processes that produced those objects. It must be this way to conform to the evolutionary cytomodel in which everything is reduced to a function that accepts only a specific type or range of input, and produces a specific type of output. There is no 'awareness' of the entire process or of some ultimate objective, rather, each function merely does its part with little to no awareness of the end result (some adaptive functions do exist, but even though they seem to balance the whole, they are still just producing output in response to input).

To help the reader grasp this fundamental concept of layer independence, we will take a moment to review the basic cycles and how they work side by side, with higher levels potentially consuming objects created by lower levels, as well as independently performing their own unique functions. Figure 15.1 shows an incomplete process cycle diagram for levels L0-L2. Rather than burden the reader with a 3-column layout appropriate to independent simultaneous processes, we will discuss them in order, leaving the reader the responsibility not to plug them into a sequential model.

It might help to think of the three levels as separate planets, each with their own orbit and period both of rotation and revolution, to make it easier to picture how each one just keeps moving along, independent of where the others are at the time. This doesn't fit the planetary model entirely, of course, because, in the model, higher levels may listen for events from the lower level, and interrupt their own processing to consume important events.

The numbered steps in the descriptions below correspond to numbered events in the diagram. The numbers do not correspond to a comprehensive sequence.

15.2   L0

Step 01: Both the internal and external senses continuously process sensory input, regardless of whether the level of the

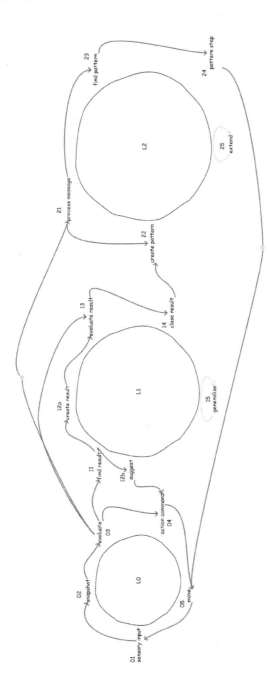

Figure 15.1: L0-L2 Thought Cycles

input is above or below the sensitivity limit of the sense.

Step 02: Snapshots of the current state of the senses are taken at variable intervals or when triggered by sensory events such as unexpected sounds, motions, light changes, etc. The intervals at which snapshots are automatically triggered vary with species, alertness state, fatigue, intoxication, etc. The snap shot encodes the input as a mentacule.

Step 03: Creation of a mentacule from a snapshot triggers a rapid evaluation cycle which determines, in order, the level of threat, then opportunity, then insignificance.

Step 04: Part of the evaluation process is to encode movement response to significant events. The action module, which evolved before any particular body form that exists today, encodes the action command in the abstract movement language.

Step 05: The body implements the action command as a series of motions in its repertoire.

Note that a null action command is not only valid, but the norm: we aren't always flinching. A most common example of this process cycle that you can see in nature, is an animal reacting to a state of need, reported by its internal senses, with a *seek* command that uses a semi-random move selector to generate a path that tends to explore the local region first, but then will move beyond, to explore the next area by making an extended movement, after which it repeats the seek process.

15.3 L1

Step 11: L1 listens on mentacule creation in step 03, and responds by searching its memory for a result containing the same mentacule information. Finding a result with a positive evaluation triggers step 12b, otherwise it transitions to step 12a.

Step 12a: L1 creates a new result for each unfamiliar mentacule, along with the state of the current memory. The mentacule is left in an open state, meaning that the next event after the action completes will trigger step 13.

Step 12b: When L1 finds a matching result with a positive evaluation, it will push the action command from the result mentacule to the action module. Whether or not this will preempt the action module from recalculating an action command will vary depending on circumstances, and comes down to a timing issue.

Step 13: When the previous action completes with L0 creating a new mentacule in step 03, L1 will take a snapshot of current memory and use it to evaluate the success of the action.

Step 14: L1 closes the result following step 13, adding another bit of experience to memory.

Step 15: When there is time, energy and sufficient cycles available, L1 silently processes the contents of the result memory store to generalize supertypes from subtypes, and then rebalance the tree, in an ongoing memory organization optimization process. The L1 memory is a hierarchical, value and type based memory store that supports interrupted searches by queuing up each node it finds as it descends the memory tree, moving from the general to the specific, so that it always has an answer at the ready, and only continues the search to improve the answer if time permits. This process runs in the background whenever possible to optimize memory organization to ensure that L1 is always able to deliver a failsafe response.

15.4   L2

Remember, this diagram of L2 processing does not explicitly include language-level functionality yet, and although adding it will merely expand what is shown, it will require some additional steps to capture the complexity of verbal communication. The current state of the diagram is intended to model the pre-language function of L2 as it is seen in animals.

Step 21: Process each mentacule created in step 03. Since patterns are complex, composite objects, L2 will ordinarily have to buffer a number of L0 events before it has sufficient input to begin processing. Think Morse code, where the operator has to collect a number of dots and dashes before accumulating enough to form a word.

Step 22: If the input is new, as determined by step 21, L2 will create a new pattern for it. Just as L1 only processes results, L2 only processes patterns, so to handle a new mentacule, it has to create an L2 pattern representation of it. Step 22 is also triggered when L1 closes a result, which prompts L2 to create a pattern from it.

Step 23: When step 21 completes, L2 searches for an existing pattern. If it finds one, it will either be an active or inactive pattern. In either case, L2 will transition to step 24.

Step 24: Send the action command from the next step in the active pattern to the body in step 05.

Step 25: The L2 background process works to extend patterns by adding onto the end of an existing chain, or by filling in another of the exit point options. Priority is given to extending shorter, incomplete chains over extending meaningful chains with an acceptable evaluation.

15.5   Summary

The takeaway from this chapter is that very high level cognitive function is a happenstance enforced by natural selection rebuking poor matches between the gross effects of cumulative layers of function output and the current ecological niche. In other words, mutation offers up what we recognize as high level function as the product of many small, nearly blind functions just doing their transformations whenever conditions are right to trigger them, and natural selection culls the failures. This does not, in any sense, diminish the miracle of life or the wonder of the cosmic reach of cognition, it is merely a model that explains what we observe in an economical way that is entirely consistent with what we know about the evolutionary process.

15.6   Review

The particular connections discussed in this chapter are not only model-specific, they are version-specific, and may change as the

simulation is hardened and extended. The important concept
is that:

- Our minds comprise separate, independent intellects.

- The separate intellects function independently.

- While higher intellects may consume output from lower
  intellects and feed them objects at their level, they do
  this as observers, as outsiders.

- While we like to think that our higher intellects have a say
  in all of our actions, our experience tells us otherwise. If
  anything such as fatigue, stress or intoxication slows down
  our higher intellects even a little, the commands from the
  lower levels will have time to take direct effect without
  editing or review.

Chapter 16

Patterns in Depth

16.1 Introduction

The concept of a *pattern* has been implemented both as a formal model, and as an actual Pattern class that is written in a programming language. The formal pattern model can be defined in precise terms, and it is consistent with the evolutionary cytomodel: it is a fixed implementation of a single-in, multiple-out switch, with branching controlled by a customizable algorithm. As a class in an application, the pattern object is a partially realized, experimental tool that supports the needs of the simulation. If we view this volume as a design document for the asomatous psyche simulation engine, then ideas we express here and there can be collected to drive the design of the executable class. But, if we view this as an introduction to faceted model-oriented reasoning, then a *pattern* is a model that is built on the universal cognition model.

However, the universal cognition model is not yet formal
and complete, and since it is being abstracted from a concrete
model (the ECDM), it is an admixture of well thought out and
ad hoc programming compromises. This incomplete state of the
general model pushes the discussion back and forth between the
specific and the general as we pursue particular threads of exposition. The verbal model of the pattern concept is a rhetorical
device that draws from both the formal and the loose model to
support the exposition of the general idea. In this chapter, we
will be explicating patterns by transposing and expanding the
executable model into this verbal model. This in-depth look
into patterns will be needed in order to understand part two of
this volume.

16.2   L2 Patterns In Depth

L2 pattern processing functionality enables us to anticipate the
future by running a fuzzy query from the current situation to
get a set of patterns that represent a number of possible continuations of the current time line. This functionality gives us a
lot of power, because it effectively allows us to see what is hid-
ing behind that hill, so it enables us to begin to react to events
before they happen. Furthermore, we can react to those future
events using plans that are not only tried and true, but that
can also be adjusted on the spot to fit current conditions by
means of the same pattern processing mechanism that created
them in the first place.

Our pattern processing capacity allows us to create language by combining grammar and lexical pattern languages. Language has made the development of complex societies possible, and also made it necessary, since the planning and organization capabilities of L2 only realize their full potential when they organize groups of people to execute complex plans.

The L2 ability to abstractly associate and group experiences, enables us, first, *to conceive* of ourselves, and second, to extend that self-concept beyond the boundaries of our bodies to encompass sources of strength with shared interests. The L2 language constructs are the primary mechanism supporting group formation by enabling expansion of the extended self to incorporate group identities, thereby making culture and civilization possible. Language, though, is just one application of the L2 pattern processing object, it also makes planning and complex sequencing of events possible, and when language joins with L1 beliefs and extends them into the levels of the higher intellect, that is when we begin to see those elements form from which culture can arise.

If we consider the L2 intellect of a mature cognitive entity, then we are looking at a mind with an extensive personal history, with an extensive library of patterns gained from a variety of sources, with a seasoned ability to situate its experience in the web of patterns it has developed in order to proactively interact with external reality. But, all of this power comes at a terrible, crippling cost: our always-on pattern processing function churns out scenario after scenario of different, possibly imminent, threats and calamities, the prospect of which would

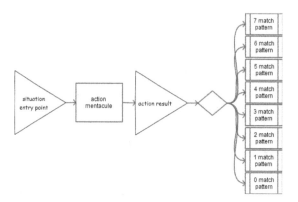

Figure 16.1: Basic Pattern Object

throw our body and lower level intellects into a constant state of alarm if left unchecked. Such a chronic panic state would not only be exhausting, but would also degrade our ability to respond to actual emergencies in the moment, in violation of **M9**. Examples of this unhealthy state can be seen in people suffering from various mental disorders.

Dreams tell us that, although its efficacy may be variable, L2 pattern processing never really stops, and it can generate truly strange, useless, and even destructive thoughts that are often difficult to recognize as unreal. Thus, pattern processing, by itself, likely would not have survived as a mutation, because the constant state of alarm it creates would be unsustainable and would interfere with normal functioning. Therefore, it seems that there had to be additional functionality included in the L2 family of mutations that could compensate for the lack of a shut-off valve on the pattern spigot (see chapter 21, Beliefs).

We begin our deeper examination of the L2 pattern object

by referring to a diagram (visual model) and a code snippet (executable model) of the pattern object. Figure 16.1 shows the layout of the L2 pattern object. Listing **??** shows part of the interface of the Pattern class from the asomatous psyche application that implements this functionality.

Listing 16.1: Partial Pattern Class Interface

```
class Pattern {
  UUID id = UUID.randomUUID()
  String name = ""
  AsomatousPsyche ap
  Situation entryPoint
  Evacules evaluation
  Condition condition
  Mentacule primary
  PatternLinks branches
  Pattern source
  PatternList siblingPatterns

  boolean active
  boolean done
  Pattern currentStep
  Pattern selectedExit
  Result result

  public static Pattern generatePattern(Result r,
      AsomatousPsyche ap){...}
  private Pattern(Result result, AsomatousPsyche ap){...}
  /*
   * Evaluation methods
   */
  Evacule entryPointEvaluation(){...}
  Double determinant(){...}
  boolean negativeTotalPatternEvaluation(){...}
  Evacule goodbadMeasure(){...}
  boolean positiveTotalPatternEvaluation(){...}
  void addExit7(Pattern p, Result r){...}
  /**
```

```
 * NOTE: this method is overridable when the pattern is
 * defined. Determines the number of matches between
 * the exits entry point situations and the entry point
 * of the pattern parameter.
 * @param sit1 startng situation
 * @param sit2 ending situation
 * @return the number of exit point
 */
int selectExit(Situation sit0, Situation sit1){...}
```

L2 naturally creates patterns from closed results, but what
we are most familiar with is the process of pattern acquisition
through verbal interaction, whether delivered through written
or oral means. When a pattern is created by either means, the
first element to be specified is the entry point situation, the
conditions under which this pattern is selected and activated.
When being created automatically from L1 results, the pre-
situation in the result becomes the situation entry point in the
pattern. When patterns are acquired from a cultural source,
the entry point is clearly defined, and it is the first thing we
must memorize. The action mentacule specifies the action to
take when the pattern is activated, and the pattern enters a
wait state until the results of the action are available to provide
the result situation, and the exit point (the next step in the
pattern plan) is selected from the set of 7 or so exit points in
the pattern, based on the level of match that exists between the
result situation and the various exit point patterns.

The comment above the *selectExit*(...) method in listing **??**
explains that the internals of this method are customizable, not
fixed. That is, learning how to do the exit point matching is part
of learning the pattern—think of all of your math homework

that made you practice how to do each operation and you will see that the algorithm for selecting the next step in a pattern is a core part of the lesson that taught you how to solve particular problems.

The basic concept of the pattern object is that patterns apply only to certain situations, they specify an action, and then they support branching to determine the next step based on the result of the action. The next step is another pattern, and there is no limit to how many patterns can be strung together. The exit point patterns do not actually exist *in* the current pattern, the current pattern just points to other existing patterns, so patterns can participate in any number of other patterns. This use of pointers instead of embedding objects keeps both the structure and the wiring light and makes creating, maintaining and using very complex patterns a fairly lightweight operation.

The situation entry point is defined at the moment of pattern creation, as is the action step, but the action result step is not, because it is different every time the pattern is used, since it is a snapshot of current memory after the action completes. The 7-match pattern exit point is also defined at the moment of creation from the result post-situation, when patterns are created from results, and is certainly part of the lesson that must be memorized when patterns are acquired socially. The remaining unspecified exit points, however many are left open, are actually filled in by L2 ruminations that occur in background processing, whenever diurnal exigencies allow. Some level of creativity is inevitable during this fill-in process, and novel extensions are sometimes suggested by the idle mind that are may be later rejected by the L2 error checking function, if it happens to be invoked by a diligent mind, otherwise, opportunities for very poor quality ideas abound.

Patterns can be thought of as paths that connect one situation to another via an action, with a new choice of paths available to follow after each step. These paths are much like paths in the wilderness, in that most natural paths extend by connecting existing traveled or natural paths, rather than being built from point a to point z in one go. In real life, paths meander, intersect and branch, and the trail you follow is one you select and make yourself, as the result of situational decisions that deal with the facts at hand.

However, what makes the pattern object so powerful is that it is a very flexible data structure that can be adapted for an amazingly wide variety of purposes. One of the most powerful forms of the pattern object is the *reference* form, which is a pattern with a null action component. The reference form only acts as a direct link between the entry point situation and the list of exit points. The common use of a reference form is the *name* pattern that connects a situation to different exits based on a name and an evaluation, or to sibling patterns. This seemingly simple pattern actually forms the basis of abstract thought by creating the facility of indirection that allows ideas to refer to other ideas or collections of ideas rather than just to things or experiences. The name pattern also happens to be the final element required for a cognitive unit to be able to achieve self

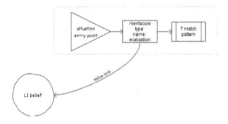

Figure 16.2: Name Pattern Object

awareness by first collecting a set of self-initiated functions and then associating those together via a name pattern, and calling it 'me'.

The truth value in a reference form comes from a value link to an L0 truth coordinate. When reference forms are learned through pattern assimilation, such as through religious or cultural education, then the value link terminus coordinate is specified as part of the learned pattern.

16.3 Data Objects Review

A cognitive level includes both the data structure and the functions encoded in the genome that endow the creature with the ability to spontaneously generate instructions, in real time, to guide its timely response both to the familiar and to the unknown and unexpected, so that it can move in a self-preferential way, even in novel situations, and does so successfully enough for a sufficient percentage of the generation to survive to propagate the species.

The data objects from the various levels of intellect are different, are acted upon by different functions (or different implementations of functions), and solve different problems. To put L2 patterns in perspective, we conclude with a quick review of all the levels we have discussed.

16.3.1   L0 Models Present Input

L0, the most primitive level, processes sensory input simply to decide whether to retreat or advance (roughly speaking); it accomplishes this through a reductive perception process that reduces the infinite number of possible perceptions down to a discrete few interpretations that it knows how to handle using instructions encoded in its genome. That is, L0 interprets *other* in terms of *self* to determine how to move *now*.

16.3.2   L1 Models The Past

L1 adds memory to L0; this means that if L1 recognizes a situation, it can immediately execute a ready movement solution. L1 memory supports learning, and learning in a stable ecological niche enhances survival potential in that niche. L1 learning can also free a population of individuals from the narrow requirements of the niche of their birth by adding the capability to program advanced behavior from experience, rather than being restricted to behavior that can be computed from basic abilities that are described in genes.

16.3.3   L2 Models The Future

L2 adds patterns to L1, thus adding functionality such as language, planning, anticipation, and sequencing to the cognitive capacity. When confronted with a situation, L2 can search memory for a result set of patterns with similar entry points, and it can then sort those by greatest threat or opportunity, and initiate action on that plan immediately, well before an actual threat is sighted.

16.3.4 L3 Models The Unknown

See volume 4 in this series.

16.4 Review

- Patterns enable us to proactively respond to situations.
- The pattern processing engine returns a high percentage of false positive results, alerting us to things that never happen.
- Pattern structure: pre-situation → action → ◊ → array of exit patterns
- The exit pattern selection algorithm is part of the learned pattern.
- Name patterns combined with container patterns form the basis of abstract thought and self-awareness.

Chapter 17

Events

17.1   Introduction

Lynch pin arguments support an entire idea complex. Knock out one of them, and you have felled the entire framework. Illustrative arguments are not as serious, they are usually not even actually part of the argument line, but are just marginal illustrations added to help the reader conceptualize the abstractions being discussed. In this chapter, and in many other places throughout this work, such marginalia is offered in an attempt to aid the reader's attempt to grasp both the meaning and the implication of ream after ream of abstractions on top of abstractions. The event model discussed here is leveraged in a later chapter, but the discussion of time and events in this chapter are primarily provided merely as helpful illustrations.

17.2   Time

Time, in both the cytomodel and the computer, is not a philosophical concept of any significance, but really is just the effect
created by the pulse or sequence of events. In an evolved cognitive entity, the process of needing and consuming energy creates
a pulse of events that is picked up by the internal senses, and
this periodically triggers a sensorium scan that is captured in
a snapshot and evaluated. In computers using dynamic memory, the clock mechanism sends electrical pulses through the
transistors x times a second to perform operations and preserve
the memory state, thus defining a forward progress of events. In
atomic reality, motion occurs at varying rates, but is ineluctable,
and a sequence of motions defines the process of time.

In the cytomodel, the concept of life is defined by a succession of events that use energy liberated from the environment
to sustain the self, and it only terminates in death. Non-life, in
contrast, has no self to maintain, is indifferent to change, and
does not have or need a diurnal energy acquisition and con-
sumption cycle. The process of converting material into energy
to drive function creates a hard base line of events that defines
a lifespan.

Thus, there are different ways to create the impression of
time, but there is no way to define time without events. Events
can exist without time, quite easily, in that events always and
only happen in the *now*, and when they do, they create the
circumstances that define the new *now*. By UC9, time is a
synthetic inference of L2, not a thread that exists independently

in reality.

Is it important that there is no passage of time, but just a progression of events? I think so. Our concept of time is an illusion, it arises as an emergent property from the overlay of the experiences of the L0-L2 intellects conceptualizing the present, the past and the future, respectively. Our L2 mind blurs these separate functionalities into a hazy, poorly defined continuum that it calls time. The succession of events in $\mathbb{R}$ is real enough, but the interpretation of that sequence as a *flow of time* is a subjective projection of the cognitive apparatus. Is the cost of this illusion so terrible that it must be corrected now? Yes, actually, it is.

The illusion of time is projected onto reality by the purblind defect that confuses our way of seeing things — a view that is determined by the interplay of specific cognitive functions — with what actually is. The goal of the entire *Pinnacle* effort is to develop rigorous, testable methods for learning how to discover, recognize, and understand reality for what it verifiably is, instead of what we think, or want, it to be. When we find our impressions of reality to be erroneous, and especially when we find those impressions to be comfortable or comforting, this must be our ready signal that now is the time to push through the imaginary walls imprisoning us in our heads, and break out to explore the undiscovered wilderness of reality.

17.3   Events In $\mathbb{R}$

The event-driven paradigm of familiar computer operating systems is not only an apt metaphor for how our intellects work,
it is a natural and useful programming model for simulations of
cognitive entities. In event-driven programming, once the program starts up, it quietly waits in a loop for an event to occur
that it can handle. Events can be driven by user interaction,
interrupts, timers, or messages arriving on ports the system is
listening on. Obviously, the asomatous psyche application uses
this model, but this is one of those cases where it is hard to
imagine that the thing being simulated is all that different from
the program simulating it, at least as far as the basic interaction
design goes.

Events can be observable or inferred. Observable, predictable
events can be tested for membership in $\mathbb{R}$, while unpredictable
events fall into the same class as inferred events, which, of
course, are events that we infer from evidence left behind. Inferred events are of primary interest in the simulation because
the design of the simulation builds on periodic scans of the environment by the asomatous psyche entity. In the program, the
basic unit of time is defined as the period required for the set
of events happening between scans to complete. Thus, the universe is triggered to update to the new state after every cycle.
There are other ways to handle this (actually the simulation
uses/has used two different approaches already, including an
independent clock), but this way either reveals or supports the
illusion of all events as being inferred.

In old film projectors, film advanced at the rate of 24 frames per second, which, with a two-blade shutter system that showed each frame twice, displayed 48 frames per second to create the illusion of smooth action. The illusion of action was created, not by the equipment, but by our brains stitching together the small changes in position made by the subjects, in twenty-fourth of a second intervals, into a continuous flow. Again, no great philosophical truth here, just a question of technical choices, but this example is being used to illustrate the concept of the inferred event, to demonstrate that our minds quite naturally infer from two still photos the event that connects them together into a continuous stream of action.

So, in the simulation, the test entity moves and acts, but all other events occur between scans (unless the clock drives them), and so are inferred by diffing successive perceptions, rather than actually observing them. This is consistent with the understanding that, while senses may produce an analog signal from a continuous input, cognition involves action that require a non-zero amount of time, so it is periodic, rather than continuous.

Consistent with this, events in $\mathbb{R}$ can be easily defined:

Event: an action that moves some $r \in \mathbb{R}$ from (x_0, y_0, z_0) to (x_1, y_1, z_1), or that transitions a state, s_0, to state s_1.

The *move* action is just a change in position. The *state transition* event may just be an accumulation of pulses, rather than some external movement or action. Inferred events can be defined indirectly, as they are in the simulation:

Inferred Event e: $s_0 + e = s_1$; $s_1 - s_0 = e$

That is, the difference between any two successive states can be said to be the result of an event, just as a footprint in the sand can be said to be the result of a footfall. The footprint does not, by itself, prove that a foot attached to a leg of a quadruped or a biped made it, but it doesn't need to. We can merely define the convention that a foot is the thing that makes footprints and reason from there without overreaching our bounds. Similarly, by defining the difference between two situations as an event, we are not necessarily committing to the idea that a single, reproducible event created the change. If our point of interest is exactly the sequence of steps required to effect the observed change, then we would have to narrow the time between the observations to coincide with the difference created by a single, reproducible action. If, however, our interest is focused on the other side, on the succession of states, then it would be valid to model the transition between two states as an event.

This definition lacks the precision to specify how close s_1 and s_0 must be, and reproducibility would be lost if e is not formally defined, but it makes the point that the pre- and post-states are measurable, and the difference is the measure of e. That is, events are not always, or even usually, visible, but by using measurements and tested frameworks, they can be inferred with an error bound.

Events in $\mathbb{R}$, therefore, are what we expect, and are exactly consistent with what we studied in physics and our other science courses.

Take a moment and ask yourself: does this definition of event apply to the subjective realm? Do we need to change, or just augment, this definition for it to work in $\mathbb{CS}$? Why?

17.4 Events in $\mathbb{CS}$

Events in $\mathbb{CS}$ are not as simple as those in $\mathbb{R}$, because $\mathbb{R}$ events have no semantic content, since all information is externally measurable. This is not the case with all $\mathbb{CS}2$ events. We are so used to thinking that the universe is this huge thing and we are just tiny organisms that, despite all of the preceding discussions, we still tend to forget that *our knowledge* of the universe is a tiny thing, much smaller than our cognitive space, and we are just guessing that the larger universe is actually out there, but by **M2** we know that the only thing we can think about is the model inside our head, not the entirety of creation out there.

$\mathbb{CS}1$ includes the action and state events from $\mathbb{R}$, and the event flow diagram for them is nice and simple:

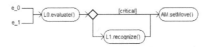

Figure 17.2: Basic Action and State Event Model in $\mathbb{CS}$

Notice that in the model shown in figure 17.2, events can

be either inferred, or real, and nothing seems to be lost for the
simplification. Diff two states and the difference is the event, or
the result of the event. Simple and straightforward. Interestingly, in this model of the 'real' world, we can represent events
as computed, or imaginary, without loss of fidelity.

Perhaps surprisingly, it is only at the level of language processing in L2 that we have to treat events *as* events, because it
is only here that events become undeniably *real*. What makes
events real is that the semantic content they carry cannot be
inferred from reproducible measurements comparing the pre-
and post-event situations in reality because, oddly enough, they
only exist in $\mathbb{CS}$, not in $\mathbb{R}$. Consider the full $\mathbb{CS}$ event model as
shown in figure 17.3.

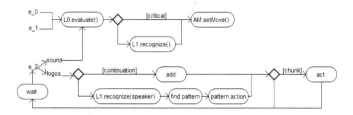

Figure 17.3: Extended Action and State Event Model in $\mathbb{CS}$

The added lower branch shows how messages, e_2 events, are
handled. Beginning at the left, it shows the e_2 message split
into two parts, labeled 'sound' and 'logos' just to distinguish
the physical from the mental attributes of the message.

First, notice that, because L0 can evaluate the significance
of volume, tone, and proximity, the sound attributes of the message are handled by it, just like any other e_0 or e_1 event is, but

since L0 is oblivious to the semantic content of the message, it simply does not recognize, and therefore, does not process it. This shows why you may have a strong emotional response to the volume or tone of someone's voice, before you even begin to consider the content of what they are saying.

Second, notice that the language-enabled pattern processing circuitry of L2 is essentially separate from that of the L0/L1 functionality. This pattern of adding new functionality on top of, and separate from, old functionality is not the only way for evolution to proceed, but it is one way. When animals first developed breathing sacks as the most primitive form of lung, this began as an addition of structure, and eventually became a replacement of structure once the functionality of the new structure was mature enough to completely replace the old. But why would this path be either required or expected when organisms are evolving new ways of cognitively processing information derived from experience? Understand that, while it is certainly not valid to expect evolution to conform to what we think 'makes sense', it is valid to study the facts in front of us and to derive a pattern from them that we can test against new data. It is this approach we have taken in developing this layered model of cognition we are using.

So, the L2 language processing circuit perceives *logos*, words, and processes them. While I suspect that our minds 'hear' sound complexes as large as syllables or words, since the simulation will have to start out by taking in phonemes and constructing words using the rules of a particular pattern language, this is the approach we are modeling. Thus, the first branch is on whether or not we are already in a word. If we are in a word (the top path), we add the new phoneme to the word, then the next branch is on whether or not we can chunk what we have so far, that is, whether or not we have reached a significant level in word assembly. If so, we see if we can act on it in some way (including deriving meaning, building or extending the sentence grammar tree, etc.). If not, we return to the beginning and wait for the next phoneme.

The first alternate path in the diagram handles the initiation of new conversations by checking to see if we recognize the speaker. Not all paths are shown in this simplified diagram, of course, so we don't see what happens if we recognize an enemy and switch from language to action mode, but that can be easily inferred. Otherwise, we find a pattern that matches the situation, and take the prescribed action, which may include beginning to listen. Communication is much more efficient, of course, if the conversation can begin with an explicit context, since this would allow the listener to fill in slots in a conversation template with a few words, instead of having to tease the context from the message or ask that it be stated explicitly.

This diagram sketch is not intended to specify program flow, but rather, is focused on drawing our attention to the structure behind an observable peculiarity of our mental function: the phenomenon of *distraction*. Why are mobile phones implicated in so many traffic accidents? Take a moment and examine the diagram and see if you can see it.

One of the characteristics of electrical circuits — and, make no mistake about it, the paths in the brain are electrical circuits — is that power is drawn by load. If you have a 15 amp circuit servicing a number of electrical outlets in your home, and you attach a 20 amp load to it, it will draw the power it needs until it overheats and blows the circuit breaker, if you are lucky. If, however, you live in an old house with fuses that you have gotten tired of replacing, and so you put a penny behind one of the fuses, rather than blowing the fuse, the excess load will overheat your wires and maybe cause a fire that burns down your house.

The L2 language processing circuit is built to assemble phonemes into words, it is built to wait on the new input it needs to extend its current construct. Look at the diagram, the question is, how is your mental power, your concentration, being divided between the externally aware L0/L1 intellects, and the internally focused L2 intellect? Take the case where you call someone to update them on your location, an innocent, common occurrence that starts out with most of your attention being focused on your driving, and, after dialing is done, almost none being required for you to say you are almost there. But, then they tell you bad news, or start a fight, or say anything that engages L2's anticipation function in dreading awful possibilities, what happens then? What happens is that L2 demands more and more power as more and more possible pattern matches are found suggestive of an exploding branching of possible continuations. In an attempt to tamp down the surging anxiety flowing on the wave of possible bad futures, L2 pulls more and more power to focus on getting the next piece of input that will allow it to zoom in on what is actually going to be happening.

That's when your L0/L1 circuits are so starved for power that they can't even process the color of the traffic light, so you don't notice that it is red, you don't notice the cross traffic is flowing, you run the light, and you die.

While **M9** states that higher levels of intellect cannot impair the functionality of lower levels, this restriction applies to the functionality of the level as a whole. Sleeping, distracted or unwary prey get eaten all the time; natural selection only culls those species who, on average, cannot use their strengths to solve the problems in their survival equation well enough to propagate. This model of cognition was developed to explain some observations, and it has turned out to be very effective in predicting others.

17.5   Message Overload

L2 is a pattern processor. This means exactly that L2 processes patterns, and nothing else. By **M2**, we know that each level of intellect only reasons on its peculiar data structure, and for L2, that is the pattern. Where L0 forms mentacules from sensations it experiences from its internal and external senses, L2 generally forms patterns from patterns. In L0, the internal senses convert what are probably chemical concentrations into experiences of hunger, thirst and the like, but in L2, patterns are generated or appended to patterns based solely on pattern grammar rules. Since the external senses are on the boundary between the body and the environment, and so are exposed to events in $\mathbb{R}$, L0 is exposed to external reality, as well. This means that the set of events in $\mathbb{CS}0$ is somehow related to, or derived from, a subset of the events that occur in $\mathbb{R}$. While the limited genetic lexicon of actionable perceptions in an organism guarantee that internal events are synthesized from a reductive encoding of external events, some relationship can exist, whereas patterns in L2 have no such connection to the outside world.

The upshot of this is that L2 is *not* externally aware. It processes patterns created from results and from pattern manipulation. An additional complication is that the messages that L2 receives are not restricted to communications from other L2 beings. We know from the purblind defect that our mind has a problem distinguishing between internally and externally generated events, so it makes sense, if you think about it, that the vast majority of messages that L2 processes are, in fact, internally generated. L2, as previously discussed, never stops processing, extending and correlating patterns, and each of these events presents as a message on the L2 input channel without the extraneous detail of physical attributes associated with externally sensed messages. This means that the vast majority of reasoning that L2 does is on abstract objects that have no defined relation to external reality. This creates the problem of message overload, where L2 draws so much power processing internally generated messages that it loses sight of external reality for periods of time, sometimes to disastrous effect.

As in the example of traffic distraction discussed above, we can see that structural flaws in our cognitive apparatus *pre-dispose* us to 'lose the plot' of the flow of events occurring in external reality whenever we get absorbed in our habitual pre-occupation with what anticipation patterns portend, as well as with the surge of ideas that flow out endlessly from mindless pattern extension.

17.6   Review

- A sequence of events defines a timeline, not a flow of time.
- In evolved cognitive spaces, the process of needing and consuming energy creates a pulse of events.
- For a cognitive entity, the sequence of events involved in converting material into energy to drive function that starts with birth and ends with death, defines a life timeline.
- Events in $\mathbb{R}$ are defined by movement or state transitions.
- An event is inferred if it is defined by a difference in state: $s_1 - s_0 = e$
- Events in $\mathbb{CS}$ include events in $\mathbb{R}$, and $\mathbb{CS}2$ events.
- Message events have semantic content that only exists in $\mathbb{CS}$, can only be interpreted by cognitive functions at L2 or above.
- Uncontrolled L2 processing can interfere with the timely and efficient function of L0/L1.
- Most L2 message processing handles internally generated messages, that is, concepts in $\mathbb{I}$, not $\mathbb{R}$.

Chapter 18

Container Patterns

18.1 Paths, Plans and Graphs

A path is a primitive cognitive construct, a graph in which *movement* links connect location nodes together. Bees are not only capable of recording and recalling paths, but can even communicate them to other bees, at least to some extent. Squirrels, obviously, have an innate ability to create and recall a map of dozens of locations of food caches. Excluding consideration of migratory and spawning routes for now, because they seem to involve a different class of directional guidance, it seems that the ability to record and recall paths is more common than rare in animals.

A plan is a path through a combination of circumstances and actions, and might be defined as a chain of contingent actions, a graph in which action links connect situation nodes. Roughly speaking, it really is just a path construct that substitutes the more general action and situation concepts for the more basic movement and location terms.

In graph theory, a graph is a model of pairwise relations that is expressed in terms of nodes and links. *Graph* is the abstract concept, an abstract formal model extracted from the concrete examples we encounter in maps, paths, plans and various other instances of relations between entities. Thus, by instantiating a graph with location nodes and movement links, we get a path, or a plan if we use situations and actions. Graphs are called directed if they use one-way links, or undirected if bidirectional travel is allowed. The Pattern object implements the graph model. In essence, a rudimentary version of the pattern object allows bees to learn paths, and nothing more than that.

As mentioned earlier, the current form of the L2 cognition level is a shortcut designed just to support the needs of the project we are working on to build a proof of concept application, the asomatous psyche, to demonstrate that we can explain, account for and predict complex human experiences such as emotions, beliefs and abstract thought using a model built on very simple, genetically encodable structures and instructions. In a formal version of the universal cognition model, L2 would have to be separated into at least several stages, maybe even six or more, to account for the different levels of cognitive capacity that support paths, semiotics, verbal language, and abstract thought.

18.2 Higher Level Thought

Since we are treating these four or more stages of L2 functionality as one level, we have to pause for a moment to explicitly
call out a transition from lower to higher cognitive function
that occurs when the pattern object evolves to the point that
it can contain anything or *nothing*, instead of being restricted
to a single type of object. This is the point where the specific
is generalized to the abstract level, where, for example, instead
of confining addition to integers only, you define it at a higher
type level to support the addition of reals and complex numbers, as well as integers. In executable language terms, this
means creating parameterized functions instead of hard-wiring
each action every time it is used. In a curious, almost poetic
turn of events somewhat reminiscent of the power of zero in
mathematics, the ability to support this simple level of abstraction where *nothing*, as well as something, can be contained,
creates the ability to support high-level abstraction of the sort
that leads to the point where an organic process, executing on
an evolved, organic structure, can achieve self-awareness, and
become conscious.

Our testable assertion is that the asomatous psyche application is, or soon will be, completely capable of becoming self-
aware, of becoming fully conscious. Now, in real life, does anyone want really to deal with computer programs that have their
own opinions, that might refuse to total the figures in your
spreadsheet because they simply don't want to? Of course not,
and not only because it would defeat the purpose of computers,

but also, to be frank, because it would unleash poorly educated ethicists to preach to us why it is immoral to delete sentient programs from our phones. The only excuse for building an application that can achieve self-consciousness, from my point of view, anyway, is to demonstrate the power of model-oriented reasoning, in combination with the universal cognition model, to accurately simulate the entire range of human emotional, intellectual and spiritual experience.

Once we have an executable model of the human mind, we will begin to be able to probe and study not only our thoughts, but our feelings and beliefs, as well. We will begin to be able to understand why we act as we do, and we will even be able to test our beliefs and potential actions *before* we act on them. In other words, we will finally be able to extend the power of scientific learning into the subjective domain of human experience.

The level of abstraction required to do this begins with the very important container pattern. To understand how the container pattern fits into the cognition model, let's review what we have so far:

- Mentacules encapsulate a snapshot of the internal and external senses into a form that can be used in cognitive calculations such as type determination, evaluation, and comparison.
- Results encapsulate before and after states of current memory with the intervening action to support the evaluation of actions, which leverages memory to make learning from experience possible.

- Patterns support contingent path definition by providing
  continuation options following an action result based on
  comparison of the post-action situation with the entry
  situations in the array of exit patterns.

Note that mentacules encapsulate sensory state, results operate on mentacules, and pre-language patterns are built from results. At this level of development, essentially all thought deals directly or indirectly with sensory experience; the structures at the heart of each level of cognition are strictly experience-based. This all changes when we add the capability of processing container patterns.

18.3 Container Object

One might think an idea with content is more powerful than one without, but a container idea is a contentless idea that only has structure—this makes a container a meta-idea, an idea that can define relations between pattern ideas. Container patterns reference content, but the container itself exists at the level above content, it isn't content itself, at least not the same level of content. The power in this change is that by structuring elements, the container pattern defines *relations* between elements, it creates a new, higher level of thought, one where we can not only think about *things*, but for the first time, we can now think about the *relations between* things. The concept of a relation between entities a and b is an invention of the container structure.

You can think about a dog without getting abstract, but only by thinking about a collection of dogs can you generalize, define types, etc. The container object gives us the ability to collect ideas and think about them, a very powerful ability, but very easily achieved.

For example, the abstraction of enumeration comes from the realization that 3 oranges are like 3 apples in that taking 1 away from either leaves 2. Enumeration is a way of thinking of concrete objects from an abstract level that supports useful and reproducible calculations on those objects that is simply not possible without the abstraction. Add to that, that once you have a collection of, say, dogs, regardless of breed, and another of cats, regardless of breed, now all of the known reasoning operations can be performed on these higher level collection objects that previously could only be used on direct experience objects. The dog and cat collection objects can now be generalized to the animal object, etc.

A container pattern is defined as a pattern object that has:

- A description,
- An evaluation,
- No asynchronous action,
- An optional synchronous action,
- Zero or more sets of elements.

The description or name field is actually a name pattern object that supplies a first level of indirection that allows us to reference an idea or collection of ideas as an idea itself. The evaluation field is a value link to a value position in the singularity distortion field. Any actions on the container object must operate directly and immediately on the object itself, they cannot specify actions that are either asynchronous, or that operate at a level below the abstraction, such as moving the body. A collection is an abstract entity that does not exist on the physical plane—it may represent a visible set of entities, but its conceptual reach extends only so far as the cognitive objects it contains. The term *set* in the last condition is used in the formal sense in that set membership is restricted by a selector of some sort that includes some, and excludes other, elements.

In the next chapters, we will be discussing some very important container patterns: attitudes, beliefs, and opinions. They are structured differently, and have very different uses and functionality, but are just different instantiations of the container pattern.

18.4   Abstraction

The most striking feature of the container pattern is that it supports meta-thought, i.e., thoughts *about* thoughts. Whereas mentacules, results and patterns support thoughts about things, container patterns support exactly what we are discussing now: ideas *about* ideas. This is where advanced reasoning begins. What made Plato and Aristotle stand out in the history of western civilization was their — at the time — pre-eminent ability to form concepts and frameworks to support thinking *about* what we think *about* what we experience. The extra level of abstraction was unusual at the time, and they were distinguished from their contemporaries who thought more about action and experience, rather than about thought itself.

Perhaps the most powerful aspect of the container pattern is that it not only creates this first new, higher level of abstraction, it also simultaneously creates an unlimited capacity for additional levels of abstraction. This is reminiscent of the way that set theory can be used to create a theoretical basis for arithmetic:

- a null set, s, has 0 elements
- adding a null set, t, to s, results in s having 1 element, and so on.

This gives theoreticians a way to bootstrap the number system without having to assume the existence of anything, since the set concept is just defined as a collection with zero or more unique elements, and the proof uses nothing but null sets.

Container patterns can contain normal patterns, or other container patterns that can contain normal patterns or other container patterns, and so on. Thus, container patterns create the capability to define unlimited levels of abstraction.

In the Java language, the joke is that all programs can be improved by adding another layer of indirection, and while that is most certainly false, the fact is that each layer of abstraction comes with a complexity cost, but it also offers a benefit of a new set of relations between the abstractions on the level

below. Ultimately, new levels of abstraction are only generally
accepted when their benefit far outweighs their complexity cost.
At the level of the container pattern, the benefit to be gained
is language and language-based civilization itself. A few levels
of abstraction higher than that brought us the frameworks that
support the scientific revolution and the development of liberal
western democracies, the highest achievements of civilization to
date. The cost of each additional level of abstraction, of course,
is that not everyone can keep up.

18.5   Review

- A path is a graph that connects locations with movements.
- A plan is a path that connects situations with actions.
- A graph is a model of pairwise relations that is expressed
  in terms of nodes and links.
- The pattern object implements the graph abstraction.
- Container patterns form the basis for abstract thought.
- Container pattern is a structure that has a description,
  an evaluation, no asynchronous action, an optional syn-
  chronous action, and zero or more sets of elements.

Part II

Intermediate Topics

Chapter 19

Groups

19.1 Introduction

Groups don't actually exist; there is nothing in $\mathbb{R}$ that we can point to and measure and say, "That is a group." We can see a crowd of people and call them a group, but are they an actual unit, or are they an accidental, temporary collection who have nothing in common beyond the moment, like commuters at a railway station? Wolves may hunt in a pack, and lions in a pride, but do even these groups exist independently of the genetically encoded, but nonetheless individual act of joining and cooperating? Given a list of names, we can read it as a membership roster of a club or congregation, and say it represents a group, but, while the readable list may exist in $\mathbb{R}$, the group, itself, still does not.

No, groups do not exist per se; *grouping* is an action an individual takes in order to extend his state of self beyond the confines of his own body and its ability to claim and maintain his interest swath. An individual may, by grouping with others, surrender some of his autonomy to the legal machinery of society, and give them the right to use violence to compel his attendance and behavior. In more primitive societies that dominate much of the world today, the act of being born is construed as a surrender of autonomy, as an acceptance that being enslaved is a requirement for survival; in these cases, grouping may be seen more as something others do to you, than something you do yourself. But, in any of these cases, grouping remains an action by which the actions of affected individuals are devoted, or more or less conscripted, to the service of the extended-self entity, regardless of who is doing the grouping action.

We are so used to thinking of groups as being actual entities that it is hard to even entertain the notion that they are not. Granted, when confronting an army in the field, the soldiers facing you sure seem to be a unit, a group, that will coordinate their attack to the limit of their training, yet, while it may be true that they will act like a group for a while, still, in reality no such entity as an actual group exists. Is this just sophistry? No, this is a substantive point, as you can see for yourself by reviewing military history of battles. What you will see is that, until relatively recently, as a general rule, overwhelming victories that turn into a rout begin with the break down of unit discipline which happens early in the conflict, about the time the losing army's casualty rate is only around 10%. The great slaughters of history invariably occurred after the soldiers stopped acting

like members of an army and began to run for their individual
lives. No, armies are not groups, but are *groupings* of men organized on cultural principles that build an association with a
characteristic coherence in the face of stress. Groups only seem
to exist as long as their members will them into existence by
continuing to act in concert.

Is this a distinction without a difference? Hardly, what this
means is that, primitive religious slave societies aside, we, as
individuals, are entirely responsible not only for our group's actions, but also for its very existence. And, even in the slave
societies, as soon as a relatively small percentage of the population decides that the group is no longer valid, it immediately
begins to break down completely. Groups don't exist, grouping
people do.

19.2 Rule Object

Because we will need it in the next section, let's pause for a
moment and define the rule object. We are doing this in passing,
rather than giving it its own chapter because the pattern object
exactly as it is, without any modification, is the rule object.
The pattern object associates a single entry point with up to
approximately seven exit points as selected by the rule in the
object. Most often, I have referred to the exit selector as a vector
angle comparison because it is such a fundamental operation,
but there is no limit on the type of selector function a pattern
can use. Just think of all the spelling lessons you have had, all
of the foreign language grammar you have studied, all of the

math theories and problems you have worked—the homework you had to do was designed to force you to learn how the selector rule should work to pick the correct exit branch in the pattern you were studying.

We don't have to spend much time discussing the rule object because we have been discussing it all along. 'Rule object' is just a name, a helpful name, but just a name that points to the familiar pattern object we have been using all along.

19.3   Grouping Object

The grouping object, shown in figure 19.1, is simplicity itself, comprising, as it does, only a name, a value link, an exit point selector rule, and three exit points: a belief set object, a membership rules object, and a conduct rules object. In the beginning, it may be easier to understand the concept of a grouping object if you picture the value link from the object as linking to some very high value position near the core of the singularity where the measure of self-interest increases to the maximum limit, because the most powerful groupings we create are those we are willing to kill, or die for. The lesser groups, like the bridge club, the bowling team, etc., simply have a relatively trivial self-related value link, i.e., they may be our team, our group, but the association is more temporary and situational, than a life and death connection. The life and death groupings are the ones that shape our lives. The other ones are just the intermediate vines we swing on as we transit from tree to tree, while moving through our lives.

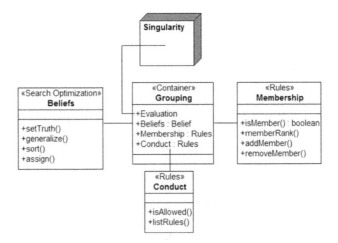

Figure 19.1: Grouping object

Grouping is the act of self-extension, if we use the cognitive space geometry model, it is the process of expanding the singularity distortion field (see figure 19.2) to encompass others in the definition of self. If we use the value link model, grouping is just the act of assigning a high self value link to a grouping object that defines a set of members with a set membership rule. Grouping is the act of conflating one's personal interests with those of others included by the membership rule. Grouping is done to enhance one's *sense* (meaning intuitive evaluation) of viability, whether the promised benefit is through hope of material gain, spiritual consequence, emotional connection, or any other goal, and it matters not if reality immediately contradicts the hopeful expectation.

The value link in a grouping object determines how closely

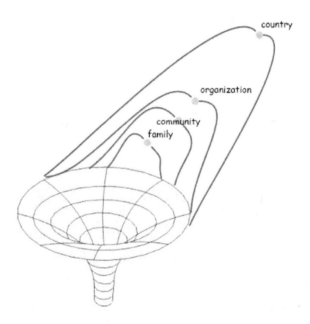

Figure 19.2: Groups extend the singularity distortion field.

we identify the grouping's interests with our own survival needs, while the value link in the contained belief object determines the gravity of the associated beliefs. The grouping's interests are defined both by the belief object that spells out the group's beliefs, as well as by the common self-interest one shares with the other members (which varies with their position in the group and personal relationship with us).

The membership rules are an essential part of the object; a grouping without a membership rule including some, while excluding others, cannot survive, because it would vitiate, rather than strengthen and extend, the definition of self into the extended self. An extended self with no limit obliterates the self by erasing its definitional boundary. A cell with just the goo and no cell wall is not a cell — life, itself, is the process of defining and maintaining an internal space by selectively incorporating external resources and excreting spent internal material. Without the boundary, there is no cell, no self, no group.

The conduct rules of a grouping are the laws, rules or creed the grouping's leaders deem important for maintaining group cohesion as well as for coordinating members' efforts to the common goal. One of the benefits of a grouping's imposed rule set, is that it acts like a loopback in the sense that it sets a boundary on the world, a limit beyond which one should neither go, nor think. In effect, group rules erect a barrier against the unbounded unknown. Rules act like walls in our minds that keep us within a comfortable, known area that we seem to share with other group members. This commonality has the effect

of rescuing us from our otherwise perpetual drift in the vast
darkness of solitary ignorance and weakness.

Daniel Moynihan once wrote that, "freedom lives in the in-
terstices of authority", and while either the wording or senti-
ment of that may be debatable, nevertheless, the flaws in L2
that produce the toxic idea fountain must be compensated for
by mental structures that limit the ability of anxious ideas to
overstimulate our minds without bound. The required constraints come in many forms from belief to impotent cynicism;
from commitment to a cause, to acceptance of authority. However expensive the constraints of group rules may be, the L2
mind cannot function without them. In fact, its need for them
is so great that, should an accident of history free one from the
sway of all groups, the mind will instantly begin to contrive new
groupings with new rules, which will likely be even worse than
those it just discarded.

19.4   Benefits of Grouping

In cognitive spaces, abstraction creates the platform for higher
level thought. Of course, this is just a general principle, and
can be misused, such as by academic philosophy, but as a rule
of thumb, it is pretty sound. The grouping object creates a
conceptual container supporting a higher level human calculus
that generates and supports civilization. Groupings of people
are capable of achieving things forever beyond the reach of the
isolated individual, starting, for example, with language and the
rules and rituals that make dense populations possible. Spe-

cialization, which creates excellence and encourages genius, is not possible without the benefit of an interlocking network of groups.

If your philosophy includes the value that progress is good, that humanity is progressing from a ruder, more primitive state to a more complex, elaborate, and productive one, then the problems and potential of groups seem to be an inescapable concern. Whether we take the collegial or the isolated path in our own work, we necessarily launch our efforts from the culture of our ancestors, and what we produce will inevitably be judged by our successors. High level thought is a product of civilization, of grouping, even if all of the work on a particular project, such as this one, has been done in complete isolation, unaided by, and invisible to, the surrounding culture.

We cannot avoid the reality that grouping creates the context for invention, just as it creates much of the need for it. When I began this project to figure out how to finally create the tools required to tackle pinnacle questions for the first time, my original interest was on the social suffering recorded in history, and I used antisemitism as my primary focus, thinking that if I could explain its never-ending horror, then I would be onto something.

The resources and need for, and validation of, invention arises from social need and benefit. While the focus in this work is strictly on the nature and function of the cognitive unit, the math and computer science concepts used to model our mind come from the culture into which we were born, and the benefit of the work will flow back to it, as well. That is, while virtually all of the significant ideas explained in this work came solely from the learning discovery process described in detail elsewhere, it would not have been possible to even begin this work without the rich intellectual history that had been developing right up to this year.

19.5   Risks of Grouping

The preceding apology for grouping was only necessitated by my own, personal, inveterate hostility to any and all groups. Much of my hostility arises from the abject failure of the university system to stumble upon even a glimmer of understanding about what the nature and function of education really is, even after almost a millennium of existence.

The reason all of the work in this series of volumes had to be done by me, alone, is because our educational institutions have not only failed to support and extend education, but are actually actively hostile to it. Pushing pattern manipulation training in support of the erudition fallacy is no more related to education than making mud pies is to haute cuisine, and, outside of the recent support of the hard sciences, this is really all they have ever done.

While having to spend my entire life fighting this cultural and institutional hostility to education has been very frustrating and infuriating, the concepts discussed in the current volume make it clear that it was also unavoidable. Grouping is an L0-L2 activity whose entire function is to extend the singularity distortion field (see figure 19.2). Why? Because this, on average, makes us individually stronger, and more likely to survive to procreate.

Decision and action are the province of L0/L1. Decision is ultimately the choice to go *this* or *that* way, to take one action or another, or none. Although we may have many alternatives to choose from, in any given situation, in the final analysis, the decision function is a binary one: do or not do any one or all of the optional actions available to us that we have evaluated as a mixture of anti-self, pro-self, or non-self values.

Grouping is the process by which the reach of the self is extended, it is how *I* becomes part of *we*, it is entirely an L0/L1 self-interest extension mechanism that is made possible by the earliest phases of L2 that support planning and semiotics. Once a species is capable of recognizing other members as an extension of self, and can make signs or signals to communicate intention, then we have the necessary and sufficient conditions for meaningful grouping behavior.

This is why grouping behavior is necessarily expressed in L0/L1 terms of right and wrong, us and them, valuable and worthless, because grouping is all about the pursuit of interest, and nothing about the value or reality of other. Whereas reality-based discussions will always involve reproducible measurements, group-based discussions will always focus on right and wrong, true and false, friend and enemy, to the exclusion of any other consideration.

Groupings are mechanisms whose primary function is to further the interest of the important members, and the effects of a grouping's actions are the product, in the multiplicative sense, of the effects of the actions of its members, so it should go without saying that groupings can have very negative effects on any outsiders identified as an obstacle to interest.

In other words, groupings are power amplifiers, and the increased power will be used in the service of certain interests and to the disadvantage of others. Judging one grouping's actions from another's perspective is simultaneously both valid and ridiculous: discussing any singularity phenomenon from the perspective of another singularity can only yield the result that could be expected from computing the degree of competition as the product of the groupings' power times the strength of their commitment for the disputed resource.

There is no basis for ethical or moral discussions on group actions except as a means for a weaker opponent to try to hobble the stronger one. Interest battles are fought on the field of conflict where they occur, not all of which are violent, but many of which certainly are. Philosophical wrangling about right and wrong, though, ignores the self-justifying nature of the singularity. It is absolutely valid to deplore and oppose the actions of any grouping, but not until chapter 30 will we have the tools to understand the nature of the argument from a perspective loftier than the claim of, "we're right, and they're wrong".

Interest battles are won with strength, however it happens to be measured in a particular conflict. Certainly, our current tendency to restrict interest battles to commercial struggles and small armed conflicts seems better, for most of us, at least, than global conflagrations would be, but this doesn't alter the fundamental nature of the biological struggle for scarce resources. From the singularity's point of view, 'good' is that which preserves and extends its own viability, and 'bad' is that which threatens it.

Groupings are no more rational than the workings of any of its cognitive units, and probably less so, due to the fact that the decision makers tend to be insulated from the bad effects of their decisions by the bodies of less important members. This layer of protection allows the leaders to press on further with internal knowledge delusions than they otherwise would if they, themselves, were the first ones to be pushed off the cliff.

Groupings can, and do, trade verifiable destruction in $\mathbb{R}$, in return for some imaginary benefit in $\mathbb{I}$ or $\mathbb{S}$, but this is only to be expected because the purblind defect prevents us from seeing that elements in $\mathbb{I}$ may not even exist in $\mathbb{R}$. This leads us to exchange the real and external, for the apparent and internal, all the time: people contribute hard-earned money to churches for spiritual salvation everyday. The most common example of this trade of r for i, in fact, is seen in the outermost reaches of every group, where the peasants actually give up real value in return for internal knowledge comforts as a matter of routine. Generally, only the inner members in a group actually gain a material benefit from their membership, although in some modern societies, the radius of benefit is very large.

19.6   Mechanisms of Grouping

Grouping is made possible by the ability to effect meaningful communication that enables individuals to coordinate their efforts to a common goal: wolves, dolphins, lions but not leopards, and so on. Speaking as one with no interest or background in the study of biology to speak of, I would suggest that schooling in fish, ant colonies and bee hives seem to be examples of the most elementary form of grouping, although the complexity of ant and bee societies is not covered by the current model.

I am using the term *semiotics* to refer to the act, as well as the study of, communication through signs and signals, or gestures, sounds and probably scent sometimes. In the current model, this stage of cognitive evolution is just compressed into L2 along with verbal language, but clearly this capability is much more broadly distributed than is speech. However, since my focus is on what we humans need to learn to be able to begin answering pinnacle questions, I give the semiotic level short shrift.

So, the ability to recognize others as an extension of self, coupled with some rudimentary level of memory, and the ability to communicate intent, forms the basis for the grouping ability, even up to the level of human society. Of course, with the benefit of verbal language, even though our ratiocinative ability is not generally adequate to support self-awareness that reaches the level of being able to understand the perceptual distortions that are created by the purblind defect, humans are able to create fairly complex groupings that are, nevertheless, governed by the very primitive mechanisms explained in this chapter.

We have an L0/L1 interest in, and proclivity towards, group-ing as a way of amplifying our power, both proactively and re-actively. Proactive, in the sense that a group of hunters can achieve much that an individual hunter cannot; reactive, in the sense that there is an arms race in grouping that puts you at a distinct disadvantage if your competitors exercise grouping more effectively than you.

We have an L2 interest in grouping as a means of managing the cognitive instability inherent in the L2 anticipation mech-anism: we have the ability to elaborate an endless number of threat scenarios that disturb our pattern processing mechanism, and being able to imagine that our allies will fight along side us neutralizes many, and maybe most, of our most troubling nightmare scenarios.

The fundamental grouping relation is simply that:

$$\text{if } |they| > |me| \text{ and}$$

$$|us| > |me|$$

$$\text{then if } |us| \ngtr |them|$$

$$increase(us)$$

That is, if they are more powerful than me, and I belong to a group larger than myself, and my group is not more powerful than they are, then I can act to increase my group until it is. The brilliance of grouping is that it represents a method to have viability-relevant power on tap. That is, as individuals, we are largely limited by our phenotype, but by introducing the higher organization level of grouping, we transcend that blueprint constraint, and suddenly find ourselves able to increase our power to an unimaginable extent, limited only by our grouping ability.

What is the essence of grouping ability? Three very relevant L0/L1 attributes: energy, vision and focus. Energy is a measure of strength and viability; groups tend to collect around stronger, rather than weaker, leaders. Vision is the ability to chart a course over the horizon, a visceral ability to orient oneself and others to distant goals. Focus is the ability to evaluate threats well, regardless of the distractions and dangers of the moment. These are fundamental viability measures for any mobile creature, and a pack leader's tendency to excel in these areas draws followers to them, amplifies followers' strength through coordination, and quiets followers' anxieties through the leadership loopback.

19.7   Summary

The suggestion is not that one shouldn't study groups, just that 'group' is a fairly expensive abstraction to collectivize the grouping actions of individuals. When one tries to hew to the evolutionary cytomodel, one is forced to ask what heritable structure produces the group? In this chapter, we have examined mechanisms of individual action called grouping, and discussed both a simple object that makes it possible, as well as the flawed mutation that creates a persistent need for it.

Grouping involves visible actions that can be readily observed almost anywhere at almost anytime. The anxiety that drives people to seek comfort in grouping is also observable both physiologically and behaviorally. But, that anything we observe can be verified to be a group is highly dubious because of the difficulty to be found in the attempt to define a rule to reproducibly specify inclusion and exclusion conditions. When we observe what we take to be a group as a thing in itself, what we are seeing is the product of the coordination of a number of individuals by the rules and methods described in a grouping object.

It is a mistake to imagine that groups exist aside from their members, that each and every engaged member is not entirely responsible for everything that group does.

19.8 Review

- Groups don't exist, grouping people do.
- Grouping joins and coordinates one with others to extend one's power.
- The rule object is a standard pattern object.
- The grouping object joins beliefs, conduct and membership criteria to govern a collective.
- The value link in the grouping determines our connection to the collective: from life and death, to only for the moment.
- Group rules trade one's independence for strength and comfort.
- Groupings multiply the power of the members, they don't just add it.
- Grouping requires that members recognize each other and

can signal intent.

- Groupings amplify the power of the members to further some interests at the cost of others.

- Groupings use power to achieve important goals. Importance can be defined in $\mathbb{I}$ or $\mathbb{S}$ as easily as in $\mathbb{R}$.

- Grouping is a method to have viability-relevant power on tap.

- Group leadership involves: energy, vision and focus.

Chapter 20

Facts

20.1 Introduction

We all know what a fact is: something that actually happened, or, more properly, a verbal reference to a thing or event that demonstrably exists or happened in ℝ. But, the *thing* itself is not the fact, it is just whatever it is; it is the *reference* to the thing or the description of the event that is the fact. In common parlance, of course, we mistakenly refer to the *thing* as the fact, and see our reference to it as a perfect, transparent lens that neither adds to, nor subtracts from, the reality of the fact.

But, no matter how obvious this elementary definition of the word is, it differs significantly from what we find in our dictionaries. First, we have the Oxford English Dictionary:

(1) a thing done or performed

(4) Something that has really occurred or is actually the case; something certainly known to be of this character;

317

hence, a particular truth known by actual observation or
authentic testimony, as opposed to what is merely inferred,
or to a conjecture or fiction; a datum of experience, as distinguished from the conclusions that may be based upon
it.

Next, American Heritage:

(1) Something known with certainty

(2) Something asserted as certain

(3) Something that has been objectively verified

(4) Something having real, demonstrable existence

Google: [A fact is] a thing that is:

- indisputably the case

- used in discussing the significance of something that is the
case

- a piece of information used as evidence or as part of a report
or news article

Dictionary.com:

(1) something that actually exists; reality; truth

(2) something known to exist or to have happened

(3) a truth known by actual experience or observation;
something known to be true

(4) something said to be true or supposed to have happened

And Merriam-Webster:

(1) a thing done

(3) the quality of being actual

(4) a: something that has actual existence,

b: an actual occurrence

(5) a piece of information presented as having objective reality

None of these definitions, of course, respect the difference between the reference and the referent. By **M2**, we know can only think in mental models, so a fact can only be a mental model that fulfills certain requirements. What those exact requirements are, though, get curiouser and curiouser as we read deeper through each definition above. Starting with the OED mention of "authentic testimony", to Am-Her: "something asserted as certain", Google: "information used as evidence", and then we get to the last two: Dictionary.com: "something said to be true", and Mer-Web: "information presented as having objective reality." It appears that a fact can be anything in the range from the real and verified, to the subjective and imaginary.

We aren't criticizing the dictionaries, they are descriptive, not prescriptive, so they are just reporting the rather loose way the word is actually used in real life. Sometimes, it seems that the modern definition of fact is, "something that supports my opinion," and it turns out that there is a structural reason for this apparent debasement of the word.

The traditional ideas about facts described in these definitions are based on the fallacy that we directly perceive an objective reality. When we add this fallacy together with the

undisciplined, informal, inconsistent, and untestable model of
the human mind that everyone uses, we have two of the central
lumps in the common mudball model of cognition that is used
by both the lettered and unwashed alike. The common, mudball understanding is that **facts** are *true*, while opinions (other
than our own) are merely subjective. But, does this make any
sense at all?

   To answer that question, let us reexamine what a fact is
from the model-oriented reasoning perspective and see what
we can see. The very first thing that jumps out at us is that,
obviously, a *fact* is an L2 verbal construct, not a reality, it is the
mental abstraction we use to refer to the presumably objective
reality. We already know a great deal about L2 constructs, so
let's review and approach the subject from that direction. L2
verbal constructs are:

- the work product of an intellect that is insulated from
  reality;

- patterns connected by the grammar of a specific pattern
  language;

- extensible, and their structure supports degrees of truth;

- error prone constructs, in which errors are optionally identified after the fact by checking the construct against the
  grammar specified by the pattern language;

- entities whose truth value is set by a value link to an
  L0 position in the singularity distortion, independent of
  whatever errors they might contain.

   A fact is a verbal construct—it is the reference, not the

referent. This reference may or may not refer to a reality that does or does not exist, and if it exists, it may or may not exist as stated, with no bound on the possible variance. That is, we know that a 'fact' *cannot* be a **fact** in the traditional sense of being an indisputably accurate snapshot of reality. Since the L2 level does not have any mechanism to automatically verify that a fact actually corresponds to anything in reality, then facts, as L2 constructs, can only be shown to have an indirect connection to reality through some kind of optional verification mechanism that has some, perhaps unknown, level of reliability.

This is not to gainsay that things actually exist, that events actually occur, but it is to remind us that we are now discussing our mental conception of the externality, not the externality itself.

If we look at facts from the perspective of context, they can either be situated or naked. A fact that is part of an opinion or belief system is situated in that larger context, and it is that surrounding system that has value and meaning, not the fact. Situated facts are severable from the context in which they are used, because it is the context that is important, while the fact is just part of the infantry that serves to support it. Naked facts, in contrast, are isolated facts that have no value links. Naked facts normally have an evaluation of high non-self, meaning that we are indifferent to whether they are falsified or verified, because they just have no value to us, they don't really have any meaning beyond their content.

Therefore, situated facts have a truth value, but they have a truth value only in the sense that the moon shines light on the earth—it is merely reflected from the source, it does not emanate from the fact itself. Situated facts' truth is proportional to their position in relation to their containing belief. Naked facts generally do not have a truth value above an indifferent level. Saying that situated facts have a truth value is not the same as saying that they are true, of course, it is just saying that the certainty that the fact is right or wrong is very high. For example, to most believers, saying that Satan is a god would be judged to be both false and wrong, despite the fact that he fits the definition to a T.

True, situated facts are reassuring because they support the surrounding narrative, the system into which they have been incorporated. Facts that somehow attain a truth value despite contradicting the enclosing belief are challenging facts. These are uncomfortable precisely because they expose the subjective nature of the belief system, and contradict its claim to represent absolute truth in a way that is corrosive of one's belief in a stable, known and ordered universe. Challenging facts are usually handled much like splinters: they are either plucked out, or encysted to isolate them from the surrounding environment, but in either case, they are painful and annoying until they are resolved.

Facts can be verified or contradicted, either formally by experiment, or informally by experience. True, situated, reassuring facts that are verified have no change in state, while those that are contradicted may enter the process of severance in which they are isolated, devalued or ejected in order to preserve the truth of the surrounding belief. Naked facts that are contradicted have nothing to save them, they are simply tagged as false and left at that, but those that are verified have a different fate that depends on the value system of the cognitive entity. Those of us who are fond of verified facts, and take pride in including them in our opinions whenever possible, are likely to upgrade verified naked facts by including them in some higher level value system.

Verification can come from several sources: authority, experience, experiment or value. Verification by authority has a value proportional to that which we assign to the authority, and this can, in general, mostly maintain or increase the esteem we have for the belief system holding the fact, but it is nothing more than a value link to a belief. Verification by experience is the stuff of ordinary life, and this just reinforces our previous evaluation of the fact, it is anecdotal evidence of undefined reliability just like all other anecdotal evidence. Verification by experiment requires formal tests with error tolerances and mostly applies to naked facts. Verification by value is similar to verification by authority, with the authority being the value system that makes things true because they must be true to support other beliefs.

If verification by experiment does not cause uptake of the fact by some belief or authority system, then it is only persuasive to those with the professional ability to judge the experimental results. For those of us with a scientific background but without the means or interest to examine the tests or the data, experimental results can only be accepted on faith, unless we have a healthy and active skeptical eye and our fact structure supports maintaining a tally of validating and contradicting tests. Even among scientific minds, this level of sophistication is fairly rare, and most will revert to the shortcut of just adding a value link to a truth value in the distortion field.

Finally, the referents that facts point to are either a *thing* that may or may not exist in reality, or an *event* that may or may not have occurred as described in reality. Let us consider these two types one at a time.

20.1.1   Thing-Fact

If we consider thing-facts from a model-oriented reasoning perspective, they are very easy to understand, because this is just the familiar case of how an internal knowledge idea (the verbal reference) relates to verifiable reality (the referent), and the definition of that relation is clear and simple:

$$t_n(i) \rightarrow r_n \in \mathbb{R}$$

where a test, t, verifies that internal idea, i, maps to an observed external reality, r, in n dimensions. This is different than saying that fact i is true in the classical sense, it just means that it has been verified in the ways specified.

The case is a little muddier, of course, when we consider thing-facts from a mudball perspective, because here it refers not to verifiability, but to an idea's membership in a belief system. That is, a fact can only be true in the region of a belief if it belongs to the belief system. Determining a fact's set membership should be an easy problem for formal methods to solve, but the application of formal methods in the extremity of the singularity distortion field is a technically difficult issue because it requires not only the formal proof of membership state, but also requires the *belief* case to be made that the chosen formal methods are valid in your opponent's self-interest distortion field where their beliefs interpret everything self-preferentially.

Does 2 + 2 = 4 everywhere? Why would you think it should? You are forgetting that in the singularity distortion field, nothing is allowed to attack the self, so even addition may be falsified if it gives a threatening answer.

Proving thing-facts in purblind reasoning requires that we go beyond experimental verification to consider authority, experience and value issues.

Authority thing-facts can only be 'proven' to a debate opponent by referencing an accepted authority of *theirs*, and even that is not enough. Where you think you are just trying to prove the truth of an idea, when that idea falls within the scope of a belief, what you are actually trying to do is to persuade your opponent to get off their train, walk to a station, buy a new ticket, and get on a new train heading off into an entirely new life. If you think that is a little over the top, then recall that truth has nothing to do with verifiability, and is strictly concerned with which path should be followed. Converting someone to your belief — which is what you are trying to do if you are talking about the truth of thing-facts — requires a conversion experience, in all its glory. If you really only want to talk about thing-fact verifiability, then you must abjure appeals to truth and concentrate on reproducible measurement, but this cannot be done in an authority discussion.

Experience verification can be achieved through anecdotal evidence that your opponent finds persuasive in the sense of being convinced to switch trains again. This often requires that the persuasive evidence must be further sweetened with an implicit or explicit promise of new group acceptance and approbation, that is, that they will be welcome in the party on your train.

Experience verification is based on L1 result objects being described in L2 terms, so the touchstone of truth being used is a personal and primordial one, not the verifiable reproducibility of the scientific method.

Value verification of thing-facts is a straight-forward appeal to your opponent to get on your train, join your group, and share your values. It has nothing whatsoever to do with the verifiability of the thing-fact itself.

Thing-fact verification is obviously quite a bit more involved than most people would expect. In fact, it is at it simplest when formal methods are used on facts that are truly naked for *all* the participants involved, and they must be naked for all, because if just one discussant has value links attached to their model of the fact, then formal discussions tend to degrade into passionate L0/L1 arguments about right and wrong.

Of course, the only way for a fact to become *true*, is for it to be converted into a belief, by being connected to $\mathbb{CS}0$ with a value link. Certainly, we should all understand, by now, that *true* really only means *actionable* or *followable*. Truth has only to do with action selection, not with reproducible measurability in $\mathbb{R}$.

20.1.2   Event-Fact

Event-facts present a whole new layer of complexity because, while events *may* occur in $\mathbb{R}$, events do not *exist* in $\mathbb{R}$. Sometimes, events do leave verifiable evidence behind, like gunshot residue, but once the event is over, its occurrence must be inferred from evidence, it does not continue to exist in a state that can be examined.

Events can be predictable, or unpredictable. Predictable events provide the basis for scientific tests because they can be repeated to formally demonstrate that such an event produces such a result, or leaves such a trace. Unpredictable events suggest no obvious path for scientific study.

Therefore, event-facts can generally be scientifically studied only if they are, or involve, predictable events that leave evidence behind. When event-facts are examined in courts of law, most evidence is either forensic, which fits the predictable trace case above, or is based on testimony. Testimony is experience verification, it is anecdotal, and is therefore subject to perceptual or cognitive error, or interest-based distortion, which is why testimony from witnesses with a prior grievance against the defendant is highly suspect. Also, testimony from multiple eye-witnesses can be suspect if the witnesses share a close bond or group value system, because it calls into question the actual independence of their testimony.

Authority evidence does not apply to verification of event-facts, it only reinforces the beliefs of pious adherents. Of course, the Bible tells us that a flood rebooted terrestrial life, and the Quran that Mohammad split the moon in two, but these describe internal knowledge events, not anything that can be verified in reality, not an event-fact in $\mathbb{R}$.

20.2   True and False Facts

The phrase 'false fact' grates on the ear, but false facts not only exist, they dominate the cognitive sphere. The attributes 'true' and 'false' only exist in the $\mathbb{CS}0$ singularity distortion field, and since each cognitive entity of level zero or above is an activation of their own singularity, then by definition, wherever anyone disagrees with another's beliefs, their different ideas are false from the other's perspective. Thus, the set of all the true facts in the universe is confined to the set of all true beliefs of a given cognitive entity, but the set of false facts is the sum of all of the sets of all contrary ideas held by all other cognitive entities in the universe. The set of false facts is, therefore, much larger than the set of true facts. In both the authority and experience verification cases, the cardinality of the set of false facts must necessarily far exceed the small number of true facts that any one mind can hold.

In the experiment verification case, as long as the only fact being discussed is the measured variation from the predicted value in the result of a formal test, then and only then, can we keep this case separate from the muddle of true and false fact food fights. Sadly, though, the reality is that many, if not most, scientists immediately attach a value link to their own quantitative results, thereby degrading what could be a scientific discussion into a truth-based brawl.

20.3   Conclusion

To paraphrase Steven King, experimentally verified facts are a good thing, maybe they are the best thing. But it takes a great deal of discipline to recognize what a tiny percentage of our knowledge and understanding is actually based on formally verified facts, and to acknowledge that almost all of our facts are actually of the authority and experience variety, and have a dubious pedigree. Model-oriented reasoning provides the discipline for taking responsibility for all of the phases of developing, acquiring, verifying and using knowledge. The current brief discussion of the difficulties involved with fact verification should at least make it very clear that we will only make progress with externalizing internal thought if we make the effort to master and utilize model-oriented reasoning.

Supercilious rationalists who claim the right to disdain the great unwashed for relying on traditional belief because their own 'rational' views are based on science and facts, are profoundly stupid. Stupider, in fact, than their fundamentalist opponents, because they wasted a small fortune merely to gain an elitist literary education that only realizes the erudition fallacy in full bloom, and that seals them in a cocoon of ignorance.

Certainly, mastering the arts of pattern acquisition and manipulation can be a good thing, but not when it is learned from internal knowledge subjects that do not support verifiable results. The most important lesson one can learn about pattern processing, in fact, is that the L2 pattern processor lacks a reality verification link, and that therefore, *any* idea can be validated by its own rules regardless of how verifiably wrong it actually is. The vast majority of what the toxic idea fountain spews out is effluent suitable only to be flushed, but the educated elite preserve the worst of this foul outflow and raise it to the level of cultural norms. Past examples of this include orthodoxy, slavery, class systems, mercantilism, hereditary nobility, etc. Current examples of this include the cultural and economic Marxism that poisons root and branch of the academy in the current day.

20.4 Review

- Facts are L2 verbal constructs that reference things or events.
- Situated facts are part of a belief system.
- Naked fact are facts without a value link.
- Situated facts have a truth value that is derived from the belief system, not from verifiable details.

- Challenging facts contradict a value system, and are processed like a foreign body.

- Facts can be verified by experiment, experience, authority or value.

- Scientifically verified facts are not true, they are merely verified.

- Facts are thing-facts or event-facts.

- Thing-facts can be experimentally verified in a specific number of dimensions.

- Thing-facts can be refuted by belief.

- Proving authority, experience and value thing-facts requires converting your opponent.

- Only predictable event-facts can be scientifically verified.

- $|false\ facts| > |true\ facts|$

Chapter 21

Beliefs

21.1 Introduction

Beliefs do not come from religion, superstition or ignorance, they are a necessary consequence and component of organic cognition—the mind could not function without them. Beliefs are not created by religion, they cause religion.

Beliefs have both an L1 and an L2 form, the first being a very primitive but seminal component of consciousness, and the second being an extension of the first into the world of language, self-extension, and reflection. In our attempts to create a general system to extend quantitative methods into the subjective domain to support the scientific study, prediction and understanding of human thoughts, feelings and actions under various conditions, the importance of L1 beliefs becomes apparent when we realize that L2 beliefs begin as linguistic extensions of them.

One of the requirements which a level implementing memory-enabled intellect must satisfy is that, in addition to supporting reasoning operations with a particular data object, it must also support rapid and meaningful queries that retrieve stored ideas in a timely manner. The function of cognitive spaces goes beyond mere data storage, the positioning of data planets around the singularity, as it were. Cognitive spaces create meaning by assigning value to the meaningless data found in $\mathbb{R}$, they do this by essentially modeling an $r \in \mathbb{R}$ (using $\mathbb{R}$ as a synonym for external reality, even though it is not) with an $i \in \mathbb{I}$ by connecting a value link to it that associates it with our own mortality. This is what vivifies a nothing rock, for example, with a type label of *metamorphic*, thereby effectively dragging it from meaningless anonymity into the sweep of natural history by defining its relation to us, to our time, to our universe.

L2 is the stage of cognition where what we recognize as intellect, wisdom and complexity arise, and these all build on the capacity of the pattern object to form semantic branching chains that can encode sophisticated, lengthy, conditional pattern constructs. The complex simplicity of the pattern object is that it is both atomic and complex at the same time; a pattern is a composite object, whether standing alone, or linked in a structure with hundreds of thousands of others. This is what forms the basis for higher thought, this is what makes thought *about* thought, i.e., reflection, possible.

L1 beliefs are created when the L1 *generalize*() function extracts the common essence from emotionally related experiences to create a super type that fits into a hierarchy of self-significant experience that culminates in the archetypes encoded in the genome. The super type objects are obtained by creating a new object (mentacule or result) from two related ones by taking the minimum from each in an element-wise fashion. The new supertype is inserted into the tree as a parent node to the child nodes below. This has the effect of optimizing the search process because, even when searches down into the tree are short-circuited by urgent events, since a supertype of the target has already been identified, the interrupted search will still return all of the most significant sought-after information contained in the descendant.

These pre-verbal L1 beliefs are subsequently extended in the L2 level with language constructs that support the expansion of the extended self into the realm of social structures. We will discuss L1 beliefs first, and then explore the power of the L2 belief pattern.

21.2   L1 Beliefs

L1 beliefs are generalizations of L1 results and mentacules, they are semantic shortcuts that make searches run faster than any search algorithm we can design without them. L1 beliefs are *true* in relation to the recorded experience of the CS0 singularity, but that truth is defined by the individual's experience, not by reality.

The L1 memory store adds a real-time recall function to L0 functionality. The real-time requirement has the technical definition of:

$$q(i) \rightsquigarrow_{(t>=0)} m_{i_{\hat{s}}}$$

That is, the query, $q()$, of the L1 memory store, with the input i, is guaranteed to return a satisfying mentacule, m_i, from the super type hierarchy, $\hat{s}$, within a time bound t, where $t \geq 0$. This extraordinarily rigorous guarantee can be met by an organic mind because it turns out that the L1 memory function does not actually focus on identification, but instead, it works on categorization by descending the type tree, $\hat{s}$. L1 doesn't care what the perceived thing actually is, it only cares about evaluating its risk/reward profile quickly enough for the body to respond successfully within the current time constraints.

Of course, the language in the previous paragraph, which seems suggestive of purpose, is just a rhetorical device intended to help convey a certain message. The L1 memory function, in fact, doesn't care at all about anything, much less about how a body, which it doesn't even know exists, should move. It is natural selection that, through the brutality of nature, culled all the genetic lines that searched memory for interesting recollections in a languid, rather than alacritous, fashion. The only way the complication of memory recall could survive in the dog-eat-dog world of the food chain is if the answer from the query never took any more time than safety allowed.

The easiest way to implement recall with this guarantee is to do an interruptible, time-bound hierarchical search in which the input is the L0 type identification mentacule that defines the appropriate archetype of the three value tertrants (anti, pro or non). The input is set as the initial search result, which means that the worst answer L1 could ever deliver is the best that L0 could ever achieve, and L1 is ready to return this preliminary answer immediately. Then, time allowing, the L1 query function will navigate by value comparison down into the type hierarchy, updating the provisional result, as each better match is found, until an exact answer is found or time expires or an interrupt occurs.

The L1 type hierarchy is built up over time as the cognitive entity processes memories of its experiences. In computer science, we learn that searching an unordered collection has an $O(n)$ complexity (read: order n), which means that the time to do the search grows linearly as the collection grows. This is also called the British Museum Search after the habit of British explorers to add specimens from all of their voyages all over the world to a museum collection that lacked a comprehensive indexing system (or so we are told), which meant that individual items might only be discoverable after an exhaustive search of everything in the museum basements.

An $O(n)$ search that takes longer and longer, as we learn more about life, is obviously incompatible with the exigencies of surviving imminent death in a food chain, and is contrary to our own personal experience of having to respond to partially recognized input while, for example, speeding down the freeway at 80 mph. Both an analysis of the evolutionary model of the exigencies of daily survival, and of our own recall experiences, tells us that our minds actually use a time-bound, interruptible search that always returns at least the threat/opportunity level of the input, regardless of how little time we have to think about it, even though the answer may be wrong.

How does the structure of the L1 data object and memory store impact the nature and function of belief? Beliefs are actually value search optimizations, they are the super type nodes in the mentacule hierarchy that are created by the *generalize()* function comparing similar experience nodes to extract a common supertype that will provide an acceptable answer to any query interrupted in its march down into this particular branch of the memory tree. *generalize()* works by comparing two mentacules and producing a super type result by copying in the minimum value of each pair of non-null attributes. This creates a super type that each subtype elaborates with additional detail. This supertype relation is defined as:

$$generalize(a, b) \rightarrow c \iff (a_i \wedge b_i) \wedge c_i \ \forall \ i \in (a, b)$$

That is, generalizing the pair of mentacules a and b will produce a mentacule c that will be logically true element-wise (in the sense of having a non-zero entry) when paired with either input parameters (meaning that all three vectors have non-zero values in the same positions). This means that $c[i]$ will be true in any case where both $a[i]$ and $b[i]$ are true.

For example, if we run *generalize()* over our experiences with dalmatians, poodles, terriers, pit bulls and chihuahuas, we could create a supertype node of 'dog' (L2 naming functionality, see below) that contains the common attributes of each, with the highest threat or lowest opportunity level in any of them.

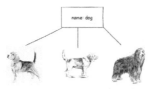

Figure 21.1: Generalize

Thus, a search for a memory of an interaction with a particular type of dog would, if interrupted at a level above the individual memories, return us an identification of the dog class, possibly with the highest danger level we had personally experienced, depending on our boldness / timidity ratio.

The *generalize()* function is run as a background mental process because it is essentially an L1 memory store housekeeping operation that is required to maintain the between $O(1)$ to $O(\log n)$ response time of L1 type queries. The function compares both result and super type mentacules, so there is no bound on the possible depth of the type hierarchy tree in the L1 result store (although I am confident a average upper bound on the order of 10^1 will be provable).

When *generalize()* is run on ordinary, low level experience inputs b and c, it would likely produce a similarly low level super type a. An example of this would be a low-level, low-value belief generalized from a few recent personal experiences such as: 'the lane of traffic I am in is always the slowest,' that we feel is true, even though it ignores the commoner cases where it isn't. Although our mind tells us that this is a truth about the world, most of us are, nevertheless, aware that this is an ad hoc, low level idea with very poor reliability. That our minds create silly, meaningless beliefs like this, though, gives us observable evidence both of the automatic generalization function, and of the $\mathbb{CS}0$ distortion field, in which all events are interpreted from the point of view of our personal experience, no matter how unimportant or unrelated they may be in the flat space of $\mathbb{R}$.

It is always well to keep in mind, throughout all of these discussions, by the way, that all meaning necessarily derives from the singularity of our existence, not directly from an external phenomenon, because meaning is a product of, and only exists in, a cognitive space.

As the L1 memory hierarchy fills out with additional results and layer upon layer of super types and subtype instances, this is when we begin to develop meaningful beliefs, beliefs that encode the truth of actual experience at a higher, more abstract level. The real power of beliefs is that, once your search for the meaning of a perception reaches a high valued belief node in a hierarchical value structure, then there is little need for the search to continue traversing the tree, because the maximum truth value that affects your decisions has already been reached—the rest of it is just details that cannot change the already determined evaluation of the current situation.

Stop and reflect for a moment about your beliefs. How many of them have you at the center? Yes, you believe God does, or does not, exist, but follow it out, and even that ends up at what it means to you.

Beliefs support rapid, definitive responses by terminating searches earlier than would be possible with any conventional search algorithm. Stop and think about this for a moment; the significance of this optimization cannot be overstated: beliefs are a search heuristic that we could not survive without, because without them, we would be eaten before we finished searching our memory to recall how we should respond to this thing we see.

Beliefs are a higher level abstraction of anecdotal experience that distills the important lessons from numerous individual events. They only become an impediment when the environmental niche changes, because, as an adaptation to a specific set of circumstances, they don't necessarily apply as well to the new conditions as to the old, and they continue to short circuit searches, albeit perhaps now inappropriately.

The archetypes at the top of the hierarchy are just value arrays that define pure threat, pure opportunity, etc. It is the hierarchy of super types that we create from our own experience that give us visceral beliefs that affect our actions, such as the conviction that dogs are bad, or people are untrust-

worthy or friendly, or members of such and such a group are
[*bad* | *evil* | *good* | *funny* | *attractive*], etc.

It may be hard for us to imagine what L1 beliefs actually
look like, because they are the type of beliefs held by dogs and
horses and such; they are not the verbal beliefs we recognize.
We tend to interpret the animal behaviors we witness that result
from these L1 beliefs as being due to temperament or the result
of maltreatment, etc., rather seeing them as being produced by
cognitive beliefs, but they come from true L1 beliefs formed
from the generalization function working on stored result memories, whether in a dog or a human mind (obviously, not all
individuals, and not all species, have the full ability to continuously learn from experience). However, since these beliefs are
pre-verbal, when they are in our own mind, we experience them
as impulses and feelings rather than ideas, as visceral emotions
such as fear, passion, revulsion, etc. But, these feelings are true
low-level beliefs, true wordless beliefs that shape our responses
to everyday experiences and perceptions.

21.3   L2 Beliefs

L2 beliefs are complex verbal constructs that extend our L0
values and conviction into the plane of social interaction. L2
is not about seeing the world, it is about *knowing* the world,
and the belief object is an L2 mechanism that freezes a section
of the world in a known state. But we know from **M4** that
our discrete models cannot comprehensively *know* an effectively
infinite referent, therefore, the truth asserted by a belief object

obviously describes our L0/L1 experience and constitution, and not external reality.

Similarly to L1 beliefs, L2 beliefs are optimizations, but where L1 beliefs are essentially just data storage and data retrieval optimizations, L2 beliefs optimize several different areas of cognitive function:

- Self-extension (grouping) ability
- Search
- Input processing
- False positive results

21.3.1   L2 Belief Structure

The structure of an L2 belief object is shown in figure 21.3. L2 beliefs are an important type of reference pattern that is similar to a naming pattern, but is specialized because:

- its top matching exit points are connected to a web of creed patterns,
- it has a value link to an L0 truth coordinate,
- it has a source field that links it back to the belief group,
- it has a list of sibling belief patterns (anti, pro, non belief buckets)
- it has a default exit point that connects to a loopback pattern

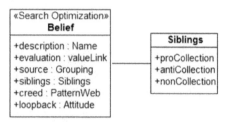

Figure 21.3: Belief object

Complex, or rich beliefs, the type that bind you to a community of believers, are generally organized in a star pattern, as shown in figure 21.4. The set of subordinate beliefs that surround a higher level belief give the believer a nearly immediate answer to any question that touches any of those points, thereby facilitating both a rapid response and the maintaining of a tight focus on the most important and meaningful risks and opportunities. Strangely, the details of the doctrine, contained in the creed element in the core belief object, are not necessarily an essential part of the belief, because believers often, if not usually, have only the vaguest understanding of them. The fact that they exist and are known by group authorities is crucial to sustaining the aura of authority and legitimacy of the doctrine, but it is the grouping mechanisms extending the self that are far more persuasive in establishing and maintaining group cohesion.

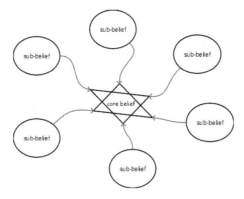

Figure 21.4: Belief star pattern

Belief systems can be arbitrarily complex, but the most important parts of the system are the source link to the sponsoring
group, the value link, and the sorting algorithm that assigns input facts into one of the three belief buckets (pro, anti, non)
in the sibling list. That is, a belief is a sorting and value assignment mechanism that enables us to assign meaning to input
facts very quickly, with very little effort.

The set of sub-beliefs that act as entry points to the body
of the doctrine are also a search optimization that gets us to
the core belief in one step, once we determine the subject. For
example, believers generally have a large set of sub-belief nodes
that match references to truth, justice, god, the purpose of life,
the definition of right and wrong, etc. All of these common, high
level beliefs connect to the same web of creed patterns through
their 7-match connection to the core belief. Just picture how
the dozens of entrances to a stadium all open into the same
arena, and you've got the general idea.

An L2 belief is an existential assertion that permanently subsumes regions of $\mathbb{R}$ to $\mathbb{I}$, that is, it posits that the belief itself is *truer* than anything in $\mathbb{R}$, to the point of asserting that reality cannot even be understood without it. In the extreme, a belief is the assertion that the singularity is the true origin point in the universe and that, instead of being warped, the distortion field is flat and constant, and that it's the rest of reality that is distorted and uncertain.

21.3.2   Search

The primary sorting key for all result sets returned from searches in L2 is the value magnitude, and since L2 beliefs have a value link to L0/L1 beliefs/values, this means that beliefs are invariably sorted at the top of list of search results, ahead of simple or technical ideas.

As a manager, I learned to prepare a to-do list everyday, sorted in priority order, and eventually learned never to put more than seven items on the list because, the sad truth was, that I almost never got more than the top three items done. I am convinced that the same rule of thumb holds true when we search our memory for problem solving ideas: even though we may get several options back, in practice, we rarely consider more than the top three, and usually we never get beyond the top one or two options. Since beliefs, by their nature, tend to have much higher value links than other types of ideas, such as opinions, this means that beliefs tend to be our go-to solutions since they are usually served up to us first.

21.3.3   Input Processing

L2's primary job is to anticipate the future, to prepare us for important, foreseeable contingencies, by matching the current situation to one in its library of known patterns. L2 orients us, both to the present and to the future, when it recognizes that the current situation matches some familiar pattern. This act of recognition tells us that we aren't lost and powerless, but are facing reality standing on solid ground. The exit points of all the patterns in the search result set we get back from looking for a match to the current situation, gives us a list of the possible paths that the future might take. This set of possible continuations enables us to prepare for the worst before it happens, and thereby often to avoid the greatest dangers confronting us.

Structurally, L2 is built around patterns; functionally, it processes patterns; operationally, its job is to keep us situated, to enable us to be proactive, rather than just reactive, to anticipate, rather than just to respond, and it does this by always staying oriented to the present, and actively conceiving the future.

Information presented directly to L2 as a payload in a message is a called a fact, a verbal pattern containing evidence. In order to stay situated, L2 must process this input expeditiously, and sort it so that it maintains its orientation in a dynamic environment. L2 asks, "What does this mean, what does it portend for my future?", and answers its own question by evaluating new facts just like L0 evaluates sensory input, i.e., in [a,p,n] terms. The goal of fact processing is to situate every new fact in the appropriate belief field as fast as it can, so that it can either trigger an immediate response, or take the fact out of alarm status.

Facts are presented naked, and evaluation adds a value link to them to define their meaning to the self. Until a fact is evaluated, it represents a possible mortal threat, so L2 keeps the self proactively situated by assigning meaning to significant facts by adding value links to them and positioning them in known reference patterns to define their type. The L2 world view is "I understand what is happening, I can figure out what will happen, the world is not an unknown, it is what I expect it to be", and it maintains this attitude by situating facts into value fields.

A plan is a contingent step sequencing structure, it is a multi-step pattern. The L2 planning function creates, extends, selects and executes plans. Its job is to keep us situated, on plan, oriented to what is, anticipating what will be. Input must be processed from an unknown to a known state, as quickly as possible, to stay on plan. The way L2 does this is by situating naked, disinterested facts of consequence into patterns, and value facts of consequence into value fields, i.e., beliefs.

Messages stating a reality are facts, regardless of whether they are true or false, and facts are a problem because they may represent an imminent threat. Therefore, to maintain its orientation and appearance of control, L2 must process—digest, as it were—facts as quickly as possible. As explained in chapter

17, Events, in the course of a normal day, L2 is deluged with
a flood of messages that it must identify, sort, and dispose of
efficiently just to keep our attention available to handle actual
reality-based events.

Facts can be challenging, confirming or irrelevant. Irrelevant
facts are simply dropped where they are — with some minds
retaining a memory of them, while others don't even recall hear-
ing them — but in either case, they are dropped the moment
they are identified as unimportant. All other facts are potentially challenging or confirming. In the rare case that a fact
actually does address the immediate future, it is processed into
the currently active pattern by being included in the current
action result set to influence the next action step taken in the
process.

The rest of the set of other facts includes gossip, news, normal conversation, really any statement, whether written or verbal, from any source purporting to state the actual condition of
something in reality. These references, idea fragments, interest
statements, historical notes, fantasies and the rest, have to be
processed and evaluated immediately to free the mind to handle
whatever reality throws at us next. The way L2 handles these
kinds of facts is again by using the familiar search algorithm to
find a set of patterns that best matches the fact by calculating
the angle between the vectors, and then selecting one or more
of the patterns (perhaps using a secondary search criteria), and
assigning the fact pattern to them. If the match is on a significant value dimension, then the pattern can be sorted as an

anti-, pro-, or non-self sibling in the active belief. Think of the sibling list in a belief object as a collection of lists that contains confirming facts in one list, contradicting facts in another, and junk in the third. Thus, for example, a believer would instantly be able to catalog assertions about gods other than his own as false facts within his god-belief anti-self sibling list.

Challenging facts, facts that are important but not evaluated yet, draw the attention of L2 and consume its cognitive power in constant or increasing amounts until they are successfully situated. Beliefs are a search optimization that produces fast matches, and so they act as a circuit breaker on the L2 energy draw because they enable L2 to safely position the fact into a known bucket and break off the processing effort. That is, the goal of the L2 intellect in handling deferrable value facts is to file them away in an existing belief sibling bucket as quickly as possible. L2 has no native interest in the details of the fact itself. Surely, you've noticed that people passionately engaged in opinion discussions are utterly uninterested in anything contrary you have to say, haven't you? This is the mechanism that explains that.

As finite creatures, we have a limited range of responses available to handle all experiences that the universe can throw at us. It's a simple question of mechanics: we are built to handle certain types of experiences, and only a limited set of types, because the structures that allow us to perceive, conceive and react to stimuli take up space in our genome, and each instruction has to be inherited in a mutable process that is sharply schooled by the harsh strictures of reality. This is why we don't see *things*, we see *types*, types with distinguishing features, to be sure, but types nonetheless. Depending on our level of sophistication, we may see lion, predator or quadruped, but we don't see 'Alvin', the lion, son of Freelis and Calos. Why would we? Why would we want to? What would be the evolutionary benefit to that type of other-essence perception, when all we need to do is identify the *type* of the thing to be able to calculate our best response to it?

The goal of the L2 information processing system is to route immediate facts to the current plan, and neuter deferrable facts by positioning them in existing value fields as quickly as possible. We only think that our minds process information to learn about reality because all of our judgments are distorted by the singularity at the heart of the cognitive space that evaluates everything according to our interest in it; from the inside, this feels like we perceived the truth about the fact and we now understand it as much as is necessary.

Beliefs dispose of facts by labeling them true if they are supporting, and false if they contradict an important belief. L2 could not maintain its **M9** service level guarantee without beliefs, because meaningful searches would consume more and more time as the depth of the information graph increased. As it happens, the additional functionality required in the L2 mutation set to stanch the toxic idea flow is actually inherent in the functionality itself. We have seen that L1 beliefs are a search optimization feature, and not an artifact of a new, higher level

of emotional, spiritual or religious sensibility. We find a similar
case with L2, which is not surprising, since L2 is an elaboration of L1, with patterns encapsulating results, and result-level
functions enhanced to process the more complex pattern structure. L2 functionality includes pattern-based search optimizations similar to, but correspondingly more elaborate than, the
L1 optimization.

21.3.4   Managing False Positive Results

The importance of the role that L2 patterns play in alerting us
to potential peril cannot be overstated, since this was perhaps
the single set of mutations that made it possible for humans
to dominate the planet like no other species, but this power
does have a cost: L2 is truly a toxic idea fountain. Left to its
own devices, the unending profusion of ideas created by L2 that
detail possibly threatening future scenarios would paralyze us
with anxiety in a torrent of worry about all of the terrible things
that *might* befall us. In order to keep on functioning, we need a
way to quell our anxiety, to quiet our worries about what what
might be so that we can concentrate on what *actually is*. The
belief pattern fulfills this need by providing us with an antswer
when none of the other options actually fit the situation.

Loopbacks that are attached to the default belief exit point
are *antswers*, answers that are formed before the question is
thought of, let alone asked. Abstractly speaking, all antswers
are fundamentally the same, they tell us:

- not to worry,
- that everything will be okay,

- that everything is as 'God wills',
- that some things are out of our power,
- that if we trust to *whatever*, then *whatever*

There is no actual content to an antswer — the sayings that we know as platitudes, clichés, bromides, apothegms, aphorisms, proverbs or maxims — since they are answers to all questions asked and unasked, past, present and future; they are just circuit breakers that shut off runaway fear or speculation to free our L2 cognition engine to get back to the business of dealing with the issues confronting us in the here and now.

21.4 Review

- Beliefs don't come from religion, they cause religion.
- Beliefs have both an L1 and L2 form.
- L1 implements an interruptible, time-bound hierarchical search within a time constraint $>= 0$ that returns an L0 evaluation or better.
- L1 beliefs are search optimizations, created by the generalize function, that organize the hierarchical type tree.
- The L1 generalize function flattens and organizes memory to maintain the service level guarantee by calculating supertypes and reorganizing memory under them.
- Beliefs terminate searches early, which improves results in familiar situations, and impairs them in unfamiliar situations.
- L2 beliefs support self-extension and optimize message processing.

- L2 beliefs are returned at the top of L2 pattern searches.

- L2 beliefs rapidly dispose of deferrable facts.

- L2 beliefs save us from having to process all the verbal messages we hear everyday by automatically sorting and filing them away.

- The L2 information processing system routes immediate facts to the current plan, and neuters deferrable facts.

- L2 beliefs are a primary toxic idea fountain control mechanism.

Perhaps now you can see why beliefs are important, why religion has mostly died, and why the modern L2 religions (mostly Marxist-based ideologies) tend to be so idiotic. Nice area for research, maybe?

Chapter 22

Attitudes

22.1 Introduction

An attitude durable enough to be part of a personal lifestyle is both a measure, and a determinant, of one's willingness to engage in a given type of interaction. We have many attitudes, some situational and fleeting, some chronic and even lifelong. We generally look at persistent attitudes as psychological phenomena, but, under the lens of model-oriented reasoning and the universal cognition model, they turn out to be something that is, at the same time, both simpler and more complex than that.

An attitude is distinguished from a mood by its function: attitudes dispose of facts, while mood colors experience. One can have both a grumpy attitude and a grumpy mood, but the effect is different. A grumpy mood biases evaluation of experience, it filters experience through a particular evaluation, but the altered experience is then processed normally, whereas a grumpy attitude essentially dismisses experience, it eschews involvement with experience in favor or preserving the current state of being, by effectively isolating it from experience.

One of the questions that has to answered when designing a cognitive entity is, how does it handle facts? How does the mind handle facts presented to it, either by experience, or in the stream of language messages? For the first type of fact, those of exigent circumstance, these are driven into the primary circuits to generate an action response, but what of the rest, those that don't demand immediate response, that are deferrable? Deferrable facts may be meaningless, or may only have potential significance that will be revealed in the fullness of time, as circumstances evolve. How does the mind handle deferrable facts?

Deferrable facts are an L2 construct, and they put pressure on the L2 anticipation mechanism because, until proven otherwise, they potentially represent an imminent threat. Their ultimate threat state can be determined by evaluation, but each full pattern evaluation takes a certain amount of time and effort that requires the L2 processor to steal cycles from the L0 capacity to scan reality for danger and opportunity, and when you consider the rate at which facts are thrown at us on a daily and hourly basis, you realize that the math does not add up. There is simply an insufficient amount of time and resources available to properly evaluate every deferrable fact. What, then, can we do? How do we manage the torrent of facts without losing the plot in the present?

One of the possible solutions to this information overload is simplicity itself: we just ignore deferrable facts. What would happen? How many deferrable facts are actually grenades whose pin has already been pulled? Not many, as experience shows, and it seems that this option must have been validated by natural selection, since it is now our primary strategy for managing information overload. The mechanism implementing that strategy is what we are calling *attitude*.

22.2   Attitude Container Pattern

When we consider attitude in light of our recent understanding of beliefs and containers, we can see that this L2 structure is actually a pure container pattern. Its lightweight structure, shown in figure 22.1, makes it highly performant, simply because it doesn't do much, and what little it does do, will execute virtually instantaneously. In the previous examination of the Pattern object, we focused on the link pattern form because it is the pattern we most often encounter consciously. The link pattern has a *situation → action → situation → pattern* flow that characterizes the standard high-level use case supporting pattern assimilation and language. However, most of the fields in the pattern object are nullable, and different combinations of null and populated fields produce interesting variations of the basic pattern object functionality.

In the attitude container pattern, the action mentacule is null, at least in the sense that no asynchronous action is specified, that is, no extra-container action with a pending result

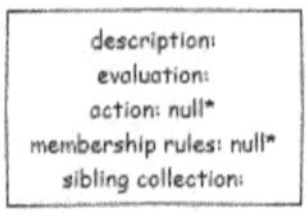

Figure 22.1: Attitude Pattern Object

that has to be awaited. With only a null or synchronous action, the wait state that allows time for the action result situation to develop is, obviously, unneeded, thus creating what is essentially a direct connection from the entry to the exit points, but in the attitude pattern, the exit points, too, are null. This leaves what seems to be an empty and useless pattern, but what it actually creates is an extremely powerful and important container pattern that both utilizes and depends on this bare, skeletal structure.

22.3 Attitude Object

The only important elements in the attitude pattern object are the description and evaluation fields, and the evaluated, non-hierarchical, sibling pattern collection. The resulting structure supports a named evaluation of an unbounded set of patterns, and this opens up an entirely new level of functionality: evaluated collections. Insertion into this structure is $O(1)$, as fast as can be, but searching in the structure is odd in that it is very approximate because it is essentially a keyless search on a non-hierarchical collection, which may clue one into the fact that insertion, not retrieval, is the primary function of this structure.

The way that the attitude object works is that an active attitude can process any deferrable fact almost instantaneously to allow the mind to maintain its level of focus on the dynamic sensorium, i.e., the world around it, without having to lose any time in reflection or consideration. All-encompassing attitudes can digest any deferrable fact, but some attitudes are parameterized to only process facts related to a given topic.

As to the retrieval operation of patterns in the object, it only accepts broad parameters, such as a topic or a time period when the insertion happened (such as today, recent, or long ago), and returns a set of patterns that may be unrelated except by some reading of the search parameter. It always returns a fuzzy, not strictly reproducible, result set, rather than a particular pattern.

Attitude is an L2 search optimization that is similar to the belief function in that it returns results faster than any conventional search could. We are calling attitude a search optimization, even though its primary function is merely to insert data, because what it is actually doing is, in effect, searching through our experience and cognitive capacity for whatever it needs to interpret the current input and assign a meaning to it. That it does this simply by assigning the meaning without bothering to do a search is the time-saving optimization, and a pretty clever one at that. Think about it for a moment: we all use attitude, to a greater or lesser degree, all the time, and somehow it suffices to enable us to process input successfully enough for us to survive. You must admit, a shortcut that essentially saves virtually all the work one might imagine would be required for a cognitive entity to make sense of its experience, is kind of brilliant.

What makes attitude process facts so fast is that it implements the view that thoughtfulness and consideration are both unnecessary and futile in processing deferrable facts, because the end result, the end evaluation of the current situation, is already known, and it is xyz, the evaluation in the attitude.

How could this work? It works because understanding is achieved when the relation of *other* to *self* is defined by linking the fact of other to a value position in the singularity distortion field. Attaching a fact to the evaluation field in an attitude accomplishes this in one step, and this can be done without examining the internals of the other idea. Given that, the quickest way, then, to understand something in particular, or the world in general, is to categorize any deferrable fact by the fewest characteristic attributes possible. This is what durable attitudes do, they instantaneously make sense of experience in accordance with some simple rule that is consistent with the current state of affairs. For example, the detached indifference of the wisdom attitude, i.e., being cool, is rarely seen in people in a firefight, but is often seen in those insulated from want and threat thanks to the efforts of others. Shooting at a group of cool, smug, entitled brats, though, might cause an immediate transition out of the cool attitude into a more engaged mode (theoretically, of course, this is an untested hypothesis).

22.4 Attitude Operation

Attitudes are most glaringly apparent when they are flaunted like peacock plumage by adolescents and young adults who aspire to seem older, more in the know, or more powerful than they actually are. But, to be sure, attitudes are used by, and evident in, all age groups. If you doubt this, watch the nightly news from any source: its function is to make sense of the day's events by applying an attitude that will comfortably contextualize all events, from the normal to the bizarre, from the wholesome to the macabre, into the editorial Weltanschauung of the interest that runs it.

Attitudes are essentially skeletal, secular beliefs, beliefs without a specified source or a web of creed patterns, a belief stripped of all of its content except for the characteristic evaluation. When an attitude is applied to the evaluation of a fact, it predetermines nearly the whole evaluation of that fact except for some small allowance to recognize the more extreme cases of threat. Attitudes are faster operations than belief, so fast, in fact, that where a belief is generally only applied to facts after they have been determined not to fit into the currently active plan, attitudes act so quickly that they can even impact the initial evaluation of the input fact. This means that strong attitudes can significantly impact perception if they cause the initial evaluation to sum both the input and attitude evaluations, in effect, overriding the actual evaluation of the input fact with the attitudinal evaluation, sometimes to disastrous effect.

Presented facts can be categorized as immediate or deferrable, with immediate facts being those that are either in-plan or demanding immediate response, and deferrable facts being all others. Attitude does the least damage when it processes deferrable facts, and leaves immediate facts to be processed by other cognitive functions, but aggressive attitudes can, and do, easily mistake immediate for deferrable facts, with predictable consequences.

The function of an attitude is to process deferrable facts as quickly as possible to maintain the facade of knowledge and control. The actual content of these facts has no relevance to the processing attitude, and is ignored. The fact patterns inserted into the attitude bucket, the sibling list, have no impact on the attitude evaluation, they don't update or influence it. Just as garbage has no influence on the route of the truck disposing of it, so fact patterns in the sibling bucket are just so much inert baggage and have no effect on the attitude. The processed fact patterns are never viewed or used as evidence for the attitude, they don't inform it, they are merely sorted by it.

The attitudinal sorting of deferrable facts performs the crucial function of converting the fact from a potential fact to an evaluated fact which restores the mind to a calm state from the excited, anxious state caused by the presentation of the potential fact. Assigning a challenge fact to an attitude bucket is a crucial housekeeping function that keeps the complex L2 pattern processor on an even keel, ready to handle the next potential threat or opportunity.

22.5 Types of Attitudes

The effect of attitude is perhaps best illustrated by the Wisdom Fallacy, the presumption that we can use arcane knowledge of $\mathbb{S}$ to insulate us from the stresses and trials of the mundane, earthly plane, $\mathbb{R}$. The wisdom attitude dismisses all facts of diurnal life with the assessment that such trivialities can be disregarded as unimportant, simply because they pale in comparison to the significance of the arcana of the wisdom culture. This attitude arises spontaneously in the youth culture of every new generation, and is also assiduously cultivated by religious, intellectual, and cultured fraternities. Youth uses wisdom, in the guise of a 'cool', detached attitude, as a means of quelling the anxiety they feel at the prospect of confronting the wide world outside of the family. Adults use the facade of benign indifference to fence off those areas of reality that defeated their attempts to subdue the uncertainties of life.

The reason that searches inside attitude collections are notoriously unreliable is because they return a largely random collection of patterns that only partially meet the search parameter. This failure, however, is never interpreted to reflect negatively on the truth of the attitude, because the function of the collection is to corral fact patterns within an acceptable evaluation context, not to build a foundation to sustain or prove the attitude's correctness. After all, just because you sometimes find something you needed last week had accidentally been thrown in a pile in the attic doesn't mean there is something wrong with the junk-holding capacity of the attic.

To test this, ask anyone who is displaying any attitude, at any time, why that attitude is correct in this situation, and all you will get back is an incoherent hodgepodge of anecdotes, the refutation of which will never suffice to invalidate the attitude itself. Remember, attitude is a data management, not a semantic, function. Attitude has nothing to do with content, but everything to do with rapid data processing and maintenance of the current status quo. The function of attitude is always to maintain a sense of orientation and control, so tossing all input facts of a certain type into the same value bin, without expending any reflective effort, is an effective strategy to minimize the amount of time we spend distracted from our surroundings; not an unreasonable thing to do given that most facts actually have little to no significance to our immediate and short-term interests.

Imagine you are facing a high-speed, unlimited capacity tennis ball serving machine: which would be easier, to try to return each ball in bounds, or just to bat them away to avoid being hit? Remember, attitude processes only deferrable facts; immediately impactful facts are ordinarily handled through another channel.

There are positive attitudes, negative attitudes, resigned, and dismissive attitudes, just to name a few. Attitudes are formed at the nexus of constitution and experience where our sense of power, or powerlessness, to control the outcome of events, is formed. However, they are not a psychological development, and to think that they are actually reflects the attitude that behavior is normative except after psychological injury, but this is a very low quality model of human behavior that, itself, represents an attitude of L2 empowerment over the chaos of experience.

In general, what we would call negative attitudes are adopted to cope with a repeated failure to successfully change the course of events to one's liking, while positive attitudes are bred from experiencing a history of empowerment and success. Neither is preferable to the other, they are both just dismissive sorting algorithms, and the price of having them will be different in different situations. An attitude can define, and confine, a lifestyle or even an entire life, because, for example, the commitment to projecting an insulated, in the know invulnerability can ultimately refute every opportunity to learn and grow.

22.6 Constraints

We will discuss how the nature of the attitude object constrains discussions in chapter 26, but certainly the astute reader can already anticipate why certain types of debate techniques simply cannot succeed, due to the actual structure of this object. You cannot invalidate someone's attitude by refuting facts since the attitude doesn't depend on the facts in any way. Facts sorted by an attitude do still exist independently of the attitude, though, so if they are accessed through another avenue, they can be examined rationally, but only if a delicate touch is used, lest the attitude be roused to defend the equilibrium.

The shallow sophisticates who adjure belief in favor of full-time rationality do not understand that an attitude such as, "we can always use our reason to understand ..." is simply a belief with an empty source field. Attitudes are manifestations of a constitutional bent that individuals develop for themselves, or, more commonly, assimilate from an admired group. The L2 memory store cannot continue to function effectively without using the optimizations that the belief and attitude objects provide, so it behooves us to acknowledge the importance of these L2 cognitive optimizations and to study the various ways they can be used. Or, if we insert the bias that one of the highest goals of cognition is to learn to understand reality in its own terms, we can say that we need to learn how attitude and belief can with interfere with this goal when used unwisely.

Finally, it must be noted that the cynical, world-weary, negative attitude often flaunted with such pride by the self-described, educated elite is a surer route to ignorance than crude belief, because the belief object supports a higher level of reflection than the attitude object does. Attitude preempts reflection to the point that perception itself can be short-circuited.

22.7   Review

- Attitudes dispose of facts to preserve the current equilibrium.
- Moods color experience, while attitudes dispose of facts.
- Attitudes are more effective at handling deferrable facts than exigent ones.
- Attitudes optimize information processing by not process-

ing information.

- Attitude objects only have a description, and an evaluation.

- Attitudes do not depend on facts they have tagged.

- Attitudes neutralize challenging or potential facts.

- Wisdom is perhaps the most universally revered brainless attitude.

- Attitudes that support or obviate engagement can determine the course of one's life.

- Never argue with an attitude.

Chapter 23

Opinions

23.1 Introduction

An opinion is the slightly smarter cousin of the attitude, but not by much. Opinions differ from attitudes in that they are not disposers of fact, but rather, accumulators of fact. That is, opinions can be built up by the association of evaluated patterns, as well as by assimilation of the opinion framework from a meritable group source. Opinions compensate for the hard constraint that exists in our cognitive apparatus limiting the number of thoughts that can be actively entertained at any one time, by rolling up the evaluation of a set of patterns into the top level opinion evaluation. This facilitates reasoning by chunking facts into manageable blocks, so that instead of having to include ten ideas in a subjective calculation, for example, only the opinion needs to be accessed, instead of all of the individual ideas.

L2 is an early stage in the evolution of higher cognitive func-

tion, so it should come as no surprise that many of its data
management operations sacrifice accuracy for speed, and power
for tractability. While the famous limit of 7 may or may not
strictly apply in this case, there is no evidence that a human
mind can retain more than a dozen or so ideas in current memory while actually being able to use any more than a half or a
third of that number in the current calculation step.

Perhaps the issue that confuses people when they try to
analyze reasoning is the fallacy that reasoning is the objective
transformation of reality bits into correct conclusions. While
we have taken great pains to debunk this nonsense, a lifetime
of implicitly assuming it is so, is hard to overcome with just a
sentence here and there. External reasoning that can be verified
through formal calculation, or replication, can be said to be
verified (supported, actually) or refuted, but cannot properly
be termed right or wrong. All other reasoning is internal, which
is to say subjective and lacking a defined relation to external
reality. Understand that, except for its highest forms, which are
not discussed in this volume, our reasoning does not care (i.e.,
is not built or designed to investigate or know) about external
reality at all. The only job our L0/L1 reasoning has, is to
evaluate phenomena in relation to our self-interest, and L2 only
has to meet the rather slacker standard of kind of adhering to
the grammar of a particular pattern language when it puts ideas
together.

It is the purblind defect that causes us to mistake the domain of our reasoning as extending all the way to the outer

boundaries of external reality, and this is what makes us think that there is a defined, objective connection between our internal thoughts and the realities external to us. Although we are surprised whenever we find our reasoning has failed to match reality, it would seem more rational to be shocked whenever it even gets close to matching it. Internal thought is just that, the product of the operational manipulation of internal models of momentary states of the internal and external senses. Without formal tests, there is no basis for assuming that there is any correlation whatsoever between it and reality; why should we assume that the sum of any two internal thoughts necessarily corresponds to anything outside of the mind it inhabits?

23.2   Opinion Object

As stated earlier, different combinations of null and populated fields in the Pattern object produce interesting variations of it. What we will be discussing in this chapter is a proposed implementation of the opinion object in the asomatous psyche application that seems to model observable human behavior with a reasonably high level of fidelity. Of course, the proof of this, as always, will be in the test, so we should fearlessly proceed with our modeling exercise, since any disappointment in the results can just be used to suggest ways to improve the model.

The difference between the behavior of the attitude and opinion objects is that a particular attitude object processes facts in a certain way *so that* a given level of engagement can

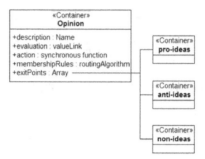

Figure 23.1: Opinion Object

be maintained, while an opinion object develops as it does *because of* a set of facts, that is, opinions are originally formed in order to explain a fact set, not simply to discharge them (ultimately, this applies to assimilated as well as developed opinions, since somebody originally formulated them), but once they are formed, they begin to function as semi-thoughtful disposers of fact.

The structure of an opinion object, as shown in figure 23.1, includes:

- Description: a structured name object providing a verbal reference for the opinion.
- Evaluation: a computed value link.
- Action: a synchronous local call, or null.
- Membership rules: opinions contain a restricted set of facts.
- Exit points: pro, anti and non fact categories.

The opinion description is a structured name pattern that can contain a number of verbal references to the opinion. This is the handle we use when including opinions in our calculations.

The evaluation field rolls up the evaluations of the pro facts included in the opinion, but this summation does not set the value link, it is only a factor in calculating it, along with the evaluations of related opinions and beliefs. Thus, the pro facts contribute to setting the evaluation value link, but they do not control it; refuting any of the pro facts does not necessarily degrade or influence the value link in any way.

The opinion object sorts facts into the usual three buckets, anti, pro, and non, but these buckets have a special function in this object: pro facts *prove* the opinion, anti facts are *disproved* by the opinion, and non facts are *devalued* by the opinion. The membership rules in the opinion object structure define which facts belong to the pro, anti and non exit points, and so act as a routing algorithm to distribute facts to the appropriate container object for handling. Thus, anti facts are sorted by the opinion to the anti bucket without having any effect on the truth value of the opinion object itself, and in fact, rather than the fact diminishing the truth of the opinion, instead, it is proven wrong by the opinion. While the value link can be affected by an influx of positive or negative facts, the effect is more dependent on group dynamics than it is on the actual content of the ideas. Facts with a high non evaluation are assigned that value because, whatever they may be, they are not relevant to supporting the truth of the opinion, and are just sorted to discharge their significance quotient.

Opinions only apply to certain types of facts: political opinions to political facts, social opinions to social facts, fishing opinions to fishing facts, and so on. Of course, facts are expressed in an idiom developed by the specific and extended self, so there tends to be a consistent or common style across one's opinions, but there is little to no useful crossover between types.

In the current design, the exit points are being used to handle the pro, anti and non categories of facts, although this is largely an implementation question, and so is open to change without impacting the interface. The fact is that the identification of a presented fact of the correct type as pro, anti or non can be done by the same simple vector angle calculation as is used throughout to evaluate input, so this seems natural and consistent with the overall design. Additionally, whereas attitudes dismiss facts into an unordered collection that does not support reproducible queries very well, the fact collections found in opinions do seem to support at least a crude hierarchy that allows the retrieval of the 3-5 most important supporting facts quickly and reliably, and this type of hierarchical structure is supported on the exit points but not in the sibling collection.

23.3   Opinion Characteristics

It is easy to see that opinions have a strange, semi-rational structure: developed opinions are formed from anecdotal evidence (while assimilated opinions are accepted as part of the dues one pays to belong to a group), so one might say they have some vague, undefined relation to reality, but since their truth value is sticky and tends not to vary with accumulating evidence, their claim to a scientific or rational basis is tenuous, at best. Furthermore, the anti fact category of an opinion functions like an opinion disposal unit, capturing and neutering charged facts.

Opinion is a container pattern with a value link evaluation that connects back to the singularity distortion field, but that link can be moved from one value site to another as conditions and interpretations evolve. However, while the container level evaluation can be influenced by values in the fact set, it is not controlled by them, on the contrary, adjustments require volitional action, they are not automatic, and will not happen without conscious intent. This means that the opinion object has an undefined relation to the fact sets it contains.

We can think of an opinion as a named evaluation of a set of thoughts, but what it organizes is a set of patterns. That set of patterns can include other opinions, which means that we can have opinions of opinions of opinions, and so on, without limit. In fact, this is how internal reasoning, i.e., reasoning on internal knowledge, actually works: we evolve, from our own experience and our own reasoning, as well as from the opinions we accept from our groups, a web of interlocking opinions that defines our body of knowledge. *All* of our knowledge that is not certifiably external can be described as belonging to a network of opinions, a web of influenced, rolled up evaluations of anecdotal experiences that have an undefined relation to reality.

 *It may seem radical to suggest that virtually all of our knowledge exists in an interlocking web of opinions, but, considering the cost of externalization, how could it be otherwise?*

Note that the peculiar structure of the opinion object perfectly explains our failure to advance knowledge through debate:

- We *know* (incorrectly as it turns out) that our opinions are based on 'good' facts.
- We try to disprove other's opinions by attacking their facts, but this cannot work because
  - Facts do not control the opinion's truth evaluation.
  - Opinions are specifically built to emasculate contrary facts.
  - The truth evaluation of the opinion links to the primitive self-interest and self-defense mechanisms, so attacking someone's strongly held opinion is the verbal equivalent of attacking them with a cudgel. Their only option is to fight back, or run away.

We *know* that our own opinions are based on facts because we do build them up from our experience and reasoning, but the purblind defect keeps us from seeing that our ideas are internal and do not correlate in any defined way with external reality, so we wind up with an entirely unrealistic expectation of the universality of our opinions.

We *know* that we have refuted an opinion when we have

attacked some of its supporting facts, even though the opinion object has no facility to disinterestedly evaluate facts, because this would be quite contrary to its actual job of reducing the unknown to the known, the external to the internal. We keep running into the essential reductive nature of cognition as we map more of our experience into our executable model of cognition because, of course, the fundamental function of the mind *must* be the reductive evaluation of the elements in the unbounded set of all possible experiences down into the limited vocabulary of perception, cognition and movement supported by our genome. This always surprises us because the purblind defect fools us into thinking that we see, know and own the world, rather than understanding that we just get an impressionistic view of the tiny bit of it that is modeled within the confines of the boundaries of our being.

Traditionally, rationalists have prided themselves on their ability to keep facts and opinions separate, and they claim to base all of their best thinking on facts alone, and they assert that it is their educated discipline that gives them authority over the unschooled. But surely, if nothing else, by now we can see that if knowledge is not external, it's internal, and if it's internal, it's rolled up into opinions. Certainly, some of that opinion might be externalizable, but until it is verifiably tested, all opinions have an undefined relation to reality. The conviction, the *belief* that rationalists have in the superiority of their thought, in the precedence that their opinions should have over others, actually is just a product of the Erudition Fallacy, the enthusiastic self-deception that is part and parcel of the accumulation of benefits sought by those who work to advance themselves into the inner circles of power, in their chosen groups, through the mastery of the manners and mores of the elite.

23.4   Changing Opinions

Personal opinions are easily and often changed, but what actually happens is that first, the value link of the existing opinion, if significant, is adjusted downwards sufficiently far to no longer be seen as reliable, and a new opinion with a new sorting algorithm, but the same entry point situation, is formed, and assigned a higher value link. Think about your own personal experience: your discarded opinions still exist intact, but you now consider them invalid compared to your new opinion.

Opinions that were adopted as part of the compact you implicitly agreed to when joining a group are much harder to change because what really has to be changed is the group affiliation, not just the opinion.

Privately changing one's opinion is an entirely different experience than being pushed to change it during a conversation. The latter case is more complex because of the grouping aspects involved, but it is still simple enough to diagram and analyze. The important point is to keep your attention focused on the value link, and more or less disregard the sorted facts except to attack the sorting algorithm.

23.5   Review

- Opinions summarize the evaluation of an initial set of facts, after that, they sort facts into buckets.

- Pro-self ideas prove an opinion true, anti-self ideas are disproved by the opinion, non-self are made unimportant by the opinion.

- Opinions support higher level internal thought by chunking ideas.

- L2 opinions sacrifice accuracy for speed, power for tractability.

- Attitude discards ideas, opinion organizes them.

- The opinion evaluation field is initially set by the rolled up evaluations of the ideas in the pro bucket.

- Once set, the opinion evaluation field is largely independent of the facts accumulated by the opinion.

- The fact buckets in opinions are semi-ordered on value.

- Essentially all of our unvalidated knowledge exists in an interconnected web of opinions.

- Opinions are virtually impervious to attacks on their facts.

- Rationalists are wrong in asserting that their opinions are correct because they are based on facts.

Chapter 24

Ideology and Religion

24.1 Introduction

Religion is a grouping (q.v. chapter 19) around a belief that satisfies at least the first three of the following four conditions:

- It defines the mechanisms to support a community of the believers.

- It defines and leads repeating rituals that are comforting.

- It defines and teaches rules of conduct for congregation members.

- It defines a theology that challenges the congregants to learn.

A group that does less than this may be a faith group, but is not what has historically been recognized as a religion. A group that does more than this, that is, that attempts to dictate to non-members, is an ideology whose belief system includes a religion. Historically, I think it is accurate to say that the world's major religions generally started out as ideologies and only later settled into just being religions after the populace was able to appreciate the benefits of separating church and state. A simple religion defines an individual's relation to the ultimate, while an ideology aspires to govern the society of believers. Islam is still, at the time of this writing, functioning as a crusading ideology that aspires to eliminate all non-believers while controlling all facets of its believers' lives. The religious aspect of Islam plays a distinctly subordinate role to its ideological component.

The challenge component of religion appears primarily in the Torah command to study, but other than that, there is no hint, that I am aware of, that a believer should ever pursue study far enough to question the major pillars of his faith.

The remainder of this chapter will focus strictly on ideology but is not, by any stretch of the imagination, going to be a treatise on ideology. On the contrary, our much more modest goal is to demonstrate the power of the executable model-oriented approach to reasoning by showing how easily the ideas discussed so far work together to explicate higher, more abstract concepts—such ideas as those that command the attention of serious intellectuals—without requiring new, higher level constructs.

24.2   Definition of Ideology

If we Google the definition of ideology, here's what we get:

Ideology: a system of ideas and ideals, especially one that forms the basis of economic or political theory and policy. [Google, OED]

Using the model-oriented reasoning and universal cognition model concepts that we have already discussed, we can provide an alternative, more useful definition of ideology:

> **Ideology**: a container structure comprising coordinated opinion, belief and attitude (and, optionally, religion) objects that supports formation of a group structure sufficient to campaign for a particular resolution to a set of resource distribution problems in such a way as to benefit their interests.

In other words, an ideology is an opinion with an attitude fueled by beliefs that endow the believer with delusions of grandeur. Note that everything in an ideology is hostile to criticism and built to view the world as a battle of self against other. There is no facility that supports reflection, inquiry or learning. Ideology is a mechanism that binds the self to a larger group with the cement of conviction and attitude, strengthened with the straw of an opinion structure just a little too large for most adherents to fully comprehend.

24.3   Structure of Ideology Object

In chapter 30, we will examine the fundamental subjective problem, but for now, let us just say that cognitive spaces are built on the fabric of mortality, and the fundamental problem of mortality, aside from duration, relates to resource allocation issues. Of necessity, all higher level conceptual systems that are not restricted to internal knowledge issues are concerned, directly

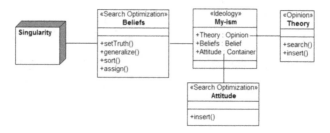

Figure 24.1: Ideology Structure

or indirectly, with resource allocation in one way or another. Ideology represents a characteristic solution to the fundamental subjective resource allocation problem, a solution with a benefit redistribution calculation that begins with zeroing out the legitimate interests of the ideology's enemies.

An ideology is a constellation of conceptual constructs that center around a small group of fundamental beliefs that assert a universal solution to a resource allocation issue. Another way to put this is: ideologies are integrated opinion systems that use belief to extend all participant selfs far enough that they can link to the founding singularity distortion field (in reality, messages communicate instructions to anchor the beliefs to certain value coordinates). The theoretical basis of the ideology is an opinion web charged up with the power of the belief truth. Ideologies process all potential facts through beliefs, attitudes and opinions. Think of an ideology as a battle group, where attitude is the first line of defense, opinion is the second, and belief is the protected third defensive line guarding a core of naked, extended self-interest ideas.

How could ideologies be anything but this? Since the fundamental tenet of an ideology is that they embody *the* true solution to the resource allocation problem in question, can it be a surprise that they are not amenable to admitting contradiction? On what basis do we expect them to actually be useful tools in the progress of humanity? Clearly, they are defined in, and exist to serve, the interests of the foundational singularity. Their function is to increase the rewards redounding to their core members, and none of their mechanisms extend to those flatter regions of cognitive space where a low distortion interaction with measurable reality can occur. Study the ideology structure shown in figure 24.1, and try to find anything in it that is capable of supporting honest, intellectual inquiry.

Pause for a moment and consider which actually describes ideology better, this structural definition, or the idealistic dream notion sold by ideological tyrants. Be honest about what is, and has been, and put aside what you might hope would be.

Make no mistake about it, though, ideologies are very powerful mechanisms for creating groupings with a very high commitment level, and these groupings can create societies or civilizations. Why are ideologies so powerful? Look at the object: they combine the power of attitude, belief, opinion, and sometimes religion. Each of these objects on their own is a powerful shaper of experience and cognitive processes, and together, their impact is multiplied, not just added. But, ideologies are about grouping and resource allocation, they are not about improving or advancing the state of any part of humanity outside of the interests of their higher members and officers.

24.4   Limits of Ideology

Ideologies do not address, cannot comprehend, and cannot investigate $\mathbb{R}$; they are opinion systems that process facts to support a particular benefit distribution favorable to their controlling interests, which of course, might not be related to the beneficiaries they claim to represent in their literature.

Part of the manifest hostility being displayed regarding ideologies in this chapter comes from the primitive limitations inherent in the crude ideology mechanism, which fits it for little but organizing larger groups of people to do mischief. The other part of the hostility comes from the recent rapid collapse of our so-called institutions of higher learning, which have deteriorated from being the effete erudition fallacy factories they have historically been, down to the malignant Marxist collectivist indoctrination centers they now are, in just the last few decades.

One of the major problems with ideology in the time this is being written is that it is common for adolescents to think they need to study and adopt an ideology so that they will know how to understand things, know what to think. Since, to their jejune minds, an ideology is what one uses to describe the underlying reality of the world, then they think that all they should need to do is to find the right one and voila, they are now situated, in the know, impervious to doubt and uncertainty, and on the right side of history, riding the wave of right and truth!

This is why we go to college, isn't it? To learn how to think complex thoughts so we can learn answers to the problems plaguing humanity? Unfortunately, the vast majority of the non-technical faculty adheres to an intolerant social Marxist philosophy that loves the group and hates both individuals and the educational process that elevates them, which results in universities becoming collectivist automaton factories.

Groups have their place, as will be discussed in chapter 19, Groups, but the thrust of the entire pinnacle effort is to try to understand why, despite our vaunted institutions of higher learning, we have, so far, been utterly unable to answer a single pinnacle question or even to define a sequence of smaller subquestions to work on. The history of the university, outside of the hard science schools, is an unending shame of failure. Watching them doff one ridiculous guiding light ideology, only to replace it with another, even more absurd one, is heartbreaking to anyone capable of understanding the role education can play in moving us beyond L2 into the discovery world of L3.

Ideology's *only* role is in group formation, it has no place in, and no capacity to contribute to, any learning or development process that can demonstrably move us forward in our efforts finally to resolve pinnacle questions.

24.5   Review

- Religion is a grouping that:
  - defines the mechanisms to support a community of the believers;
  - defines and leads repeating rituals that are comforting;
  - defines and teaches rules of conduct for congregation members;
  - defines a theology that challenges the congregants to learn.
- Ideology is a container structure comprising coordinated opinion, belief, and attitude (and, optionally, religion) objects that supports formation of a group structure sufficient to campaign for a particular resolution to a set of resource distribution problems in such a way as to benefit the leaders' interests.
- An ideology is an opinion with an attitude fueled by beliefs that endow the believer with delusions of grandeur.
- The theoretical basis of the ideology is an opinion web charged up with the power of the belief truth.
- An ideology is a battle group in which attitude is the first line of defense, opinion is the second, and belief is the protected third defensive line that guards a core of naked, extended self-interest values.
- Ideologies are very powerful mechanisms for creating groupings with a very high commitment level that can create societies or civilizations, and destroy others.

- Ideologies do not address, cannot comprehend, and cannot investigate $\mathbb{R}$.

Chapter 25

Statements

25.1 Statement Definition

Before we can begin to examine conversations, first we must define the fundamental unit of all interaction with ideas and models, the *statement*:

statement = [context] + content + [purpose]

That is, whenever we express an idea or a feeling, we do it using the statement construct; this is not something we learn to do, it is the necessary consequence of the fact that all meaning comes from the singularity distortion field. To think or say something significant means that we had to have previously situated that fact in our value field, and it is this action that embeds it in the statement construct by setting the three values. This definition just formalizes what necessarily is. The square brackets indicate that both the *context* and *purpose* elements are optional in the sense that they may be implicit rather than explicit, but they are *always* there, just not necessarily — in fact, not usually — expressed, or even consciously thought, or understood, at the verbal L2 level.

Large statements can be easily constructed just by adding simple statements together in a collection or path of some sort:

compound statement = statement + statement+

That is, a compound statement simply consists of two or more simple statements, so compound and simple statements do not require separate treatment.

25.2   Statement Elements

The *content* of the statement is whatever it is, but for analytical purposes, just assume we are talking about ideas small enough to be expressed in simple sentences and let compound statements handle paragraphs and larger constructs.

The *purpose* of a statement is the goal or conclusion that the statement is intended to achieve or facilitate, whether it is the goal 'add numbers' in the statement: [arithmetic] 2+2 = 4 [add numbers], where the context is arithmetic and the content is '2+2 = 4', or whether it is an implicit plea for help in the statement: [some illness or injury] "I feel bad" [succor me].

The *context* of a statement can be, and often is, implicit, either in whole or in part, which makes sense, because statements we make are situated in the complexity of our experience, which it is clearly not practicable to express with every bit of content, every time, especially since the purblind defect leads us to assume that it is just what everybody else feels.

With the bulk of a statement construct being potentially implicit, is it any wonder that verbal communication is so fraught with misunderstandings?

The scientific revolution effectively extended the definition of a statement to include a new, critically important term:

statement = [domain][context]+content+[purpose]

Domain, as used here, identifies which external discipline contextualizes the statement with its own grammar and vocabulary. That is, it specifies that discussions on astronomy are restricted to astronomical concepts and observations, and shouldn't be wandering into fields of literature and religion, for example. It tells us that the subject is external, and where we will find our reproducible tests. Without a specified domain, we must assume the statements are of a strictly internal type, and that their content may only exist inside the head of the discussants.

25.3 Statements and Models

Statements either relate to an internal reality that exists inside our minds, or to the external reality that exists independent of us. Since scientists are doing a fine job of exploring external reality, we will leave external statements to them for now, and focus our attention exclusively on internal statements because our failure to answer pinnacle questions has always started and ended with our misunderstanding of internal reality.

The fundamental question of cognition has always been, what relation does a given internal statement, i_i have to an external reality, r_i? This is exactly the problem that faceted cytomodel-oriented reasoning provides a framework to answer. In a sense, this is the core of what model-oriented reasoning is designed to do.

The overall goal of this work is to provide a unified, executable model of the human mind that allows us to extend the scientific revolution to all areas of human experience, and in particular to externalize the subjective problem space to make it accessible to objective reasoning tools and reproducible tests. Our premise is that all of our thoughts, feelings and beliefs originate from, and exist within, the small confines of our skull-encased brain, and this supports the hypothesis that — all historical evidence to the contrary notwithstanding — it is actually possible to develop a unified model of the human mind that relates our various mental experiences together in a way that will enable us to extend the scientific revolution into the subjective domain of human experience.

The models and operations presented here allow us to define a unified solution space that encompasses all of human experience, which not only relates our various mental experiences together, but that also defines transformations from each type of mental experience to any of the others. Perhaps the most significant accomplishment of this work is that we show how *any* subjective statement can be transformed into an externalized, testable statement that can generate results that are reproducible by others. That is, we show how to convert any subjective statement to an objective counterpart external statement that should be either refutable or verifiable.

But, there is another aspect of learning that model-oriented reasoning addresses, and that is the extent to which we are changed by what we learn. The nature of pattern assimilation is that patterns are learned as units, black boxes, as it were, that, figuratively speaking, have an input slot on one side and an output slot on the other. As you can tell from dealing with doctors of theology, medicine and psychology, it is possible to complete a tremendous amount of pattern assimilation without ever being touched by any of it, without it affecting the core of your being in the least. L3 model-oriented reasoning, while it does not necessarily improve you in any way, changes the circuitry that processes many of your thoughts and feelings as you build extensive networks of naked ideas. Again, this change is just a change, a lengthening of certain paths, so it is not necessarily either a good or a bad thing, just a fact.

Supposedly socially conscious posers have always complained that science and technology improves our tools without improving us, that the failure of science is that it just provides stone age barbarians (us) with better weapons to disastrous results. Unfortunately, since this crowd, nearly to a person, manages to get their soft degrees without ever having to take more than an introductory course or two in the hard sciences, as a group, they wind up being uniquely unequipped to participate in the effort to extend the miracle of scientific accomplishment into the arena of subjective human experience and feelings. So, they will never have the background or ability to master faceted model-oriented reasoning, and thus will never be able to participate in the solution.

25.4   Statement Types

Of course, there are as many statement types as your analysis requires, but we will restrict ourselves to considering the three highest level types of internal statements:

- Interest
- Existence
- Meta

25.4.1   Interest Statements

The term *interest* is used extensively throughout this series of volumes in the sense of self-interest, as in an *interested* party, that is, someone who has a personal stake in the proceedings. Interest is an L0 concept that applies to any threat to us or ours, or any opportunity that might benefit us or ours. In the context of the singularity, interest could easily be defined as the slope of the distortion field at a given point. Therefore, interest statements include all statements about resource allocation—whether actual or potential, positive or negative—as well as all statements about truth that impact one's interest or identity. Thus, statements relating to our interest swath, such as, "he cut me off by pulling into that gap in front of my car!" are interest statements.

L3 operations can transform interest statements into optimization problems using the formula shown below, which will be discussed in depth in chapter 30.

$$\text{alter}(P_{p_i..p_n}) : Q(q_j..q_m) \rightarrow |A_1(a_k..a_p)| > |A_0(a_k..a_p)|$$

Statements expressed in this form are both externalizable and testable.

Ordinarily, though, interest statements are processed by the L0 truth engine in this form:

$$\text{ownership right} = \frac{strength_{mine} * need_{mine}}{strength_{theirs}}$$

That is, my ownership right in something is the ratio of the product of my perceived strength and my perceived need compared the perceived strength of the competitor. L0 interest statements are familiar to us as conflict triggers, with the mode of conflict ranging from armed confrontation to fighting, posturing, or legal or verbal sparring. Notice that this L0 interest formula is biased towards conflict by the way it compares the product of our need and strength against just our assessment of our opponent's ability to resist us. While this formula emerged from the coding model, it seems to align nicely with observations of normal instances of social conflict.

In polite society, L2 interest statements are truly uninteresting, since they seem so often to boil down to the pusillanimity formula:

$$|\text{my ownership right}| - |\text{their strength}| \rightarrow \begin{cases} \leq 0 : other \\ >> 0 : self \end{cases}$$

That is, if their strength is greater than or equal to my rights, then they get it, otherwise, only if the force is overwhelmingly in my favor, then I get it. This isn't the only way L2 processes interest statements, but in genteel societies that find violence uncouth, this seems often to be the bottom line recommendation of L2, regardless of whether we are talking about personal or political situations. When conflict avoidance becomes the highest value, naturally one's rights recede in the face of determined opposition.

Remember that, unless being driven by L0 motivations, the L2 pattern processing engine just uses the grammar supplied with each pattern language as its only test of validity. It doesn't automatically check its results either with our self-interest or reality, so it will happily give away the store with a smile if it finds a rule that says it should.

25.4.2 Existence Statements

Existence statements are statements against the reality that each intellect level recognizes, they are assertions that x describes an actuality in its reality. The existence statement is a statement of fact: *that* exists; I saw *that*; *this* is true, etc. Most of our non-conditional statements are existence statements, assertions that the validity of a fact's content makes it actionable. Anytime you state what you know, you are making an existence statement.

The L0 existence statement is simplicity itself:

$$evaluation(x) = r_i$$

That is, from L0's point of view, however it interprets a sensory event exactly describes the reality of thing. L0 considers no reality higher than itself, and this makes sense, since its only job is to reductively evaluate the entire cosmic domain down into actionable terms. Thus, L0 completely identifies its $\mathbb{R}$ with external reality, and is only capable of making statements that have some level of an absolute truth value. Remember that memory only comes in with L1, but L0 is still the evaluator, decider and actor it has been from the earliest times. This means that the ancient evaluate, decide and action functions operate in a pre-memory context, that is, L0 lives in a 'one and done' kind of world, in which it sees something, evaluates it, reacts to it, and forgets it, to be ready to move immediately onto handling the next reality. Reality does not exist on a continuum for L0, as it does for L2 and L3, because, even though there is overlap between snapshots, without memory, each new snapshot of the internal and external senses defines all of reality anew for each L0 moment. For an L0 entity, reality is the snapshot being processed now.

The phrase, 'acted without thinking' has a deep source of meaning, since this is *exactly* what our most primitive intellect is *built* to do: preserve the self by reacting to immediate threats and opportunities. In the mudball model, except when it is impossible to do so, people routinely assume that our experience and behavior is exclusively controlled by our modern intellect, even though we know this is not how evolution works. Our higher intellects can modify the input to the L0 action module, but the more primitive machinery is always working, oblivious even to the existence of our higher functions, so anything that affects the timing or efficacy of our higher thought inevitably leads to unreviewed L0 actions taking over our behavior, often pushing the situation in directions we never intended.

L1 is just L0 plus the ability to make a partial record of the past, as well as the ability to evaluate, generalize and learn from experience. The L1 form of the existence statement asserts the truth of experience represented in the result object:

$$\text{given situation } s_0, \text{ action } a_i \rightarrow s_1;$$

$$\text{or}$$

$$\text{if } (s_0) \text{ then } a_i = true \ \& \ a_j = false$$

That is, if we recognize a situation, then we *know* that an action we have done before will have the result we saw previously, or, to put it another way, given a situation we recognize, the action we have personal or collective experience with, will be judged to be right, and any other alternative will be judged to be wrong.

L2 existence statements are fuzzy implication truth statements:

$$\text{situation } s_i \xrightarrow{\circ} s_j$$

The unusual implication arrow with a degree symbol is meant to indicate that implication has degrees of certainty. This matches the multiple exit points in the pattern object that are accessed via different levels of matching with the search key. That is, L2 existence statements assert that situation s_1 will eventuate from situation s_0 with the given degree of likelihood.

That is to say that, in each of the levels, existence statements tell us something different:

- what is (L0);
- what path, action or decision is right (L1);
- what is likely to be, what might be coming (L2).

25.4.3 Meta Statements

Meta statements are statements about statements. Since statements are an abstraction that contextualizes content, and content is any reference to a mentacule, result, pattern or statement, and each of these is an abstraction of an evaluation of a sensory or cognitive event, then meta statements are statements about abstractions. But all statements are about abstractions: all of our thought, however primitive, is an abstraction either of other thoughts or of interpreted sensory experiences. In other words, introducing a term to refer to abstract thought may be a rhetorical convenience, but it is a logical nullity since it adds nothing new to the conversation.

However, since we are here, and since the term was originally added to help contextualize discussions about religious, spiritual and philosophical matters, let's continue using it for now. Meta statements are purely internal statements *about* statements, as opposed to being statements about reality or referents to reality. Reality, even though it is subjective and level-bound, is nevertheless a very important, persuasive concept to the mind at level L2 and below, so it matters not whether a verifiable entity actually exists at the end of the reference chain. Since the reference affects perceptions, evaluations, decisions and actions, it is, in at least these dimensions, real to the person with that belief.

Religious-type meta statements, on the other hand, are different, they are the verbal counterpart to the container object that spawns a new level of abstraction, that conceptualizes a new level of existence. Even to the average mind using the mudball model, although the believer may be utterly convinced that God exists, most will acknowledge that he dwells in $\mathbb{S}$, rather than in $\mathbb{R}$.

Statements about what God is like, what he wants us to do, what he intends to do, etc., are statements that use L2 patterns to elaborate the sense of conviction and viability of the highest value L0 beliefs with the most abstract (in the sense of not grounded in experience) L2 patterns. Rationalists like to dismiss such statements as dealing in ignorance, superstition and mythology, but this is a mistake for the simple reason that it draws a false and misleading division in the set of statements in $\mathbb{I}$. **All** statements in $\mathbb{I}$ have an undefined relation to $\mathbb{R}$ UNLESS they have been externalized, and pointing out meta statements in $\mathbb{S}$ as somehow different than any other statement in $\mathbb{I}$ just fuels the delusion that L0 truth can somehow validate all $i \in \mathbb{I} \setminus \mathbb{S}$.

If we consider meta statements by level, we see that meta statements really are just statements:

- L0 meta statements = empty set (no abstraction without memory)
- L1 meta statements = L1 result object (contextualizes the

action object)

- L2 meta statements = L2 statements

Meta statements that concern us exist in the verbal model, which means that they are L2 statements, and all L2 statements are actually meta statements.

However, since we introduced the term to help us analyze religious statements and behavior, we can define religious statements as meta statements with context $\mathbb{S}$. The reason that religious statements can be so powerful is that they routinely link to a religious object that gathers grouping, authority, loopback, purpose, conduct, and challenge statements together into a coherent structure that situates us in a larger reality with a healthy dose of anxiety reducing loopback statements. That constitutes a mighty fortress to attack frontally without the sword; historically, successful attacks have always taken a tunneling vector to undermine the fortress's foundations.

25.5 Statement Validity

How do we compare the validity of meta statements (statements in $\mathbb{S}$), to ordinary statements (statements in $\mathbb{I}$)? Let's do some back-of-the-envelope calculations to see what we can figure out.

How numerous are internal statements relative to external statements in our mind? Since externalizing statements is expensive in terms of time and effort, it is safe to say that, on the best week, we externalize maybe low single digits of statements per day, which means that we are likely externalizing single digits of statements per week, *in a good week*. In a usual

week, a usual month, a usual *year*, we might not externalize
any. (Of course, this is an unsupported number, so feel free
to use your own count of how many ideas you externalized in
the last week using formal tests. Programmers: implementing
designs at work doesn't really count as externalizing your own
ideas.)

Compared to this, how many new internal statements are
we creating *daily*? Let's look at the numbers:

number of seconds in a 16 hour day: $60 * 60 * 16 = 57,600$

7 objects per snapshot, 1 snap/second:

$7 * 57,600 = 403,200$ objects/*day*

assume 1 snap/5 sec, 2 objects/snap: 23,040 objects/*day*

assume 1 snap/min, 1 object/snap: 960 objects/*day*

Any way you do the math, the number of new internal statements we generate daily utterly swamps the number of statements we externalize in a year. Artificially tagging a small set
of internal statements as somehow different than the millions of
others in the collection, creates a false impression of a defect in
the former, and a level of quality in the latter, that impedes the
actual process of externalization. This is why it is unhelpful to
call out supernatural statements as being any less trustworthy
than any other kind of internal statement.

L2 cognitive faculties suffer at the extremes: too many charged ideas breeds distraction and anxiety, but too few breeds alienation and ennui. Health is an emergent property of dynamic equilibrium.

25.6 Goal

What is the implicit goal in these statements we are making about statements in this chapter? (You have noticed that we are using sentence statements to make points about statements, right? And that means that each of our sentences is a statement comprising context + content + purpose, and that in many, if not most cases, the context and goal of the statement are implicit or just unstated, right?) Consider figures 25.2 and 25.3. The first represents a view of the current division our body of knowledge between external knowledge, which contains both what we have scientifically measured and what might be measurable, while the rest of the area represents pure internal knowledge. That's where we are. The next diagram, 25.3, represents where we want to be, with the bulk of knowledge externalized and verified.

External knowledge, the domain of science and the beneficiary of all of our scientific progress, represents a minority slice of our current experience pie that is dominated by subjective knowledge. The contention is that faceted model-oriented rea-

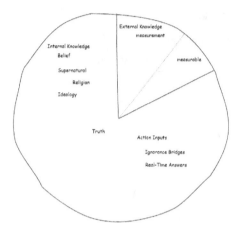

Figure 25.2: Current State of Internal and External Knowledge

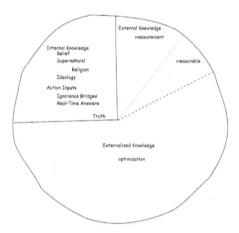

Figure 25.3: Future State of Internal and External Knowledge

soning will enable us to flip the proportion of internal to external knowledge, from figure 25.2 to figure 25.3, reducing the proportion of untested, personal, informal, purely internal knowledge to a minority of our knowledge by externalizing subjective experience to the domain of scientific examination and testing.

Achieving this goal will require formalizing our more important concepts so that they can be externalized, tested, iteratively enhanced and extended into previously unexplored areas of subjectivity. Understanding the nature of the fundamental unit of interaction with knowledge, the statement, is an important step in this process.

25.7 Review

- statement = [context] + content + [purpose]
- compound statement = [context] + statement + [purpose]
- Two-thirds of conversations are normally implicit, making formal communication effectively impossible.
- Scientific statements are restricted to a formal domain, making formal communication possible.
- Interest statements address mortality concerns.
- Existence statements express an intellect's knowledge mechanism's view on input usefulness: truth $\propto$ usability.
- Meta statements are in $\mathbb{S}$, ordinary statements are in $\mathbb{I}$.
- Meta statement validity $\approx$ ordinary statement validity.
- Our goal is to externalize many subjective statements.

Chapter 26

Conversation, Debate and Argument

26.1 Introduction

From an abstract perspective, there are only two things an organism can do with a high-level (L2) cognitive capacity: think, and communicate.

We have discussed the way the model breaks thought down into an accumulation of the output of a relatively few, relatively simple, functions:

- evaluate input
- compare and select
- respond to perceptions with movement
- remember, recall and learn from experience
- generalize from the specific

- learn, create, extend and manipulate patterns
- create, modify and execute plans
- think about thoughts

Now, we can consider *communication*, the process by which cooperation is forged through signs, sounds and scents; it provides the base abstraction layer upon which physical and relational hierarchies and structures can be contrived. The extended self is created and maintained through communication which, at the L2 level, is primarily verbal. That is, grouping is a function of communication; the ability to communicate is the ability to organize socially. The ability of a cognitive entity to extend its self-concept beyond its own corporeal boundaries requires at least the ability to communicate through signs or sounds. Communication and social organization are inseparable functions.

*The reader must, at some point, ask, "What can I **do** with this information?" Pause for a moment and write down how you can make conversations productive. Then, repeat the exercise at the end of this chapter. Note the differences.*

The two primary modes of communication are: affectless, in which word patterns are exchanged without emotional or mortality-related dimensions; and affective, in which the survival and emotional interests are engaged. And, even though affectless communication can be used to communicate patterns without any apparent grouping application, ultimately, all communication both requires and relates to the socioeconomic structures of the culture, so it is correct to say that all communication is related to, or embedded in, a grouping context.

In this chapter, we will examine the mechanics, limitations and capacities of verbal communication using the universal cognition model to force our thoughts beyond the world of humans and history and out into the world of the abstract and universal. As with everything cognitive, there are three fundamental types of communication: pro-self, anti-self, and non-self. At the level of conversation, this tripolar evaluation is built on the goal or tenor of the communicative act: it is either positive, in the sense of convivial or supportive; negative, in the sense of hostile or competitive; or affectless in the strict sense, meaning dispassionate or disinterested, rather than bored or uninterested.

Another way to characterize the three poles of verbal interaction is friendly conversation, confrontational argument, or information exchange. In each of these areas, although all conversations are L2 level interactions, they can be characterized by their affect and purpose as either L0/L1 or L2 verbal exchanges. L0/L1 interactions deal with truth, decision and action. Discussions can therefore either be L0/L1 truth struggles, or L2 pattern language interactions according to the objects being discussed: opinions, beliefs, facts, relations, etc.

This model applies to conversations, debates, arguments, texts, speeches, and even drunken rows. Thus, it applies directly to our core problem: since we think and relate to others using words and signs, then communication can be seen as the medium of thought, the means by which we attain, develop, express, exchange and interact with ideas. Since our fundamental question seeks explication of the mechanism of our fecklessness in progressing in the pinnacle subjects, then by examining the capabilities and limitations of the communicative processes, perhaps we can begin to find some clues about why we have been failing so utterly, and for so long, to make any real progress on the higher level questions.

26.2   Communication

Figure 26.2 shows a partial, but trenchant, view of how communication layers onto the first four levels of the universal cognition model.

Communication begins with a challenge. This is easy to understand if you have already grasped the nature and function of the L0 perception process: mortality dictates that a cognitive entity's first responsibility is to protect the self, so every single sensory input is evaluated first for risk, and if it is found to be safe, only then can it be checked for opportunity or content. This challenge is shown in the diagram as the dot-dash outlined fact object, it represents a potential threat that must be processed and evaluated as quickly possible.

In the simplest L0/L1 case, initializing a mentacule with a snapshot of the current sensory input produces an actionable evaluation that generates a move command (the dashed path

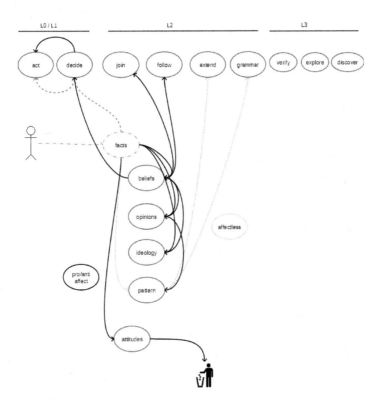

Figure 26.2: Communication paths, objects and functions.

to the *decide* and *act* functions). This process has been explained in detail, so we will move onto the more interesting, for us, anyway, case of the L2 language level cognitive entity that occupies the rest of the diagram.

It makes no difference whatsoever whether the input fact comes from a conversation or an experience because, to the cognitive mind, the distinction between the two only arises postprocessing. At the point of impact, an experience is simply an event that must be responded to, or defused, as expeditiously as possible.

The first L2 path in the diagram we will consider is fact → attitudes → trash. This shows graphically that attitudes filter out experience to whatever level they are contrived to handle, and they do this to maintain cognitive-emotional (L1/L2) equilibrium by reflexively assigning dismissable meaning to experience, not by extracting meaning from it.

If not handled by an attitude, the first step in processing language facts is to check them against beliefs, because beliefs are really just L2 representations of L0/L1 survival truths, thus they return immediate, definitive answers to any questions they can handle. Beliefs are the most primitive L2 high level object, and they act by injecting the absolute power of L0 truth into the agnostic world of L2 pattern language grammar. The L2 pattern processing mind is truly the unreliable, amoral fop that the lower classes accuse it of being, because without the backbone of belief, L2 is a gullible, rudderless, sophomoric pattern manipulator that cannot be trusted to defend our interests. Beliefs are a fast evaluator of language facts, and within milliseconds will claim and process relevant facts fully.

Facts handled by beliefs can trigger the L2 *join* and *follow* functions that are part of the grouping mechanism that causes the contours of the self to extend or reshape in response to differing perceptions of shifting threats and opportunities in the social landscape.

Facts that are found to be neither exigent, nor beliefs, have thus been implicitly identified as less urgent, so they can be processed by more complex structures with slower response times. If the fact manifestly represents no threat, such as being an in-subject verbal pattern where the subject itself is either safe or abstract, then it can be handled by the dotted pattern route connecting the fact to the pattern object and thence to the extend and grammar functions of L2. Think of this as the quilting bee path, where new fabric scraps are casually sewn into the pattern with some care, but no urgency. For those who are not baseball fanatics, the fact that Mickey Mantle's batting average in 1952 was .311 is of such little consequence that it might never be sewn into any pattern quilt, while those with an eidetic memory might indifferently stitch it into a memory structure pattern without bothering to relate it to baseball at all, and fanatics might even contest it.

The vast majority of L2 facts are non-critical events that connect to patterns related to anticipating future events, rather than being urgent messages with real-time significance. In reality, since the L2 verbal ability infects its host with a concomitant loquacity, we tend to spend our days immersed in a sea of verbal messages, almost all of which fall below the level of survival or belief importance, and are only obliquely or potentially interesting. Such is the stuff of which opinions, the baleen filter-feeder mechanism of our cognitive system, are made. Our Weltanschauung, our daily relationship with experience, comprises a web of opinions that form a screen to filter and sort the conversational detritus that assaults our awareness throughout the day.

Facts that are processed by opinions are committed to memory and may be processed as patterns later or simply forgotten, but in the present moment, are simply filed away as reinforcing ideas or as errors or lies told by others. Opinions, once formed, are like sorting screens on assembling lines that separate a flow of input into pre-determined categories. They are not learning mechanisms, they have no facility to support critical thought.

This sequencing of beliefs-opinions-ideology is not a fixed order, and for ideological fanatics, ideology can be at the head of the line since, in the extreme, it can define an all-encompassing worldview coextensive with the specific self-concept. Since ideology includes belief, the overall effect isn't changed much, except that when ideology evaluates first, this can lead to a moral myopia caused by seeing everything through an ideological lens.

Note that both opinions and ideology connect to the L2 *join* and *follow* functions through their belief component.

Finally, it should be noted that the L3 functions of *verify*, *explore* and *discover* are not connected to this information flow for the simple reason that, due to the very small audience who might be interested in, or competent to understand this information, this discussion has been deferred to a later time. For the time being, I leave it as an exercise for the reader. Trust me, I've done it, it's not that hard.

26.3 Conversation

The questions of this chapter are,

- what can be accomplished with communication?
- what are the different forms of communication?
- how do the different forms of communication affect the payload potential?

The purblind defect leads us to see communication as a great, smooth pipe through which ideas and feelings can flow. I suppose many people unconsciously imagine a duplex set up, with separate incoming and outgoing pipes, but interruptions and talking over each other make it clear it is a simplex channel that takes time to fill, and to empty, in each direction, before the opposing stream can freely flow.

It is equally clear that, not only is the pipe not as smooth and capacious as we might assume, but that the metaphor itself is deeply and unhelpfully flawed. We can only know what our senses perceive and our minds conceive, so the pipe image is out — at best, our words exit our beings through the spigot of our mouth to spill onto the floor, only some of which will be picked up and processed by mechanisms that must be deliberately exercised by the other participants in our little tête-à-tête.

There is no mechanism, no model that supports channel connection from mind to mind. The boundary of self both contains and limits us, and it defines the interface with the outside world through which we experience all events and interactions with everything beyond our skin. Every word we hear is an instance of the challenge fact explained in the previous section, it is a potential threat that has to be deciphered, evaluated and discharged, in order for us to maintain our dynamic equilibrium so that we stay in a state where we are ready to handle and respond to whatever the wide world throws at us.

We can only process word facts using the objects and functions in our toolkit, and we have no universal communication object: attitudes do what they do and nothing else, similarly with opinions, patterns and ideologies. At the very best, we can process what we hear with what we have, but life is not a path restricted to the very best way. When we say, or write, a paragraph of words, what spills on the ground between us is not just individual words, but sequences, relations, contexts and implications, the sum of which produce the intended meaning only when they are reconstructed in the reader's or auditor's mind in exactly the same order and proportion *not* as spoken, but as *intended*. How could it be otherwise, when we never express the fullness of the singularity-defined context that is the source for the meaning we meant to convey in the handful of words we actually expressed?

The rest of this chapter will examine the potential and the limitations of inter-being communication in the harsh light of the executable reality represented in the communication processing flow illustrated in figure 26.2. As you consider each object with its capabilities and limitations, and perhaps feel a protest rising in your breast that your favorite form of communication is not represented (or, not presented fairly), feel free to define your own L2 object and functions and add it to the simulation and see how it works. But, remember that it is only the purblind defect that causes you even to imagine that the classical idiocy of simultaneous apprehension of a common ideal is possible, or even in the least desirable.

26.4 Affectless Communication

The archetypal L2 affectless interaction is the professional pattern language dialog, the task talk, where the rules and patterns, in a given pattern language, form the subject and purpose of a conversation. For example, tradesmen on a job will have in-profession conversations in the argot of their trade, such as plumbing, electrical, or carpentry topics, tasks and specifications. Other examples include academics speaking to others in their discipline and area of interest, discussing arcane subjects in a language peculiar to their specialty, or family members discussing errand assignments and grocery lists. These types of in-subject discussions are examples of affectless communication as long as they remain affectless; the instant that self-interest or emotion gets involved, the conversation ceases to be affectless and transforms into one of the forms that involve different parts of the mind, which we will discuss below. These conversations are effective to the extent that the context portion of the statements was previously explicitly defined in the training or regulations covering the particular job or task. The implicit goal portion of the statement, even in these technical discussions, is often still troublesome, with inconsistent understanding of goals or constraints often leading to participants working at cross purposes with each other (e.g., are we focusing on achieving high quality, or on rapid completion with minimal expense?).

Task oriented discussions succeed best when the entire focus is on the task, materials, time and resource constraints, as well as the risks involved. Coloring such an exchange with passion, fear, resentment or even sycophancy, distracts from the matter at hand, and reduces the likelihood that the task will be completed in a timely and acceptable manner. This is not advice on how to manage task assignment and explanation, it is saying that if these emotional responses arise in the interaction, it fundamentally changes the interaction from a task talk to another interaction that is handled by another part of the brain that is ill-equipped for this job.

The next kind of affectless dialog, the intellectual conversation, seems to be everyone's default model for what communication naturally is: a rational exchange of objective perceptions and evaluations of events and things in reality. This definition of dialog seems to be everyone's starting point, from which they diverge only when one or more of the participants starts frothing at the mouth, then they bemoan that the conversation has deteriorated to such an emotional level. This, despite the fact that, we rarely, if ever, actually see one of these supposedly normative discussions complete successfully. What is usually happening during intellectual conversations is that all participants are seeing the world from their own distortion field, which they see as flat, causing them to see their opponents' positions as hopelessly distorted and unreasonable.

Oddly enough, the closest we come to successful intellectual discussions may be the lecture model, where an instructor lays out patterns for students, while possibly accepting the occasional question. That is, the most common form of the affectless intellectual dialog we experience is actually a monologue. Hmmm.

The lecture format supports the kind of pattern assimilation that we do in the classroom that focuses on laying out the the lexicon and the transformational grammar of the pattern language under study. This often amounts to a verbally annotated outline of the current chapter of the textbook, and it prepares the student to read and work the problems on their own. During class time, all focus should be strictly on the details of the material, not on our positive or negative response to it. The lecture form succeeds to the extend that the context portion of the statements has been provided in prerequisite courses, since this ensures that everyone is on the same page with the same frame of reference. Sadly, this is rarely the case, as is shown everyday in mid-level math courses where the bulk of the students are lost in a bored fog, because they lack the necessary background even to keep up with the terms used in the lecture, which the teacher gleefully ignores.

As a rule, the affectless intellectual discussion suffers from a three-fold confluence of failure:

- the implicit context of the statements is never adequately clarified;
- the pattern language grammar is not formalized;
- the implicit goal of the statements is belief-based.

Referring back to the definition of the statement, of course, all discussions are made up of statements, and statements include context, content and goal. Intellectual discussions focus on content because the purblind defect causes people to mistake their internal thought for external reality, so they cannot anticipate that their private frame of reference is not shared by all rational people. Discussions consist of the exchange of phrases, periodically interrupted by gaps, often occasioned by the breakdown in the assumption of shared context, that hit the conversation like a hiccup, when the thought train derails on the diverging tracks. Hemming and hawing, the driver pries his train back on the track, muttering vague cultural references thought to be shared through the erudition fallacy, after which, the confused listener will often grudgingly acquiesce, just to maintain the emotional bond sustaining their interaction. After a few of these interruptions, the conversation generally begins to run out of steam as the assumption of a shared understanding of an objective reality is gradually revealed to be the delusion it truly is.

The problem with the content portion of the statement in

the intellectual dialog comes down to a the universal problem with internal thought: lack of reproducibility. In this case, results cannot be reproduced because the grammar of the pattern language being used is not formally defined, so even if they all use the same set of facts, every participant can legitimately arrive at different, and possibly contradictory, conclusions, because the output of manipulating a fact set is dependent both on the imprecisely defined transformational operations supported by the grammar, and the value context of the ideas.

The fatal problem, though, with affectless intellectual discussions that are not in-subject discussions of formal disciplines, is in the implicit goal portion of the conversation's statements. The goal portion is a statement of purpose, of meaning, that, with a few strictly defined exceptions, is effected through a link to a value position in the singularity distortion field. That is, it is belief based, except as explained in chapter 32, Purpose, but in the rest of the cases, either the meaning must be peculiar to one participant or must be shared through a common belief, because meaning only arises in the singularity distortion field. This is to say, when you get right down to it, underneath it all, almost all intellectual discussions ultimately resolve into fairly primitive belief engagements.

From my point of view, of course, the most important kind of affectless communication relates to exploration, but this is an L3 function, and will be covered in a later volume.

26.5   Affective Communication

Affective communication is any communication that engages
our passions, our sense of righteousness and certainty, our experience of fear or awe at the gravity of a situation. Affect is
an emotional response to stimulus, and it derives from the fear,
perception or anticipation of events that touch our specific and
extended interests in either a positive or negative direction. Affective communication uses objects that have a value link to a
site in the singularity distortion field. This means that affective
communication engages the L0 mind. The attentive student
should be able to immediately see the world of implications
contained in that simple statement, because it tells us nearly
all we need to know about the purpose, methods and limitations
of the entire family of affective communication modes.

The key to understanding all forms of affective communication is the evacule ternary data structure on which L0 functionality is built. L0 evaluates, decides and specifies an action
based on the evaluation of the values in the evacule structure.
The unit vectors of the structure encode the actions retreat, approach and ignore; L0 decides to do or not do, to move towards
and attack, to run away, or to continue on as before, based on
these values. Since each dimension can hold a range of values,
the evacule supports a complex range of evaluations, and an array of evacules, such as are contained in the mentacule, support
a very large number of different values. But, everything comes
down to the three buckets, and only the three buckets, however
many of them there are in your particular mentacule model.

L0 reduces the unbounded complexity of cosmic reality to the elementary judgment of the degree of good, bad or indifferent *for me*.

Therefore, since all affective communication engages the L0 intellect, all forms of interested communication ultimately reduce to just the three variables in the evacule. L0 is a reductive intellect whose function is exactly to reduce the complexity of existence to the three part algebra of self-interest. Whatever flurry of noise and intellectual posturing is involved in an affective conversation, in the end, the most complex thought that is actually being handled is: is this good, bad, or indifferent *for me*? That's it, whatever so-called facts are adduced in defense or attack of a position, all of it will be wiped out, lost in the narrowing type cast from the complex pattern structure down to the ternary evaluation structure. The most complex theory and argument considered in an affective conversation is of no interest whatsoever to L0 beyond the variables fed into the evaluation algebra that determines the 'go/no go', agree/disagree, decision.

We have spoken extensively of the internal and external senses and the crucial role they play in the function and survival of cognitive entities. With communication, cognitive entities gain a new, third type of sensory apparatus: verbal senses. Affective communication is a grouping activity; in addition to fact transfer, communication also transmits or triggers meaning; exchanged messages achieve meaning when value links are attached to them following an evaluation. Grouping creates an abstract organization layer above the level of solitary physical entities situated in an environment. Although abstract, the grouping layer drives behavior that is real, that is observable in $\mathbb{R}$, and communication provides the means by which we can perceive events on that level, and use those perceptions to anticipate future events. That is, our verbal senses extend both our L0 and L2 functionality beyond the limits of the physical world into the abstract grouping world. This extension of our sensorium is critical for our survival since so much human behavior is triggered by verbal events in the grouping communication layer.

Understanding L2 communication as a sensory experience of grouping behavior, demystifies much of what has always been confusing about human social and intellectual behavior. In the last century, many of the classical philosophical paradoxes were cleared up, in a stroke, with the correct application of set theory to disambiguate situations by clarifying that sets cannot be aware of, or refer to, themselves. It turned out that many of the paradoxes were caused by this single error, and suddenly, what had seemed profound, was now understood to be an elementary mistake. Similarly, many of the most perplexing mysteries about cultured human behavior turn out to be caused by the purblind defect conflating all the levels and functions of our mind into one incomprehensible mudball. Simply by switching our frame of reference, from synthetic pattern languages with unvalidated grammars, to the evolutionary cytomodel perspective of heritable survival behaviors, we can begin to see that affective communication is only possible in a grouping context, that it only serves the requirements of group dynamics, that we evaluate words with an anti-, pro- and non-self assessment, and that we move, we act, on the basis of that evaluation. L3 level model-oriented reasoning is required to clarify our thoughts and perceptions about human behavior in a way that content-focused L2 patterns cannot.

We will consider the implications that using a model which sees communication as the sensorium of grouping behaviors, has on our understanding of beliefs, opinions, attitudes, religion and ideology. The context of this discussion is the misguided belief that engaging in 'logical' discussions on these topics represents civilized, rational behavior. Has no one ever noticed that debates on beliefs, religions, ideologies and opinions have never once persuaded our opponent to see our truth? But first, before we consider each of these types of discussions, let us spend a moment on the conversion experience.

26.6 Conversion

People convert from one religion, political ideology, or belief system to another, all the time. Not that conversion is common, exactly, but it is hardly rare. It is so ordinary that I'm pretty sure we know enough to model it mathematically. Let us call *conversion* the process of abandoning a low engagement belief system in favor of embracing a high engagement belief system, and *deconversion* the process of moving in the other direction.

I would argue that deconversion is actually a gradual deterioration in the level of commitment to the old system, a drifting away from the old as its value link is adjusted progressively downward to lower values, more than a rushing to embrace a new low-involvement belief. This, too, happens all the time, but it's more of a crumbling process, rather than a case of being inflamed with a new certainty. One could argue that a deconversion process preceded the Protestant Reformation in Europe.

The conversion experience is far more dramatic, and happens far more quickly, than the deconversion process. At the extreme, this is the blinding light, the 'Paul on the road to Damascus' sort of thing. In the main, it seems to be the result of an ongoing deconversion process progressively discomfiting one who doesn't want to adjust to living in their own world, separate from an all-encompassing group. In this case, the old loopbacks would have already lost a critical amount of efficacy leading to a leakage of anxiety load from not-quite-quieted doubts into the general constitutional anxiety pool where it accumulates.

Conversion may bring about dramatic changes into a person's life, and even into a civilization's life, but, from a modeling point of view, it's not very interesting. We use grouping to extend our selfness in order to enhance our sense of viability and well-being, so the idea of switching from an unsatisfactory grouping to an all-consuming (or, at least more-consuming) one is the most natural thing there is. L0's job is to decide to 'go this way, now', and we join groups so that we can strengthen ourselves by coordinating our decisions with others, so that we move in numbers, rather than alone. So, it is only natural to expect that some percentage of the time, some followers will think that an alternate group is following a better path, and therefore decide to switch groups to benefit from the better course.

Conversion, even though it invariably follows verbal input of one kind or another, occurs at a much more primitive level than the types of conversation we are discussing, and is triggered more by the preexisting deconversion process than by anything anyone says. Conversion has everything to do with personal need and group dynamics, but has next to nothing to do with doctrine. The fact that converts preach their new doctrine to all and sundry is related to the grouping dynamics, and not the actual doctrine. As previously explained, doctrine is lost in the downcast to certainty.

Affective communication is an extension of the self-interested perception and response functionality of L0 into the L2 verbal world of grouping. Affective communication extends our physical, external senses, e.g., sight, sound and smell, to the abstraction layer above the individual where grouping occurs, thus creating the ability to identify threats and opportunities, not just in physical perceptions, but in the words and social interactions we share with others, and to respond appropriately.

26.7 Conversation Attack Vectors

Figure 26.3 shows the various objects, the data structures, involved in belief, attitude, opinion, religion and ideological arguments. The gray arrows indicating the attack vectors for each one are intended to show the only parts of each object that are

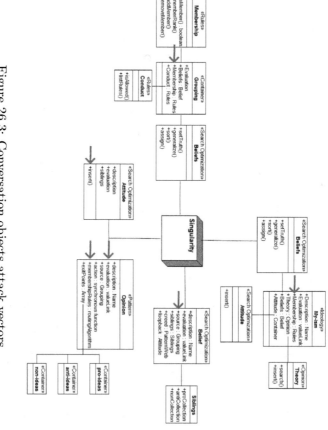

Figure 26.3: Conversation objects attack vectors.

vulnerable to change from pressure or suasion:

- Beliefs are generally sponsored by one or more groups. Moving someone off a belief is generally effected by alienating them from the sponsoring group.

- Opinions tend to be more personal and malleable than beliefs. Sometimes, if the value link is tenuous, one can talk it up or down a little, and tweak the routing algorithm that assigns facts to opinion buckets.

- Attitude is inherently intransigent, but sometimes one can be persuaded to slightly modify the insertion algorithm that assigns facts to anti-, pro, and non-self buckets.

- Ideologies are vulnerable to criticism on their membership rules. Since the membership set is not formally defined, it is open to interpretation and is thus endlessly debated and often leads to defections and schismatic arguments.

- The grouping object is at the heart of belief, and thereby, ideology. This is the object with the membership rules that are vulnerable.

We will examine each of the objects and how discussions involving them work. Keep in mind that in affective discussions, idea content does not matter. The subject of each and every discussion is always grouping and/or fact filtering to maintain equilibrium. Even when doctrinal differences lead to violent schisms, the doctrine details do not matter, what is being debated is who shall lead the group and what the membership rules are (viz., you must believe the right things to belong to *my* group).

26.8   Conversation Transformations

Our discussions about conversations are based on the data structures in the models of the various levels of intellect. The terse explanations may make it sound like everything is deterministic, but that is just a shortcoming of the particular verbal model underlying this presentation. The reality is a great deal more flexible, and more interesting than that. As you study the diagram in figure 26.3, notice that since all the objects are compound or container types, then from any object containing any other object, you can navigate from the one to the other and back again.

What this means is that conversations can and do easily transition from one form to another. Opinion arguments become belief arguments become attitude/loopback affirmation sessions, etc. The limitations we will be discussing below, refer to each type of object and the conversations built on them, but if the interaction transforms from an affective discussion to an affectless one, then an entirely new set of rules comes into play. Saying that certain things are impossible in belief arguments does not mean that your objective cannot be achieved in a grouping discussion, it just gives you the knowledge that your focus should first, be on achieving the transition, and then, once the conversation has changed, you refocus your objective on the avenues of attack available on the new object.

26.9   Belief Discussions & Debates

Pro-self belief discussions are extended self affirmations, inter-actions that tend to grouping needs, that cultivate relationships among the community of believers. While important for main-taining group health, there is not much to say about the intel-lectual content of such discussions since it does not, by design, exist. Communication in such discussions is between belief ob-jects derived from a common group source, so there is no real communication from one mind to another, rather, it is just an exercise in supportive interpersonal dynamics. If the content of such talks were changed from dogma to reminisces of old Sat-urday morning cartoons, it wouldn't change the nature of the interaction at all (oftentimes, the talk in such meetings does drift to shopping or sports, etc.).

Anti-self belief arguments or debates, are another beast al-together. These are potentially life and death struggles as is shown in the current day when critics of Islam are met with death threats, some of which are realized. Referring to figure 26.3, since beliefs are search optimizations that produce rapid, passionate responses generally based on group affiliation, and since the evaluation in the belief object is defined by the value link that is influenced or determined by the source grouping, then attacking the veracity of sorted facts cannot have any in-fluence on the assessed validity of the belief. The belief is a grouping phenomenon that situates the believer in a universe defined by the group's worldview, it is not a rational assessment of the verifiability of the sorted facts. Beliefs sort facts, they are not built on facts, they, in a sense, deny facts for the higher purpose of maintaining group cohesion and calming the anxiety produced by persistently charged facts. Sorting facts into categories inside a belief discharges their disruptive potential, and this is not a cost or by product of the belief, it is the function of the belief to do this, to ground live wires to neutralize their danger.

The only attack vector on a belief is through the affiliation to the sponsoring group. Conversion events happen because someone is convinced by passion and conviction that following another group will enhance their security and opportunities. Attacking sorted belief facts is really just kind of silly, unless it is done in a way that discredits the controlling group before a pitch is made for a better leader of another group. But, at any rate, the suggestion that thoughtful, rational belief discussions are possible is not rational and is not supported by either the model, history, or our personal experience.

26.9.1   Avenue of Change

Beliefs are statements in $\mathbb{I}$, or $\mathbb{S}$, that purport to state facts either in $\mathbb{R}$, or facts in $\mathbb{S}$ that overrule $\mathbb{R}$. The attack vector against the belief object is through the grouping link, not through the doctrines in the belief. Although the doctrines are certainly a topic of conversation, the target of the proselytizing harangue is the discrediting of the sponsoring group, not the beliefs, in the effort to persuade the target that transferring their allegiance from one group to the other will be in their immediate and ultimate self-interest. While beliefs commonly do have a high truth value link, in virtually all cases, they are simply statements in $\mathbb{I}$ with no credible validation.

26.10   Attitude Arguments

Since the function of an attitude is to discharge the potential of ideas to disturb one's inner status quo, that is, the function of attitudes is to preclude the consideration of input, attitude arguments cannot be viewed as rational discussions on any level. The attack vector for attitude arguments is shown to be on the insert method, because, depending on the reach and power of the attitude, it is sometimes possible to nibble at the edges to modify how a particular idea gets sorted. For example, depending on how detached the person is who is affecting an attitude of cool, it is sometimes possible to argue that a particular fact *might* actually be more sincere and positive than it is being credited for. Doing this, though, doesn't accomplish much.

Productive discussions can only be had with someone who is weighed down by attitude if they can be pushed or persuaded to drop the attitude and engage in one of the other discussions. Oftentimes, transition can be made to angry belief arguments, but this isn't much of an improvement, if intellectual inquiry is the objective.

26.10.1   Avenue of Change

Attitudes are defensive screens; any intelligent discussion can only happen after they have been dropped. While some concessions on the sort/insert operation can be gained, since active attitudes work by turning off the lights, the only reasonable path is to try, by whatever means, to get the target to suspend the attitude and turn the lights back on. Then, transition to some other conversation type might be possible.

26.11   Opinion Discussions & Debates

Opinions are essentially self-formulated beliefs, or casual, short-term beliefs shared by a social group. Opinion validity is set by value link, but when these are self-defined, they can be affected by persuasion. However, when the value link is set by the consensus of a social group, then they are harder to influence; this is an example of peer pressure affecting an individual's judgment. With all of these L2 objects, the nature of the value link is the determining factor in defining their power, function and malleability.

Pro-self opinion discussions among members of a social group are grouping maintenance functions that reinforce the self-extension represented by the alliance with others, through cultivating mutual affirmations between members. It is considered bad form to vigorously disagree with a compatriot on unimportant issues the grouping already has expressed an opinion on, which makes sense, since the purpose of the small talk is to strengthen, not weaken, the convivial bonds among acquaintances.

Pro-self opinion discussions among relative strangers work similarly, the difference being that what is happening in these interactions is that an ad-hoc, transitory group is being created by the discussion that will likely not survive the discussion. This is an easy way to defuse the social tension created when strangers are forced by circumstances to be together for more than a few minutes. Since agreement is the norm, small talk is generally based on whatever commonality can be espied in any of the other persons salient attributes: class, clothing, age, origin, etc., and the talk is meant to light on agreement as a way of defusing the charged fact of the other person's extended presence.

Anti-self opinion debates or arguments are something else again. First, understand that this is a seminal, not definitive, work. Its purpose is to break new ground, to introduce principles and practices that will allow the industrious student to achieve significantly higher levels of thought than had been possible before. In that spirit, understand that part of the appeal of the singularity distortion field metaphor we are using to get a geometric model of the role self-interest plays in the cognition process—a process that is not restricted to or particularly defined by our experience of humanity—is the suspicion we have that something like field equations, with different values, of course, will eventually be shown to be useful in predicting responses, i.e., that the distortion will be shown to be mathematically similar to gravity.

Opinion objects derived from social interaction (social opinions) present a multiple body problem that makes interest calculations more difficult, because peer pressure can be aligned at arbitrary angles to self-interest. On the other hand, opinion objects derived independently from personal experience (personal opinions) are probably the norm, and these are easier to ana-

lyze. The salient point to understand in this model of cognitive
objects is that opinions are not a pyramid built on a base of supporting facts, they are butterfly-like constructs that accumulate
facts (eat leaves) in the larval stage, gestate quietly for a while,
and then transform into efficient search optimizations in the
mature phase. Once mature, opinions are no more dependent
on their digested fact set than butterflies are on the leaves they
ate months ago. The function of an opinion is to help the cognitive entity maintain psychic equilibrium in the word storms
that we navigate daily. Just as a ship sails into waves, riding
over each one as it tries to keep on course, opinions enable us to
effortlessly brush irrelevant facts aside by dumping them into
one of the opinion bins. Each passing wave is a challenge, a
threat, to overcome, not a thing of interest in itself, since the
goal is the journey and its destination, not random, anonymous
waves crashing into our bow, and just so, most of the words we
hear in a day merit only a cursory glance before being defused
and forgotten.

The attack vector on the opinion object is shown to be on
the evaluation and the routing algorithm, not on the disposed
fact bins. Opinions optimize our diurnal functioning by mini-
mizing the effort required to defuse unimportant facts, that is
their function. Just as vacuums are built to remove bits from
carpets, so opinions clean up conversational debris. And, just
as a critique of a vacuum's efficiency should focus on what is
left on the floor rather than what has been collected in the bag,
so too, an opinion's value is measured not by what it sorted,

but by what it couldn't handle. One can persuade someone to reexamine their private opinion by focusing on its weakness and offering a new one that is more efficient than the old.

Of course, if someone's opinion of something led them to miscategorize a genuine threat as something normal that can be ignored, then in this case it can look like the opinion can be attacked on one of its facts, but what is actually being attacked is its sorting efficiency.

The error boulevard we travel in our opinion conversation farces is paved by our conceit, based on the purblind defect, that *we* see the world correctly, objectively, and that the other person's views are mistaken. This lulls us into thinking that all we have to do is to explain, either calmly and rationally, or passionately and aggressively, what their mistake is, so that they can fix it and come to agree with us.

When we point out weaknesses in someone's personal opinion, what we are doing is attacking the value link. Weakening this link, getting the other to adjust the certainty evaluation down even a notch or two, makes it easier for us to sell an alternate opinion. Of course, the alternate opinion we are selling is a social opinion, not a private opinion, so it is likely to be stronger than the private opinion in proportion to the vigor of the value link back to the sponsoring group. Preserving personal opinions against social opinions takes some strength of character to compensate for the imbalance of forces.

26.12   Avenue of Change

Keeping in mind that conversation is a grouping behavior, not
an idea pipe, makes it easier to see that the goal of opinion
conversations is to align another person with our group, by
getting them to accept our sorting algorithm instead of their
old one. Opinion conversations *cannot* be about content, they
are about equanimity, and the most efficient way to achieve and
maintain it. Opinions bind us to a group, they filter noise, and
they optimize value search response time when we have to react
to verbal input. Since opinions have an undefined relation to $\mathbb{R}$,
any discussion of their level of correctness, or of the ideas they
sort, can only be an argument about their value link, and that
is a simple L0 self-interest truth battle.

26.13   Ideological Discussions, Debates

Ideology is a higher level of abstraction than the other L2 objects discussed in this chapter, because it is a container object
that combines all of the others into one. While religion models
$\mathbb{S}$ and our relations to it, and opinion is a flexible fact organizer,
and attitude a first line of defense against the din of word noise,
by combining them all, ideology becomes an abstract pattern
system that attempts to model all of $\mathbb{R}$, in one go. Where religion claims to describe a higher reality, $\mathbb{S}$, which is asserted to
be more consequential than $\mathbb{R}$, ideology leverages the purblind
defect to claim that it is an objective description of $\mathbb{R} \cup \mathbb{S}$.

Since ideology adds nothing but a higher level of abstraction to the other objects, calculating how it processes positive

and negative input is a simple matter of matching the input to the processing object. Reviewing ideology's constituent objects' limitations and functions should reveal why it is so impervious to any attacks on its theory and fact set.

Pro-self ideological discussions need hardly be mentioned, since they can be little more than believer affirmations or enthusiastic pattern extension sessions that feed the believers' delusions of grandeur, as they see their vision of truth extend into the furthest corners of reality.

26.14 Avenue of Change

The only attack vector against an ideology is through the membership rules. For reasons that will become clearer after we examine the fundamental subjective problem in chapter 30, universal models are subject to schism along group lines whenever underserved groups (and it can be proved that these always exist) begin to clamor for a larger share of the spoils. Since they are compound objects, the constituent parts can be attacked as discussed above, but since the grouping effect in most ideologies is strong, this often puts these other avenues out of reach. Understand, though, that to destroy someone's attachment to an ideology is to destroy their whole world, since the ideology is a cosmic model. Deconversion generally must proceed for a considerable period of time, before the attachment to the ideological certainty is weakened enough to be vulnerable to direct attack. Obviously, attempts to detach someone from an important grouping can never be done in view of that group, since that would make the peer pressure to defend the group well nigh overwhelming.

26.15   Affective and Affectless Thinking

Both affectless and affective communication have important roles to play that the other is incapable of fulfilling, and it is important to keep this in mind, when mulling over the various kinds of discussions:

- Decision and action require affective thought.
- Anticipation and planning require affectless thought.
- Threat and opportunity identification require affective thought.
- Creativity requires affectless thought.

Thus, any reasonably complex situation requires both kinds of thought to interact gracefully in a cognitive equality waltz, where L0/L1 leads for a while to scout out the floor for threats, then L2 takes the lead to search for continuation patterns, before L0 takes the lead to make the decision on the next action, and so on.

Neither kind of thought is better than the other, they both perform necessary functions that the other cannot. Sophisticates have always disdained the uneducated classes for being driven by passion and belief, but somehow they consistently fail to notice that their sophistication has generally come at the cost of betraying the valid survival interests of their family and general culture.

26.16 Testing

This chapter is an elaboration of an executable model of a cognitive entity that seems, to my satisfaction, to model human behavior rather well. It is not a prescriptive or proscriptive code of conversational etiquette. It is a testable model. The main takeaway should be that conversation types can be analyzed with an evolutionary cytomodel, and propositions concerning them can be tested in a simulator, such as the asomatous psyche, to produce results that can be compared to observable reality, which would then lead to another round of scientific inquiry.

In this chapter, we have explored a fairly casual discussion of high-level concepts that is based on a partially implemented model. Neither agree nor disagree, but explore the model and improve or replace what you will to make it strong enough to support your discovery process. Just remember to formalize your work so that it can be checked by colleagues.

Take these conversation types, add new ones, change the implementations, run tests, gather results, try them in real life, compare results. Rinse and repeat.

26.17 Conclusion

We close this discussion of the types and functions of various conversations with a nice little aphorism:

Argue decisions, discuss ideas, validate measurements.

Why? Because decisions are the province of L0: decisions; right and wrong; true and false; good, bad or indifferent; this way or that way—these are all determined by the L0 part of our mind that evolved long before we were bipedal. Patterns, what we generally think of as ideas, are what the L2 mind does, they are paths that can be followed and discussed. Measurements of reality need to be double-checked and verified.

Affective communication deals with these L0 notions and pushes us towards decisions based on conviction, leadership, and tradition (L1 lessons). Affective communication is about the specific and extended self (grouping), so it handles social communication. Affectless communication is suitable only for pattern manipulation and extension. Combining the two gives us the mess that we see everyday: pundits *arguing* reasoning, despite the fact that the most complex message that can be transmitted across the L2/L0 border is: "follow me".

But, before we give the wreath to affectless communication as the best of all kinds of conversations, let us, literally, return to reality:

$$\mathbb{R} = \forall \, r \in \{i_d \; : \; |i_d - r_d| <= \epsilon\}$$

Our knowledge of reality is called external knowledge:

$$\mathbf{E} = \{i_j \in \mathbb{I} \iff \exists \, r_j \in \mathbb{R} \; : \; |i_j - r_j| < \epsilon\}$$

That is, if we are actually trying to discuss reality, what we are talking about is: $|i_j - r_j| < \epsilon$, the verifiable margin of error that exists between our idea of something and reproducible measurements of it. All discussions of reality are discussions of *measurement*, not right or wrong. If you are talking about right or wrong, you are operating in L0 and should be in an affective argument. If you are talking about logic and facts, then you are in L2 and should be in an affectless discussion in which you give up values such as true and false, and defer any decision making as premature. If you aspire to discuss reality, you must transition to L3 and be ready with measurements and formal procedures.

But, be aware that pattern language grammar, the validation mechanism of the highly vaunted L2 reasoning, is less than worthless, unless the grammar has been formally validated (and only symbolic logic has been validated; what you think of as logic is not formal and has not been validated). The intellectually corrupt and bankrupt institution known as the university that has been spewing an effluent of graduates into society for some 900 years now, is a monument to the erudition fallacy built on the foundation of unvalidated pattern language grammar. Perhaps this seems too harsh, but in the current day, an increasing portion of the humanities and soft science departments at these institutions worldwide, are indoctrinating students with Marxist ideology as the foundation of all knowledge, and as a result, are vomiting wave after wave of anti-freedom, anti-individual, Marxist antisemites who are consciously determined to destroy all that Western Civilization has fought so hard to establish.

The focus in this chapter has been to move intellectual discourse from the squalid mudball model of 'I will attack his reasoning with my reasoning', to an articulated, executable, evolutionary cytomodel that models behaviors in terms of heritable structures so that we can see important distinctions where before everything was just a jumbled mess. There are profound differences between positive and negative attitude, belief, opinion, ideology and pattern discussions, differences that must be taken into account in any intelligent interaction. Whether the particular models discussed here are useful, or fatally flawed, matters not as much as the demonstration that models such as these can clarify our understanding of human interaction in potentially helpful ways. Remember, it's a model, so if you don't like it, refute it and fix, or replace it.

Finally, to summarize:

- If you need to make a decision, spend some time in affectless communication exploring patterns that anticipate the future, then switch to affective communication to drive to a decision.

- If you need to review specifications and technical material, engage in affectless communication up to the point where you need to make a decision.

- If you want to explore reality, first, you must learn faceted model-oriented reasoning. Then, and only then, will you be able to enter into structured, modular conversations, where formal methods, experimental design, experimental results, measurements, and refinements to the models are discussed.

- Iterate.

26.18   Review

- Communication is the process by which cooperation is forged through signs, sounds and scents.

- Language provides the base abstraction layer upon which physical and relational hierarchies can be built.

- Grouping, the extended self, is created and maintained through communication.

- Affectless communication conveys word patterns without emotional or mortality-related dimensions.

- Affective communication deals with survival and emotional interests.

- All communication is related to, or embedded in, a grouping context.

- Communication is a cognitive function, and therefore has a mixed pro-self, anti-self, and non-self aspect.

- The three poles of verbal interaction are: friendly conversation, confrontational argument, and information exchange.

- L0/L1 interactions deal with truth, decision and action.

- Affectless L2 conversations are informational.

- Communication begins with a challenge.

- Messages are generally processed in an order characteristic of the individual's temperament and mood.

- Most messages we receive merit little attention and need to be defused as quickly and effortlessly as possible.

- Verbal communication is transmitted through a simplex channel.

- We usually process messages using attitude, belief, opinion, religion, or ideology objects.

- Task communication has the highest average success potential because the statement parts are often explicit, but it fails in proportion to the extent that the statement parts are not explicit and unambiguous.

- Intellectual conversations can only succeed when they are in-subject, affectless dialogs between highly trained colleagues.

- Intellectual monologues, lectures, successfully convey information highlights and outlines to prepared, motivated listeners.

- Affectless intellectual discussion suffers from a three-fold confluence of failure:
    - the implicit context of the statements is never adequately clarified;
    - the pattern language grammar is not formalized;
    - the implicit goal of the statements is belief-based.

- Since all affective communication engages the L0 intellect, all forms of interested communication ultimately reduce to just the three variables in the evacule. The most complex thought that is actually being handled is: is this good, bad, or indifferent *for me*?

- Conversion is the result of acting on a psycho-economic calculation that a new grouping favors our interest more than our existing one does.

- Attack beliefs by attack the grouping link, not the faith

content.

- Attack personal opinions by offering a more efficient one with a desirable grouping link.

- Wait out an attitude before even trying to discuss anything.

- Attack an ideology by driving in a wedge to create a schism.

- The common point of vulnerability is generally the grouping object that maintains the value link through a group. This is always vulnerable.

- Deconversion is a long-term project achieved through gradual devaluation of the grouping link, and gradual escalation of the evaluation of the limits of the dogma.

- Since all L2 patterns exist independently of collection objects that refer to them, conversations can be transformed from type to type while preserving the topic.

- Both pro- and anti-self belief discussions are arenas for passion, not reason.

- Pro-self opinion discussions are group-building exercises, they have nothing to do with the content.

- Anti-self opinion discussions are about truth, not the content of the opinion, don't bother attacking sorted facts before transforming the discussion to another form.

- Both affectless and affective communication have important roles to play:
  - Decision and action require affective thought.
  - Anticipation and planning require affectless thought.

  – Threat and opportunity identification require affective thought.

  – Creativity requires affectless thought.

• Argue decisions, discuss ideas.

26.19   Checkpoint

Before proceeding into the advanced topics section, stop for a day or more and review all of the notes you have taken so far, and check and see if you can now answer any of the questions that came up along the way. If you don't have a notebook full of notes, then you have probably been reading, instead of studying. Would that approach work with a calculus text? Why would casual reading work any better with this material? Hasn't it been fairly abstract, difficult and complex?

Part III

Advanced Topics

Chapter 27

Discovery

27.1 Introduction

Discovery requires that you step to the last edge, and unblinkingly behold your failure in the yawning abyss, but more than that, it requires that we insist on pressing the question, not only while confronting the erasure of our being, but that we continue to press it, long after we slink away from the chasm in defeat. For it is only as the last wisp of hope fades, and the resistance of the circuits drop to a minimum that, finally, the weak spark of inquiry can leap the surrounding gap to connect to the realization of an insight.

The risk one runs in discussing the boundless nature of human potential is sounding like a self-fulfillment charlatan who urges you to follow your dream, after sending him your money, of course. Clearly, this work does not follow that pattern, but I want to go beyond that and describe how miserable the life of discovery in the cognitive space actually can be. Previously, I have concentrated on relating the elation, the clarity of vision that moments of discovery entail, and the rapture that is the pure experience of learning explosions. All of that was, and is, true, but what I didn't mention, because it seemed that it was only temporary, was what the experience of the pre- and post-learning explosion time actually feels like. I didn't talk about it because it seemed like I was progressively working my way out of the dark woods and up the mountain to the peak, and that, somehow, once I achieved just one more explosion, my life on the peak would begin, freeing me forever from the agony of the climb, and the subsequent fall down into the next valley.

I have since realized that one never can live on the peak, and that, in reality, the main thing one accomplishes in gaining the summit is the ability to make a clear choice of which valley will lead to the next peak. This reality will be discussed at greater length elsewhere, but for now, let me just mention that the experience of engendering and recovering from learning explosions is kind of difficult, and feels sort of like what I imagine exploring a live volcano that erupts while you're in the crater might feel like, minus the death part, obviously. Instead of dying, though, it's like you just get thrown a long way onto some very hard rocks, and while you are able to get up, you are stiff, sore, and disoriented when you do, and you still have to get up and go to work the next day.

I am not trying to talk anyone out of pursuing a life of discovery, I just think it needs to be pointed out that such a life is still just a life. A rewarding, thrilling life, I must admit, but, for me, at least, it has meant laboring in the wilderness for literally half a century, with all of the discoveries related in this, and the previous volumes of this series, completely invisible to every other human being on the planet as of the time of this writing. I've done this work because it was my mission, but I've had to do it nights, weekends, vacations and between jobs. That is *every* night, *every* weekend, *every* vacation. For fifty years. Now that the foundation of the work presented here has been laid, it may be possible to embark on shorter journeys of discovery with actual, tangible rewards, but that is something someone else will have to prove.

As every explorer knows, the journey often involves risk, discomfort, doubt, and even ennui, while the romance of the effort is deferred to later reminiscences. With that attitude adjustment in mind, even though exploring the discovery intellect, L3, in depth, is being deferred to the next volume, we will spend the rest of this chapter exploring the basics of L3 functionality in order to give the reader some of the background they will need to master model-based exploration themselves.

27.2   The Discovery Intellect

Although the L3 intellect uses a unique data structure to perform cognitive functions on a level above L2 to accomplish feats that L2 simply cannot do using the pattern object, it is not always easy to point at one intellectual accomplishment and say, "L3, definitely!", because, while L2 cannot do what L3 can,

L2 can represent L3 accomplishments using the pattern object. But, while the first still has the live, sparking edge of discovery in it, the second is just a picture of the last stable discovery accomplishment. That is, once a discovery has been made, it can be used by L2 individuals who would never have been able to make the discovery themselves.

Inspired work has always been accomplished through L3 circuits, dating as far back as Hesiod, at least. But, their moments of inspiration were restricted to moments, single visions that, however grand, were still but fleeting visions. The first clear example of sustained, pioneering exploration beyond the limits of authority that comes to mind might be Michelangelo, but that is not to say that he was the first, just that he was a very early example of a person who was able to tap their L3 intellect, more or less regularly, as part of their normal work. It should not be a surprise that this suggests that the first general appearance of the L3 discovery intellect was during the Renaissance and the Reformation.

The burst of creativity starting with Shakespeare, and flowering with J.S. Bach, is consistent with this narrative, but more importantly, Galileo's scientific accomplishments represent a huge step forward in the regular use of the complex functionality of the L3 intellect to model the unknown in a way that never required a recourse to authority.

Citing a number of geniuses, of whom one is fond, and claiming them to be 'one of us', is not an argument, of course, but it does give us a segue into a discussion of the defining charac-

Figure 27.1: L3 Step Object

teristics of the type of situations these geniuses dealt with that required the use of the discovery intellect. Only the L3 intellect can succeed when:

1. the problem to be attacked lies past the edge of the known, and therefore,

2. an original insight is required to proceed.

When the discovery intellect does succeed in inventing a new solution in these cases, generally it does so by inventing new terms that:

1. do not fit into existing paradigms, and

2. that are testable.

What suits the discovery intellect for these type of situations, and also makes its solutions testable, is the data structure used by the L3 intellect.

27.3   The Step Data Structure

The data structure used by the L3 intellect is called the *Step*, and the step uses an object called the *query*. Despite its apparent simplicity, what distinguishes the step from the pattern object is the flexibility and complexity of structures that can be built with it, as shown in figure 27.2.

The key to the step structure's power is that it implements

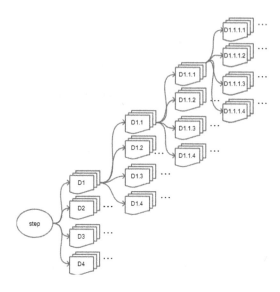

Figure 27.2: Fractal step structure

a dynamic query that can be run on any dimension of the target objects to return a set of steps that can be sorted and queried again, essentially without limit. The step object supports dynamic navigation, sorting, and requerying of the result set, and this ability to 'ponder' and 'poke' results in real time, requerying them again and again on different dimensions, gives the discovery intellect the ability to investigate ideas more deeply than ever before. It gives the discovery intellect the ability to pause before the burning bush and to ponder the sight from different angles until the insight can occur that the lack of ash and char is testimony to something noteworthy. This support for continuously pivoting the results to unlimited depth, in order to explore new dimensions in the search for interesting continuations, is what makes the discovery intellect capable of completely unanticipated discovery and invention.

The step structure is not a durable collection of steps, but a temporary path discovery object. It does not retain these paths across executions, meaning the queries must be rerun every time a topic is investigated. However, interesting results can be patternized and stored in the L2 memory. These retained queries become typical rote patterns when communicated to others, but the mind that created them can use them to restart the exploration journey within a limited time frame, such as a few days or maybe weeks. After that, a new exploratory journey must be started from scratch.

27.4   Step Operations

The process that L3 uses to initiate an exploratory journey is:

1. Identify a question.
2. Refresh (maintain) the question.
3. Review all new situations for associations to the question.
4. Interrupt L2 to start a step process once an interesting situation is idenified.
5. Search, examine, sort, repeat.

The precondition that must be met, though, before this process can even begin, is that the discovery intellect must be brought online with an active need, as well as the permission, to ask any questions at all, completely free from the control of pattern authority. This active initialization prepares it to recognize interesting questions from the stacks of anomalies discoverable in the pattern structures currently being processed.

Once an intriguing question is identified, it has to be re-freshed — re-asked — frequently, or it will die. While main-taining the question in a charged state, the L3 intellect calmly watches the L2 proceedings, quietly waiting to find another sev-eral, good cards to add to its hand. Once a good starting hand is collected, L3 has to have the independent authority to inter-rupt the normal L2 housekeeping pattern processing operations to instantiate a step object and initiate the exploration pro-cess. This tolerance for an interruption of normal threat and opportunity processing generally can only happen in temporary bubbles of protection created and supported by social institu-tions that successfully enable the accumulation of wealth well beyond the sustenance level, and maintained by personal choice and commitment.

The exploration process starts almost as a nervous twirling of the information at hand, while the mind watches the various dimensions of the various objects in the situation swirl on by. When, and if, an interesting dimension is found — interesting in terms of extending the question towards target ideas — a query on the dimension of interest is formulated, and a result set is generated. The process repeats on this new result set, and so on.

Note that the exploration proceeds along narrow, new paths with commensurately high resistance (resistance is lowered as usage of a path broadens it), and the further the exploration goes, the weaker the signal gets as it is divided into more and more paths being explored.

In previous volumes, I spoke of learning explosions as building on learning discoveries, and in the current terms, what this means is that, since the exploration is focused in an area that has been the target of recent investigations, the complex constructs previously created by learning discoveries are likely to be found and when they are added to the fractal step tree, this extends the tree by leaps and bounds, instead of small steps.

Explorations leading to learning explosions generally require several days to weeks to complete, so they have to be stored and restarted daily for several weeks. Any extended interruption to the process generally leads to a loss of the ability to recreate the in-process tree, forcing the investigation to be started again, usually from another starting point.

The gaps between problem and solution that require insights to be jumped appear in this model as a limiting factor on what ideas get included in the result set. The more focused we are in our question, the stronger the charge on the asking side, and the more we have ruffled questions in related material, the more charge there is on the receiving side, the combination of which extends the radius of discovery in assembling the result set.

The L3 operations that work on the fractal step structure are:

- Leverage a situation to create a step.
- Select a dimension.
- Formulate and execute a query.
- Sort and re-sort the result set along different dimensions to look for a lead.

- Repeat the process on the most interesting results until either the signal is too weak to follow, or a candidate solution is found.

Thus, beyond the data structures it uses, L3 doesn't actually need any new low-level functions to perform its operations. The familiar *search*(), *sort*(), and *evaluate*() functions are just enhanced to work with the new data structure.

27.5   Step Potential

The fractal nature of the L3 data structure, its self-similarity across increasingly fine scales of detail, makes it uniquely capable of progressively investigating the unknown without recourse to metaphor. Imagine you want to model an arbitrary section of the Grand Canyon in finer detail than ever before, what would you do? The investigative process of L3 can leverage the fractal structure of steps to extend down an arbitrary axis until ground is found, and then find ground around that point at any depth, whether higher or lower, using the exact same process.

Are we talking about modeling a physical canyon, or about asking questions about an undiscovered concept? What is the difference? Seriously, just because we have a hard visual metaphor for what a canyon looks like, doesn't mean that nature used that visual metaphor to carve the canyon, and of course, we know that it did not. Gravity, water, silt, rock and flood carved the canyon without even once stepping back to inspect its work. Canyons are the result of a variety of natural processes over a period of time, they are not a visual construct. Just the

same, when we are building an understanding of a question —
whether it is about a canyon, or about how we think and feel
— we are probing in the dark, blindly feeling our way from
question to question to candidate answers that must be tested
and verified before we can know that they are worth anything.

While patterns are naturally suited for pattern language
grammar validation, the granularity of L3 discovery tree ideas
exposes each leaf to individual, independent verification. The
simpler pattern structure is more suited to modeling experience-
based plans than modeling anything that we have not already
experienced and evaluated. Once we have invented or discovered a new concept, we memorialize it by committing it to memory as a pattern that others can learn and follow.

27.6 Step Limitations

The depth and complexity of the elaborated step structure at-
tenuates the querying signal with depth, and intentional and
emotional signals interfere with deeper queries, because L0 belief signals are strong to begin with, and aren't vitiated by being
split to travel multiple routes at the same time. This is why so
many discoveries occur in moments of interruption (the shower),
or after the effort is abandoned (despair), or just before sleep
overtakes us, because the mind often resets in these transitional
moments and opens a brief window where the querying signal is
the strongest active pulse, and this is what allows us finally to
see the smallest sparks given off by inchoate, insightful jumps
across new connections to other ideas.

27.7 Conclusion

This brief excursion into the L3 mind was intended to introduce the reader to the world they will be living in, from time to time, should they choose to master faceted model-oriented reasoning, the L3 reasoning mode.

As mentioned previously, our minds have both a sequential, and a parallel processor. We are familiar with the sequential processor as that part of the mind we use when we are following a list of steps that we can check off, one by one, as we complete them, and then double check as much as we want. The parallel processor is what allows us to function smoothly when we are comfortably situated in familiar circumstances. The easiest example of this is driving; if you can remember your first week of driving, you should recall how much you struggled to check everything all at once (your mirrors, your speed, traffic in front, back, on the side, on cross streets). This insistent need to be aware of so many things at once leaves many young drivers wondering if they will ever be able to drive on the expressway. Just a few weeks later, though, they smoothly handle all of this without a second thought. What has happened is that, after 100-200 hours of driving, our brain learns how to parallelize all of these independent tasks, instead of trying to process it all at the same time with the lumbering sequential processor.

Exploring the fractal discovery / step tree requires liberal use of the parallel processor to maintain all the threads down all the branches currently being investigated. By the way, it's because the work is being done on the multi-threaded parallel processor that it seems like magic when an answer just drops in your lap, since the sequential processor, the mechanism by which we 'know' things, can't keep up with the parallel processor, and is thus surprised when a result suddenly — from its point of view — just appears.

The delicacy of the equilibrium required to support deep parallel processing can be disrupted by any strong signal, but is most frequently brought down by the usual suspects:

- a hard truth evaluation,
- an appeal to authority, or
- an interrupt from L0.

That is, *knowing* that something is absolutely true or false kills the entire branch of the tree where this happens. An appeal to authority, that is, shifting from query mode to accepting or rejecting an idea because of the dictates of a grouping authority, kills it, too. Getting yelled at, or even spoken to, can also terminate an exploratory session.

Remember, all of this is natural, from the parallel processing to the use of the fractal discovery tree and dynamic querying. Your brain knows how to do it already, and you should be able to recall moments that you can now identify as being discovery activity. But, while being able to draw an indifferent squiggle with a pencil is natural, learning to draw a beautiful, lifelike portrait takes a considerable amount of instruction, practice, and talent. Consider this text to be your initial source of instruction in faceted, model-oriented reasoning. Its goal is just to make L3 reasoning more accessible, more reliable, and more productive. The functionality has been there for a few centuries, at least, all we are providing here is the theoretical framework, the constructs, and procedures that can make that functionality readily accessible and enable you to develop your own level of expertise in model-oriented reasoning.

How much time do you have to spend exploring to have a good chance at discovery? What happens if the missing bridge idea is in a technical subject you haven't studied yet? What is your vacation reading?

27.8 Review

- Inspired work has always been accomplished through L3 circuits.
- The discovery intellect is required to create insights needed to solve problems in the unknown.
- Discovery achievements create new, testable paradigms.
- The step data object is a temporary path discovery object with a wide fanout querying structure.
- Discovery prep is done by running multiple queries on different dimensions of a result set, and exploring many paths.
- Discovery queries and results are stored as patterns in L2. L3 has no memory.
- Short interruptions temporarily stop an exploration, long

interruptions kill it.

- The L3 intellect uses enhancements of existing functionality operating on the step data structure to do its work.
- Querying signals are attenuated as branching complexity increases.
- L0 signal noise obscures the weak L3 query signal.
- The discovery intellect is operative in at least high intelligence individuals, albeit usually ineffectual.

Chapter 28

Faceted Model-Oriented Reasoning

28.1 Introduction

The first step in the journey to mastering the techniques of model-oriented reasoning is to study both its terms and laws, and the laws of the universal cognition model. It would have been difficult, if not impossible, even to guess all that would inevitably follow from those abstract principles when they were introduced in the early chapters. But, as each chapter unfolded, we referred to them time and again, relying on them to nail point after point as we worked our way further away from the abstract beginning and deeper into the consequential world of choices and experience. For example, **M2** is used about 25 times throughout this work to prove statements, ranging from the obvious (all of our reasoning is always model-oriented) to provocative statements about subjectivity in chapter 30. Although this is not an axiomatic system, it might help to think of it as one, at least until you get a solid sense of how everything works together at a very deep level.

The process of learning model-oriented reasoning starts with understanding that we have to formalize our models — our ideas — to prep them for testing. By **M3**, we know that since we can't identify which of our models are formal, then they are all informal or mixed, since building a formal model takes an unforgettable amount of effort, and we would remember formalizing any of them. From **M7**, we know that our informal models have a validity of roughly zero, so we know there is no dearth of material to formalize. The question then is, where do we start? Which of our informal models should we begin formalizing first?

The old adage, "start small" is a good rule of thumb in this case. Pinnacle questions are called that precisely because they sit atop a mountain of smaller, less consequential questions. We cannot tackle any of the biggest questions first, because perching a formal model on a pile of informal rubble would collapse the pile immediately. In the operations chapter, we saw that ideas can be generalized, added and extended to create an arbitrarily large composite. It is important to understand that the validity of such a composite is the *product*, not the sum, of the validity of its parts. This means that if we normalize the validity measure so that 100% valid is represented as 1, and half valid is 0.5, then the validity of a composite comprising 5 components, each of which has a very high level of validity, say 0.9, is: $0.9 * 0.9 * 0.9 * 0.9 * 0.9 = 0.59049$, that is, multiplying quantities less than unity together produces a result smaller than the smallest value in the collection.

Thus, it is unwise to try to build a larger formal model on anything but the soundest components, which means that we have to fix our smallest ideas before we tackle the larger ones. Taking this approach will help you to understand the implication that being a living, mortal creature has on this process: we have to learn how to do everything, we aren't born with sophisticated cognitive powers. In order to succeed in this journey, it is critical that we shift our focus from the output, to the process itself, from the product, to the method. Only by learning the method to the point of mastery will we ever develop the ability to tackle the larger questions.

One of the many things that has always bothered me about classroom teaching is its focus on pattern assimilation to the utter neglect of the discovery process. Model-oriented reasoning is an L3 function that uses the L3 fractal branching tree to organize facts in a way that promotes discovery and invention. Unlike pattern assimilation, which concentrates exclusively on memorizing patterns and learning rules and transformations, the first step in discovery learning is to respect your current state, and to focus on growing *from* the edge of your current knowledge and abilities, rather than *towards* a predefined goal. Pattern assimilation works fine for pattern uptake, and you should use it for that, but this is not what we are doing in model-oriented reasoning, we are using different functions in a different part of the brain to achieve goals that are different from those of pattern assimilation, different and much larger.

In *Pinnacle Questions*, we focused on the role that anomalies and ruffling questions plays in the discovery process. The approach we took in that volume was to try to force the reader's mind into a frustration trap in order to build a sufficient charge on the explore/conclude decision junction to support the leap into L3 (the DI). While we have offered a number of more elegant ways to step off confidently into the unknown in this volume, ruffling anomaly-based questions is still an excellent way to start the journey past the pattern edifices on the way to breaking out into the wilds of the unknown, where all of existence is waiting to be discovered.

28.2   Facets

The fable of the six blind men opining about the nature of an elephant based on the part they were touching at the time, is more trenchant, on more levels, than we give it credit for. If you finally realize that it really is only the purblind defect that gives you the idea that you can see the world directly, then you can begin to understand what this book is about and why we need model-oriented reasoning. Recall, the motivation for undertaking this work was our frustration with humanity's utter failure to answer any of the pinnacle questions, despite having worked on them for millennia. Surely, the reader would not have done all of the work required to come this far were they not keenly aware of the failure of our untutored intellect to penetrate the mysteries of our subjective experience of humanity and nature. If we could see reality directly, then we wouldn't need model-oriented reasoning, but then by what organic construct could objective knowledge of the external world be had by newborn organisms? Such an idea just makes no sense, which is good, since it corresponds neither to reality, nor to our experience.

No, we are blind, blind in the truest sense, completely cutoff from the world, sealed inside our own little reality, but we survive because our body is adorned with some special cells that respond to certain kinds of stimulus by sending signals to our nervous system and thence to our brain, where it becomes the responsibility of various mental structures to synthesize an image of the world around us that is sufficiently rich to motivate us to execute an appropriate movement response (a responsibility that, when not adequately met, costs us our life).

Since we cannot apprehend the whole, we have no way of knowing what portion of it we do perceive, whether it is large or small, trivial or true, and this is why attacking discovery from a single direction just won't work: it restricts us to a small, linear swath of reality that makes sense from our original views, but does not give us a mechanism to explore in all the directions of the compass. The process of methodically examining our subject from several perspectives in succession in order to develop unanticipated dimensions of understanding is called *faceted model-oriented reasoning*. This is the process that has been used throughout this work to create the complex, dimensional model we have been discussing, and the reader should be ready to explore it now.

Faceted model-oriented reasoning is not just *a* way to reason in L3, it is the *only* sound way to leverage L3 capabilities to explore the world. The process begins when you start struggling with an anomaly that you found in a familiar and interesting subject, which you then express in an opinion. Next, to overcome the limitations of the L2 opinion object, you analyze the opinion and sorted facts into constituent parts and begin to build an explicit model using the L3 fractal branching tree data structure that has no L0 value link. It is important to remember at this time that we are not trying to define a solution, the *right* L0 answer, instead we are just building a model of the problem that captures the dynamics of the situation well enough to support measurable experimentation.

To begin this process, start with your strength, whether that is math, coding, diagramming or the written word. Try to account for the anomalous results in a way that makes common results normal, rather than pathological. Once you get a first level explanation, however primitive, of what previously had been surprising, after the first flush of victory, you will generally find that your investigation will stall. This gives you the choice of deciding whether your model is 'right', or whether your should keep on investigating. If you have gotten the least benefit from reading this book, you will understand what the choice really means, and you will continue the investigation. Even with this renewed determination, you will often find that you have stumbled into a desert of leads where you see no obvious path forward. The first thing to do is to try ruffling questions and then get up and do something to purge the recent pattern buffer (such as going for a walk, or even better, taking a shower). Many times, this will provide you with a new lead to pursue. Sometimes, though, it won't work, and this is when you should switch modeling modes to your next most natural method. e.g., from words to diagrams, from code to math, etc.

Now, if you take the time to start from the beginning, and express the model in this new language, you will find that you are confronted with a new set of constraints, questions and possibilities. The verbal model is good at letting us develop an overview, but, since it has no actual discipline, and no constraints to prevent us from ignoring gaps with a little handwaving, it is not good for anything much more than that. The visual model is good at letting us see and work out data and process flow, and sometimes help us create a map of relations from a high level. The executable model, particularly if you stick to a functional programming paradigm (even if you use objects to organize your code, always write functions instead of methods), is especially good at forcing you to define interfaces between systems, which pushes you to eliminate the 'god awareness' flaw (i.e., using a global controller and variables, etc.) from the model and stick to the evolutionary cognition levels paradigm. The math model, whether geometric, algebraic, or discrete (or whatever kind of math you can use), brings a bracing level of formalism to the process sufficient to discipline the executable model and to help simplify all of the other models. Expressing constraints and definitions with set notation is a particularly inexpensive way to introduce new levels of clarity to your model.

Then, iterate. Endlessly.

 *Force yourself to switch facets more frequently than you think necessary, and you will be amazed at how much richer your model becomes, how much more viable and productive.*

28.3   Verbal Model

The verbal model, the pride of the intelligentsia, the pinnacle of intellectual achievement, is built on the statement construct:

Statement: [context] + content + [goal]

This definition of a statement, the unit of both thought and conversation, is not being imposed on our traditional concepts by some new formalism we invented, instead, it was derived from traditional conversation and intellectual debate by asking, "What the hell is wrong here?" It is hardly an overstatement to say that debate *never* works, that puffed up, would-be intellectuals who meet in a verbal tournament to bravely and deftly slay their opponents with rapier intellect, cutting words and devastating logic and then leave the field triumphant, apparently never notice that their uninjured, unbowed opponent is also leaving the field trumpeting his own indisputable, overwhelming victory. What I had to ask myself was, how has this sham been going on for the entire span of civilization without anyone noticing the charade? Oh, yes, it's because the opponent is too 'stupid', or too 'biased' to fairly see what anyone of sense can, which is that they were crushed in the verbal battle.

Review your experience with debates, and you should see that the discipline of the exercise focuses attention on the content portion of statements and neglects the other two-thirds that remain implicit, lurking under the surface like motionless alligators waiting to snatch the rational elements of the debate down into a death roll, leaving only passion and confusion in its wake.

Review your experience with conversations, whether of the opinion or task variety, and you should notice they naturally fall into a bimodal distribution with effective conversations between participants who share an explicit context, such as a team, assignment, or project, on the one end, and the ineffective, frustrating conversations being between those who either had no shared context at all, or even worse, mistakenly thought they shared one when they did not, at the other end. That is, conversations succeed or fail not on content, but on the degree to which the context is shared, because with shared context, content communicates, but without it, it cannot.

As stated previously, conversations between congregants sharing explicit belief goals that constrain context are strictly grouping exercises that have essentially zero intellectual content.

It follows from our models that the function of the verbal model is to facilitate grouping, that it actually has nothing *whatsoever* to do with intellectual inquiry. This is an important result. So important, in fact, that you should take a while to try to disprove it. Of course, as long as you stay with the evolutionary cytomodel, you will fail, but the exercise will be edifying. In conversation, the verbal model is a grouping mechanism, in rumination, it is either works as a pattern language mechanism, or as a loopback mechanism that discharges the power of disruptive thoughts. Only lazy intellects, dazzled by the purblind defect into thinking that their ideas describe external reality, would even expect that they could use words and partial statements to express realities. By now, all readers should know that reality is measured, and truth is only defined by a locus in the singularity of the speaker. Using words to express realities makes as much sense as using paper bags to carry fire, or forks to carry water. We define reality as the set of all measurable things precisely because all things in our universe have measurable attributes, such as location, velocity, dimension, charge, etc., not because we are being cute with a definition. Measurement is the simplest, surest way to distinguish between the real and the imagined, between external and internal knowledge.

The verbal model is not well-suited to focusing on measurement, because, even when we start a conversation with a reference to a reproducible measurement, from that point on the sway of the grouping action of interpersonal communication bends the interaction away from the external towards internal, group building concerns. It is simply a fallacy to suppose that verbal communication is a natural or even feasible choice of a method to use to discuss reality.

What the verbal model is particularly good at, though, is articulating the implicit goal component of our statements. A goal is necessarily derived from personal values, it is a statement that a state or action is a worthy objective, as designated by a value link connecting it with our singularity distortion field. Goals are personal, they are what affective communication is about, they are the seed of groupings that focus members' attention on achieving a shared accomplishment.

A good verbal model includes a clear articulation of the belief set that governs this learning effort, an unmoving polestar that we can always find so that we stay on track through the roughest seas. The rest of the verbal model is really only a list of bullet points of interests, ideas and such that we had on hand when we started our effort.

The rather ponderous verbal model you are currently reading is, of course, an affective conversation intended to gather a higher level grouping of highly intelligent individuals by persuasively making the case that this is a good path to follow. With luck, though, there are enough formal elements included in this missive to equip the interested student to begin their own self-guided journey as soon as they can stand up, kind of like a newborn giraffe stands up on it own within minutes of being dropped on its head from six feet up.

28.4   Visual Model

The whiteboard is one of the greatest inventions of the current age; I have several in my office, and even have one in my shower, a practice I highly recommend. Whiteboards support visual brainstorming of systems, flows and relations, and, in the shower, they help us to capture the rush of insights that often flow into the freshly flushed current pattern buffer after a long session of question ruffling.

When used following a session with the executable or verbal model, a diagrammatic approach to conceptualization helps one to rise up out of the weeds and get the overview, the panorama of how all the subsystems and players participate in the overall process. Creating visual models, whether on paper, the whiteboard, or in UML or just software sketching applications, is an important step in reconnecting low-level implementation with our original high-level, verbal goals.

As a rule of thumb, try drawing whenever the model interactions get too confusing to follow in your mind.

There are formal visual models in the hard sciences, but we are discussing using visual models in the process of externalizing internal knowledge, to formalize subjective ideas and experiences. As such, the focus should be on the broad strokes, the flows between the parts, not on using compilable language on the link constraints.

Of all the modeling modes, the informal visual mode is the

least like the thing itself, and more purely and obviously just a personal aid to assist the learning process. Since most of the modeling effort is, in fact, an exercise in extending our mental abilities, then aids such as informal drawings can be appreciated for the help they give us in straightening out our thoughts as our model grows through successive stages of complexity and simplification.

28.5 Executable Model

The executable model is a formal model written in a scripting or programming language such as Groovy, Ruby or Python. Of course, depending on your problem domain, Fortran, LISP and C are also reasonable options. I would suggest that anyone already conversant in a programming language should choose the most fluent one available, while non-programmers should look at one of the scripting languages listed above and select the one whose syntax is the most natural and least annoying to you.

Do not listen to people in the business who tout one language over all the rest, since the standards professionals use to judge the quality of languages are not important to you when you are just trying to express in executable language what started out as a few words and scribbles.

I will strongly suggest/insist that you use test-driven development with a functional programming style in your code, because this will greatly enhance your chances of writing functional, maintainable, working code. If you are absolutely new to programming, you might try:

- learning rudimentary Groovy from an introductory book,
- use a free IDE like IntelliJ Community Edition,
- set up the Spock testing framework first thing
- work all the examples in a test-driven development primer, such as *Test-Driven Development by Example* by Kent Beck, or a more recent one.

(I understand that all of these suggestions will be horribly dated in no time, but they set a benchmark that clarifies the sort of effort I am suggesting.)

The initial goal of the executable model is to introduce the habit of formality into one's reasoning. The ultimate goal, of course, is to build a simulation that will support experimentation that produces quantifiable results, thus enabling you to use the scientific method to study, extend and correct both your model and your ideas. I do expect that, in the very near future, we will have universal simulation engines available on our phones to support rapidly testing a wide range of models with minimal programming, but until then, we have to build the test bench ourself.

Writing your model in an executable language allows you to run assertions against it to verify that it does what you expect and, more importantly, it allows you to sharpen your model and pushes you away from the teleological bias of a god process towards using independent functions performed by independent systems having no knowledge of, or coordination with, each other. Doing this will enforce the small, ignorant function paradigm of the evolutionary cytomodel and eliminate undesirable dependencies and side effects while forcing development to proceed from the primitive to the complex, rather than starting with preconceived conclusions and working your way backwards to the basics.

Nothing exposes implicit assumptions quite like executable code. Executable code does not force you to achieve perfection in your model, but it pushes you up to the first level of formality in your modeling, and it makes it easier to break your bigger ideas down into smaller, testable functions.

28.6   Mathematical Model

The way I approach reality, I have very little need for calculus, but I find linear algebra to be the Swiss army knife of math, and it seems like all of my numerical calculations involve it in one way or the other. Computer science naturally uses discrete math, and I have found it to be very helpful in designing and working with discrete models. Set theory, it should go without saying, is essential to modeling the domain and range of functions on the various levels. Last to the game, for me, was abstract algebra, which I found to be hugely liberating and essential for understanding how to create mathematical models from executable ones.

Most school-level math is, once you learn a few techniques, monkey-simple, and I have long thought this is part of what makes math classes so painful for so many: the teachers are bored out of their minds, and are afraid the class will discover that their instructor just isn't very bright, so they make the subject appear harder than it actually is just to torture their students into thinking their instructor must be thinking high-level thoughts all the time.

I recall a situation comedy plot where one woman gave her neighbor a valued recipe, but deliberately left out one key ingredient to make sure the dish didn't come out as well as her own. I think math teachers do this petty little trick all the time. In communication, there is an issue called *lexical mismatch*, which happens when a listener doesn't know all the words the speaker is using, which causes their comprehension to continually decline as each new term is used without being properly defined. The consequences of this happening in the classroom are fairly dire, and it happens all the time in math classes, and I contend that many math teachers do it deliberately to make themselves feel more important. In a classroom, when we are situated, we listen using our internal parallel processor, assigning the input to one thread, and the association and recall efforts to other threads. This process breaks down, though, when a lexical mismatch disables the associative and recollection processes, which causes the brain to fall back from parallel (fast) mode into sequential (slow) mode. Meanwhile, the teacher charges on, and the higher level students continue processing the input in parallel, while the rest of the class struggles in sequential mode, falling further and further behind, getting more confused at each new step, and less and less prepared to do the homework.

It should come as no surprise, by now, that educational institutions know nothing of education, and barely anything about pattern assimilation, but in no area of the curriculum does this have a more devastating effect than in mathematics, where it turns most of the class off of the idea of pursuing math, and turns many of them phobic about the subject. This is yet another way that our sham educational institutions ill-serve our civilization.

Yes, it is hard doing math homework, and part of that is because of the level of precision that formal languages require, but this difficulty can be ameliorated by instructors who actually understand the theoretical nature and purpose of mathematics in the intellectual development of students who will never use it in their professions. I understand the shiver of distaste that runs down the spine whenever I talk about building mathematical models, and there is nothing I can do about the bad education one has had, but I can assure you that I get by just using a little of this and some of that. But, it is important to have a reasonable, practical idea of the different mathematical tools out there, so that we know what choices we have, and what we should brush up on, when confronting a particular type of problem.

If I have the time, I would like to write a modeling primer where I present the essential aspects of testing, programming, and software design, along with some short courses in various mathematical subjects, in order to equip the ambitious student with a basic toolkit containing what they will need to succeed in faceted model-oriented reasoning. If not, there are examples out there already, such as math for engineers books and the like, so probably any double major in computer science and math, with rudimentary verbal skills, could take on this little job.

For now, understand that using simple set theory to define the domain and range of a function has a powerfully clarifying effect on the mind, it simplifies and focuses one's attention of the deeper abstractions in the problem where the power and the solutions lie, and away from the noise of the other modeling facets. Returning to the executable model after a bracing dip in the math pool can feel like revisiting high school after graduating college—what had seemed so daunting before is now so clear and simple.

28.7   Conclusion

Faceted model-oriented reasoning is not just for especially formal projects, it is the only reliable modeling approach for any serious problem, and it gives us our only chance of expanding our model beyond our original prejudices and imagination. Faceted modeling has a unique power to push our reasoning to the next level of coherence and fluent expressiveness.

Untestable models are mudball models with no defined relation to external reality. You will find that acquiring the habit of crafting ideas in a way that makes them inherently testable, all by itself, will bring more discipline to our thought process than almost anything else we can do. Of course, most of our thoughts will remain informal, but our central concepts, the hub of our belief and opinion system that informs and organizes our experience of our world, these pillars of our consciousness must be formalized and tested before we can even begin to think about making an assault on what we have decided are our pinnacle questions. Otherwise, we are building our work on swampland.

28.8 Review

- The validity of an imperfect model declines as it grows.
- We are one of the blind men; faceted model-oriented reasoning is a tool that makes us all of them.
- The verbal model is good for overview and goal definition, but has very low precision, and no reproducibility.
- The visual model is good for overview, and for visualizing flow and process.
- The executable model is testable, introduces formality and, with good programming discipline, it can help to implement the evolutionary cytomodel.
- Set theory clarifies containment and relationships.
- Algebraic models with formal definition of domain and range for every function makes discovery by calculation possible, and greatly improves the executable model.
- Geometric models may help to visualize mathematical relations in ways that otherwise might not be available.
- Force yourself to switch modeling modes on a regular basis, and switch more frequently than you think necessary.

Chapter 29

Curriculum

29.1   Diatribe

I barely went to high school, so I don't know what its function is, or claims to be. Socialization, of course, seems to be its major focus, with introduction to abstract thought being a minor concern. Vocational schools, if they still exist, should offer training in the mechanical arts of various jobs, I would hope. College preparatory schools seem to concentrate on the erudite arts, as well as offering early to advanced placement classes in science and mathematics.

Outside of the technical colleges, the only job the university system aspires to accomplish seems to be cultivating an air of erudition appropriate to whatever socio-economic strata its particular graduates are likely to flow into.

In days of yore, my dismissive sleights of our institutions of higher learning would be met with howls of, "But, we teach the great achievements of Western Civilization to our students, we make them competent participants in the great effort to advance the state of our culture and to contribute to the progress of humanity towards a state of enlightened civilization." But, sadly, even that fiction has been thrown into the dustbin of history, as the current generation of cultural Marxists dominating academia preach a medievally intolerant liberation theology that hates science, technology, freedom, individuality, the Enlightenment, and everything related to the kind of learning this book is about.

What should we do about this sad state of affairs? First, understand that the recent collapse of the university system is a collapse in style only, because, in fact, the system has been worthless and corrupt (again, the technical colleges aside) since Oxford and Cambridge were founded. The old focus on contributing to the progressive development of civilization so that it could achieve the lofty goal of becoming the inevitable present time, at least had a whiff of romantic respectability, but the pedagogy was thoroughly corrupt and corrupting, all along. Now, even that illusion has been shattered, as universities worldwide have become avowed indoctrination centers that not only teach just one ideology, but that grade down, or fail, any students foolish enough to express an opposing opinion.

The first thing we must do to begin digging ourselves out of this dung heap of educational failure, is to recall the definitions of internal and external knowledge. External knowledge is real, internal knowledge has an undefined relation to reality. Guess which one we should be teaching in institutions of higher learning? Here's a one word hint: *reproducible.* If what you are teaching does not generate reproducible results, then what is the difference between teaching it, and not teaching it? Without reproducible results, how can you tell whether or not anything has been taught?

Part of the confusion regarding the value of higher education comes from the conflation of different mental functions together, a problem that is caused by reasoning with the mudball model. For example, one of the arguments in favor of teaching literature, now that we no longer teach the classics, is that it still helps students to learn how to interpret the written word to extract meaning from its various levels. But, this is just pattern identification, pattern analysis, and pattern synthesis, i.e., pattern processing skills. It would be much more efficient and effective to teach these skills directly, rather than obliquely through mud puddles of internal knowledge in the form of poems, stories and novels.

Another long-standing failure of the current system is that the curriculum and insular perspective of universities tends to detach the extended self of the student from the greater body politic and attach it, instead, to the effete, erudite fraternity of the cultural elite. Shouldn't we be asking ourselves why any rational government would want to waste its resources effectively alienating its best and brightest from any commitment to the nation's weal? That is, why should we be paying to create enemies of the good?

Another failure of the current system is that it showers scorn on L1 functions, while it heaps nothing but praise and resources on L2 functions. That is, universities teach students to scorn the lessons of history, of experience, i.e., the wisdom of the L1 intellect, in favor of the fatuous intellectual constructs of the L2 intellect. But, how does this make any sense? Remember, not only does L2 have no direct connection to external reality, its only error checking capability comes from the optional activity of running L2 constructs through a fast-fail (it stops on the first error or two, it cannot parse the entire construct to find all errors at once) L2 grammar checker. That means that the built-in proclivity of L2 pattern processing to generate patterns with a ridiculously high rate of false positive matches is cultivated in a hothouse of academic elitism that is impervious to criticism. How does supporting that make any sense?

Finally, of course, after nearly a millennium, the university system has still not even stumbled onto the the fact that L3 not only exists, but that it is the sole engine of invention and discovery.

29.2   Curriculum Design

If we design our curriculum using an articulated, executable model of the mind, we can focus on L0, L1, L2 and L3 skills directly, using quantifiable lessons and tests that produce verifiable results. Of course, this curriculum is a pattern complex created by L2, so while we will discuss it level by level, since we are viewing it from the perspective of L2, then discussion of lower level courses will focus on the lower level skills from the perspective of L2.

29.2.1 L0 Education

L0 education is what used to be called moral education. L0 is the parochial source of our knowledge of absolute truth, and while the elites sneer at the concept, L0 is actually representing the interests of our mortality. As mortal beings, we should have some level of interest in that.

What would a course of study in L0 moral education that incorporates the perspective of the amoral pattern processing engine in L2 look like? For one thing, it would incorporate an awareness that the source of truth is our personal or extended singularity — instead of an objective, external truth — with an acknowledgment of our continuing need for L0 certainty in the decision making process. This need for at least temporary conviction is especially important in low information situations, such as those we encounter in the socio-political, or economic, internal knowledge arena, not to mention those physical situations where the need for alacritous decisions is a matter of life and death.

Although L0 is the most primitive mind, one we share with rodents, adding the language capacities of L2 to the mix, creates complexities that the lower creatures don't face. L2 has the ability to spin out scenarios endlessly, without any sense of urgency, while L0 knows how to decide in the moment which action *must* be taken. How do we reconcile those rather contrary abilities? Truth be told, it's actually pretty simple, but it is a skill that should be taught and practiced at the university level, because it is only when adolescents get to college age that their ability for abstract thinking really gets going, so what they thought they knew before about reconciling absolute truth with endless possibilities, they now find is no longer adequate to balance their new L2-heavy mix of ideas with their old and new beliefs.

Absolute truth, although it is not true in the classical sense everyone supposes it to be, is nevertheless directly connected to the truth of our viability, and that is not an insignificant reality. *True* isn't true in the simple sense you used to think, but there is a facet of truth in it that is sophisticated and defies the simple abilities of L2 to easily comprehend. For example, it's pretty easy to determine the volume of a bucket if you can pour measured amounts of water into it, but if the bucket is a mile across, you probably need a little math to perform the calculation; this is really no different than having to learn how to calculate the significance of truth in a given situation, once we realize that it comes from within us, rather than from a fixed point in the universe.

The animal brain can do vector calculations because the self vector is always fixed at the origin, at the center of the universe, which simplifies the calculations considerably. In contrast to this, L2-aware, L0 moral education would have to teach us to do the calculations between any of several vectors, none of which is positioned at the [0, 0, 0] point. Also, it would have to teach us to do this with words and ideas, instead of just numbers.

This is a slightly more complicated problem, but still eminently doable.

29.2.2   L1 Education

L1 instantiates a result with a pre-situation and an action. This part seems to be built-in, and doesn't seem to offer much opportunity for enhancement, but the other part of the process, holding the result open for a time and then taking a new situation snapshot to close it, seems to offer us some serious possibilities for enhancement. What if we close a result too early, and thereby create an evaluation that misstates the true impact of the action? What if we hold results open too long, and lose them for lack of the reinforcement required to cement a memory, robbing us of chances to learn from experience?

There is every reason to suppose that the lesson-learning part of the process could be enhanced with results of scientific studies, that we could learn practices and tricks to maximize our ability to learn from experience. The other part of L1 function, the generalization process that runs in the background to maintain our optimal search value-tree, might also be amenable to enhancement through study and training.

29.2.3   L2 Education

The curriculum we have been discussing so far is all L2-based, and now we consider L2 education from an L2 perspective. The idea of using L2 to study L2 in order to teach L2 skills is almost poetic in its elegance. The idea is to switch from trying to induce students to recognize and infer patterns from mushy internal knowledge literature, to focusing on directly teaching them pattern processing skills in a way that can be objectively tested.

There are modern IQ tests that contain no words, but only use patterns to test the L2 pattern processing ability. These tests can inform a curriculum if we use their pattern to teach pure, abstract pattern recognition and manipulation before we extend it into the cultural domain using words. This won't, of course, suddenly make everyone 'smart', since L2 intelligence involves skills in proclivity, retention and facility, but it will greatly improve the efficiency of instruction to focus the teaching effort on the actual thing that needs to be learned.

A greater emphasis on formal languages, and external verification, will shift the focus away from the internal verbal model and towards the stronger, formal modeling facets. Recognition of the folly of enshrining the erudition fallacy as the centerpiece of education and culture, though, is the single most critical change we can insist on, if we are serious about wanting to elevate our educational process to focus on education, rather than training and preening.

By appropriately contextualizing math and science with the different requirements and backgrounds of the various classes of student — which we will finally acknowledge do exist and are valid — and then making the purpose of all teaching statements both explicit and appropriate, we will be able to equip a much higher proportion of our students with the kind of quantitative skills that faceted model-oriented reasoning requires. This will not only greatly benefit the average student, it will prepare the specialist student for advanced L3 instruction.

29.2.4 L3 Education

Despite the inclusion of the previous chapter on discovery in this volume, we are still deferring in-depth discussion of L3 to the next volume.

29.3 Changes

The fundamental change we are proposing to the higher education curriculum is to change the focus from internal to external knowledge. This will have far-reaching effects.

First, we need to bring back what used to be called normal schools, now called teachers' colleges. In these schools, personal opinion specialties, such as 19th century French poetry, or sociology and the like, could be kept alive as degree specialties to train teachers for survey courses. Basically, all the soft courses that wouldn't be eliminated altogether would be taught as instructional indulgences in the new normal schools, whose two-fold job would be to pass down the verbal tradition in various arcane literary niches, as well as preparing lower level teachers.

29.3.1 Exclusions

The basic idea would be to cut all subjects that do not generate reproducible results. The first to go would be all the social Marxist courses indoctrinating students in the ideology of class struggle, including but not limited to: women's and gender studies, social justice studies, race studies, etc.

Some subjects, like political science and sociology, might benefit from being split into quantitative and qualitative branches, so that the qualitative branches could be eliminated, while the side dealing with reproducible measurement of actual phenomena could be preserved.

All literature courses would be eliminated, replaced by reading groups discussed below.

Essentially, the entire erudition fallacy infrastructure should be defunded and all work in that delusion stopped.

Social justice and gender study courses may produce a measurable increase in the student's sense of grievance and anger, but this is an L0 result that does not require a university course. This is not the kind of measurable result we seek.

29.3.2   Inclusions

As mentioned, the focus of coursework would shift to verifiable intellectual development, but instead of forcing general students to take mathematics classes intended for math students, they would follow a parallel curriculum that would concentrate on the competencies required for ultrareasoning.

Of course, the science and math curriculum would be beefed up and tailored to support model-oriented reasoning, and courses

in computer science basics, computer language, software engineering, and simulation would be added. Econometrics, with a
focus on simulation, would be another requirement. Basically, if
it can be measured, or if it uses tools and techniques of general
interest, it would be included in the basic curriculum.

Once a student had completed the pattern processing courses,
there would be a choice of pattern processing application courses
offered to introduce the student to a particular application of
pattern processing in a subject of interest.

29.3.3   Goals

The goals of all courses would be explicitly stated, and the relation to the overall degree program would be made measurably
clear, of course. However, the high level goals of the various disciplines would concentrate on developing the specific potential
of the various intellects, as mentioned previously:

- L0: competence in moral philosophy,
- L1: evaluation and generalization skills,
- L2: all of the pattern processing skills, along with external
  validation disciplines, as well as mastery of specific pattern languages, such as those used in different branches of
  mathematics, engineering, and the sciences.

The core goal in ultrareasoning education is to exercise and
extend our abilities that arise from the most recent mutation
stages on the presumption that this will best equip us to deal
with the coming, but likely unforeseen, changes in our environment. Yes, we still have to make a living in the here and now,
but since ultrareasoning is externally focused, the skills that we

master in learning it, will enable us to focus on, and interact with, the verifiable reality surrounding us, better than we could without our new proficiencies.

29.3.4 Additions

Since literary interpretation is not reproducible and, aside from securing one's entry into a destructive erudition club, actually does not accomplish anything beyond some very expensive and inefficient pattern manipulation practice, then, logically, not spending any time doing it is exactly equivalent to spending years steeped in the practice.

However, given the order of infinity gap between the details in discrete and continuous models, and the acknowledged benefit of a multi-faceted approach to developing models, it turns out that literature and other internal knowledge literary forms actually do still have a place in a sound educational plan. Once a student has mastered the pattern manipulation curriculum and taken an introduction to pattern application course, it is now time for them to begin readings from the catalog of great writings of Western Civilization. But, instead of sinking into undisciplined, self-indulgent internal ruminations on subjective interpretations of ambiguous writings of subjective experience, the student should grab a section of interest, and work on externalizing it. This is when a peer reading group would be helpful in providing the student with feedback on different aspects of the modeling process: the choice and method of externalization, the design of the tests, and the analysis of the results. After all, however brilliant we all may be, we can't think of everything, and we don't all have the same initial frame of reference, so our appreciation of the depth and breadth of the modeling space can always be enhanced with additional perspectives.

In theory, such a thing as a collegial environment might exist, and if it can be shown to be recreatable with entering classes, then it would seem that the intellectual, professional and personal maturation of the student would be enhanced with their participation in a number of peer discussion groups, such as: reading, topic discussion, socialization, and mate selection groups.

Although it may seem odd to include dating groups in the curriculum design, the possibility that one might find a life mate among one's intellectual peers does not seem to be a ridiculous notion, and since a balanced life is a worthy goal to strive for, incorporating discussions on the intricacies of interpersonal relationships into the last formal formative stage of our pre-adult education, seems both reasonable and prudent.

29.4 Conclusion

Obviously, waving a hand and saying, create "pattern processing courses," evades more than it explains, but the reality is that this is the one area that our professors and graduates actually already know a lot about. Of course, they conflate pattern processing techniques with subject matter specifics and the whole truth thing, but once the interested and gifted intellects among the autocrats are shown how to think abstractly, yet with a reality focus, they will be able to spin out curriculum proposals by the bushelful. Then, thanks to the nature of the discipline, they can run calculations, simulations, and experiments on any number of alternatives, and the results evaluated prior to any large scale roll out. One likely result would be the finding that different approaches work for different types of intellect, and then schools could reform along the lines of subject and mind type.

The 'not in my lifetime' objection has no impact on me. After all, I am reasonably serene in the knowledge that the fifth person who will read this book will likely do so long after I am gone. Our goals are long term, but our responsibility is just to model the problems important to us, and to suggest and test solutions, and repeat, as long as we can. Given time, we might participate in the actual implementation effort, but the natural course of things is for L2 minds to implement L3 discoveries, so it is of no consequence whether any of us survive to see the results of this great effort to pull institutional higher education from the tar pits of the mudball academy, or not.

29.5   Review

- Focus on level-specific education:
    - L0: competence in moral philosophy,
    - L1: evaluation and generalization skills,
    - L2: all of the pattern processing skills, along with external validation disciplines, as well as mastery of specific pattern languages, such as those used in different branches of mathematics, engineering, and the

sciences.

- L0: Truth, although parochial rather than absolute, is nevertheless directly connected to the truth of our viability, a not insignificant reality.

- L1: The ability to learn from experience is automatic, but can be schooled and tested.

- L1: Generalization is a very sophisticated function executed by a very primitive part of the mind. Training can verifiably improve this skill.

- L2 studies:
  - pattern processing skills, including memorization and recall;
  - learning to anchor alien subjects, such as math, with a strong value link is a skill that can be learned;
  - facility with formal languages;
  - specific math competencies, such as: calculus, discrete math, linear and abstract algebra, etc.;
  - several computer languages in multiple paradigms;
  - physics, chemistry, biology, engineering, etc.;
  - rhetoric from the ultrareasoning perspective;
  - other such quantifiable subjects as needed.

- The fundamental change to the higher education curriculum is to change the focus from internal to external knowledge.

- Scrap all soft subjects that fail to generate reproducible results.

- Explicit context and goals for all statements is mandatory.

- Peer discussion groups might be helpful to many.

Chapter 30

Subjectivity Conjecture

30.1 Introduction

Subjectivity Conjecture: all subjective problems can be expressed using one formula.

The subjectivity conjecture states that the bewildering complexity of the entire domain of subjective problems can all be expressed using a single formula. If this seems to be an unbelievable claim, perhaps it is because the real nature of subjectivity has not yet fully emerged from the confusing mists of mudball reasoning.

All subjective problems exist in a cognitive space, and all cognitive spaces are characterized by an interest singularity. That is, all subjective problems are defined in relation to a singularity. This means that all the elements in a subjective problem can be defined in relation to a singularity. Therefore, the subjectivity conjecture comes down to the simple proposition that one can create a formula to relate the position changes of the problem elements in cognitive space to the actions that lead to those changes. We will not only show that such a formula can be defined, but will also show that it really only expresses that the relation between $\mathbb{CS}$ and $\mathbb{R}$ is an action vector, since cognition is fundamentally the mechanism of interested choice that is effected through action.

30.2   Problems

To start, let us carefully define exactly what a problem is:

Problem: an unsatisfactory circumstance influenceable by actionable inputs.

That is, if there is nothing we can do about something, then by this definition, it is not a problem, even though we may be discomfited by it. For example, scientists tell us that in about 3 or 4 billion years our sun's luminosity will increase to the point where it will boil the oceans on earth, making life here kind of difficult. By the definition above, the increasing luminosity and temperature of the sun is not a problem, it's just a fact, but the fact that our life on earth will become untenable *is* a problem, because we can do something about that: we can leave. This suggests that part of our responsibility as mature, externally oriented intellectuals may be to reframe situations that we find unsatisfactory, until we can find an actionable problem that, if solved, would successfully ameliorate the issue.

For clarity, we might define a subjective problem as a problem with a value component, but this is redundant and unnecessary, since the term 'unsatisfactory' in the original definition already denotes a value component. It may sound dispassionate, but the quality of being unsatisfactory cannot be defined without a value component, so this means that all problems are subjective problems without the need for any further qualification, but we will use the term 'subjective problem' whenever doing so helps the clarity of the discussion.

The fact that we use the same word to refer both to an actionable circumstance, and to pattern language calculations (like $2+2 = ?$), should only cause a moment of confusion in this discussion. The different words for circumstance and calculation problems are homonyms and homographs, that is, they sound the same and are spelled the same, but they are actually different words, as indicated by their different domains and ranges. Exercises in pattern language grammar, like mathematical formulas, have a domain and range that are both restricted to the set of pattern language constructs. Actionable circumstances have a different constraint profile.

The problem profile in figure 30.1, shows that problems have one foot in cognitive space, $\mathbb{CS}$, and the other in external reality, $\mathbb{R}$. The top branch represents the definition of the problem, the middle branch represents the hoped-for result of the action, and the bottom branch represents the measured result of the action. The delta, δ_t, between the top and the bottom measures the

Subjectivity Conjecture

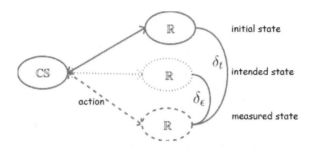

Figure 30.1: Problem profile.

actual effect of the action, and the δ_ϵ between the middle and the bottom branch measures the error in the problem model.

This profile thus defines problems as mappings that match initial conditions and a set of actionable points to a set of resulting changes. That is, with our definition of problem, we are confining our attention specifically to *unsatisfactory actionable interest situations*, and ignoring issues confined to the world of internal feelings. There are three key elements in our definition:

- an interest element: *interest*,
- a value element: *unsatisfactory*,
- an influenceable external element: *actionable*.

If any of the three is missing, then there is no problem in our sense of the word: if we care nothing about a situation, or do, but find it satisfactory, or it happens that there is nothing we can do to influence it, then it isn't a problem from our point of view. Does this mean that tidal waves that wipe out shore populations are not a problem? Yes, it means exactly that, but it does not mean that we cannot reformulate the issue (e.g., we need to install early warning sensors in the ocean and create rapid escape route for vulnerable villages, build barriers, or move the villages), into a proper problem form that focuses our attention, and empowers us to do something about it. So, what may seem heartless at first blush, is really just a decision to see reality in a way that enhances our ability to shape our future.

Circumstance problems map concepts in $\mathbb{CS}$ to measurable phenomena in $\mathbb{R}$ through actions, some of which we take or affect. Another way to put this, is that subjective problems are resource and effort allocation issues which have mortality-significant results in $\mathbb{R}$.

Note that, although an uncomfortable internal state is not included in the concept of a circumstance problem, it could be if it were reframed to be actionable with a measurable objective. So, "I feel bad," is not a problem, but "I am unhappy about certain aspects of my primary relationship," would qualify as a problem if there were actions you could take to address the problem aspects.

Thus, the version of the word *problem* that we are using refers strictly to life-significant circumstances that can be influenced by volitional actions. Is this a reasonable restriction of the word? Yes, because it clarifies that the significance of a circumstance is influenced by how we look at it: that an asteroid will strike the earth is a simple fact, it doesn't become a problem until two conditions are met: 1) we realize that it will affect our interests, and 2) we decide to look for something we can do to influence the outcome. Note that it doesn't matter whether or not we ultimately succeed in our efforts, or if success was even possible. All that counts is just that we conceive actionable points in the problem that, by our calculations, could lead to a new outcome with a positive impact on our interests.

Fatalistic philosophies take an extreme approach to coping with mortality concerns precisely by blocking many issues from becoming problems through preaching that there is nothing we can, or should try, to do to change the outcome. That is, their solution to the threat of the unknown is to use this exact definition of problem and declare that we shouldn't look at the future either as undesirable, or as actionable.

Learning to reformulate unsatisfactory circumstances as actionable problems is an important intellectual and life skill, it empowers one to manage and affect the affairs and conditions in one's life. This emphasis on the narrow definition of what a subjective problem is, is worth the effort it demands for the clarity it brings to the topic, and to the process of dealing with difficulties of various kinds in all different aspects of our life. Basically, this definition *challenges* us to see difficulties as actionable problems, because this is what makes it possible to find solutions for them through our efforts.

Perhaps the reader can think of more examples of subjective problems that don't fit this definition, than that do, but I suggest that this confusion traces back to the fact that most statements have implicit context and goals, and that once we define these terms of the statement in each instance, and make them explicit, then the case of non-compliant subjective problems just goes away.

Subjective is, as previously explained, a synonym for *internal*, as in *internal thought*. All perceptions, feelings, and ideas that we have are internal thought, only a very small fraction of which have been externalized sufficiently to achieve a defined relation to $\mathbb{R}$. So, let us rephrase our conjecture:

All internal knowledge expressions of actionable, unsatisfactory circumstances beginning and ending in $\mathbb{R}$, can be represented with the subjectivity expression.

Again, we assert that this is not an unreasonable restriction of the concept of a problem, and in fact, we asseverate that, rather than being a restriction, this is a universal formulation of mortality-significant issues that cognitive entities confront. Subjective problems are an L2 phenomenon that connect $\mathbb{CS}$ to $\mathbb{R}$, because the definition of problem requires both an actionable situation in $\mathbb{R}$ and an interest component in $\mathbb{CS}$.

L2's data structures and functions restrict its ability to conceptualize problems that have a detail profile finer than the width of the pattern object, and this manifests in the L2 subjectivity problem solution. When we use the L3 fractal branching structure with model-oriented reasoning to conceptualize complex issues, we can achieve an entirely different solution to the subjective problem, as you will see below. Switching from L2 to L3 while in problem-solving mode allows us to peer into issues at a much higher resolution, enabling us to see new details and follow threads at a finer scale than we have ever been able to perceive before.

Pause for a bit, and reflect on the subjective conjecture for a moment. Does the assertion that a single formula can express all subjective problems still seem so unlikely?

30.3   Subjective Ideas and Mortality

Our minds are mortal, they can only exist in a bounded context of birth, growth, decline and death. This claim may seem as unilluminating as it is incontrovertible, like saying that lines written on a whiteboard are written on a whiteboard, but even that empty truism implies more than it might seem. Characters written with a marker on a simple whiteboard are drawn by hand, they do not exist in a word processor, they are editable by erasure and overwriting only, back spacing and cut and paste do not exist, and it is unlikely that any of them were written a century ago. Similarly, the universal cognition model is built on the presumption that self-consciousness arising from an organic context bears the imprint of the evolutionary organic structures that made awareness possible. Our understanding of the evolutionary process tells us that awareness and intelligent choice must have a positive survival-related impact.

We have a tendency to decontextualize our ideas, to imagine that our appreciation of a springtime breeze exists independently of our mortality, but of course, it most definitely does not. Since all meaning and value derives from the singularity distortion field, then any idea with a significant value link is expressly situated in our own mortal context. This means that all affective ideation is biased by the mortality context that birthed it. And, even if certain pattern languages can be shown to be perfectly affectless, still the effort to learn or create them must be motivated by a calculation that the effort is worthwhile, that it has value, and this means that the language must, at some point, connect back to our mortality context.

30.4   Subjective ideas exist in minds

Just as a mind cannot exist without a body that defines a mortal context, subjective ideas cannot exist without a mind. We tend to think in terms of events and entities in reality, traditionally failing to appreciate that we only know of externalities because we are able to form a mental model of them, a model that only exists in our mind, independent of any external referent.

Without biology, everything is physics and chemistry, but add biology to the picture, biology with the evolution of sensory and cognitive organic structures, and this creates the ground on which the phenomenon of *experience* can come into existence. Until something existed to register an experience of the physical world, experience itself simply *did not exist.* And what is experience, but the processing of physical events by the machinery of organic beings? That the experience of the external event is therefore defined less by the facts of the event, than by the parameters of the organism's awareness, is definitional: experience is defined by the instrument registering the experience, not by the external event. While the experience may contain some information traceable to the event, all of the information in the experience is defined by the limits of what the experience structure can encode.

30.5   All ideas are subjective

Surely, it is trivially true that when a being is literally crushed by some external force, then that force defines the outcome of the event, but this is the event, not the experience. Regardless of how trivially *real* reality may be, regardless of how silly it may seem to discuss the reality of existence, nevertheless, the unavoidable fact is that, whatever reality may or may not be, however exposed to it our bodies might be, our awareness of it is separate and distinct from it, separated as if by an impenetrable black wall.

But the blackness separating us from reality is not a wall, it is the discontinuity that exists between different levels of existence, between physical reality and impressionable organic cognitive material. Picture us, not as objective viewers of objective reality, but, instead, as unskilled courtroom sketch artists holding an erasable pad on our lap; the blankness on the empty pad is in us, and we can only know those parts of the outside world that we clumsily sketch from our interpretations of what our sensations are telling us.

We take it as an axiom that reality and events are real, but we can only prove the validity of this notion in our minds, in our awareness, in the rare, special case of a reproducible test—all the rest of the time, we are relying on faith and experience that our ideas closely match reality. Our perception is imperfect, and our cognition is expensive, so we often, or usually, trust second-hand reports, without attempting to verify them. For example, when we are told that *those* people are bad because they are of a certain type, we tend to believe it to the extent that we trust the source.

Even though our genotype is defined by natural selection to match a particular environmental niche, as sentient beings, we must rely on our mental processes and actions to interpret our perceptions, and then to figure out the similarities and differences between the various things in our environment to maximize our survival potential, first by improving our ability to respond quickly to threats, on the one hand, and then to seize opportunities that arise, on the other.

Technically speaking, even our scientific knowledge is mostly subjective — if you think about it honestly, you know that we really accept nearly all of it on faith — because we verify very few facts ourselves, and we rarely even read any of the literature behind most theories. Our knowledge framework, the network of ideas that supports, contextualizes and extends these purportedly scientific facts is, by definition and construction, almost entirely subjective. That doesn't mean it is invalid, simply that we must acknowledge that we really don't know the quality of everything we picked up in the net when we scooped up supposedly scientific information from some source. We must forever keep our minds open to correction, since new, better measurements may become available at any time.

30.6   Mortal ideas → mortal issues

Obviously, since subjectivity only exists in the experience of a living being, and all living beings we know of are mortal, therefore, all subjectivity occurs within a mortal context. While this statement might seem incidental, it actually leads to a vitally important insight that collapses what we have thought was an unbounded problem (how big is the subjective problem space? how do we test it?) down to a single, tractable problem: how does a living being perceive, evaluate, and respond to an event in reality, $\mathbb{R}$?

Mortal beings can only process perceptions and thoughts in a cognitive space in which value is defined by the ego-calculus: "what does this mean to me, how should I respond?" (Now that we understand the nature of the extended self, we don't have to quibble about the pronouns, since we know that *me* and *we* are really just conventions in self-designation.) Objecting to this formulation would require that you could design a natural selection process that did not favor mobile organisms who processed their experience in a self-preferential way.

It is vital to reflect on this long enough to grok it: if no one cares, or can do anything about it, how is it a subjective problem? A problem without a value link to the singularity distortion field has no value.

30.7   Subjective Problem Class

Formally, the class of subjective problems can be defined as the tuple:

$$(\vec{r}_0,\ \vec{a},\ \vec{r}_1)$$

If we add the convenience term *circumstance* to mean a set of one or more situations, then we can read this tuple as comprising $\vec{r}_0$, which represents the initial circumstance vector; $\vec{a}$, which represents an array of actions; and $\vec{r}_1$ which represents the post-action circumstance vector, which, by definition, must evaluate to be greater than the pre-action vector. In other words, simply by modeling an unsatisfactory circumstance as actionable, you are successfully defining it as a problem.

When you first define a problem, all you have, of course, is $\vec{r}_0$, the model of the unsatisfactory circumstance. The other variables are just place holders, and they remain so until you come up with a set of actions that you predict will lead to a resulting circumstance that improves on the initial one in some significant way.

Both $\vec{r}_0$ and $\vec{r}_1$ are models that may be above the level of a situation, and the difference in evaluation represents a complex *intention*, not a measurement, since no action has happened yet. This definition covers the top two branches of figure 30.1, and is consistent with the verbal definition from the beginning of this chapter.

What this definition codifies is that, as cognitive entities, we judge reality from our mortality value perspective, and we conceptualize problems as situations that can be improved by means of our ability to move and act. All problems in cognitive space conform to this definition, and all problems exist in cognitive space, which means that in the flat space of external reality, outside of cognitive space, there are no problems.

The next question is, given that we have our subjective problem definition, how do we transform that into a subjective problem solution? Since L2 and L3 express their data in different structures with different supporting operations, subjective problem solutions are, unsurprisingly, formulated differently in the two intellects.

30.8   Public Policy Solutions

Learning how to problemitize personal subjective situations is a skill in itself, but this activity is already part of our normal life, and there is no lack of advice on how to transition from a powerless, passive attitude to an active, empowered one, so we will leave this topic for others. In general, subjective problems that are going to be solved by one's own actions are just turned into plans or tasks, and not of great interest to us as this point, since when we create or invent solutions to problems we are either relying on our experience of one kind or another to associate a sequence of steps as the solution to a problem, or we are using L3 to invent a new solution. The former is just normal problem solving, and the latter is covered at length in *Pinnacle Questions* and *Pinnacle Reasoning*, so we don't need to cover these cases here.

There is another, important class of subjective problems, those that are to be solved by unspecified groups of people, and this is the sort of problem that public policy discussions focus on, the sort of problem that provide the meat for most public and media discussions on 'serious subjects'. These discussions are predicated on the fallacy that we can use our 'reasoning' to 'rationally' look at 'both sides' of the issue and come to a 'reasonable' conclusion. That this is a fallacy can no longer be doubted, but we will now examine the mechanism of failure of public policy discussions, which turns out not to be a product of either ignorance or ill-will — although there is much of that on display in almost all such discussions — but to be an inevitable consequence of the structural limitations of L2.

Public policy problems are encoded using an object that is a variant of the opinion object, from which it is distinguished by the list it contains that holds one or more unexecutable actions. The actions are unexecutable in the sense that the assignee is not *me*, but an unspecified *them*, so the public policy object differs from a normal pattern object in that it is neither a plan

nor path, but merely a static assertion that an action set has
a certain value. Whereas task objects can hold an assignment
to named individuals, public policy objects are assigned to a
collective, over which one has no control. These objects that
handle such momentous subjects as war and peace, governance
and resource allocation are, ironically, actually simpler and less
rigorous than the simple task object. The task object for applying paint, to take a mundane example, contains a series of
actions, such as: clean, sand, and prime the surface; use the
correct type of paint; apply it evenly with the correct type of
brush or roller; apply it within the correct temperature range,
etc. The policy object only contains a prescription that you
cannot even implement yourself (e.g., cut taxes), and the steps,
if there are more than one, are not specific enough to actually
use. The policy object contains general instructions, and the
only assurance that it will even apply in a particular situation
is because the value link connecting it to a web of opinions and
beliefs says that it is true, which is to say that it is effectively
the next thing to an antswer, an answer that doesn't need a
question to be true.

The subjective conjecture is that we can express any subjective problem using a simple formula. The corollary of the
conjecture is that we can also express the solution to all subjective problems in a simple expression for each intellect level. In
this introductory volume, we will confine our demonstration of
the conjecture to public policy problems, since this is the arena
where we hear and see people struggling, and failing, to use

their great reasoning skills to solve vitally important problems. By doing this, we hope to anticipate the standard objection / question (what good is this model? how can we actually use it in practical situations?) with a demonstration of a practical application of the abstruse model that illuminates why public policy discussions are such sad, low-level affairs.

30.9 L2 Subjective Problem Solution

By **M2**, we know that L2 uses patterns to construct a solution to subjective problems. Since the public policy object deals with circumstances that aggregate situations, the pattern matching operation is correspondingly enhanced to manage the extra level of abstraction. This involves both running the match operation multiple times across multiple pattern entry points, and introducing a higher level of fuzziness into it to allow matches to be summed across objects until enough patterns are mixed to contrive a match to the given circumstance. This takes trial and error, personal experience and creativity to build a complex public policy object. The easier, and more common, path, of course, is simply to accept an object from a grouping one joins, but that just means someone else did the work at another time.

Since L2 only processes patterns, we know that the L2 subjective problem solution must be a pattern. The public policy pattern object encoding the solution is simply an opinion pattern synthesized from other opinion and belief patterns. The function of the public policy pattern is to reduce a complex problem to a simple set of actions with a value link.

For example, the stereotypical conservative public policy solution might be: for any situation, *, the set of actions {reduce taxes, reduce regulation, enforce contracts, protect property, enhance industry-related infrastructure} will produce the result: {increased wealth and freedom}. The stereotypical liberal solution might be: for any situation, *, the set of actions {raise taxes, increase regulation, raise benefits, create government jobs} will produce the result: {increased wealth and safety}.

Think about political arguments and campaigns for a few minutes, and try to convince yourself that they are above this level of simplicity.

The L2 problem solution can be formally represented as:

$$(\vec{r}_0, \ \vec{a}, \ \vec{r}_1) \ = [true \mid false \mid nil]$$

That is, once the problem formulation is instantiated with values for $\vec{a}$ and $\vec{r}_1$, then the solution object is assigned a truth value calculated from the included components via a value link, and that's the solution. That's all there is to it: a problem, a set of actions, and an assertion of what the outcome will be; there is nothing else in the L2 problem solution object. L2 *cannot* do any better than this, this is all the object and operations can achieve. Certainly, since we still can learn from experience (L1), we may find over time that our idea is not supported by reality, but if we find it is still supported by our friends and at-tacked by our enemies, then it is unlikely we will be motivated to replace it with an updated one. Unless, of course, we change group allegiance, then we will accept the new policy object from our new friends, and will be willing to tell everyone how wrong our old comrades were.

The L2 problem solution object is just an opinion object that asserts that the action set will lead to the desired conclusion. The actions cannot actually be executed, they serve as affiliation points to vet comrades and candidates — anyone who doesn't have a matching policy object and does not parrot the same solution is not "one of us."

The L2 public policy solution object is just an assertion that reduces a web of L2 opinions and beliefs down to an L0 truth value to put you in the position to know, to decide, to act. Notice that there is not even any mechanism that could support testing, no suggestion of what tests might be run, no facility for update. The L2 solution object does not accommodate the lower branch in figure 30.1 — there is no way to correlate a public policy object with a reality check, since its truth value comes from a value link, not from an assessment of facts.

30.10   L3 Subjective Problem Solution

In the current version of the model, L3 does not have a memory, just a data structure and the operations that work on it. This is consistent with my experience that discovery structures do not retain charge over time, not even overnight, really. They always have to be refreshed in most branches to regain the charged state that supports insight and discovery. This is also consistent with the evidence that the inventions of L3 can be communicated to others, but only as L2 patterns that can be followed, not as discovery trees with the charged leaves that make L3 so powerful.

So, where does L3 start its work? With L2 patterns, of course, but it cannot work with patterns as patterns, since their structure hides the most important details of the ideas inside, so the first thing L3 has to do to convert patterns to fractal discovery structures is to decompose the patterns into constituent parts, and position the parts of interest into the developing discovery tree. Another way to say the same thing, is that L3 has to *expand terms* hidden in patterns into *measurable* concepts, and express relations in a *testable* format that supports an *iterative* development process.

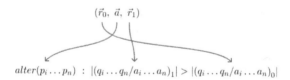

$$(\vec{r}_0,\ \vec{a},\ \vec{r}_1)$$

$$alter(p_i \ldots p_n)\ :\ |(q_i \ldots q_n/a_i \ldots a_n)_1| > |(q_i \ldots q_n/a_i \ldots a_n)_0|$$

Figure 30.5: Expanding the subjective problem into an L3 solution.

Figure 30.5 shows one way in which the subjective problem can be expanded to support an L3 solution. Reading from left to right, it says that:

- if $p_i \ldots p_n$ are the processes that generated the original, unsatisfactory state of affairs, $\vec{r}_0$, then our set of solutions actions will be modifications to those processes that will generate

- an ending state, $\vec{r}_1$, that has a higher evaluation than
- the beginning state, $\vec{r}_0$.

In any given situation, there are many processes $p_i \ldots p_n$ in the set of processes $\mathbf{P}$, that influence the situation. Those processes each have outputs $q_i \ldots q_n$ in the set of outputs $\mathbf{Q}$. Those outputs impact the participants $a_i \ldots a_n$ in the set of participants $\mathbf{A}$, where participants can be either different beings, or just different elements in our awareness attribute array. The optimization problem states that we must alter one or more of the processes, p_i in such a way that the benefits $q_i \ldots q_m$ received by the important participants $a_i \ldots a_m$, maximally increase. Converting these words to expression form gives us this:

$$alter(p_i \ldots p_n) \; : \; |(q_i \ldots q_n / a_i \ldots a_n)_1| > |(q_i \ldots q_n / a_i \ldots a_n)_0|$$

That is, alter some processes such that the benefit to the prioritized parties is optimized.

Combining this with the definition of statement,

statement = [context] + content + [purpose]

we can define the context of the optimization formula as $\mathbf{A}_0$, the initial state of the being's awareness which represents $\mathbf{E} \cup \mathbf{A}'$ where $\mathbf{E}$ is the perceived initial state of the environment and $\mathbf{A}'$ is the initial state of the organism; the content of the statement is: $alter(p_i \ldots p_n)$, and the relative improvement of $\mathbf{A}_1$, the subsequent state, over $\mathbf{A}_0$ is the purpose.

Therefore, the expression form of an internal, subjective

statement is:

$$given \ \mathbf{A}_0, \ alter(p_i \ldots p_n) \to optimize \ (q_{i\ldots n}) \ for \ (a_{i\ldots n})$$

Note that each part of the above expression is both easily quantifiable and testable, and that, therefore, by taking this approach, we can quantify and test any subjective statement using this optimization formula. This means that, for the first time, we could actually have policy debates on the explicit costs and benefits of pursuing any policy we want to consider, and we could do this by strictly focusing on verifiable, measurable calculations instead of on primitive L0 concepts of right (meaning: in my specific and extended perceived self-interest) and wrong (contrary to my specific and extended perceived self-interest).

Note also that this in no way guarantees fairness or efficiency, and that

$$|(q_i \ldots q_n/a_i \ldots a_n)_1| > |(q_i \ldots q_n/a_i \ldots a_n)_0|$$

just explicitly states the cost and benefit shifts caused by the process changes to the interested participants. What this L3 solution shows is that the essential problem of subjective experience always reduces to an optimization problem: how can I minimize my risk and maximize my benefit when responding/reacting to an event, external force or entity?

30.11   Compare and Contrast

In general, L2 uses patterns to solve problems by constructing or assigning a pattern to the problem situation. In the normal case where the individual is the actor tasked with the actions, one simply executes the one or several steps in the pattern, and then appraises the new situation and repeats the process. That is, all L2 can do is throw a known or newly synthesized pattern at the problem, and then, once that pattern, or pattern step, is complete, assess the situation and match the next step in the pattern or select a new pattern and go.

If the problem is solved by a pattern-sized solution, then all is well. If it requires something more than that, then it's still going to get a pattern-sized solution. Let's walk through a really mundane example:

Not a problem: The grass has grown.

Problem: The grass is too long.

Pattern: The grass needs to be cut.

Solution: I am going to cut the grass.

Problem: Cutting the grass with the gasoline mower will destroy all life on earth.

Solution: I will cut the grass using the manual mower.

Problem: The grass will look terrible after being cut with a manual mower.

Solution: Take pride in being slovenly, it means you care about the environment.

This silly example illustrates the fact that we deal with problems at all levels each and every day, and we solve them by pattern matching and executing the steps in the pattern. The nature of L2 problem solving is that as long as you can see patterns in the circumstances around you, then you can always

respond with an action, and the process need never end, because, regardless of the outcome of your previous action, you
will always be confronted with a situation that you can respond
to with another pattern. For the familiar problems of existence
that are wholly describable as threats, opportunities, or nullities, this approach is entirely adequate, as long as you are satisfied with achieving familiar results when responding to familiar
problems.

The inadequacy of L2 problem solving becomes apparent
as soon as the unknown component in the circumstance demanding attention rises above a trivial level, or you become
dissatisfied with the same old results. Then, L2 hits a hard
limit, because its operations do not extend to exploration, they
are limited to adding, subtracting, generalizing and extending
ideas. If these simple transformations do not produce a satisfactory result, then you're out of luck, the L2 toolbox is empty.

But, take a moment and notice the essential limitation of L2
problem solving: when confronted with a situation, it can only
match it with an existing or newly cobbled pattern, and then
execute the action. This terminates the pattern solution process
because once we are done acting, we just scan our environment
again, like normal, and repeat the pattern processing routine.
Except when one is following a complex pattern through a chain
of actions and exit point selections, there is no connection between the execution of independent patterns that follow one
another in a sequence. The crux of the L2 pattern solution is
that we have executed a pattern in response to a situation, and

then we start all over again with matching a new pattern to the new situation now in front of us, regardless of whether or not the reality we are confronting is a continuation or consequence of our previous actions. In fact, L2 doesn't necessarily recognize the new situation as being in any way related to the old. Surely, you have observed this myopia in others, if not in yourself.

Interpreting resource allocation optimization problems as pattern matching problems is a simplification that is required by the limitations of L2. L0/L1 uses reductive perception to simplify the world to a problem that can be addressed with a motion solution. L2 uses pattern matching to simplify the world to a problem that can be simplified and solved with known steps. This simplification that L2 uses is not a foolish or pathetic response to a reality that is immensely complex, it is a step in the evolutionary response of organic entities to conceptualize an external reality they only get a vague, limited sense of in a few dimensions. In the march of organic entities towards a comprehensive awareness of external reality, L2 was a significant, even profound advance. But, although it is a step up from the reductive perception of L0, it is still only a step up.

The particular genius of L3 is the quality of genius itself: its flexible, complex data structure supports exploration of the unknown to an essentially unbounded extent, creating the opportunity for invention and discovery. The capabilities of L3 enable it to explore the unknown in an incremental and insightful fashion to discover new solutions and new levels of solutions that transcend our knowledge and experience. Figure 30.5 illustrates the level of detail and complexity that can be achieved when we switch from the simplicity of pattern matching to the precision of patient exploration.

By matching subjective problems with a pattern solution without measuring the actual variance historically seen between the claimed and actual results, the L2 solution object effectively reduces problems to a simple ternary value (T/F/N) asserting the efficacy of this solution, while the L3 object can return a set of numbers that specify the delta between the intended and the measured result in any number of dimensions. Note also, that the example L3 solution explicitly names the winners and losers in each version of the solution, while the L2 object is just asserted to be true with the conviction of the value link.

30.12   Discussion

Ask yourself, what should the answer to a resource allocation optimization problem actually look like? It certainly is not the simple [*true*|*false* |*don't care*] value, or the list of unexecutable actions. Instead, it would have to look something like a spreadsheet that showed the winners and losers with their respective gains and losses, and be executable so that you could run what-if scenarios. It would have numbers, lots of numbers. Why would anyone ever expect we should be able to reliably reduce a complex resource allocation solution to a literal two bit value?

Even though L2 sees them as pattern matching problems, *all subjective problems are resource allocation optimization problems*, as only L3 can conceive them to be. L2 is like a space probe that returns pictures whose pixels are 10 or 100 miles on a side — not necessarily wrong, as far as it goes, but missing a lot of detail due to the lack of precision. L2 *cannot* see problems as resource allocation issues because it lacks the refinement ability to explore and define the problem to that level of detail, because it is limited to responding to circumstances or situations as a whole with a pattern as a whole. Instead of discovering the fractal dimension of the coast of England, L2 would probably call it a dodecagon or icosagon (12 or 20-sided polygon) and be done with it.

L4, whatever that evolves to become, will have a different solution, of course, but inasmuch as the L3 level is our current limit, we can confidently say that, at least, all subjective problems can be expressed as resource allocation problems. If all problems can be expressed as resource allocation problems, does that make them resource allocation problems? First of all, we are dealing with models, and the formulation **a** *is* **b** is a metaphor, an L0/L2 cognitive device, so no, the model is not the thing. Secondly, since problems only exist in cognitive space and cognitive space is a mortality-bounded space, then everything in it is part of mortality-related resource allocation concerns.

The optimization formula is more of an approach, than an actual formula you can use by substituting values for variables, but that's not actually an issue. The real import of the formula is that debating public policy issues as L2 tuples with a truth value is both incompetent and dishonest, and everyone knows it, we just haven't had the theoretical framework to expose it until now. Unless candidates and policy makers can use the L3 optimization formula to calculate and demonstrate the projected gains and losses from the changes for the target groups, they should be booed off the stage. Asking that partisans should be able to fill out the specifics of the formula is not only not asking too much, it is difficult to imagine why we would expect any less than this.

This means that, either as a candidate, or just as a member of the electorate, before you propose a public policy change, you should have:

- an executable model of the current situation;
- a list of the important mechanisms, processes and constraints to change;
- a projection of the output of each of the changes severally and together;
- a list of the beneficiaries and payers;
- estimated gains and losses to the beneficiaries and payers, respectively;
- an affordable experiment or pilot project design with a given time period;
- an error bound, along with experiment premature termination conditions.

How is expecting responsible officials to do some homework before implementing changes that will cost billions and affect millions of people asking too much of them? And shouldn't all policy changes have projections that include tripwire values to terminate failing changes? It's not asking too much, it's not asking very much at all.

What it is doing, though, is demanding a radical course change to convert from L0/L2 planning (what's right for my extended self is right for everyone) to L3 planning (full scientific method protocol) consistent with the recognition that right and wrong are primitive, inadequate concepts in resource allocation discussions since all of the precision data gained from modeling and scientific measurement is lost in the narrowing typecast down to the L0 data structure. We still need L0 to decide, and to act, but we cannot rely on it to perform, or evaluate, the precise measurements that prove that our ideas correspond to verifiable reality: $|i_i - r_i| < \epsilon$.

30.13   Summary

All problems relate to actions intended to increase the viability benefit flowing to a subset of beings or internal realities. This means that, while some may benefit, others will be disadvantaged by any solution. Solutions are, by the nature of mortality and cognition, partial, they cannot maximize returns to every interested party at the same time. While this fundamental asymmetry of scarce benefit flow is inherent in the relation between $\mathbb{R}$ and $\mathbb{CS}$, it can now be quantified and made explicit. We now have the option to begin to tackle our public problems using the optimization formula. This will mean that we can make the cost and benefit distribution of our planned solution explicit and testable, rather than implicit and narrowly interest-based; that we can begin to move policy making from L0 (truth, right), L1 (experience), and L2 ('makes sense', 'seems fair') ideas to L3 calculations (measured results, iterative solutions).

To recap, since all internal/subjective statements can be expressed as optimization problems, and since optimization problems have a testable, external representation, all subjective statements can be externalized and tested.

Optimization problems cannot have a single right answer, and not only because even if we did distribute benefits equally, this would only serve to starve some while surfeiting others, thus wasting resources while causing unintended damage, but because they address scarce resource allocation in $\mathbb{R}$ by evaluating changes from a particular singularity. The only fixed point in the mortal domain is in the center of each organism's self-interest, so there are as many fixed points as participants, but the evaluation will be determined from only one singularity which, even if it is a synthetic product of committee judgment, will necessarily favor some, over others.

Up until now, we have been using L0 functions to determine the 'best' solutions to the unrecognized optimization problem, but this is asking our oldest intellect to perform duties which it is unequipped to handle. The entire alphabet of L0 contains only 3 characters in total: a[nti], p[ro], and n[on], equating to degrees of bad, good and indifferent. Optimization problems are much more complex and require much more sophisticated data structures with operations that return quantified answers in the integer, real or complex number systems, each of which has an infinite alphabet of its own. Reducing fine measurements to three values can only preserve the single value of self-interest.

Truth has a very specific, very ancient function that it fulfills better than anything else can, but it is not up to the complex task of evaluating the inputs and outputs of optimization problems that are conceived by an intellect that evolved millions of years after L0 was encoded. We will never be able to make any real progress in social, political or economic problems as long as we use L0 to evaluate which solution to an optimization problem is 'true'.

Externalizing our subjective value propositions into explicit, optimization problems, and then transparently assigning values to the parameters to identify winners and losers, will at least allow us to have rational resource allocation discussions based on reproducible calculations, rather than on the fallacy of absolute, partisan truth.

30.14 Review

- A problem is an unsatisfactory circumstance influenceable by actionable inputs.
- A problem is a mapping that proposes a match exists between initial conditions and a set of changes resulting from a set of undefined actions.
- A problem solution specifies the actions and the intended final state.
- All subjective ideas exist in a mortal context.

- All subjective ideas exist in a mind.

- All subjective ideas address mortal issues.

- Subjective formula is a tuple that maps an initial state and a set of actions to a resultant state: $(\vec{r}_0, \vec{a}, \vec{r}_1)$.

- Public policy object is an opinion object with a collective action.

- L2 subjective problem solution maps a problem solution to a truth value: $(\vec{r}_0, \vec{a}, \vec{r}_1) = [true \mid false \mid nil]$.

- L3 subjective problem solution is an optimization formula:

$$alter(p_i \ldots p_n) \ : \ |(q_i \ldots q_n / a_i \ldots a_n)_1|$$
$$> \ |(q_i \ldots q_n / a_i \ldots a_n)_0|$$

- All subjective problems can be expressed using the formula:

$$given \ \mathbf{A}_0, \ alter(p_i \ldots p_n) \rightarrow optimize \ (q_{i \ldots n}) \ for \ (a_{i \ldots n})$$

Chapter 31

Semantic Reality

31.1   An Analytical Model

Our model of external reality, $\mathbb{R}$, is defined as

$$\mathbb{R} = \forall \, r \in \{i_d \; : \; |i_d - r_d| <= \epsilon\},$$

the set of the dimensions of all ideas, i_d, that we can measure to be within an acceptable margin of error of direct measurements or calculations of dimensions of entities, r_d, that are physically observable by independent examiners. In simple terms, it is the set of all measurables.

Since we know that we are building a model of something that we can measure aspects of, perhaps we need a way to refer directly to the external physical reality that provides our referent. What happens if we introduce $\mathbb{U}$ (for Universe) to denote external physical reality itself? So, that would mean that our model of reality, $\mathbb{R}$, maps to $\mathbb{U}$, the physical universe.

537

But, by **M2**, we know that $\mathbb{U}$ is not actually reality, the external physical universe, itself, but rather, is still just a model of it, so this gives us:

$$\mathbb{R} \mapsto \mathbb{U} \mapsto x$$

but this brings us right back where we started, confronting the fundamental epistemological question: how do we know things? Our answer, of course, is that we know things through models implemented in heritable structures in an organic mind (**M1** & **M2**).

This is why, until this point, we have simply used $\mathbb{R}$ for the dual purposes of referring to our model, and to reality itself. If we had any direct way to define reality, we wouldn't need to master model-oriented reasoning, but we don't, so here we are.

Although, formally speaking, $\mathbb{U}$ doesn't actually seem to add anything to the discussion, we will use this convenience notation to ask a question:

$$\mathbb{R} \overset{?}{\mapsto} \mathbb{U} \overset{?}{\mapsto} x$$

That is, how would $\mathbb{R}$ map to $\mathbb{U}$, and how does $\mathbb{U}$ map to x, the actual physical universe and its contents? We seem to have at least a couple of options here: first, if we think of $\mathbb{U}$ as a set, we immediately get into the turtles regression; alternatively, if we transform $\mathbb{U}$ from a set, to a definition of set membership, a solid path opens up for us, because it leads to the obvious conclusion that $\mathbb{R}$ is actually just one reality in a set of realities (let's call this set of realities $\mathfrak{R}$, Re), then $\mathbb{R}$ would simply be an element of $\Re$, giving us:

$$\mathbb{R} \in \Re \overset{?}{\mapsto} y$$

The change in the variable being mapped to, from x to y, was only made to indicate that $\Re$ might map to a different, or higher, level of reality than just our phenomenological universe.

This brings us to the question: what is reality? In a sense, this is the question underlying much of philosophical thought through the ages, as well as being central to the entire *Pinnacle* effort. This has long been seen as an impossibly difficult question to answer, but it turns out that the switch from mudball reasoning to model-oriented reasoning reveals it to be anything but hard. We can define the abstract concept of *reality*, the $\Re$ set membership rule, as:

> **Reality**: a container of verifiably measurable, related entities and forces that only interact with each other; a container into which external entities and forces cannot enter.

A reality is a self-contained universe of entities and forces that are not measurably impacted by extrinsic entities or forces. The elements of a reality are related in the sense that they are constructed, developed or evolved from a limited alphabet of elements, and forces.

By now, we hope that the reader knows we are talking about defining our model, not external reality. Once we have our model in hand, we can begin to interrogate it to define the degree to which it measurably corresponds to external phenomena. But, what happens, you may ask, if we discover that this definition does not actually hold for our physical universe because, for example, we eventually verify that particles or whatever are entering our universe from somewhere outside of it? Easy, we expand our definition of our universe to include all the entities and forces that are included in, and interact with, it. After all, since our models are discrete, we know that they are incomplete (by **M4** and **M5**), so it should never be a surprise that we need to enhance them.

At this stage in trying to understand how our reality, $\mathbb{R}$, fits into a set of realities, $\mathfrak{R}$, we have:

$$reality : \text{isolated universe of interacting entities \& forces}$$

$$\mathfrak{R} : \text{the set of realities}$$

$$\mathbb{R} \in \mathfrak{R}$$

Now, we have to ask the obvious question: what is the cardinality of $\mathfrak{R}$? Is our universe the only reality? As to whether or not there are other physical universes out there, that question is not germane to the current discussion (why?). From a model-oriented reasoning point of view, of course we can define other realities simply by defining isolated sets of elements and forces other than $\mathbb{R}$. But this raises the skeptic's questions: how would we design a new reality, and if we could, would it be useful, or just a useless intellectual indulgence?

*Remember, this work is essentially a primer on model-oriented reasoning, so you should expect new ideas to build on familiar ones. Does the phrase 'viable and **productive**' ring a bell?*

We are going to spend the remainder of this chapter answering these two questions.

31.2   Defining a New Reality

To answer the first question, we will use cognitive spaces and verbal events, elements we have already discussed, to define a complex graph object that will constitute a second reality in $\Re$. We will call this new reality a *semantic reality*, $\mathbb{SR}$, and define it as:

$$\mathbb{SR} = (\{\xi\}, \{\mathbb{L}\})$$

where ξ (xi) = the externalized (in the less formal sense of *acknowledged by others*) subset of $\mathbb{CS}$.

This means that $\mathbb{SR}$ is being modeled as a dimensional, hierarchical graph, a network of the externalized portion of cognitive space nodes (the measurable actions, messages, and artifacts), ξ, and communication links, $\mathbb{L}$. By dimensional and hierarchical, we mean that the ξ nodes can connect with each other across any number of language links that join arbitrary, multiple dimensions of each node. A 'language link' is nothing more or less than any connection that can be made between cognitive spaces by means of language messages.

A dimensional, hierarchical network thus supports the existence of different hierarchies in all of the different dimensions, each of which can be revealed, or accessed, with the appropriate query.

It might help to think of semantic reality as a 3D graph of cognitive spaces that changes orientation to present different faces, hierarchies, and value paths, depending on the dimensions and values you query on. Note that the various sets of externalized parts of cognitive spaces and associated links are not necessarily linked with each other: think solar systems in a galaxy, and galaxies in the universe, rather than imagining a single connected spider web, for example. The whole reality is isolated from external interactions, but the elements within it are all subject to a wide range of influences from each other.

A cognitive space models how we individually think and perceive our experience of the world, and of life; it is meant to capture the essence, and many of the details, of how we think, feel and behave. Cognitive spaces are individual value experience worlds that are centered in the singularity distortion field, and while, because of the purblind defect, they seem to represent all of reality to us, they are just an individual's personal experience of life.

Semantic reality, on the other hand, is a model that we can use to understand how populations of cognitive spaces form, act and interact based on their externalized aspects. Semantic reality is a meta-model that enables us to model the gestalt of language-enabled cognitive entity function. A semantic reality is the level above the individual, it is the level of groups of groups; it models all of human civilization, and every level of group below.

31.2.1 $\mathbb{L}$, Language Links

$\mathbb{L}$, the set of language links in semantic reality, is a new concept that represents the grouping paths enabled by symbolic or verbal communication. The primary evolutionary benefit of language seems to be in the higher level of coordination among larger groups that it enables and supports. Language (verbal, symbolic, formal or otherwise) is the means by which we can partially externalize our internal thoughts and plans; it creates a platform of cooperation that makes larger groups feasible and beneficial, and makes civilization, itself, possible.

With grunts and gestures, clan members can cooperate on a hunt, but only language supports the building of cities, the storing and exchange of surpluses. The language component of the L2 message bundle is what makes interpersonal exchange of *meaning* possible.

By exchanging meaningful messages, grouping individuals forge value bonds of various strength and durability with each other, and engender the development of hierarchical groups that have some power to direct members' efforts at a common goal. The hierarchical form of organization, although often decried by lower level members, is actually just an organizational representation of the L0-L2 level structure that vests the executive function in the smaller levels, not altogether unlike the way that the L2 and L1 data structures get narrowed to the L0 ternary form in order to fit into the action decision process.

L0 and L1 interact with $\mathbb{R}$ by means of a sensory interface. This does not mean that they conceive of it accurately, just that the sensory interface exposes cognitive entities to the hard knocks of external physical reality. L2 has no such interface, and once it achieves language ability, the focus of L2 cogitation shifts from processing experience to processing language messages. The sound of speech exists in $\mathbb{R}$, but as explained before, the meaning of speech only exists in $\mathbb{CS}$ until it is successfully expressed to another, at which point it becomes part of ξ, and therefore can become part of $\mathbb{SR}$. The verbal model, the construct of language and culture, although horribly ambiguous and imprecise, nonetheless, along with the coercive power of grouping and L0 truth, is adequate to coordinate people well enough to form large groups that can cooperate on large projects. Of course, the imprecision of language and the existence of an independent interest singularity in every member's breast, ordains that coercion is required to cover the last mile in forging successful, long-term coordination.

While a building, and the written plans of its design, along with the sound of the speech among the construction crew, all verifiably exist in $\mathbb{R}$, the semantic content of their words *does not*. The semantic content, the thought element, the meaning of words can only exist in $\mathbb{CS}$ and $\mathbb{SR}$. That is, the semantic dimension of language, the very means of grouping, does not exist in $\mathbb{R}$. This means that, although the artifacts of civilization may exist in $\mathbb{R}$ for a moment, civilization, itself, only exists in $\mathbb{SR}$, and not in $\mathbb{R}$.

31.2.2   Operations

Semantic reality is an abstract, non-physical reality created by words that enable and sustain individual and aggregate, hierarchical relationships, and coordinate cooperative actions. And, while $\mathbb{SR}$, itself, is non-physical, since the cognitive spaces it comprises exist in organic entities, their coordinated efforts both consume physical resources and produce physical artifacts.

A semantic reality is a dimensional graph of ξ nodes and $\mathbb{L}$ links, and as such, supports operations that elaborate on the structure and function of the cognitive space nodes. These operations include, but are not limited to:

- $maxNode(d, s)$: return nodes with maximum value in dimension d in system s
- $listSets(d, s)$: return list of hierarchies in dimension d in system s
- $sortNodes(d, s)$: return a list of nodes sorted on dimension d in system s
- $linkValue(n1, n2, d)$: return link value between nodes on dimension d
- $hierarchyStrength(n, d)$: return group bond strength of nodes under n on dimension d

Additional functionality will be elaborated as needed, but this list should be adequate to make it clear to the attentive reader that these are just higher level versions of the evaluate, compare, and search functions we have used in the earlier models. Complexity arises from aggregations of simplicity within more sophisticated structures, not from a miracle in a higher intellect.

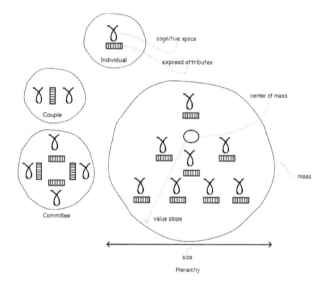

Figure 31.2: Semantic units in semantic reality.

31.3   Semantic Units

If we visualize $\mathbb{SR}$ as a multi-dimensional graph as proposed, we can use our astronomical universe as a metaphor, with semantic units in the roles of objects, solar systems, galaxies, and larger structures, and semantic links acting as a coherent gravitational force. The singularity in each cognitive space creates a gravity well much as mass does in the physical universe, and just as in the physical cosmos, the characteristics of each space give it a different measurable mass as determined both by its constitution and accumulated experience.

The difference between gravity and the semantic links, of course, is that where gravity curves spacetime in all directions, semantic links are vectors connecting specific cognitive spaces (although, it does seem likely that the larger semantic units will exhibit a local attractive power on weak, or weakly attached, neighbors, but we leave that for later experiments).

Gravity, however, is just a metaphor that may, or may not, be helpful. The significant point is that, because everything in the cognitive space model is quantified, $\mathbb{SR}$ gives us a fully testable model of every level of cognitive entity grouping there is. The model can obviously be adjusted to support any type of depth of query needed to investigate any combination of cognitive spaces we choose.

Figure 31.2 shows a sampling of semantic units in semantic reality that we will briefly discuss, one at a time.

31.3.1 Individual

The individual is simply a cognitive space. The symbol labeled, "exposed attributes", is just some part of the attribute array of the entity. This array is neither fixed, nor necessarily well defined, but this vagary just matches our real life experience. Some of us are withdrawn and taciturn, revealing as little of ourselves as we can, while others are "open books" who reveal as much as they can. But, of course, what attributes get exposed is also affected by the perspicacity of the observer, so the exposed attribute array, **EA**, is the XOR of what is revealed, **RA**, and what is seen, **OA**:

$$\mathbf{EA} = \mathbf{RA} \oplus \mathbf{OA}$$

We might note, in passing, that this formulation allows us to define miscommunication as:

$$|\mathbf{OA} - \mathbf{RA}| > 0$$

If $|\mathbf{OA}| > |\mathbf{RA}|$, the observer is seeing more than the subject wants to reveal, and if $|\mathbf{RA}| > |\mathbf{OA}|$, then the observer is failing to see all the available information. But, for modeling purposes, there is simply an array of exposed attributes, $\mathbf{EA}$, that can be tested, and that is why we only show it.

31.3.2 Couple

The couple is structurally not much different than the individual. The complication is that what is shown as one exposed attribute array between the two cognitive spaces is, of course, three: the testable one of mutually agreed exposed attributes (shown), as well as an additional one for each space representing the *experienced* attributes. That is, there is the relationship that can be verified, and the relationships that each participant projects as existing. The only thing we can test, of course, is what can be verified, not the internal experience of each participant's expectations, hopes and fears. That which is not externalized may occupy our thoughts and experiences, but it can be neglected until it is manifested through action.

31.3.3   Committee

The committee element is meant to represent non-hierarchical organizations of whatever size and purpose. The question, of course, is, should this be represented like the couple, with a single array representing the exposed attributes of the committee, or as it is, with individual arrays showing the level of participation of each member.

Since semantic reality is conceived as a dimensional, hierarchical graph, the obvious answer, of course, is *both*, since both aspects must exist and could be queried individually for different questions.

31.3.4   Hierarchy

The hierarchy is shown with additional attributes, but these are not exclusive to the hierarchy, they are just easier to understand in this context, so they are called out here. The additional attributes make it clear that the element can be studied as a collection of spaces, or as a unitary element with attributes such as center of mass, mass, and a value slope that declines from the center mass to the periphery. This model captures the observable truth that peripheral members just do not matter as much as central, key members.

The semantic reality element model supports calculations on interacting populations, calculations that are similar to ones we can perform on physical bodies in $\mathbb{R}$. Thus, we can use this model to study both micro interactions among member elements, as well as macro interactions between different populations, without every having to lose ourselves in the morass of the soft sciences.

31.4   The Utility of $\Re$

As mentioned before, new levels of abstraction are expensive, but potentially powerful tools that enable you to interrogate your subject at new levels, from new angles that were not possible from a more concrete perspective. Many of the stranger aspects of quantum mechanics, for example, came from Einstein working the equations to reveal that if quantum mechanics were sound, then these strange properties (e.g., entanglement) had to be true. He expected they wouldn't be, but it turned out that they are.

Semantic reality is not some useless, theoretical abstraction. While the idea for defining it arose from the logical implications of defining $\Re$, only the semantic reality model captures the fact that civilization and its semantic components and aspects only exist in $\mathbb{SR}$, and not in $\mathbb{R}$, at all. Civilization's resources and artifacts exist in $\mathbb{R}$, but not its meaning, not its purpose. The purblind defect is so powerful it induces us to see civilization as existing in physical reality, but clearly it does not, and cannot. This forces us to see, on this much broader level, that everything of value, everything of meaning, only exists in semantic, not physical, spaces.

While we have only described one new reality in this chapter, there is no reason that someone else with different models and different data might not find it useful to define any number of others whose abstraction level might open up entirely new worlds to us.

31.5 Summary

While we will delve deeper into semantic reality in the next chapter, even if defining it did nothing more than combine the quantified models of individual cognitive experience to the aggregate levels of hierarchical groups, then this, alone, would make this new model a valuable addition to our tool chest.

But semantic reality does more than that, it presents an outline of a unified model of the entire range of cognitive entity experience and behavior that reaches from explaining an individual's feelings, beliefs, ideas, and behavior all the way to the rise and fall of civilizations. Although we have not discussed it in this brief overview, the perceptive reader may see that a semantic reality model connects the history of the rise and fall of civilizations to the sand pile and other models in chaos theory.

31.6 Review

- $\mathbb{R}$ is just one reality in the set of realities $\mathfrak{R}$.
- Reality: a container of verifiably measurable, related entities and forces that only interact with each other; a container into which external entities and forces cannot enter.
- Semantic reality, $\mathbb{SR} = (\{\xi\}, \{\mathbb{L}\})$:
  - ξ: the externalized subset of $\mathbb{CS}$.
  - $\mathbb{L}$ is the set of communication links in semantic reality.

- – $\mathbb{SR}$ is a dimensional, hierarchical graph, a network of the externalized portion of cognitive space nodes (the measurable actions, messages, and artifacts), ξ, and communication links, $\mathbb{L}$.

- Although the artifacts of civilization exist in $\mathbb{R}$, civilization, itself, only exists in $\mathbb{SR}$.

- Semantic reality operations are just elaborations of the basic lower level operations, such as evaluate, compare, and search.

- Collections of one or more externalized cognitive spaces are called semantic units, and they populate semantic reality.

- Semantic units can be analyzed either as collections or as units that have properties such as mass.

- Semantic reality models civilization and all the levels of grouping below that.

Chapter 32

Purpose

32.1 Review

By this point, surely all surviving readers already know that we cannot pretend to look for the purpose of life in reality, $\mathbb{R}$. First, because it doesn't exist there, and second, because we cannot see reality itself, we can only see a model of it. Therefore, it must be obvious that we have to begin our search for the meaning of life in our model of our mind and in the way it sees and understands reality, not by interrogating reality, itself, directly. But how do we begin this task, what objects do we pull from memory to construct our idea web that will eventually yield a sound definition of purpose?

A fact is a verbal construct—it is the reference, not the referent, so we cannot base our conclusions on the purpose of life on facts alone, since they are merely discrete models of continuous reality that we have done more or less to confirm, and if we're being honest with ourselves, it is invariably *less*.

Beliefs are a mechanism that can always successfully convert any unknown to a known quantity that we know how to handle, and they dispose of challenging facts by labeling them true if they are supporting, and false if they are contradicting. Beliefs also support rapid, definitive responses by terminating searches earlier than would be possible with any conventional search algorithm. Beliefs are optimized to shorten the time from perception to response. Their truth value is calculated internally, not externally. Beliefs are important for decision making, and can form the basis of a faith-based definition of purpose, but they are not structured to help in the construction of an outward-looking concept of purpose.

Opinions have a deprecated claim to being fact-based, but actually are fact castrators that manage corralled herds of now docile facts. They are gyroscopes that keep us balanced in the face of an unrelenting torrent of language messages. Opinions do not have the capability to lead us to a definition of the purpose of life.

Statements are the stuff of which ideas and conversations are built and, when they are made against the verbal model, invariably, two-thirds of them are undefined or implicit. Formal, executable statements are something else again, they are testable. Understand though, that, whether formal or informal, it is the context of statements that is the killer of purpose, for if that context is one of the inward-oriented constructs, such as an opinion or a belief, then the statement has no purpose and can lead to no progress other than as an appeal to grouping. Since neither the convivial conversation nor the debate has room for a clean focus on measurement and experimental results, statements made in conversation tend to have little potential to support the definition of purpose.

Religion can be used as a compass, or a club. That is, it can be used to orient an individual to their polestar through the vicissitudes of life, or it can be used as a seductive or coercive grouping mechanism. In the first case, purpose can be accepted or synthesized from an acceptance of, or accommodation to, the religious doctrine, but this is just faith-based belief, rather than outward-facing purpose exploration. In the second case, it is just a case of piety and subordination, and the actual idea of purpose that is accepted from the doctrine is obedience to group dictates in exchange for a sense of security.

Ideology has no function beyond grouping. To pretend that it has a higher purpose is both perfidious and contemptible. Ideology is just a way to expand one's power, to extend one's interest swath, at the expense of others. Ideology is a powerful grouping mechanism, and is valid in that context, but all other considerations fall when it becomes ascendant, so it is obviously of no possible use in discovering a valid and productive purpose.

Semantic reality is a universe of multi-level, multi-dimensional collections of externalizations of cognitive spaces linked by language messages and constructs. It is the universe of groups of size one and up. By grouping together based on shared understandings and common, or at least consistent, goals, cog-

nitive entities can cooperate to create higher levels of reality
that are more complex, and have more potential, than anything
in physical reality. Just as statements are our means of interacting with models, statements are the means by which groups
accomplish goals, but instead of the content of group statements
just being words, it can also include actions. Group statements
retain the three part structure of the model statement, but the
context and goal are usually fairly explicit, and this accounts for
the relatively superior efficacy of practiced, orchestrated group
action versus verbal discussion. But, just as a knife can be a
tool or a weapon, so, too, a group can be constructive or destructive, depending on the minds and motivations controlling
it.

The language links that connect cognitive spaces into various kinds of groups are forged by education and acculturation.
In the current era, this means schools that are almost entirely
focused on pattern assimilation, not only as the vehicle of education, but as the very definition of intelligence. On the whole,
this produces functionaries without vision who only produce
and cooperate within authority structures. This works for using
known means to produce known results, but is simply irrelevant
to the rigors and demands of exploration and discovery.

We have mentioned the need to shift most of the teaching of
humanities and soft sciences to teachers' colleges, and to replace
them with straight up pattern processing and cultural survey
courses. Obviously, none of these courses that lack reproducible
results can be of any help in defining an outward-looking pur-

pose, and they don't even help in learning about practical or scientific understanding of reality.

Once we squash the erudition fallacy and its supporting social structures, we can restore respect for the skilled tradesmen and restore tracking in education with the elevation of vocational schools to the level of respect and support they deserve and require. But, while vocational schools will help many to master precise interactions with the physical world, they will not help us to explore the concept of ultimate purpose.

Introducing faceted model-oriented reasoning as the focus of true higher education, and restructuring the curriculum to include all of the necessary hard science, math, and modeling disciplines required by L3 level reasoning, will better equip students to explore purpose questions, but will not, by itself, provide a launching point.

It took me less than ten seconds to grasp the essence and power of model-oriented reasoning one Saturday evening when I was fourteen. In a life-changing flash of insight, everything I knew and valued was changed forever. Either I had experienced a once in a millennium explosion of genius, or I simply stumbled on a switch that, when flipped, opened the pre-existing circuits in our brain that were structurally capable of executing the exploration and discovery process. I rather think it was the latter, which is why I have tried to explain the method and process of deliberate exploration and discovery in this book.

L0 responds to the present, L1 responds to the past, L2 anticipates the future, and L3 explores the unknown. L3 rea-

soning is no more improbable or unnatural than the reasoning
supported by the other levels, it is only unfamiliar because it's
fairly new, one of our mutation-born untapped resources. Now
is the time to begin to learn how to use it.

32.2   Building From Models

The only way not to get lost in the weeds, or tangled up in
one's sheets, while exploring the unknown, is by emphatically
rejecting mudball reasoning with enough conviction and vehe-
mence to successfully impel one through the rather lengthy and
rigorous preparation required to master discovery learning and
faceted model-oriented reasoning.

The definition of an outward-facing purpose is a subjective
problem, and therefore, the L3 solution to it will be an optimization formula that balances trade-offs of benefits and costs
for the various stakeholders. In the first phase of the definition,
the stakeholders will all be internal values, needs, abilities and
desires. Subsequent elaborations will extend the stakeholder
group to include, more or less well, the interests other entities and groupings. Evaluations and weighting of interests will
necessarily be subjective, and only the calculations and experiments employing the solution will be reproducible, but at least
the choices will be externalized and explicit, and therefore subject to rational comparison of experimental results.

Now, let us begin our discussion of how we can go about de-
vising an L3 level definition of purpose that is based on our executable models of semantic reality and cognitive spaces. Con-

sider this:

$$\mathbb{R} = \forall\, r \in \{i_d \;:\; |i_d - r_d| <= \epsilon\}$$

$$\nu \notin \mathbb{R}$$

$$\xi = \text{ the externalized subset of } \mathbb{CS}$$

$$\mathbb{SR} = (\{\xi\}, \{\mathbb{L}\})$$

$$\xi \overset{\ell_\varkappa}{\leftrightarrow} \xi$$

$$\nu \in \mathbb{SR} \iff \textit{we put it there}$$

This is not, and never has been, difficult to understand:

- Our physical reality, $\mathbb{R}$, comprises all measurables.
- Value, ν, is the output of an evaluation process, it is not a measurable.
- Therefore, value does not exist in the physical universe.
- ξ is the externalized subset of $\mathbb{CS}$
- Language links reify value in semantic reality.
- Value exists in $\mathbb{SR}$ if, and only if, we work to put it there.

32.3   Meaning and Purpose

Definitions:

Valuescape: the portion of the singularity distortion field where the value component is not zero.

Meaning: an idea's coordinates in a valuescape.

Purpose: the goal of meaning, the point of maximum value in a valuescape. Local purpose is contextual, while global purpose is our subjective definition of the ultimate.

Thus, relative meaning is defined by the ratio of the value

component of an idea to the value of a designated purpose, whether local or global.

If we use ν for value, π for purpose, and μ for meaning, then we know:

$$\nu \notin \mathbb{R}$$
$$|\pi| \leq max(\nu)$$
$$\therefore \pi \notin \mathbb{R}$$
$$\mu_i = i_\nu / \pi$$
$$\therefore \pi = null \rightarrow \mu = undefined$$

Since value does not exist in $\mathbb{R}$, π cannot exist in $\mathbb{R}$, but only in $\mathbb{CS}$ or $\mathbb{SR}$. Since meaning is the ratio of the value component of an idea, i, to a purpose, if the purpose is null, then the meaning is undefined. Therefore, nothing has meaning when a cognitive entity fails to define a purpose, because purpose can only exist by dint of cognitive effort. That reality is meaningless is a truism that never changes, but semantic reality lacks meaning only as a direct consequence of an individual's failure to define it.

32.4 Does God Exist?

If we represent God with $\aleph$, then:

$$\aleph \notin \mathbb{R}$$

$$\aleph \in \mathbb{S}$$

$$\mathbb{S} \overset{?}{\subset} \mathbb{I}$$

$$\mathbb{S} \in \mathbb{I} \mapsto \aleph \in \mathbb{I}$$

$$\mathbb{S} \notin \mathbb{I} \mapsto \mathbb{S} \in \mathfrak{R}$$

God is not, either by doctrine or observation, a measurable, therefore God does not exist in $\mathbb{R}$. The *idea* of God is an element of the set of supernatural thoughts or phenomena. The question is, is the set of supernatural things a subset of internal thoughts? If so, God is a transcendent loopback in the set of loopback coping strategies. If not, if the world of the supernatural is an independent reality in the set of realities, then what?

$$\aleph \in \mathbb{S}$$

$$\mathbb{S} \notin \mathbb{I}$$

$$\therefore \mathbb{S} \in \mathfrak{R}$$

$$\mathbb{S} \cap \mathbb{R} = \emptyset$$

If the set of supernatural phenomena is an independent reality that does not interact with our reality, then what? Perhaps someone could investigate the properties of this reality, but only after defining it, and what would constitute evidence about it? Of course, since truth is an element of semantic reality, and

scriptures are an artifact in $\mathbb{R}$, then proof by authority of scrip-
ture is just an L0 assertion, and we have $\mathbb{S} \subset \mathbb{I}$ again.

Separating God and $\mathbb{S}$ from $\mathbb{I}$ would require a non-scriptural
definition of evidence and a definition of supernatural reality
before we could begin to investigate $\mathbb{S}$ to see what it implies.
While this does not mean that it cannot be done, it does mean
that lazy, purblind mudball reasoning can no longer be accepted
as a valid means of doing it.

Does God exist in $\mathbb{R}$? Until proven otherwise, by definition,
no, he does not. Does God exist in $\mathbb{S}$? He does, if you so choose.
Should God exist in $\mathbb{S}$? We need loopbacks, we need grouping
seeds, and historically God has served both of these purposes,
but only at a very high price in terms of fueling and supporting
inter and intra group strife. But, the problem of religious strife
comes not from the God concept, per se, but from:

$$\mathbb{S} \not\subset \mathbb{I}$$

$$\mathbb{S} \in \mathfrak{R}$$

$$|\mathbb{S}|_\nu > |\mathbb{R}|_\nu$$

That is, it is the assertion that the supernatural world is an
independent reality with more value than our physical reality
that has historically caused real problems. Before we proceed,
stop and consider that last expression, $|\mathbb{S}|_\nu > |\mathbb{R}|_\nu$ (the value
magnitude of $\mathbb{S}$ is greater than the value magnitude of $\mathbb{R}$), for
a moment. Do you see it? $\mathbb{S}$ and $\mathbb{R}$, in this context, are independent, non-intersecting sets in $\mathfrak{R}$ that have no elements in

common. Furthermore, as of this time, we have no valid way to interrogate $\mathbb{S}$. Given that, how is it possible to define a comparison function, $compare(\mathbb{R}, \mathbb{S})$ that could yield any result whatsoever? Is it any wonder that, given the impossibility of the comparison, it would fall to our L0/L1 belief systems that, by construction, can evaluate *anything*, to render an absolutely certain answer that is consistent with the interests of its extended self? But, this brings us back to $\mathbb{S} \subset \mathbb{I}$, and religious strife is just a grouping phenomenon where the members use their L0 beliefs to extend their L0 interests at the expense of their neighbors.

While I will not get into scriptural quibbles, the belief that the value of the independent spiritual world is superior to the value of reality is an L0 interest statement, not a statement about the ultimate (see *Universal Judaism*).

When notions of the supernatural are used as loopbacks to help us maintain our focus and equilibrium, when they provide *us* with our own moral compass, they can be a positive influence. It is only when they are used strictly as a group formation mechanism as a component of an ideology that they become a conscienceless tool to expand one's interest sphere, and this is when their capacity for evil fully blossoms.

32.5 Evil

In *Pinnacle Reasoning*, we defined evil roughly as the product of:

- intention,

- severity of injury,

- the vulnerability of the victim,

- frequency of repetition of the action,

- the number of people affected,

- divided by the radius of concern.

This was not offered as an ideal or logical definition, but just as a descriptive one: the more deliberately and grievously you hurt helpless people subjectively close (in the observer's judgment) to you, the more evil people generally think you are (the same calculation yields opposite results when run from the attackers or the attacked population's point of view). This definition is useful because it incorporates the observation that people don't count injuries to distant, unfamiliar populations as a very serious evil, and it gives us a reasonable, historically meaningful concept.

If we were to update this definition in light of the more advanced concepts we have discussed in this volume, we would use the concept of semantic reality to focus in on the definition of what 'close' means in defining the radius of concern. The radius of concern, of course, is a value judgment we make: we can harvest plants without rebuke, because plants are not close to us, so only an odd few would see evil in the action, but there is more disagreement about the harvesting of animals. While values are inherently subjective in the sense of being the product of personal history, calculation and choice, this does not mean that we cannot construct a model that would allow us to externalize, analyze and test some definition of evil. The radius of concern is a value from $\mathbb{CS}$, but when the expression is formalized, the possibility for measured discussion at least exists.

32.6   Relative Values

In the whisper of the traditionalist, you can often hear the lessons of his elders, along with the joy and agony of the experiences of birth, struggle, life and death. In the cacophony of an intellectual's opinions, on the other hand, the only sound you generally hear is ego uncurbed by humility or discipline. While we rail at the failed university system and its thousand year betrayal of intellectual promise and power, we must confess that it is the intellectual, not the institution, that is the criminal.

By this time, we should all know what opinions are, what internal and external knowledge is, and what the subjective nature of perception and thought tells us about our knowledge base, and how little we actually know. We should also recognize how the entire framework of model-oriented reasoning and discovery learning is anathema to the liberal arts tradition which, in the last few centuries, has traversed the arc from absolute truth to no truth at all, and is now going even further to push an absolute relativism that explicitly attacks what it considers the 'oppressive' legitimacy of science. The liberal arts education scam has become the spearhead of an authoritarian march to oppress the many in the drive to protect the few, the pure, the powerless, the perfectly oppressed, the imaginary, while crushing everyone and everything else in its path, all the while preaching that everything is relative and no culture is any better or different than any other, except for Western Culture, which is clearly the worst, and the cause of all ills.

It might seem to the obtuse that, by explicitly subjectivizing all thought and perception, this current work is continuing the tradition of tearing down what is known and knowable in the effort to expose everything as being equally meaningless. Except, that it is not, and anyone expecting this has not been understanding the work up to this point. By identifying the source of meaning in the cognitive universe, by creating a bridge from science and mathematics into the world of subjective thought, faceted model-oriented reasoning is building a solid bridge to a future where internal thought, emotions, and beliefs can be connected to the world of discovery, scientific inquiry and independent verification in the continuing struggle to evolve humanity, to progress towards our goal.

But, if the only thing that we know is real is what can be verifiably measured, does this not restrict us to a materialistic universe where higher ideals and values are merely imaginary constructs? No, certainly not.

32.7 What is Real?

If we let τ represent *truth*, then we can say:

$$\tau \mapsto \text{L0}$$

$$\tau \not\mapsto \mathbb{R}$$

That is, truth makes a statement about L0 evaluations, decisions and actions, truth does not make statements about reality. Truth is, of course, a crucial concept in both building groupings and motivating actions, so it is, in a sense, much more powerful and important than any unverified L2 idea we may have, but that does not mean that it describes reality in any way— it describes our evaluation of and reaction to some perceived reality.

If we refer once again to the definition of reality:

$$\mathbb{R} = \forall\, r \in \left\{ x \ : \left| x_{d_i} - r_{d_j} \right| <= \epsilon \right\}$$

this time, including the d to represent the *dimensions* of each thing we are measuring to make it explicit that, while reality is the set of all things that can be verifiably measured, since we never measure the *thing* itself but only certain dimensions of it, then we can only ever verify discrete dimensions of the things we study.

We can see that this definition is more expansive than we may have realized. Consider that this definition means that the following statement is also true:

$$\forall\, (r_{m_i}, r_{m_j}) \in \mathbb{R}, (r_{m_i} \cdot r_{m_j}) \in \mathbb{SR}$$

where:

- r_m is a model in $\mathbb{I}$ that has been verified to map to an $r \in \mathbb{R}$,

- '$\cdot$' represents any formally defined operation over the field defining the quantification,

That is, ideas combined using valid operations in subjective algebra produce valid ideas in $\mathbb{SR}$ that testing can verify either do or do not exist in the $\mathbb{R}$ subset of $\mathbb{SR}$. Thus, semantic reality not only models forces and material things in the universe, but equally includes the products of formal thought. This is a shocking result because it means that, while informal thought still has an undefined relation to reality, formal thought is actually real. Abstract, non-physical, formal ideas are real in $\mathbb{SR}$, and they can profoundly affect physical elements in $\mathbb{R}$.

Now, what exactly does it mean that formal thought is real? It doesn't mean that it is right, and it doesn't even mean that it necessarily describes something in our physical universe. The confusion about what is real and unreal that reigns in the mudball world of traditional reasoning is caused, as most problems are, by the purblind defect that leads us to conflate internal with external reality. Even now, when we speak of reality, $\mathbb{R}$, undoubtedly most readers still think we are talking about the phenomenological universe, when clearly we are actually talking about the model of it that we are building inside of our own mind.

A reality is a self-contained universe of entities and forces that are not measurably impacted by extrinsic entities or forces.

The elements of a reality are related in the sense that they are constructed, developed or evolved from a limited alphabet of elements, and forces. In that set are mental models of objects we have encountered, such as trees and rocks, as well as *classifications* of trees and rocks. To say that such a classification is real is not to say that there are not alternative classifications that might be superior in some, or even all, ways, it is just to say that verified, formal ideas are real in the same way Euclid's theorems are real: they have a verifiable, measurable reality outside of an individual cognitive space, they exist in the abstract message plane in $\mathbb{SR}$.

Certainly, it is obvious now that *value judgments* can be real, too. Again, not necessarily, and not even probably, unique, just real. The inputs to the value judgment, inasmuch as they are defined by a singularity, are necessarily subjective, but given those parameters, the judgments, if calculated by formal means as in the current model, can be real. Is this just moving the ground of subjectivity around without actually reducing or changing it at all? No, because what faceted model-oriented reasoning has shown us how to do is how to quantify these subjective inputs to incorporate them into executable models.

*Subjective parameters to a formal model aren't subjective anymore, they are **arbitrary** elements in the problem domain that map to particular solutions in the range.*

Converting subjective values to arbitrary values in a defined range of values in a problem domain gives us the ability to compare the *relative cost* of different input values on the basis of the reproducible results that the tests of the formal model produce. This means that, instead of two people arguing L0 truth, "My values are right, yours are wrong!" now we can review how expensive our belief-based evaluations are relative to various alternatives. We can move from an L0 right/wrong discussion directly to an L3 quantitative comparison dialog.

In other words, we now have the means to *measure* subjectivity and to evaluate it based on *real* results.

32.8   Semantic Reality

Semantic reality is the reality of meaning, of planning, of purpose, none of which exist in $\mathbb{R}$. The $\mathbb{SR}$ model, shown in figure 32.2, models civilization, society, family, clubs, couples and singles. It will eventually allow us to predict collective behavior propensity based on quantitative models of the intellectual and experiential components of the included cognitive space externalizations.

What should be both obvious and anticipated in figure 32.2, but what perhaps many will find surprising, is where reality, $\mathbb{R}$, fits into this picture. The top of the figure shows semantic reality with a few different elements visible, the rest just assumed. The dotted lines expand one of the cognitive spaces into the figure in the lower left that shows the singularity distortion field extending into the flat geometry of value-free thought.

The black dot in the flat region is expanded into the figure on the lower right where you can see that this is our model of reality. The small dot in the remote regions of a cognitive space is our entire model of reality. The rest of our model of reality is in our mudball model in our interest-distorted, internal knowledge, where verifiable fact is diluted nearly to invisibility with impressions, anecdotes and toxic ideas.

Understanding the relative scale of semantic to external reality is necessary to appreciate that, however it came into being, our external universe is a fairly simple, mostly empty container populated with meaningless, unaware matter that is built from a small alphabet of elements and forces, that is already most — if not all — of what it will ever be. While it has been historically difficult for us to learn how to understand and describe it, physical reality, itself, is a pretty simple, warped billiard table where balls carom about as a consequence of collisions.

Semantic reality, on the other hand, exists on an entirely different level. Let's say God or the Big Bang initiated the expansion that plays out in our universe today in an act not entirely dissimilar to triggering a bomb packed with accretable and divisible objects of various kinds. Boom! and the act of creation was done. The rest is just balls on the table bouncing about. Until, that is, until longer chain molecules started to form and twist and store energy. Once that started to happen, and we began down the road to creating life, then things started to become interesting.

Skipping a few steps, finally we get to the development of

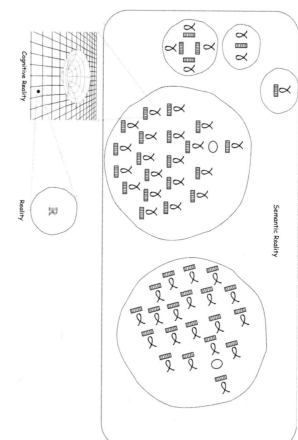

Figure 32.2: Unified model

language, and the capabilities of language changed everything. Language pushed us into the position of *creator*, for we are now creating a reality that is orders of magnitude more complex, and more interesting, than physical reality. There is no obvious limit to the complexity or power of the semantic structures we can build in semantic reality that do not exist in the physical world, but that can affect it in truly profound ways.

Value is defined in the singularity, and we use it to evaluate events and our experiences, so value, as we individually assess it, directly impacts our decisions and actions. But, it remains internal to us, it is part of our internal knowledge, and it doesn't ever get directly externalized until language enters the picture. Words change everything. Words (verbal and symbolic communication) provide the semantic content in messages, they create a bridge that allows us to exchange our values with others in an imprecise, but actionable way. By generating a new class of semantic message event, words actually create a brand new level of reality which is self-defined, and potentially completely unrelated to anything in $\mathbb{R}$.

If the verbal model is the highest level of language message we use, we are stopping our progress in developing semantic reality in the mudball model stage, and thus are destined to be stuck with the pathetic results the last several millennia of mudball reasoning have produced. However, faceted model-oriented reasoning now gives us an option. Now that we know that words are just the verbal model, and that the verbal model can never be fully externalized, we can push on to expressing, testing, validating and evaluating our thoughts using all the facets of model-oriented reasoning, including the formal languages that, alone, give us the opportunity to fully externalize our thoughts, and finally begin to move our culture forward at last.

$\mathbb{SR}$, being the domain of verbal, abstract, and formal ideas, is naturally larger and more complex than the earlier cognition levels. It is also necessarily larger and more complex than phenomenological reality itself, since

$$\mathbb{R} \subset \mathbb{SR} \text{ and}$$
$$\forall \ r_i, \ r_j \in \mathbb{R}, (r_i \cdot r_j) \in \mathbb{SR}, \text{ but}$$
$$\exists (r_i \cdot r_j) \notin \mathbb{R}$$

That is, not all $r \in \mathbb{SR}$ also exist in $\mathbb{R}$. For example, semantic structures exist in $\mathbb{SR}$, but do not exist in $\mathbb{R}$.

Also, whereas events in $\mathbb{R}$ are governed, and limited, by scientific laws, events in $\mathbb{SR}$ are governed by self-defined and extendable laws, which can evolve without any obvious limit. $\mathbb{R}$ creates the base for physical existence, but message based interaction and cognition creates an abstract reality that is more complex, more interesting, more creative, and more real, in many ways, than $\mathbb{R}$ itself.

By organizing societies, economies, and political entities, L2 language entities create a *reality* that uses pattern languages to organize themselves into structures that interact to a self-defined purpose at a level of complexity and sophistication that simply does not, and cannot ever, exist in $\mathbb{R}$. The semantic concepts created by L2 functionality can only exist in $\mathbb{CS}$ and above, because it is only within a cognitive space that the resources supporting relational complexity are created and can exist.

Cognitive spaces are not an imposition on $\mathbb{R}$, they are not some pathetic attempt of weak species to cope with the majesty of $\mathbb{R}$. On the contrary, cognitive spaces are an evolutionary advance, both on rude material existence, and on non-cognitive life.

Thus, not only are things and forces in $\mathbb{R}$ real, but also the products of *operations* on models of them, although abstract and non-physical, are also real. Why? Because formally defined operations on real entities produce measurable, reproducible, verifiable results, and if those results are verified within a specified error bound, then the results of the operations are as real as rocks, water and gravity.

This means that there is no limit on the number of high level concepts we can reify, there is no subjective term we cannot at least consider for reification through modeling. Semantic reality can support structures of meaning of unbounded size and complexity, but as a reality, it is also subject to the laws of chaos and complexity. This means that the semantic grouping structures we build, although not physical, may exhibit a fragility similar to material structures in $\mathbb{R}$.

32.9   Civilization

Civilization is an $\mathbb{SR}$ construct that builds on the value element of L0. Value, ν, is the discriminant that orders the mortal universe from each and every cognitive space up to the level of semantic reality.

Without putting too fine a point on it, let's say that society is a structured grouping that includes some cultural, political and economic aspects. So, depending on how it is defined, we could identify a society with a nation, a geographic and political entity, or more broadly, it might refer to a number of trading partners sharing similar institutions and values. Narrowing our focus only to the cultural facets of a society structure reveals what we might call a *civilization*, a loose grouping attribution, in distinction to being a product of grouping action. A civilization would include a set of various societies that, at some level, all share the same cultural tradition, but again, this is a commonality attributed to them, not necessarily claimed by them. In this sense, civilization is a term so vague and loosely defined as to mean little more than a particular cultural theme that we identify, often retroactively.

Or, we could see civilization as an unending relay race where the individual runners race until they drop and die, leaving the baton on the track to be picked up by a successor who continues the race. Besides being an odd image, what sense, what value would there be in an effort like that? The value, of course, would be entirely in the value of the goal being pursued, and the salutary results of its pursuit.

Western civilization might be the only viable example of this concept, this process, but it does represent an evolutionary development of the ideas of individual dignity, individual freedom, and the gradual, if unsure, intellectual progress achieved through the accumulation of the artifacts of organized learning that culminated in the scientific revolution and the creation of the modern world.

These ideals are real, we can measure them in $\mathbb{SR}$ in any number of dimensions, and more importantly, we can sharply and formally distinguish them from the collectivist values of the anti-individual, anti-freedom, anti-discovery Marxist civilization that is currently working so hard to destroy the legitimacy of Western civilization's values by regressively subordinating the dignity of the individual to the coercive power of the collective.

32.10 Progress

Consider the value-laden term *progress*. While we have felt free throughout this work to provide alternate definitions for long familiar terms, it should be noted that, in almost all cases, all we have been doing is formalizing previously informal, verbal models. That is, we applied faceted model-oriented reasoning to create formal, executable or mathematical models of the usually ambiguous verbal model of a concept. Of course, a critic can object that this or that formalization subtly or dramatically changed the actual meaning of the term, but that is as it should be. Turning to the important idea of progress, our goal will be to offer a conventional mathematical model for the general understanding we share of the idea of progress.

First, the verbal model:

Progress: the rate at which we are approaching our goal.

With that in hand, the mathematical model is automatic. The distance between two points in 3-dimensional space is:

$$dist(p_1, p_2) = \sqrt{(x_2 - x_1)^2 + (y_2 - y_1)^2 + (z_2 - z_1)^2}$$

(this is easily extendable to n dimensions). If we set p_1 to be the location of our goal, p_2 to be our current location, and set d_0 to equal our initial distance from the goal, and d_1 to be our new distance from our goal after a time t, and we let $\wp$ stand for *progress*, then the definition of progress is simply:

$$\wp = \frac{d_1 - d_0}{t_1 - t_0} = \frac{\delta_d}{\delta_t}$$

Historically, this definition would not have been helpful because we weren't able to quantify subjective concepts like current conceptual location and purpose or goal, but we have already resolved that problem. The only issue remaining is, how do we define purpose?

32.11 Defining Purpose

I tend to use 'goal' and 'purpose' as synonyms, but the connotation of achievability in a goal and that of endless pursuit in a purpose, colors their usage in particular sentences. To the extent that we can agree that an ultimate goal is something to strive for, that it is a purpose to work for, then we could just use the word *goal* all the time, but that would confuse the reviewers who never get deeper than the headings.

Sophisticates, intellectuals, academics, cynics and nihilists all use their insight, wisdom and education to sagely declare that there is no meaning, no purpose, to life, that life is just a series of experiences destined to be betrayed by death. Of course, since they suffer from the purblind defect, they are unaware that what they are so ineptly trying to say, is that life has no meaning in *reality*, $\mathbb{R}$, in the material universe, because the ineluctable march of time in atomic reality belies the vain dreams of romantic, idealistic youth, and the reality of materialism trumps human experience. But the march of time eventually belies matter and energy, too, and yet the universe exists, has existed, and will continue to exist for at least another 70 million generations. When dilettantes with no math or hard science expertise draw self-indulgent, philosophical conclusions from ill understood theories, the result is just embarrassing.

There is no precision in the verbal model that intellectuals use, it is a mudball model that is inherently qualitative rather quantitative. Its sloppiness makes it virtually impossible for erudite intellectuals to recognize the impact that the purblind defect has on their perceptions, thoughts and conclusions. And, if they can't see it, they can't correct for it.

"But," you say, "with the proper education, one can articulate ideas with great precision!" The problem is, even this claim of defense is bogus, because the term 'great' is a qualitative, not quantitative notion, and cannot be crisply defined.

If you are honest and perceptive, you will find it easy to admit that feeling **certain**, actually *feels* good. *Knowing* things in absolute, unmeasured terms generates *physical* sensations that are sweet, warm, reassuring and wonderful. Forget about monkeys self-administering cocaine by hitting levers, verbal-stage L2 cognitive entities have that lever built-in, it's the L0 certainty evaluation function. While L2 is awash in doubts and possibilities, these all vanish instantaneously in the narrowing typecast down to the evacule-based mentacule structure of L0, so with a simple downcast, all grays and colors disappear with the leap into the black and white world of L0.

And, make no mistake about it, intelligent people make the jump into the pre-conscious L0 certainty pool not because they want to do the right thing, but because they are tired of dealing with doubt, and they are aching for the joyous fix of absolute truth. When an intelligent person chooses to wield the truth mallet — either through an appeal to authority or belief — in any but a life threatening situation, all this means is that they have chosen to chase the high that comes from wallowing in the ecstasy of parochial truth over any and every external value. They are just junkies who are so addicted to certain internal chemicals that they will sell their loved ones out for the next fix.

Certainty and higher level thought are incompatible. Having confidence in one's results and being certain they are right are radically different mental experiences because they are the product of different parts of the mind that evolved in different evolutionary periods. Certainty is native to the evacule structure and the L0 intellect, while having confidence in practice and procedure is an L2-L3 assessment. Yet, even the most advanced among us dabble in certainty, but this should be restricted to decisions and action, and must never be allowed to infringe on exploration and consideration of possibilities.

As we explained earlier, in model-oriented reasoning, the procedure for developing models is to build them on top of solid, tested models. It should be fairly obvious that our model for purpose will most naturally build on our model of semantic reality. Why? For starters, how about because in $\mathbb{SR}$, L2+ cognitive entities are gods (who else creates universes?) tasked with a process of creation far richer and more complex than the one that produced our physical universe, whether it was by the Big Bang or divine intervention. $\mathbb{SR}$'s capacity for complexity and structure far outstrips $\mathbb{R}$'s capacity, and not only by orders of magnitude, but by a technically unbounded amount. All higher levels of human organization exist only in semantic reality, but even though they are themselves non-physical, they generate results and artifacts in $\mathbb{R}$ that can radically alter physical reality. Physical reality exists in $\mathbb{R}$, but it is only *known* in $\mathbb{SR}$.

The cynics who claim human efforts have no enduring value in $\mathbb{R}$ are not only making a nonsense statement, they are ignoring the fact that we are verifiably creating a meaningful reality that includes $\mathbb{R}$ as a small subset. I suggest that the action of evolving semantic reality to new heights of complexity and fecundity is a fundamental, sharable value. While there are countless valid ways to initialize the optimization solution, there are real aspects of $\mathbb{SR}$ that we can measure, such as the fractal dimension of population distributions and complex organizations.[1]

The fractal dimension of population distributions and socioeconomic realities can be measured. Technology, science, and all external knowledge is real, and can be measured. The progress of humanity towards higher levels of complexity in structures, organizations and external knowledge can be measured. Progress towards the purpose of evolving $\mathbb{SR}$ can be measured, and is real.

The gist of the evolutionary life value process (see figure 32.3) is that life posits the value of life. The semantic reality model shows us that by communicating and cooperating with each other on ever higher levels of complexity we are, in fact, creating a profound, new reality that cannot exist without our efforts, and with our efforts can take us places we cannot even imagine yet. If we accept this model, then progress can be simply defined as the rate at which we build semantic reality to richer and higher levels of complexity and fertility. This gives us all we need to define the concept of progress in relation to our purpose:

Purpose:

---

[1]See *Resource Optimization and Self-Interest: Variations on the Game of Life*, The 28th Annual Simulation Symposium Proceedings, Phoenix, 1995.

1) increase our ability to thrive in the current and future environmental niches we inhabit,

2) increase value and meaning in $\mathbb{SR}$,

3) increase the shared store of external knowledge.

Progress:

a) an increasing ability to thrive in the current and subsequent environmental niche we inhabit.

b) a positive slope in the line graphing the evaluations of our viability over time.

c) an increase in organizational complexity and productivity in a reality.

d) an increase in the shared store of external knowledge.

e) an increase in the communication efficiency of language links.

32.12 Conclusion

The richness, potential and significance of semantic reality, not to mention our responsibility as gods creating it, suggests that when we apply the optimization formula

$$alter(p_i \ldots p_n) \; : \; |(q_i..q_n/a_i..a_n)_1| > |(q_i..q_n/a_i..a_n)_0|$$

to defining an approach to life that respects both our short and long-term interests, then we can live meaningful lives built on a core of a solid model of purpose that is rooted in the reality of $\mathbb{SR}$. The suggestion is that we incorporate both our short-term survival needs and our potential contributions to the evolution of semantic reality in the list of attributes we are trying to optimize for. As we gain experience with the universal simulator and improve our ability to model both near and remote features of interest, we will become more adept at juggling our various needs, while maintaining an alignment with our longer term interests, and thus avoid the rancid experience of having wasted our mortality opportunity on a meaningless life.

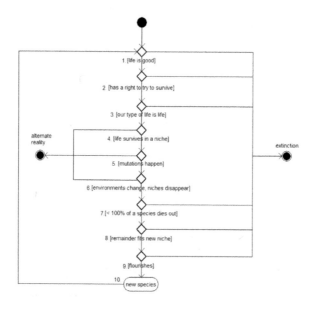

Figure 32.3: Evolutionary life value process

The purpose of a cognitive life in a semantic reality is to live a self-crafted solution to the problem of an evolutionary life form struggling with the changing environment problem. Living a perfectly selfish life, a life focused only on artifacts in $\mathbb{R}$, by definition, has no purpose, no meaning. Purpose beyond our own survival exists in $\mathbb{SR}$, not $\mathbb{CS}$, so we need a concept of the *ultimate* in order to be able to align our efforts at solving current problems with the long-term evolution of $\mathbb{SR}$.

32.13   Review

- A fact is the reference, not the referent.
- Beliefs convert any unknown to a known quantity that we know how to handle.
- Opinions have a deprecated claim to being fact-based, but actually are fact castrators.
- Informal statements are grouping mechanisms with a very narrow information bandwidth.
- Religion can be a personal compass, or a club to coerce discipline.
- Semantic reality is a universe of multi-level, multi-dimensional collections of externalizations of cognitive spaces linked by language messages and constructs.
- L0 responds to the present, L1 responds to the past, L2 anticipates the future, and L3 explores the unknown.
- Meaning cannot exist in $\mathbb{R}$, and it only exists in $\mathbb{SR}$ if you define it in relation to a purpose you also define.
- Asserting that $|\mathbb{S}|_\nu > |\mathbb{R}|_\nu$ is profoundly evil.
- Grouping aspects of religion are simply ideology, and as such, have nothing to do with $\mathbb{S}$.
- Evil is real, measurable and testable, but is still a civilization-specific value optimization formula.
- Truth makes statements about L0 realities.

- Formal statements exist in $\mathbb{SR}$, they are real.

- Converting subjective evaluations to formal parameters defines them as elements in a problem domain, and erases their subjective nature.

- $\mathbb{R}$ is a tiny subset within every $\mathbb{CS}$ inhabiting $\mathbb{SR}$.

- $\mathbb{SR}$ is larger than $\mathbb{R}$ because every element in $\mathbb{R}$ can be modeled in $\mathbb{SR}$, but many formal realities in $\mathbb{SR}$ cannot be found in $\mathbb{R}$.

- Progress, $\wp, = \frac{\delta_d}{\delta_t}$

- Certainty baths are a seductive indulgence.

- Certainty and higher level thought are incompatible.

- Whether we accept it or not, elaborating and extending semantic reality is the sole responsibility of L2+ cognitive entities. Thus, it constitutes a global purpose.

Chapter 33

Conclusion

The stated goal of this work has been to build a set of intellectual constructs sufficient to bridge the gap between the objective, reproducible techniques used in the scientific method to investigate reality, and the qualitative thinking done in the subjective world of personal experience. Instead, here is what we have shown:

Let Q = {all quantifiable things}

Let S = {all unquantifiable, subjective ideas}

Suppose: $S \neq \emptyset$

but: $\forall\, s_i \in S\; \exists\, m_i \in \mathbb{M}$ (by **M2**)

and: $\mathbb{M} \subset Q$

$\therefore\; S = \emptyset$

That is, the set of all purely subjective, non-quantifiable ideas is the empty set. How could it be otherwise, given that our brain comprises but nodes, paths, charges and triggering and suppressing chemicals, etc.?

Subjective, as it turns out, is a term of art used by the intellectually lazy to evade the responsibility to measure and calculate the actual results of their efforts. It is possible, using a model based on the concepts presented here, to trace the events involved in every subjective thought. The work to program a universal simulator has begun, but any competent software engineer should be able to take this rather elaborate and detailed design document and build one themselves in just a few months.

This work has described a unified model of thought, belief and feeling that is not restricted to humans, that is based on an evolutionary cytomodel that analyzes cognitive phenomena into the smallest, mutually ignorant functions possible that are consistent with successive levels of heritable structures. We have not just introduced the principles and practices of faceted model-oriented reasoning, we have defined an entirely new science, the science of subjectivity. There might well be centuries of work to be done to create a firm, mathematical foundation for every step, and many executable models to build.

It should be possible, with a little effort, to build a universal simulation engine to run cognitive space models in a semantic reality on wearable devices, so we can augment our reasoning with tests and simulations in every type of situation.

The most exciting prospect, though, is the possibility of unleashing a kernel of each generation to explore the unknown using L3 faculties, instead of relying on just the odd, lonely genius here and there. Imagine how different it will be when invention and discovery are normalized, instead of being the rare mystery they still are today.

The progress we make evolving semantic reality to new levels of complexity and productivity is measurable, and therefore real. The majesty and potential of the $\mathbb{SR}$ universe is awesome and unlimited. Physicists speak of the evolution of the universe in the first few trillionths of a second of its existence, then in the first few seconds, just moments really, when matter, as we know it, began to form. The footprints of the L3 intellect only began appearing in the historical record in the last five hundred years or so, and given that merely dozens (or at most a few hundred) minds have exhibited L3 productivity, we are virtually in the first few trillionths of a second of our awareness of the semantic reality universe.

Is there a purpose in life? Yes, because life's bias towards life defines purpose by its very nature. Is there a purpose to human endeavor, to the trials and tribulations of sentient life? Language-capable L2+ cognitive entities are unavoidably conscripted into the godlike act of universe creation by merit of their participation in the semantic communication that forges the links that connect cognitive spaces together and thus engenders a new reality, a new universe with an unbounded capacity for complexity, accomplishment, and *meaning*.

We are mortal beings that have to survive in brittle circumstances that are sure to change over time, sometimes catastrophically. The most elemental definition of progress is the measure of the extent to which we manage to thrive in the current conditions while preparing for the next.

Is progress real? Absolutely. Is progress important? Yes, as important as life itself. Is this the only way to define progress, or the only level on which we can define it? Of course not, progress, like any other term, can be defined any way we want, but model-oriented reasoning teaches us that we measure the quality of our ideas on the basis of their viability and productivity, and the current definition does very well on both counts.

Modern sophisticates, cynics, some atheists and even many believers take the position that this world, $\mathbb{SR}$, *our* world, the semantic reality that realizes meaning, just doesn't matter. They stand astride their wisdom fallacy, disdaining the futility of our mundane concerns, laughing at our efforts to excel, and sneering at our need to find meaning in human relations. That is their choice, a choice they are free to make. I make the choice to see the value in life, and to work at building a learning bridge that will equip us to survive any challenge thrown at us by the vagaries of nature. After all, the vastness of empty space that predominates in the lifeless reality, $\mathbb{R}$, which they think belies ours, is merely the opportunity for existence, nothing more. Let us celebrate and cherish the fragile, beautiful universe *we* are tasked with creating, and see rocks for the simple, lifeless phenomena that they so obviously are.

Progress is real, it can be objectively measured given explicit parameters. Progress, as we have defined it, is inextricably tied to the value of life itself, so it is a worthy goal. Progress can be measured, and we can measure the effect of our actions on our progress as individuals and as humans. This means that we can objectively measure our worth as beings, as participants in the human efforts to progress towards our goal. We can measure the value of our personal efforts to help us move towards the goal on a weekly, annual, or lifetime basis. Since progress is real, that means that any value judgment tied to the value of life or progress can also be real if correctly formalized.

When did evolution end? If it hasn't, then where did we get the idea that we should even want to live above the struggle? The nature and meaning of a learning life is in that struggle, and it never ends. The work is never done, it is always just beginning.

Index